The Rise of the Semi-Core

The Rise of the Semi-Core

China, India, and Pakistan in the World-System

Samee Lashari

LEXINGTON BOOKS
Lanham • Boulder • New York • London

Published by Lexington Books
An imprint of The Rowman & Littlefield Publishing Group, Inc.
4501 Forbes Boulevard, Suite 200, Lanham, Maryland 20706
www.rowman.com

86-90 Paul Street, London EC2A 4NE

British Library Cataloguing in Publication Information Available

Library of Congress Cataloging-in-Publication Data

Names: Lashari, Samee, 1981- author.
Title: The rise of the semi-core : China, India, and Pakistan in the world-system / Samee Lashari.
Description: Lanham : Lexington Books, [2024] | Includes bibliographical references and index.
Identifiers: LCCN 2024006520 (print) | LCCN 2024006521 (ebook) | ISBN 9781666942866 (cloth) | ISBN 9781666942873 (epub)
Subjects: LCSH: China—Economic conditions. | India—Economic conditions. | Pakistan—Economic conditions. | China—History, Military. | India—History, Military. | Capitalism—Political aspects | International organization.
Classification: LCC HC427 .L35 2024 (print) | LCC HC427 (ebook) | DDC 330.951—dc23/eng/20240418
LC record available at https://lccn.loc.gov/2024006520
LC ebook record available at https://lccn.loc.gov/2024006521

∞™ The paper used in this publication meets the minimum requirements of American National Standard for Information Sciences—Permanence of Paper for Printed Library Materials, ANSI/NISO Z39.48-1992.

In memory of
My Mother

Contents

Introduction

This study is an effort to provide a structural explanation for the complex transformation the capitalist world-system has been going through since its inception in the sixteenth century. I try to analyze the positional standing of the Asian empires of China and India before the emergence of capitalism in the sixteenth century, their fall when capitalism expanded and integrated these regions through colonial projects, the postcolonial attempt of the states to develop their own model of development, and their eventual rise after they were integrated into the world-system. The three phases of the world-system—colonial, postcolonial, and the latest, post-integration—are analyzed by looking at the policies the core adopted to maintain its central position in the globalizing economy. From the start, this study tries to explicate that the core had a distinct edge regarding superior military power, which enabled it to occupy vast areas of India and China, coerce the Chinese Qing dynasty to concede discriminatory terms and conditions after its defeat in the Opium Wars, and govern India through colonial administration. This study also discusses the increasing complexification in the trimodal structure of the world-system in the postcolonial phase, the latest being the emergence of the semi-core. Moreover, the study discusses the presence of two world-orders within the world-system: economic world-order and strategic world-order. Whereas the economic world-order imposes a peculiar division of labor facilitating the accumulation of capital in the core, strategic world-order ensures deterrence through the coercive powers of the core. This study argues that the positional standing of any given country in the world-system depends on its positional standings in both world-orders. The core is composed of countries that are both military as well as economic powers. However, looking at the uneven pace of development within the developing world, the semi-core is argued to be a group of countries that essentially are either military powers or economic powers. The phenomenon of the semi-core shows an endeavor on the part of the core to impede the transfer of technology from the core to the periphery, spread and compartmentalize production processes, and create a complex interdependence within various tiers of the economy to ensure the survival of the capitalist system and procrastinate its eventual collapse.

Moreover, based on utilitarian ideas and comparative advantages, some of the developing countries are found to be more fit to serve strategic purposes and utilized accordingly. Since the developing countries found it suitable to cooperate with the core to accrue material benefits regarding industrialization, infrastructural development, growth in per capita income, and financial ability to spend more on national defense, this study argues about the survival of the world-system for the foreseeable future.

The first chapter of the book provides a detailed explanation of the model mentioned above. A literature review of both the classic and contemporary studies guides in identifying the discourse about the dynamic structure of the world-system. The logical argument about the changes in the positional standing of rising and falling powers in world history requires new explanation, particularly the one that may explicate the latest phase of contemporary globalization and the rise of China and India. This chapter provides a theoretical framework and debates in favor of the rise of the semi-core in the contemporary world system. This debate is based, whenever possible, on empirical evidence showing the emergence of the semi-core. Since I am arguing to include military power as an indication of national power when attempting to classify the positional standing of a country in the world-system, indicators about the military powers are also analyzed. I have endeavored to provide a logical and measurable definition of what I mean by the core, the semi-core, the semi-periphery, and the periphery. These definitions help me identify a set of countries that I label as the semi-core. This chapter provides a solid foundation to move forward to look at the countries of my interest: China (1757–2014), India (1757–2014), and Pakistan (1947–2014).

While looking at the origins of capitalism in Europe, recent studies have relied on the concept of "the great divergence" during the fifteenth and sixteenth centuries, which transformed Europe into the center of world economy, whereas China and India became peripheries after they were integrated into the capitalist world-system. Within the limits of my theoretical framework, I argue that Europe could expand its new system of world trade—capitalism—and impose it on non-European lands primarily because it had gone through a military revolution by that time. Superior military power and strategic skills, therefore, enabled Europeans to coerce and subdue the Chinese and Indian empires once they decided to occupy these lands, plunder local economies, and impose terms and conditions suitable to their commerce and accumulation of capital in Europe. The Industrial Revolution of the eighteenth century, therefore, took place *after* the fall and looting of China and India. This looting could have been possible because Europeans used their superior military power to impose their new economic system of mercantile capitalism on these and other regions. The chapters on China and India explain the premodern world-prominent position of those two regions in world trade, the consequences of their fall, and their recent rise within the structure of a capitalist world-system. Since they are emerging economies but not military powers, particularly when compared to the core countries of Western Europe and North America, they are put along with other emerging countries to create what I call the semi-core.

The complicated nature of the world-system helps identify the interplay between the system and these states. The desire to develop could not be materialized without integration into the world-system dominated by the core. The core, for its part, wanted to expand into and penetrate these regions. Since the end of the 1970s, a new wave of integration of China and India into the world-system took place. They are now becoming new capitalist societies as they witness economic growth and development. The core economies and their stakeholders are also benefiting through the diversification of production processes and complex industrial interdependence. The rise of the semi-core enables the core to assuage newer aspiration of non-European economies by helping them become semi-core countries—powerful economies yet less confident militarily. They are new allies of the capitalist core and help it procrastinate the eventual collapse of the system.

The chapter on Pakistan shows the imposition of the strategic world-order. Since its independence, Pakistan was found to be far more significant militarily than economically. Since the core maintains a deterrent presence of its forces in the world, it uses various countries to perform assignments. Regarding South Asia, Pakistan's military power can be explained using the structural framework I have developed. It also helps me explain why Pakistan could not develop a strong economy. Together, these three cases help me explain the fall and rise of non-European powers in the world-system.

Chapter One

From the Periphery to the Semi-Core

The Fall and Rise of Powers in the Modern World-System

This book is an endeavor to propose a new version of the theoretical lens of world-systems analysis in order to revamp it to address an increasing level of "complexification" in the global capitalist world-system. This said system is posing new challenges in the form of transformational developments, the most important being the re-emergence and resurfacing of economic powers in what is termed the "global South." This book argues that in response to these new challenges, the world-system is "complexifying" itself horizontally as well as vertically in terms of its structure, scope, and operations. Historically, since its inception in the sixteenth century, European capitalism has been dominating world trade and economic growth because of its imperial control across Asia, Africa, and South America. The global relations of productions were maintained through a two-tier system whereby the core grew by inflicting underdevelopment on the periphery by exploiting the resources of the latter. The system worked well throughout the colonial period and the initial decades of decolonization. Using its economic as well as military powers, the core could maintain its position determining the fate of economic development in the global South. An interplay between the system and the states determined the global division of labor and ensured accumulation of capital in the core though increasingly raising the share of the fast-growing semi-peripheral states. The integration of the developing states into the capitalist world-system was based on the extension of the global division of labor and the compartmentalization of production at the global scale. However, as some of the countries in the global South started "developing," the world-system had to increase their share of the politico-economic power.

One of the main consequences of this shift was a rise in the share and leverage of the non-Western powers, thereby taking global politico-economic leverage beyond Europe. The transformational shift, which is still underway, has posed new theoretical questions to approaches particularly interested in looking at the discourse of development-underdevelopment through a critical lens. This book tries to revamp world-systems analysis by arguing in favor of the complexification of the relations of production and proposing the insertion of a new tier in its trilateral global economic structure. This new tier, named here the "semi-core," is a necessary tool that allows me to reflect on the contemporary nature and outlook of global economic structure. In the following chapters, I apply this new tier to study the fall and rise of China and the Indian Sub-Continent over a period spanning more than two and half centuries.

This chapter delivers the central argument of the study; it discusses the emergence of the semi-core and the difficulties in its proper recognition so far. These central claims of the book have been laid down in the form of a set of five hypotheses that, put together, argue about the emergence of a new tier in the contemporary capitalist world-system and the integration of military power as a source of power determining the positional standing of a state in this system. Using the narrative of world-systems analysis, it builds a theoretical framework to discuss the transition taking place within the operational mechanism of the global capitalist system. This theoretical framework argues that despite the apparent rapid transformation in its functioning, the core is still dominating global trade and business. It is because the core has complexified the system of production, assembly, and consumption through an intricate network of decentralization and compartmentalization at the global scale. It has accommodated the aspirations of the faster developing states in a relegated manner; it has facilitated the emergence of the semi-core in the hierarchical structure of the system. These countries, as reflected in the data, are mainly economic powers but lacking in military power. In other words, the core is able to remain the epitome of the world-system primarily because it possesses *both* military *and* economic power. Dominated by the transnational capitalist class, the core is still capable of dictating the nature and magnitude of growth in various areas of the world. It has co-opted and encompassed the probable resisting powers within the developing world by coercively luring them in the name of economic development and modernization. The semi-core countries are coerced to allow the accumulation of capital in the West primarily because they lack military power, find it far more convenient to cooperate than resist, and are unable to develop or find any plausible alternative system to adopt. Given these reasons, it becomes necessary to analyze the functioning of the system in a historical manner. This framework serves as the bedrock for the next chapters looking at the historical fall and contemporary rise of China and the Indian Sub-Continent from the perspective of world-systems analysis.

MAJOR RESEARCH QUESTIONS

This study provides a structural explanation of the fall and rise of non-Western powers in the modern capitalist world-system by looking at the history of more than two and half centuries. In doing so, it deals with the economies of the world-empires of China and the Indian Sub-Continent and their transition from a tributary world-system into the capitalist world-system through colonization and its implications in terms of the loss of their erstwhile positional standing during the nineteenth and twentieth centuries, as well as the recent reversal of historical trend, resulting in another rise of China and India. It ponders how the capitalist world-system could effectively inflict a plunder on the regions under study in order to expand the venture of capital accumulation. It asks and explains how contemporary disparity between Western powers and non-Western powers was generated during the past two and a half centuries. More importantly, this study tries to explain how, once having been integrated into the capitalist world-system, the states under study remained underdeveloped unless they agreed to partially surrender their sovereign powers and embrace neoliberal capitalist policies by opening their economies to the dictates of global capitalism. More precisely, this study addresses following major questions: (1) As capitalism emerged as the leading politico-economic system of the world during the sixteenth century, how and why did China and the Indian Sub-Continent fail to maintain their erstwhile central position in the world economy? (2) Why did these regions remain underdeveloped for a good time after they had gotten political independence? (3) How did the capitalist world-system deny any endeavor of development in these regions unless it ensured its most vital interest—accumulation of capital? (4) How did it enforce the transformation of the national political economies in the states under study? (5) How has it complexified itself in order to remain the "only" workable politico-economic system in the world? This study tries to resolve these and other related puzzles by looking for answers based on historical and, whenever possible, empirical analysis using the theoretical lens of a modified version of world-systems analysis. These modifications try to expose emerging incompatibility of the theory in the light of apparent "Asianization" of global economic development. Simultaneously, these modifications claim to reflect the increasingly complexifying nature of the global capitalist world-system whereby states play subservient, co-constitutive, and facilitative roles in ensuring the accumulation of capital in the core.

THE ARGUMENT

In an endeavor to find answers to these questions, the study develops a set of arguments. Within the broader parameters and grand ontological positions of world-systems analysis, they aim at presenting a model that redefines the emerging structure of the global capitalist system. This model covers three distinctively different phases of world-systems: the era of the world-empires (two-tier world-system), the postcolonial era (which gradually transformed into a three-tier world-system), and the contemporary era (emerging four-tier world-system). This study agrees with the broader posture of world-systems analysis that, before the emergence and expansion of the modern capitalist world-system in the sixteenth century, world trade was governed through world-empires. However, with the inception of the modern world-system of capitalism in Europe during the sixteenth century, the nature of economic relations between various regions of the world was transformed. Therefore, it is immensely important to differentiate between the two different world-systems; the premodern or precapitalist world-system was the one under which free-trade relations existed and empires facilitated the conduct of trade across seas and land routes. The second and third chapters—in which I study the central position of China and the Indian Sub-Continent in world trade before the emergence of capitalism in Europe and the consequences of their forceful integration into the modern capitalist world-system—emphasize the difference between the two world-systems. Since this study encompasses a period during which this whole transformation took place, it is immensely important to keep in mind the difference between the two economic systems.

The main arguments of this study are the following. I argue that the world-system is dynamic, includes economic as well as military dimensions, and has been continuously complexifying itself since its inception about five hundred years ago. Initially, it was a two-tier structure comprised of the core and the peripheries. The core became the core because it was the home of capitalism, and it could turn some other European and then non-European areas of the world into a periphery. This transformation has been continuous and took place primarily because the core had acquired superior military capabilities due to the military revolution of the fifteenth and sixteenth centuries and it could impose its politico-economic policies on the regions to turn them into peripheries. The origins of the expansion of the capitalist world-system can be found in the ability of the European powers, particularly the British, to militarily coerce both China and India to accrue economic gains. The idea of the great divergence can better be explained by encompassing the superior military power of the British into the broader outlook of development that took place during the sixteenth, seventeenth, and eighteenth centuries; the Europeans, particularly the British, could subjugate, occupy, and decimate these regions and their premodern yet powerful economies primarily because they had far more superior military technology and skills. In both China and India, the British (and other Europeans, and Americans in the case of China) could impose unequal treaties primarily because of their ability to militarily control the regions. It was a combination of *both* fiscal and military power that enabled the British empire to defeat other European contenders in the Indian Ocean and occupy China and the Indian Sub-Continent to unleash colonialism. It used mercantile and colonial policies, de-industrialized these regions, peripheralized their economies by redefining their role in the international division of labor, exploited their resources, and imposed unequal and discriminatory terms and conditions of trade over them. The division of labor was evident in the military dimension as well; whereas the core countries maintained superior destructive powers, they assigned their respective peripheries the role of supplying financial resources to strengthen militaries further and recruited foot soldiers to fight their wars. Therefore, though the division of labor was prevalent and overwhelming in economics, it nevertheless prevailed in the military as well; the core developed, advanced, and maintained its exclusive control over superior military capabilities and exploited states to provide raw materials of the war, particularly the "human resource."

The postwar years show the continuation of the complexification process. Colonialism ended primarily because it was no more beneficial for the Europeans, and particularly war-torn British, to afford the administrative and political expense of maintaining physical control of Asia and Europe. As the world economic order transitioned from colonialism to postcolonialism, the core had to come up with new processes to overcome the challenge of newly developing nationalisms in the postcolonial world. The complexification process promoted the redefinition of the world economic order as well as world strategic order. On the one hand, due to the uneven pace of economic development, some of the countries within the periphery turned out to be transitional economies, or the semi-periphery. The world-system, therefore, turned into a three-tier system with a core, a semi-periphery, and a periphery. Whereas the core was defined as comprised of the developed states, the semi-peripheral countries were considered as developing economies, and the periphery as the agrarian countries. Controlled by transnational and elite capitalist class, the core was capable of determining the fate of development in various states and regions in accordance with the global division of labor. It further refined the division of labor on two parallel lines; it created an economic order wherein the division of labor in terms of production and consumption of resources was arranged according to the interests of the core. The states were classified—or promoted to be classified—as the core, semi-periphery, or periphery depending on their relative "positional standing" based on their respective roles in the division of labor. The core institutionalized this structure by incorporating inter-governmental organizations, financial institutions, and multinational corporations to complexify the functioning of the system. The states found it convenient to cooperate—they played a co-constitutive and facilitative role by serving their interests and those of the powerful core—and the quasi-monopolistic status of the states facilitated the division of labor and the reproduction of economic relations between them and the core.

On the other hand, since there prevailed a parallel world strategic order, the core redefined this hierarchical structure well. It relied on its military power to protect, promote, and deepen capitalism across the globe. In doing so, it forwarded a utilitarian approach of development whereby some countries were urged to develop economically while some others were lured to adopt a watchman character and serve strategic interests. I argue that since the process of complexification has been continuous, the magnitude of uneven development within the semi-periphery has stratified further, and the factor of nonstate actors and institutions has gained greater magnitude of influence, it strengthened the parallel world-orders. Every country, therefore, possesses a positional standing in both world-orders. The two world-orders are highly intertwined, hugely reciprocate each other, and precede as well as follow each other. They, however, are separate facets of and within the world-system. The two realms are affected by the scale of technological growth trickling down from the traditional core in most of the cases.

Within each world-order, the positional standing of a country is dependent on its retrospective powers. These forms of power are influenced by a complicated interplay between the country and the world-system. The structure of the world-system influences the fate of a country's positional standing primarily from the perspective of its utility in the system; a country grows militarily or economically when it is in the interests of the system. Simultaneously, any such positional standing is also subject to change following the patterns of development in the realms of national economy and security. The change in the positional standing of the states in the world-system depends, *primarily*, on the "needs" of the world-system and, *secondarily*, on the aspiration of the state to develop. Historically, the core had the power to arbitrarily and coercively define the positional standings of the regions by exclusively following its own needs. Contemporarily, though it still dominates the scope of development, the state develops a cooperative relationship to acquire a say in the process. A state develops when it submits to the terms and conditions of the world-system and thus agrees to facilitate it in serving its various interests, including, primarily, the accumulation of capital. More importantly, it develops more readily in those sectors that serve the interests of the core the most.

The complexification process facilitates integrating the state further into the system, promotes its material interests further, and develops its stakes in the survival of the system. Since the stability factor of the positional standing of any given country depends on how *symmetrical* both the facets of national power are, the core ensures that a noncore country may develop in one dimension only. A country, therefore, may progress militarily but not economically, and vice versa, and thus may occupy varying positions in the global security system, as well as the economic system, within the world-system. The study, one can infer, assumes that the greater the disparity between the two positional standings, the higher the instability and thus greater the dependency on the core to survive. The change in the positional standing of a state in either of the two world-orders takes place when the core redefines its role in that particular world-order. The change in the overall positional standing of a state in the world-system, however, takes place when, with the help of the core, it makes significant inroads in redefining its role in the global division of labor. Thus, unless a paradigmatic transformation in the core takes place, the utilitarian nature of the noncore states changes only to the extent of the acquiescence of the core and the aspirations of the state.

Furthermore, though the global economic system has undergone a fundamental change, it is *still* dominated by the Western economies led by the United States, and contrary to Immanuel Wallerstein and others, this study argues for its continuation for the foreseeable future. It is because the modern world-system, due to a set of five factors—vertical and horizontal globalization; the complex interdependence between production, assembly, and consumption; specialized and parochial industrialization of the global South; co-option of non-Western powers in the world-system; and an increase in the magnitude and scale of war and violence—has complexified the economic division of labor across the globe. Simultaneously, variations in the "positional standings" of different states in the interstate economic and political system, whereby China has become the second top economic power after the United States while Russia has fallen from its superpower status since its disintegration in 1991, has complicated the classification further. Wallerstein defined "semi-periphery" to hierarchize the structural outlook of the production processes of the capitalist world-system. This study argues that in the wake of rapid technological growth and its transfer away from the core to non-Western countries, faster economic growth and the embracing of global capitalism by some of these states, such as Brazil, China, India, South Korea, among others, the trilateral hierarchical structure has further complexified itself by the creation of yet another layer, which this study names the "semi-core." More importantly, this layer allows the core to remain intact while saturating the quest of these rising economies to transform the capitalist system. I argue further that this new layer enables the capitalist system to survive for the foreseeable future. I, in other words, do not anticipate the demise of the system *as soon as* Wallerstein and others predict. A long-term analysis of the fall and rise of Asian powers, by interlinking history with their contemporary status, is, thus, a timely attempt to magnify the relevance of world-systems analysis with the contemporary global economic structure. By disagreeing with one of the fundamental positions of Wallerstein, and by bringing in a factor of change *and* continuity in the case of the two most important states in BRICS (Brazil, Russia, India, China, and South Africa), this study attempts to deliver an alternative explanation of transformations within the capitalist world-system.

SIGNIFICANCE OF THE STUDY

This study addresses two omissions in contemporary theoretical literature within world-systems analysis. These two omissions, in other words, are the contributions this study claims to make in the existing literature. First, it tries to provide a structural explanation of the fall of China and the Indian Sub-Continent after they had been forcefully integrated into the capitalist world-system. The world-system exploited the economic resources of these regions under study during mercantile, imperial, and colonial times in order to accumulate capital in the core. These regions, more importantly, remained underdeveloped unless the states submitted to the demands of the capitalist world-system. The modernization and development in these states, particularly China and India, started when they agreed to play the crucial role of proactive facilitator to integrate their respective national economies with the capitalist world-system. The contemporary wave of "development" in these states is supported by both the capitalist world-system and the so-called "developmental" state because, I contend, there is an apparent convergence of interests of the two entities led by the national and transnational capitalist class. Even more significantly, the divergence in the "development" policies of the postcolonial states of South Asia can better be explained by bringing in the "structure" of the world-system as the most significant factor. Pakistan was quick to embrace the capitalist mode of production *before* its domestic economic infrastructure could mature. It adopted economic policies that suited Western capitalist interests. A rentier capitalist structure could not support the growing demands for employment opportunities and market diversification. The contemporary economic condition of Pakistan shows the repercussions of a wholesale acceptance of the capitalist world-system. This study endeavors to contextualize the historical developments and relates them to the latest complexified outlook of the global capitalist system. It accepts the significance of economic history in the same manner as emphasized by Andre Gunder Frank, Immanuel Wallerstein, Hamza Alavi, Giovanni Arrighi, Christopher Chase-Dunn, and other leading scholars of the tradition. Simultaneously, however, it identifies the role of the capitalist world-system represented then by imperial and colonial powers and now by the core countries, global financial institutions, and multinational corporations run by the transnational capitalist class to argue that capitalist expansionism has globalized production processes. As a dynamic system, it has caused transformation in its composition and structure by influencing the pattern of economic and/or military power in the countries of the global South.

Second, with establishing the claim that states develop when they submit to the terms and conditions of the world-system, and thus facilitate in serving its interests, a very important inference can be drawn. As developing states witness prosperity, they accrue stakes in the existence and continuity of the system. The same can confidently be claimed for China, India, and other states reaping the benefits of integration into the global capitalist system. Contrary to the burgeoning literature connecting the looming demise of American imperialism with the eventual termination of the capitalist world-system, this study argues that Asianization of the world-system, or the rise of Asian economies in the world economy, has been capitalist in nature and essence. Besides the ideological or material costs that both China and India had to pay in order to grow and develop, what remains significant to identify and explain is that their elevation in the global capitalist system has burgeoned their stakes in the survival of the system. Simultaneously, the system has been able to enforce its terms and conditions on those countries that agreed to submit to its "procrustean bed" (Perelman, 2011). The scarcity of literature offering a structuralist explanation of the phenomenal rise of China and India can also be attributed to the fact that the world-system has *still* not let either of the two countries, as well as Brazil, South Korea, Japan, and perhaps more, become powerful enough to challenge the location of the core, though it has let them become part of an influential club of countries dominating the world-system. This study argues that varying paces of development and economic growth in different countries and regions, as influenced by the world-system, have complexified the world-system to an extent that it has facilitated the emergence of another tier in the hierarchy of the global economic structure: the semi-core. The rise of China and India, in other words, is a deeper penetration and globalization of the capitalist world-system.

Some important terms are introduced in this study. Together, they are the essence of the arguments this study forwards. To restate, this study argues that in the wake of rapid and comprehensive changes in the "positional standing" of countries and regions in the global economy, the capitalist world-system has "complexified" itself to such an extent that a new tier in the hierarchical structure—the semi-core—has emerged. "Complexification," then, is a term that explains the nature and impact of the inclusion of state as well as nonstate actors in production processes, thus escalating the diversification and decentralization of the production processes by taking them away from the traditional core. Taking an analogy of horizontal and vertical nuclear proliferation, this study coins the terms "horizontal complexification" and "vertical complexification." Horizontal complexification takes place when some countries shift their positional standing from one tier to another or when they create a new tier within the world-system. As countries join the semi-periphery from the periphery, or when they create the semi-core from both the core and the semi-periphery, they complexify the production system and the reproduction of social processes and cause changes in the development, underdevelopment, or maldevelopment of various countries and regions across the globe. Simultaneously, the term indicates the emergence and growth of new nonstate actors, particularly the economic elite class and the rise of multinational corporations in global capitalism. Vertical complexification, then, is a process whereby every entity diversifies its productive capacities and increases its contribution to the global production of marketable products. Vertical complexification globalizes class alliances and competitions and thus compels state actors to follow the dictates and act as facilitators of the accumulation of capital.

It is important to see how and why economic neoliberalism falls short of offering a theoretical solution to the question this study is trying to answer. Without denying that economic neoliberalism, whose one concrete form can arguably be found in the Washington Consensus, has been the dominant policy prescription in the second half of the twentieth century. It is the newer prescription of economic ills derived from the old philosophy of liberalism. The globalization of capitalist production and reproduction in the wake of postwar politico-economic development has affected the pace of economic growth and underdevelopment throughout the regions of the world. The neoliberal approach not only condones historical developments but also downplays their deterministic role in defining, explaining, and resolving the phenomenon of underdevelopment in the global South. Its parochial perspective neglects not only historical developments but, more importantly, the long-term consequences of the colonization of Asian, African, and American continents by European imperial powers. The ahistorical approach of economic neoliberalism allows it to condone the "structural" factors that have prolonged global inequalities caused by colonial and postcolonial policies. Instead of recognizing the factors that created an unbridgeable gap between the West and the rest of the world, such as colonialism, a variety of other reasons are forwarded. A deliberate attempt is made to condone the unequal terms and conditions imposed on the developing and the underdeveloped world by neoliberal institutions and economic powers. It is ignored that world trade had been governed through imperial policies. Galtung (1971) termed the postcolonial policies "structural imperialism," by which he meant that the global structure of economic relations was comprised of center and periphery nations. He argued that structural imperialism "is a system that splits up collectivities and relates some of the parts to each other in relations of *harmony of interest*, and other parts in relations of *disharmony of interests*, or *conflict of interest*" (p. 81, emphasis original). In such a system the nations in the center have mutually reinforcing interests, primary of which is the accumulation of capital, while the peripheral nations have "incompatible goals" to pursue. The neoliberal theory disagrees with this approach and simply condones the criticism. It ignores "how, after the end of colonialism, the West managed to push ideas of free-market fundamentalism—many of which reflected the perspectives and interests of Wall Street—on developing countries" (Stiglitz, 2015: 64). The consequence of the dominance of this approach is that history is sidelined; Eurocentrism and inequality are naturalized.

While economic neoliberalism offers an ahistorical analysis of economic development and underdevelopment, the dominant approach in world-systems analysis appears to be nostalgic in referring to the "thousand" years of history, as if it is in competition with the European description of global economic history led by modernization theorists. There is no denying that a long-term historical analysis does help in predicting the likelihood of future patterns of developments from a number of competing versions only if a theoretical framework aims to do so by providing a due space by relating the history with contemporary affairs. Analyzing history, however, can make little sense in explaining the contemporary issues of the global South if a theoretical approach does not provide a balanced focus. The world-systems analysis approach is credited to have made commendable intellectual contributions by denying "modernity" as being an exclusive European phenomenon and placing it back on Asian soil. More importantly, it should be credited to have contextualized the genesis of underdevelopment and the accumulation of capital with the colonization and economic pillage caused thereafter. Even more importantly, using a neo-Marxist theoretical lens, it has successfully exposed the phenomenon of structural subjugation established by the Western-dominated interstate system and institutional paraphernalia.

What, however, it has been unable or unwilling to explain is the relevance of economic history in the rapid industrial and technological transformation of the last four to five decades that ushered the politico-economic resurgence and rise of Asian countries as the new dominant powers in the world-system. In particular, while macroscopic analysis provides a long-term development perspective, it falls short of explaining the rapidity of transformation in cases where it is fundamental and comprehensive, thus showing its inability to theoretically explain the changes in the "positional standing" of various states, including, most importantly, China and India. It has not offered a plausible explanation for the complexification of the global economic production and reproduction process whereby global capitalism has been able to control the transformation of production processes and the reproduction of social relations through the invention of technology and its replacement in the periphery. The fundamental concepts of the approach, such as the binary spatial *and* temporal division of global production and the reproduction of economic relations between "the core" and "the periphery," remain unchanged to a larger extent. For example, while discussing how global economic integration has been fatal to the global South, Samir Amin argues that "the world expansion of capitalism is accompanied by increasing inequality in social distribution at the periphery, whereas at the centre of the system it does create conditions for lesser social inequality" (Amin, 2011: 220). The underlying definition of the periphery in binary opposition to the core or center stands very similar to what he described some forty years earlier in his seminal work (Amin, 1974; Amin, 1976).

While there is no doubt that dependency theorists have delivered remarkable contributions by offering alternative explanations for underdevelopment in the global South, they have been stagnant in offering a methodical approach to delineating the rapid structural transformations in the postwar world where the rise and fall of powers has been quick and affected global politico-economic development. The capitalist world-system was led by Dutch, British, and American hegemonies in the eighteenth, nineteenth, and twentieth centuries, respectively. The rise of competitors to the United States, however, has been phenomenal. By the mid-1970s, China was still the peripheral state. In the last forty years, other states have risen from peripheral status to the semi-periphery level. In particular, the BRICS countries have turned themselves into a group of new aspiring states collaborating to redefine the global economic order. Japan, despite having been defeated in World War II, was able to rise again. South Korea, Taiwan, Singapore, Malaysia, and, to an extent, Indonesia have also been successful in elevating their positional standing in the global economic order.

The binary scheme of dividing countries and regions into the two opposite categories of the core and the periphery was somewhat modified when Wallerstein claimed a new tier in the system—the semi-periphery. While it turned the appearance of the world-system into a trilateral structure, it did not bring any fundamental transformation in theoretical perspective. Wallerstein defines the semi-periphery as "a mix of the core-like and peripheral products" (Wallerstein, 2004: 29). In other words, to Wallerstein and others, the principal feature determining the positional standing of any country in the economic world-system is dependent on "the production processes," which are based on the scale of invention and the application of modern technology.

Since the West, particularly the United States, is the epitome of technological invention and its applications, and since the technology being born there affects production processes throughout the semi-periphery as well as the periphery, the real significance of the semi-periphery stands as nothing more than a transitory level with two primary objectives. First, it should happily perform the core-like tasks assigned to it by the core. Second, the transfer of proliferating technological inventions in the West to peripheral states could be slowed down. Given that these two features reaffirm the dependence of both semi-peripheral and peripheral countries on the core, it looks unattractive to create a new tier in the system.

This might have been truer had there been no fundamental changes in the production processes of the global economic system. A number of unprecedented factors, the most important being the rapidity of invention, the growth of technology, and the shift of their location away from the core, have not properly been incorporated into the theoretical framework laid down by Wallersteinian world-systems analysis. More importantly, it has become inevitable to respond to one of the central questions that world-systems analysis has been condoning: Why do some states—within the periphery—develop faster than some other states? A utilitarian thesis about the variations in the pace of growth of developing countries may not suffice to answer the intellectual queries contextualizing the long-term macroscopic history of economic development and underdevelopment. This study claims that a fundamental shift in the global economic system is underway and needs to be acknowledged. The production process has been complexified. The United States is increasingly losing its position as the "exclusive" center of modern technological development. Rapidly, the BRICS nations are taking assertive positions with an increasing capacity and ability to develop modern technologies on their own.

Far more significantly, world-systems analysis condones the role of national strategic power in the functioning of global capitalism. Being a neo-Marxist perspective, the tradition adopts a genealogical-cum-intellectual propensity to define economic power as the most significant mode of national power, which is understandable. However, neglecting coercible strategic power in the world-system or considering it of trivial significance in a world where relations among territorial entities depend on their capability to defend or defeat, it is necessary to take into account the facilitative role military power plays to enable the core to maintain its economic control over various parts of the world. Imperialism in the eighteenth century could expand its control over the vast African and Asian territories primarily because of its superior military power; in the postwar world, the core maintained its status by relying on the combined military power of North Atlantic Treaty Organization (NATO). I will explain this further while pointing out the emergence of the semi-core as a resolution to address the rising aspirations of fast-industrializing countries of the global South. Suffice it here to say that a country can become a member of the core only if it elevates its positional standing *both* economically and militarily. Progress in one of these two forms of national power deprives it of gaining any such status. This issue helps me explain why some states have developed militarily but not economically, and vice versa. The core has ensured that its collective military power, with the United States at the center, remains far too great to be destroyed.

COMPLEXIFICATION OF THE CAPITALIST WORLD-SYSTEM: THEORETICAL FRAMEWORK

The State and the World-System

This book follows the grand postulates as laid down by leading critical political economists who look at the developments in and transformation of the politico-economic structure of the whole world over a long period of time. In general, the critical tradition of political economy defines the global politico-economic system in hierarchical terms dominated by a class structure that has globalized its control. Within this theoretical tradition, however, various approaches disagree about the role and comparative power of the actors involved. While a Marxist approach underscores the role of the state as an "instrument" of the international bourgeoisie devised to "facilitate" the accumulation of capital, a neo-Marxist understanding emphasizes the "structure" within which the transnational capitalist class rules over the institution of the state. In other words, a predominant understanding of the political economy designates the state as an important character in the conduct of international economic activities. A sub-group within the neo-Marxist approach, called dependency theorists, emphasizes the role of "structure" to refer to the "development" in some regions of the world at the cost of the "underdevelopment" in some other areas of the world. World-systems theorists take a long-term approach to show the correlation between the underdevelopment in some areas perpetuated due to their historical "exploitation" and the rise of global capitalism. The institution of the state, here, is considered an important factor in providing conspicuous growth to the accumulation of capital directed toward the core.

One of the main shortcomings of this tradition, however, is a dearth of recognition of the so-called "quest" of the state to develop, something neoliberal economists concentrate on. In other words, while critical political economists concentrate on the structure, neoliberal economists look toward the agency role of the state in the discourse of development; while critical political economists look at the idiom of "development" being defined by the Western modernization scholarship and its deleterious socio-ecological consequences, neoliberal economists emphasize that the state has a predisposition to develop. This book, however, argues that because the institution of the state has played an instrumental role in facilitating the accumulation of capital in the core, the nature of development and underdevelopment could better be explained by looking at the global economic structure while taking into account the valuable significance of the role of the state. Within critical tradition, therefore, there is a lack of recognizing the accurate sense of interplay between global *and* domestic forces that results in failing to acknowledge the varying paces of development in the global South. Analyzing the "rise" and "re-emergence" in the global economic system of countries including but not limited to BRICS asks for theoretical reformulations and adjustments.

It is not the case that critical political economists have just ignored the institution of the state while zealously labeling the structure as the most plausible source of explanation for the development of the global economic system. They, such as Karl Polanyi (2001), have looked into the role that the state played in the emergence and growth of the free market economic system in Europe, in general, and Britain, in particular. With an aim to term "the idea of a self-adjusting market" as "a stark utopia," Polanyi refers to the fundamental conflict between the so-called self-adjusting market and the society whereby the market emerged, "annihilating the human and natural substance of society" and compelling the latter to take "measures to protect itself." These measures, however, "impaired the self-regulation of the market, disorganized industrial life, and thus endangered society in yet another way," by which he means the "disruption of the social organization" (p. 3). It places the state at odds with either society or the market. The "double movement" characterized by the resistance of society to its disembeddedness from the market results in either protectionist policies whereby the state has to support the effort of the society to control economics, or laissez-faire policies whereby the state supports the disembeddedness of economics from society. Polanyi argues that it was in fact the state that had always been there to support both kinds of ventures. In other words, it is the state, not the independent autonomous market, that determines the outlook of economic policies. In times of need, neoliberal economists also yearn for the support of the state to take care of the "dirty consequences" of market failures.

The role of the state, therefore, remains a crucial one. Neoliberal economists acknowledge this role but argue that the "necessary" and minimal role of the state is meant to both protect and support national economic interests in order to "facilitate" the conduct of business by developing rules guaranteeing the right of property and blocking monopolization. Smithian economics argues that a strong state is necessary to enforce private property rights, ensure the honoring of contracts signed by independent actors, discourage monopoly and ensure competition, maintain public order through the policing and administration of justice, and guarantee national defense. Milton Friedman and Rose Friedman (2002) argue that the best way to establish a true competition and spontaneous order in economy and society is to adopt a free market mechanism whereby the exchange of goods and services is administered through an entrepreneurial spirit, leading to greater individual freedom and an efficient allocation of scarce resources.

Economic neoliberalism asks to ensure the functioning of the free market economic system, which, the critics argue, cannot be provided without the patronage of the state. According to David Harvey (2005), in neoliberal economics, "the role of the state is to create and preserve an institutional framework appropriate to practices" such as "strong private property rights, free markets and free trade" in order to ensure that "human well-being can best be advanced by liberating individual entrepreneurial freedoms and skills within an institutional framework" (p. 2). In doing so, contrary to the rhetoric of minimal role of the state as espoused by neoliberal economists, the state is required to "set up those military, defense, police and legal structures and functions required to secure private property rights and to guarantee, by force if need be, the proper functioning of markets" (p. 2). John Maynard Keynes argued that markets were essentially unable to, and often did not, adjust on their own the way neoliberal economists believed. He argued that "in those situations the state's economic interventions can correct or offset market failures or inadequacies" (quoted in Wolff and Rensick, 2012: 115). He, therefore, argued in favor of an embedded liberalism, a mixed economic approach whereby government intervention was termed necessary primarily to stabilize economic growth by creating full employment opportunities, circulating finance in the market, and facilitating its trickling down to address the issues of abject poverty.

In almost all theories of political economy, the role of the state remains crucial, though the ontologies of significance remain starkly different. In world-systems analysis, the state is assumed to be a co-constituent and a facilitator in the growth of the capitalist world-system. The state played various significant roles in submitting to and facilitating the needs of the capitalist system. These roles ranged from autarkic, mercantile to liberal, and so-called noneconomic. Historically, the state has been assigned *and* denied various prerogatives. It, nevertheless, has been a quintessential ingredient in facilitating the primary interest of the capitalist world-system, which, as I have argued, has always been the accumulation of capital in the core. The state has been providing the principal framework within which, until now, *international* politics has been conducted, processed, and analyzed. It was empowered with exclusive control over the human, material, and political means available to the world. Currently, it is the master of individual and collective political identities. It still controls the citizenship and movement of individuals across geographical units, and it claims to be sovereign, at least and in theory, in its internal political affairs. Simultaneously, the world-system has relinquished it from a number of its historic "duties" and "prerogatives." Particularly, it largely has been defanged from its mercantile capacities. The capitalist world-system, using its self-manufactured forces of globalization, has "taken over" many of the roles erstwhile associated with the state, including but not limited to the nature, magnitude, and dimension of development.

Throughout the history under discussion, the institution of the state kept playing a facilitative role, ensuring the smooth functioning of the modern capitalist world-system. It has been the frontline agent of the capitalist system. Today, the core of the world-system is comprised of developed capitalist states controlled effectively by the transnational capitalist class. The system wields the interests of both entities in such a way that the political outlook of the state is made to serve the economic interests of the capitalist class. The world-economic system, therefore, controls the political-administrative units called states and determines the fate of development, underdevelopment, and/or maldevelopment in an effective manner. The states, in essence, do not enjoy sovereign autonomy in economic ventures. Contrarily, they are controlled by the superstructure of the world economic system. This book follows the neo-Marxist understanding of the state that the primary "function" of the state and its institutions is to serve the capitalist mode of production (Barrow, 1993: 51). In other words, the very "structure" of the state itself was designed as capitalist in order to preserve a peculiar kind of mode of production. Therefore, the ruling political class was simultaneously the ruling economic class. The post-Marxist theory of the state concentrates more on the contradictions within the systematic features developed and put in place by the capitalist order. Given that world-systems theorists emphasize the structure of global capitalism *and* its propensity for crisis and eventual termination, it can safely be argued that the state plays a necessary facilitative role in serving the interests of the core within the constraints enforced on it by the global capitalist structure controlled by the transnational capitalist class.

Wallerstein has explained in more than one place the role of the state in the smooth functioning of the world-system. In this system, a stronger state is the one that facilitates the maximization of profit-making. Multinational corporations, the frontline organizations of the capitalist system, enable themselves to survive, burgeon, and accumulate capital depending on their ability to screw the states to serve their interests (Wallerstein, 1984). In particular, the institution of the state facilitates the functioning of the system by subjecting the production and movement of products to varying territorial and legal controls. It also ensures taxation, price control, monopolization of economic processes, internalization of manufacturing costs, enforcement of patent system, and subsidization. These functions, Wallerstein argues, enable the capitalist world-system to function smoothly (Wallerstein, 2004: 46). The state, therefore, performs certain actions that cannot be performed in a political order envisioning a global state. In fact, Wallerstein argues, "The modalities by which states interfere with the virtual market are so extensive that they constitute a fundamental factor in determining prices and profits" (Wallerstein, 2004: 26). He admits that in a constant struggle over the allocation of surplus value, "the state is a central actor in shifting the allocation in one direction or the other" (Wallerstein, 2004: 50–51). In such a struggle, weaker (peripheral) states succumb to powerful (core) states. The core states are captivated by the firms owned by the transnational capitalist class. The capitalist system, therefore, utilizes the core states and their powers as a compulsive tool to maneuver the weaker states to facilitate these firms. Since markets or economic forces cannot function on their own, they are in need of continuous assistance and support from the state and its institutions to facilitate the process. Therefore, instead of entering the bickering and the tiresome job of doing politics, the economic elite class controls national politics by pouring in finances and determining the fate and direction of national political developments.

Despite that there is a disagreement about the origins of the modern world-system, theorists nevertheless place an overwhelming emphasis on the structure of the global economic relations that gave birth to and enabled the rise to contemporary domination of the Western powers about five hundred years ago. According to Tariq Amin-Khan (2012), the institution of the state has changed since its modern conception as the capitalist driving force. Capitalist development was initially supervised and patronized by the state, and its expansionist nature asked the state to turn itself into an imperialist entity in order to protect the interests beyond territorial boundaries. There is, in other words, a "link between the rise of the nation-state and the expansion of capitalism" (pp. 22–25). The role of the state, therefore, remains undeniable. It is essentially the imperial state of the West that played the frontline role in establishing the modern world-system. The state, as mentioned, acted under the "system" of global capitalism to promote trans-territorial trade and commercial ventures, facilitated the growth and burgeoning of the transnational capitalist class, and enabled the capitalist class to accumulate capital by imposing territorial control in the name of abstract ideas such as nationalism.

Despite being the fundamental ingredient of an international system, the status of the state has been precarious and fickle. Contrary to general understanding, the theoretical approach adopted by Eurocentric historians whereby the Westphalian nation-state was pronounced to be the fundamental pillar of the global system of governance, it has been attacked by leading scholars from all theoretical approaches of international politics. Leaving all other "Great Debates" in the theories of international relations aside, I keep my focus on the interpretation of the role and status of the state in the growth and complexification of the capitalist world-system as espoused by world-systems analysis. World-systems theory argues for the existence of the state as a territorially defined strong institution in the pre-Westphalian world. This book recognizes the validity of this argument. I, however, take this argument further and argue that the Westphalian system was crafted in order to facilitate accumulation of the capital. Because Europe was able to define and establish its relations with the world firstly and primarily through commercial activities, the state facilitated the accumulation of capital by adopting mercantile policies that later turned colonial and imperial in nature and essence. The institution of the Westphalian state was made to fit into the schema of global capitalism.

PHASES OF COMPLEXIFICATION

The First Phase: Asia, the West, and the Great Divergence

Based on historical facts available today, such as *International Historical Statistics*, I argue that before the West could rise, the structure of the world-system was Asia-centered. It remains one of the most significant topics of intellectual wrangling as to why Europe, and neither China nor India, experienced an Industrial Revolution. Termed the "great divergence," this historic development receives opposite narratives and arguments from scholars peering into the world socio-economic history. As a matter of fact, the role of intercontinental trade, mainly through the ancient Silk Route, and factors impeding its growth during 1300–1500, such as the rise of the Turkish empire in Asia Minor and the Mediterranean region and the consequent European push to explore "all-sea" routes of this trade, are among the most prevalent ideas explaining the origins of the rise of capitalism, the first globalization, the West, and colonization (Duzgun, 2018). It was primarily the question of safe trade routes to India and China that pushed European sailors such as Vasco da Gama and Christopher Columbus to go on voyages that resulted in what we know today as the "Age of Discovery." Disagreement arises as to how this first globalization resulted in the great divergence. On the one hand are those who refer to geo-ecological and economic reasons that compelled northern Europe, particularly England, to utilize coal as a source of fuel. Kenneth Pomeranz (2000) argues that although coal had been used in China since at least the eleventh century, it did not become the primary source of energy because of an abundant stock of wood as a source of fuel. Similar circumstances on the Indian Sub-Continent also hindered utilization of coal as a source of energy. More importantly, it is argued that while Europe could not utilize its land resources much, it went on developing resource- and energy-intensive technologies, and China went on increasing its grain productivity in order to ensure a food supply for its larger population.

In the long run, the European decision to capitalize on coal energy led it to develop an industrial base dually supported by its control of the Americas. This, however, was achieved much later as compared to what Eurocentric development theorists claim. Even by 1789, Pomeranz argues, "Western European lands, labor, and product markets were on the whole probably *further* from perfect competition than those in most of China" (p. 17, emphasis original). Prasannan Parthasarathi (2011) argues that while advanced regions of Asia and Europe grew at an almost equal pace, it was by the end of eighteenth century that the gap started widening to an increasingly vivid level. In particular, Britain faced stiff challenges to its economic growth from the Indian textile industry dominating world trade from the Americas to Japan. It led to the invention of spinning in Britain during the Industrial Revolution. In addition, facing a shortage of wood for fuel, they found coal, which later led to the invention of the steam engine and newer modes of transportation. Recently, two crucial contributions have been made rejecting the dependency theorists' argument. Roman Studer (2015) argues that the great divergence started not as the consequence of coal exploration and its widespread use, but that it had already started in the seventeenth century when European commercial links had been established with East Asia, China, India, and Africa. In the same manner, Peer Vries (2015) also attacks so-called "Eurasian similarity thesis" by arguing that in fact there were huge differences between the two areas of the world whereby "the Great divergence is caused by the emergence of modern economic growth in a specific part of the world and its absence in the rest of it" (p. 3). This, however, needs to be contextualized with the fact that both the Dutch and British East India Companies were chartered one hundred years before the Europeans could develop the first commercial steam engine. The cotton-spinning machine was invented even later.

Some recent studies have offered different explanations. Pim de Zwart (2016) looks at the living standards in Dutch East India Company settlements in the seaport areas of India and Africa such as Bengal, Ceylon, Java, and Cape Colony and compares them with European standards. He argues that "evidence about Asian standards of living is generally thin and contradictory" (p. 80). He uses real wages as an indicator of living standards and takes into account the role of globalization in converging prices of consumer goods. Based on his analysis, he argues that "the real wages for Cape Town show a slightly increasing trend over the seventeenth and eighteenth centuries," whereas "living standards were generally lower in the other case-study areas, where, in contrast to the Cape, the evidence for indigenous workers, rather than for European settlers" was used (p. 140). In other words, he argues that the income and living standards of indigenous populations were already lower before the penetration of European traders in Asia and Africa. Similarly, Daly (2020) argues that "the Industrial Revolution, the Great Divergence," and in general "the rise of the West" were not accidental, not a stroke of luck, not unexpected, but precisely the result of "a deep, slow evolution out of centuries of particular conditions unique to early modern Europe," prominent being the "Europeans' willingness and ability to build on cultural foundations and achievements from around the world" (pp. xi–xii, 12).

The rise of the West, according to another group of scholars led by eminent intellectuals such as Andre Gunder Frank and Hamza Alavi, was in fact made possible at the cost of the economic collapse of the Indian Sub-Continent and China starting with the arrival of Western traders and merchants. This group is dominated by Indian nationalist economic historians and postcolonialists such as Bipan Chandra, Dipesh Chakrabarty, R. S. Sharma, Mubarak Ali, Ayesha Jalal, and others. This groups looks at the history from a different perspective. According to these scholars, the rise of the West would not have been possible without the compellingly coercive power of an increasingly influential economic class that utilized private military resources under the patronage of the state to occupy Asian lands. It was, therefore, a *consequence* of the fall of China and the Indian Sub-Continent in the world-system. In order to control the global economy, it was necessary to plunder competitive production houses in Asia. The capitalist world-system, therefore, inflicted on the economic structure of China and India a pervasive and prolonged destructive campaign of imperial control. Throughout the colonial period, spanning over two hundred years in the case of the Indian Sub-Continent and over a hundred years in case of China, the mercantile and imperial states of Europe were assigned to be guardians of the interests of the home-based economic class through self-serving terms and conditions applied to Asian and African lands. The prosperity of the West was secured at the cost of the impoverishment of China and the Indian Sub-Continent. The institution of the state in the West adopted all economic policies, including autarky, imperialism, occupation, colonialism, and arbitrary oppressive looting of the resources from the colonies and occupied areas and bringing this wealth to the West.

World-systems theorists argue that as capitalism rose to be the most prominent economic system in the world, it penetrated into the areas of Africa and Asia through trade. The European disadvantage of silver was met through the discovery of the same in the Americas. During the initial periods of modern capitalism, the burgeoning economic class pushed the state to adopt mercantile policies to advance imperialist designs aimed at physical control of the lands in Asia. The expansive Western capitalism in the early eighteenth century utilized the institution of the state to transform national economic orders in accordance with the dictates of the capitalist class. Contrary to neoliberal claims, therefore, the state has always been there to facilitate the processes of production and the accumulation of capital. Though this book agrees that Europe used South American silver to set aside its chronic trade deficit in Asian trade, the real benefit of this turn of events was the development of military skills that, together with mercantile-imperial policies, ensured territorial conquests in Asia. The fact is further delineated in chapters 2 and 3 where I analyze the notion of military power as a principal factor in ensuring the great divergence of Europe toward industrialization and of China and India toward a fall from the pinnacle of economic power to the periphery in an expansive world-system.

There are credible historical facts to corroborate the claim that Asian empires, particularly China and the Indian Sub-Continent, were the leading economic powers during the famous "Dark Ages" of the West. Andre Gunder Frank and Barry Gills (1993) refuse to credit Europeans for the creation of either the world economic system or capitalism. They argue that while Western and southern Europe had a trade deficit, which they tried to meet through the silver and gold trade, India and China had a trade surplus mainly with Europe and West Asia. According to them, "By comparison and instead, Ming/Qing China and Moghul India, as well as Ottoman Turkey and perhaps Safavid Persia politically and economically far outranked any of the individual West European economies and states, and probably all the European ones put together" (Frank and Gills, 2000: 7–11). At another place, Frank argues that China and the Indian Sub-Continent were the geographic and economic epicenters of the world for three consecutive centuries starting in 1400. Both countries, he argues, fell prey to the imperial world-system led by the British (Frank, 1996).

Wallerstein's concentration on the contemporary world-system from 1500 onward and its location of origins in Europe has been criticized by scholars likeminded to those who argue that the world-system is as old as five thousand years and Europe was not the founder of this system. Hamza Alavi, for example, criticizes both Marxist and non-Marxist approaches claiming the origins of capitalist structure in Europe and its subsequent expansion in colonies. Refuting the argument that "the core" of the modern world-system has always been northwestern Europe, he argues that the reverse was rather a fact: Indian economic structure, though with a feudal mode of production, was far ahead of the European states (Alavi, 1982). Angus Maddison (1971) and others have argued that the two regions of the Indian Sub-Continent and China produced about half of the world's gross domestic product (GDP) and more than half of industrial production. In 1720, India contributed about one-fourth of the world's GDP, equal to the whole of Europe put together. To put it in context, it was only in the mid-1980s that the whole continent of Asia was able to reach the level of GDP share in the world that India had produced in 1720 (Chaudhuri, 1978, 1985; Hobson, 2004; Maddison, 2003, 2005; Mielants, 2008; T. Roy, 2006, 2012a, 2012b). Pomeranz (2000) observes that "it seems likely that average incomes in Japan, China, and parts of Southeast Asia were comparable to (or higher than) those in Western Europe, even in the late eighteenth century" (p. 49). China and the Indian Sub-Continent, in other words, were producing more than half of the world's GDP before the Europeans could occupy these lands. Though India was not as advanced as the Europeans were when they occupied it, particularly in military power, it still remains a fact that the colonial experience affected Indian society and economy negatively and immensely. Its industrial exports were halted and then deserted. Palat and others (1986) argue that while the taxation system under the Mughals did not allow the middle and lower-middle working classes to grow to play a decisive role in economic development, it was primarily the colonial venture that, by squandering material and fiscal resources, de-industrialized and de-urbanized the Sub-Continent. A somewhat similar outcome was observed in China. For more than two hundred years, the European-led world-system was able to accumulate capital in its center while the colonies saw a sharp decline in their contribution to the world economy. Had there been no colonial history or had India (united) been liberated by 1880, "it is likely that both income and population growth would have been accelerated" because of "a smaller drain of investible funds abroad, greater tariff protection, more state enterprise and favors to local industry, and more technical training" (Maddison, 1971: 37).

I argue that pre–Industrial Revolution world trade and commerce was dominated by the Indian Sub-Continent and China. Before the Europeans could rise to dominate the world, the textile industry in the Indian Sub-Continent was far more advanced than in any other part of the world. For three hundred years—from 1200 AD to 1500 AD—the Indian Sub-Continent was a flourishing urban society with large-scale production of crafts through spinning wheels and treadle looms, wine, paper, sugar, and, most importantly, textiles exported to the Middle East, Central and West Asia, and China (Mielants, 2005: 123–24). According to Lin Chun (2013), at the time when Europe was a primitive periphery in the world-trade system, China was the leading producer of silk and many other products (p. 10). Andre Gunder Frank disagrees with Immanuel Wallerstein and Giovanni Arrighi about the origins of the capitalist system in the world, as he considers the middle of the nineteenth century the time when a paradigm shift took place culminating in the rise of the West and an accumulation of capital there. Wallerstein, however, argues that the invention of capitalism as a large-scale system of economic competition and surplus accumulation started in the sixteenth century; the eighteenth century was the time when the domination of the modern capitalist world-system spread throughout the globe through imperial-colonial policies. Arrighi (2010) argues that every century since the fifteenth has witnessed a shift in the core. During the fifteenth century, Genoa—a city-state of modern Italy—was the leading power accumulating capital by dominating trade routes throughout the globe. The central significance in capital accumulation, according to Arrighi, went from Genoa to the Portuguese capitalists, followed by the rise of the British empire in the eighteenth and nineteenth centuries. The twentieth century was called the American century. The most significant threat Arrighi identifies is the "financialization" of the world economy. As financialization reaches its apex level, surpassing trade and production, the crisis of speculations starts and brings a downward trend in the capitalist system. Since this has been the case in the later years of the twentieth century, the systemic crisis is not a surprise. In this sense, Arrighi comes closer to Wallerstein by predicting a looming collapse of modern capitalism.

With a vivid disagreement about the origins and the nature of world capitalism, however, both Wallerstein and Arrighi agree with Frank that the Indian Sub-Continent and China were the leading economic powers before the West could rise. Frank argues that from 1400 AD to 1800 AD, China was the "super accumulator" of economic power in the world "based on its unrivaled manufacturing efficiency and export of silk, porcelain and other ceramics" (Frank and Gills, 2000: 8). A recent study by Christopher Chase-Dunn and Bruce Lerro partially supports Frank's claims. While they agree about the Sino-centered nature of the world-system before Europe could rise, Chase-Dunn and Lerro (2014) argue that "the long rise of the West" started much earlier than the eighteenth century as claimed by Frank. More importantly, this rise was not abrupt or quick; it took place in a series of what Arrighi calls "systematic cycles of accumulation." Chase-Dunn and Lerro argue that "a strong urban and agricultural capitalism" emerged in Europe "in the sixteenth and seventeenth centuries" due to the confluence of "structural features"—"the existence of appropriately commoditized institutions" such as "money, market, contract law" and "the weak and decentralized nature of European tributary structures"—and "conjectural elements" (p. 214).

Frank is particularly important in establishing the case of historical Afro-Eurasian supremacy in world economic history. He argues that "contrary to widespread doubts and denials, there was a single global world economy with a worldwide division of labor and multilateral trade from 1500 onward" (Frank, 1998: 52). The Eurocentric modernization theory erases historical evolution by restricting world development history to the last two hundred years or so. This, according to Frank, is due to "Eurocentric bias and civilizational arrogance" (p. 19).

Frank (1998) argues that because the Eurocentric social theory "distorts all perception of, indeed even blinds us from seeing, the reality of the world outside the West" since it is "innately incapable of coming to any terms with the (economic/systemic) reality of one single world," "an entirely differently based world history and global political economy" is required (p. 28). He fulfills this challenge by "reorienting" his readers with *world* history and *world* economy during 1400–1800 when Europe possessed a marginal position in the world economic system. During this time, Frank argues, world trade was dominated by India and China, with the former leading exports of textile products and the latter being the top silk producer and maintaining a trade surplus with almost all the regions of the world. At the same time, Europe needed to develop trade relations with both leading economic powers of the world in order to meet its own requirements. In order to grow, Europe had no other option but to attach its commercial and trade activities with those of China and India. By 1500, therefore, Europe was an underdeveloped periphery compared to China and India. Two important discoveries—the new sea trade route through the Cape of Good Hope and the Atlantic Ocean route discovering the Americas—enabled Europe to look at its trade relations from an optimistic perspective. In particular, the discovery of precious metals proved befitting to its needs. It was able to meet its trade deficits through the massive extraction of gold and silver from mines in the Americas, thus enabling it to shift the balance of trade in its favor. Frank argues that Europe "used its American money to buy itself a ticket on the Asian train." In other words, "the West first bought itself a third-class seat on the Asian economic train, then leased a whole railway carriage, and only in the nineteenth century managed to displace Asians from the locomotive" (Frank, 1998: 37).

The history of Eurocentric modernization starts its discourse within the timeframe only when Europe was able to occupy the dominant position in the world economic system after it had physically colonized India and opiumized China. In the sequel to *ReOrient*, *ReOrienting the 19th Century*, his last intellectual contribution and posthumous publication Frank (2014) re-establishes his case by arguing that the notion of "centuries" of European domination is a "myth." Looking at economic history through a global framework of analysis, it can be found that the Eurocentric theory misinforms historical scholarship on economic growth and development. Once a global framework is adopted, discontinuity is replaced by continuity. According to Frank, the rise of the West due to the shift of economic dominance from Asia to Europe started around 1870 (p. 4). In other words, it was a small period of European domination that spanned just over two hundred years at maximum. At another place, he claims that historical scholarship shows that the East was never the one the West made it to be. More importantly, the West was not the same or as developed as it claims to have been. The fact is more palpable once we compare the East with the West over a long history from 1400 onward (Frank, 2000). The shift in leadership from the East to the West was a phenomenon of the nineteenth century and happened mostly due to the decline in economic and military power of the Asian countries.

The genesis of the decline of Asian contributions to the world economy, thus, needs to be explored in the prolonged maldevelopment and under-development caused by European mercantile, imperial, and colonial policies. Before the Europeans could develop paraphernalia for the Industrial Revolution, they were reaching India and China for trade. According to Om Prakash (1998), when the Portuguese discovered the all-water route via "the Cape of Good Hope" in 1488, there was exponential growth in the volume of trade between the two continents. The Portuguese monopoly of the route was challenged and taken over by rival European companies by the start of the seventeenth century. These companies restructured the production, procurement, and transportation of goods from and to the Indian Sub-Continent. The increasing volume of trade could have dried Europe of silver to be paid for goods purchased had there been no discovery of the Americas and extraction of silver from the mines, which increased the Europeans' stock of the metal hugely. The price revolution in Europe in the sixteenth century enabled them to turn the trade deficit with China and India into a trade surplus by placing what is called "bullions for goods" (Prakash, 2004; Bowen, 2006). Europeans, in other words, used booty from one place to exploit and monopolize the terms of trade at another place in order to accumulate global wealth in the West. The competition to colonize these regions, however, was a prolonged effort based on inter-imperial competition. Given that the Dutch empire, the leading European economic power during the sixteenth century, was able to establish an effective trade regime in the Indian Ocean through its East India Company, it can safely be argued that imperial competition for domination in the Indian Ocean continued for more than a century, resulting in the terminal defeat of the Dutch, the decline of the Mughal empire, another defeat of the French, and the penetration of the British East India Company into the Indian economic system from 1757 onward. Dennis Owen Flynn argues that had there been no discovery of American silver, and had it not been extracted to such an extent as to turn the other European imperial powers to envy the Spanish empire, world history could have been very different (Flynn and Giráldez, 1997).

Frank (1998) cites some other reasons for the rise of the West, including, too, that it occurred after 1750, not since 1500 as mentioned by Wallerstein and others. More importantly, he does not see any indigenous reasons ushering the growth and development in Europe to the extent of world domination.

Contrarily, he seconds Janet Abu-Lughod (1989) when she argues that "of crucial importance is the fact that the 'Fall of the East' preceded the 'Rise of the West'" (p. 88). In the first half of the eighteenth century, the dominating stable monarchies started to decline. The Mughal empire in India started disintegrating with the demise of the last of the powerful Mughal kings, Aurangzeb Alamgir, in 1707. The Safavid monarchy in Iran collapsed in 1723. The control and influence of the Chinese kingship in its vast empire also started waning around the same time. Meanwhile, during the sixteenth and seventeenth centuries, the role of American silver and gold bullion had brought a paradigm shift in the nature of the very equation of European trade with Asia and Africa by turning it into surplus from deficit. This transformation in the nature of trade relations enabled European empires, especially the British, to develop strategic fangs to seize the vast lands of Asia and Africa. The pattern of long cyclical economic growth of Asia had already reached the "A phase" by the end of seventeenth century and was starting to witness the "B" phase around that time. Around 1750 started the "A phase" of Europe.

The invention of capitalism in the West during the sixteenth century and its expansion in Asia, Africa, and the Americas during the next two centuries resulted in the emergence of the modern world-system. Whereas China and India were the core of world trade in the premodern world, expansion of imperialism in these regions and beyond since the sixteenth century eventually deprived them of any such status. The shift in the economic core from Asia to Europe starting in the eighteenth century was made possible mainly due to the policies that imperial powers imposed on these regions. Because the imperial project of global economic restructuring was meant to serve the new core of the modern world-system, the West, it was necessary to destroy the competitors. The genesis of "the rise of the West" is located in the unprecedented accumulation of capital that European mercantile states were able to accrue from Asia, Africa, and South America. Hamza Alavi and Angus Maddison argue that the British had two very significant interests in the case of India: a monopolistic trading position vis-à-vis Indian foreign trade, particularly its textile exports, and the potential role of India in global politics and the power structure "in terms of geography, logistics, and military manpower" (Maddison, 1971: 35). In order to monopolize the market in favor of the British trading companies, the pattern of development was crafted to destroy local industrial production to such an extent that the term "de-industrialization" of the Sub-Continent was coined in order to reflect the magnitude of adversarial consequences the area had to face under colonial rule (Thorner, Thorner, and Bhattacharya, 2005). While analyzing the implications of imperial policies, scholars have argued that the special targets of such policies were the handloom and other traditional industries of fabric production. During the nineteenth century, the share of handloom industries in national production declined from 21 percent to 9 percent. Most of this economic mayhem took place during the first half of the nineteenth century (Bagchi, 2010; Clingingsmith and Williamson, 2004; Seth, 2014). According to Prabirjit Sarkar (1992), the purpose was to expand the market to dump the surplus production of European textile industries in the Sub-Continent. In an unusually short span of time, India ceased to be an exporter of cotton and textile products. Instead, it became one of the major importers and dumping grounds of European textile products made from Indian raw cotton.

While the second and third chapters of this book explain in detail the role of Asia in the Industrial Revolution, suffice it here to say that the eighteenth- and nineteenth-century world-system led by the British empire accrued every material benefit from the "golden sparrow" that was necessary to industrialize the West and produce cheaper products to be sold at arbitrary prices back in the colonies. In terms of raw material production, the primary prey was the agricultural system. The East India Company paid special attention to it. In 1764–1765, the last year of an Indian ruler in Bengal, the land revenue collected was £817,000. The next year under the company's rule, it rocketed up to £1,470,000. In 1793, it had reached £3,400,000 (Alavi, 1989: 9). The purpose of empire building in India, thus, served the requirements of the burgeoning capitalist system.

Any investment in infrastructural development in India was meant to reward the project of capital accumulation in the core. For example, according to Stuart Sweeney, the British empire invested about £274 million in the Indian railway system during 1853–1908, about 80 percent of the total industrial investment made in the colony by the empire, mostly accrued from the Indian taxpayers. The motivation of such an enormous investment was purely economic. The primary purpose was to utilize local tax money to develop monopolistic control of the government over the commercial transportation system to the utmost benefit of British traders and commercial enterprises. According to Sweeney, a memorandum prepared in 1909 informed that the system had produced a net cash surplus of about £30 million in 1908, with total benefits exceeding £100 million, mostly to the trading sector. The irrigation system developed by the empire had resulted in about an 8 percent growth of returns, with £32.5 million only in that year (Sweeney, 2011: 1–2). Simultaneously, the imperial machinery either refused to invest in sectors of least economic attraction or invested merely to the extent of convenience and the advancement of economic benefits. In the education system, for example, the purpose of the investment was to "form a class of persons Indian in blood and color, but English in tastes, in opinions, in morals and in intellect" (Macaulay, 1835). According to Alavi, the economic pillage under colonial rule was primarily based on huge levies eked out of impoverished rural peasants, particularly in Bengal. According to Maddison, "The British were not averse to Indian economic development *if it increased their markets* but refused to help in areas where they felt there was conflict with their own economic interests or political security" (Maddison, 1971: 35, emphasis added). Aditya Mukherjee (2010) argues that "at the heart of colonialism lay surplus appropriation from the colony to the metropolis or the colonizers" (p. 74).

The nature of the European imperial encounter with China was unique. Instead of its physical occupation, as European empires did across the world, China was perceived as a hot cake too big to fit into any one imperial mouth. As mentioned, by the end of the eighteenth century, China had a trade surplus with every region of the world, including British India, thereby creating a silver crisis for the Europeans in a bilateral trade. Due to an insufficiency of silver to pay for the tea, silk, and porcelain, Europeans "enforced" barter trade with China by exporting Indian Sub-Continental cotton to mainland China. However, that was not sufficient to address the trade deficit and, therefore, did not satiate the lust for capital accumulation through so-called "open trade" (Klein, 2012: 789). British merchants, ultimately, found a commodity to dump in China: opium. Though the British had started exporting it to China by 1700, its exports rose and became a challenge for the Qing empire by the middle of the eighteenth century. In 1757, British merchants attacked and exhibited superior military skills to impose opium on mainland China. From 1790 to 1832, the British dumping of opium in China produced a generation of addicts there. It was in 1838 when the Qing emperor decided to ban the import of British Indian opium in China, arguing that "trade with the West was neither necessary nor desirable for China" (Scott, 2008: 20). The outcome was two Opium Wars fought over the next five years, resulting in what is called the start of "the century of national humiliation" for China. By the end of the eighteenth century, Frank's "super accumulator" of capital found itself peeling in the face of almost every regional and global imperial power, including Japan, Russia, Britain, the United States, and others. The Treaty of Nanjing, the first of the unequal treaties, ratified at the end of the second Opium War in 1842, comprised the terms exclusively dictated by the British army to the Qing dynasty. It annexed Hong Kong to Britain; set Five Treaty Ports at Shanghai, Ningbo, Fuzhou, Xiamen, and Canton; and enforced extraterritoriality, something later called "legal imperialism" (Scott, 2008: 24). With this, opium flooded into the country. The first military encounter and defeat of China at the hands of an imperial power termed it an "uncivilized" and decadent country, easy prey for other powers in Europe and beyond. It is, of course, significant to infer that China was forcefully integrated into the world-system and at the dictation of the system.

With the forceful inclusion of India and China in the capitalist world-system, Europe gained the central and core position. For about next two hundred years (1757–1948), Europe colonized these two empires and the African continent. The colonial empire used the enormous wealth accumulated from these regions to propel its own economic growth. I will examine colonial policies and their implications in detail in the next chapters. Suffice it here to say that Europeans, and especially the British, built their own economic and industrial power by extracting wealth and raw materials from these regions, banning the import of Indian and Chinese products into their own countries, and imposing self-serving commercial terms and conditions leading to the de-industrialization of these two regions, along with others. It produced a stable two-tier world-system consisting of the center, or core, and the periphery. The core, comprised of imperial powers, eventually kicked off mass-scale industrialization—the Industrial Revolution—whereas the periphery was restructured to produce and supply raw materials. By the time the two-tier system started vanishing after World War II, regional economic inequality had completely flipped; India and China were left far behind, whereas Europe and North America had gained unprecedented economic and political prominence in the world.

The Second Phase: Postcolonial Expansion and Complexification (Three-Tier System)

After remaining under oppressive colonial and imperial rule, the Indian Sub-Continent and China got independence by the mid-twentieth century. Decolonization was deemed necessary because the colonial empires—the core—found no further attraction in accruing capital through direct political control. As the decolonization process began, the glaring divide between the North and the South allowed the former to dictate the terms of the global economic structure. The core, after having accumulated capital and created the great unbridgeable gap between itself and other regions of the world, was able to determine the fate of development patterns across the world.

One of the major patterns observed in China and India has been their consistent underdevelopment or low scale before they liberalized their economic outlook. In the case of China, this happened in the mid-1970s, and India found it suitable to surrender to international neoliberal economic order in the early 1990s. In other words, before they willingly embraced a neoliberal economy, both states remained largely outside the orbit dominated by the dictations of the core of the world-system and could develop only to a little extent. Mao's China, as far as it did not "open up" its arms to the global capitalist system, remained poor, underdeveloped, and backward. The Indian National Congress, the oldest political party of the Sub-Continent and the one that ruled India for a large part of 1947–1987, preferred the state-controlled protectionist economic system, and thus developed at a slower pace. In both cases, it was only after they embraced the capitalist world-system that they could grow. The miracle of contemporary history, in other words, could not dawn until the respective states submitted to the terms and conditions of the capitalist world-system. Most of the literature justifies the growth of China and India as a triumph of these countries without mentioning that it was facilitated by the capitalist world-system in order to keep the venture of accumulation intact.

As compared to China, which in the wake of the failure of "ideology-led" economic policies of Mao made a swift move to liberalize its economic policies and open its economic and industrial sectors for foreign direct investment while keeping a strong control of the state on economic development, India remained under what is now called "license raj" until the late 1980s. While comparing India with Brazil, South Korea, and Nigeria, Atul Kohli argues that development in India was delayed because of socio-political issues, thus leading him to argue that "the way state power is organized and used has decisively influenced rates and patterns of industrialization in the global periphery" (Kohli, 2004: 9). Following his argument, it can be argued that China's swift move and India's reluctant behavior toward economic liberalization were due to their difference in regime type and political system.

One of the major impacts of the glaring economic progress made by China during the last thirty years is deliberate oblivion of the economic performance of the country. During 1948–1978, the Chinese economic system came "close to collapse" and the Chinese growth rate was slower compared to other economies, though its "GDP trebled, per capita real product rose by 80 per cent and labor productivity by 60 per cent from 1952 to 1978." It was mainly due to state-controlled industrialization; the industrial sector outgrew the agriculture sector by 1978 (Maddison, 2007: 24).

It was before the launching of the Comprehensive Economic Reform in 1978, the official claim of which was to "create a socialist economy with Chinese characteristics." The intra-China Communist Party (CCP) struggle about ideology versus prosperity led the latter to dominate the politico-economic system of the country and the embrace capitalist traits of an economic outlook, such as private property rights, a farewell to income egalitarianism, and the implementation of a market-based labor productivity system. Though the state kept occupying the driving seat of economic modernization, it increasingly collided with the market forces (Xu, 2012).

Though it is usually believed that China performed poorly on economic development during the Mao period, it was nevertheless able to establish strong foundations of subsequent industrial growth when the state eventually let the neoliberal capitalist policies reign. More importantly, China was able to integrate with the capitalist world-system by luring foreign direct investment (FDI) through the establishment of Special Economic Zones.

The argument that the state determined the nature and magnitude of FDI belittles the fact that both the state *and* the capitalist world-system found it profitable to launch economic ventures whereby the world-system was able to introduce its own version of economic progress, though only within those sectors opened by the state. The world-system approached China and welcomed it in its orbit in order to accumulate capital by exploiting cheaper labor and lower production costs in the country. Instead of letting the state determine its role in the chain of global production in sectors opened by the state, the world-system implemented a fragmented part of the whole process, thus developing economic stakes of the country in a smooth functioning of global production processes. According to Deming (2010), "made in China" is a part of the whole process; capital and technologies are provided by transnational corporations based in the core, whereas raw materials and semi-finished products are provided by Asian countries. Industries in China, then, are meant only to process, manufacture, and assemble these products at cheaper prices. It integrates the national production process with the global level, thereby allowing the core to reap the joys of the technological and communication revolutions. Though integration into the world-system has enabled China to become the fastest growing country in the world, surpassing many European countries to become the second largest economy of the world after the United States, the process has not materialized all intended or desired benefits for China. Instead, while the reforms made possible a rising standard of living for the majority of China's population, they came at the costs of weakening the central government, increasing inequalities, and fragmenting society (Goldman and MacFarquhar, 1999: 19; Naughton, 2007: 209–16). Jonathan Fenby (2014) argued that the wealth gap in China is increasing and leaving millions resentful of the process whereby the rich are becoming richer while the poor are becoming poorer. Using data collected by various research organizations in China, a recent study concludes that "China's income inequality not only surpasses that of the United States by a large margin but also ranks among the highest in the world." The major reasons cited include "structural forces attributable to the Chinese political system, most notably the urban-rural gap and the regional variation in economic wellbeing" (Xie and Zhou, 2014: 6928). In other words, it is the paradoxical relationship between an apparent socialist political system and a burgeoning capitalist economic system that is leading the state to a socio-economic crisis.

The economic development of China, nevertheless, has enabled the state to accumulate valuable fiscal resources. Currently, China possesses the largest stock of foreign exchange reserves in the world. Its collusion with the capitalist world-system has "Asianized" the global production system, though the core has been able to ensure the transfer of global wealth to itself. What is most important about China's growth is that the outcome of its experience with the modern capitalist system has been a combination of both benefit and loss. Michel Aglietta and Guo Bai (2013), for example, argued that Chinese economic growth is mired with a number of issues and challenges at both the domestic and global levels. During the last thirty-five years, the country's GDP has grown five times compared to what it was in 1978. However, there have emerged structural disequilibria that have consistently been affecting otherwise rapid economic growth and social progress.

At the global level, China has established itself as the second largest economic power after the United States. Wallerstein and others, however, do not consider China as part of the core. Contrarily, a larger group of scholars insist that China is still a part of the South and semi-periphery. As I mentioned in my hypotheses, this book argues that the modern world-system is increasingly complexifying its structure in order to preserve the core and secure its primary interest of capital accumulation. It is rather logical to argue about another tier in the hierarchical structure of the global capitalist world-system: the semi-core. Given that industrial production processes have been offshored and devolved to the lowest possible levels, and that the core has been able to control the direction and magnitude of the flow of capital throughout the world, there remains little doubt about the fragile capacity of China as the state to transform the global economic structure. Contrarily, what we are observing is a convergence of the economic interests of both the state and the global capitalist system whereby the state is eagerly submitting to neoliberal economic policies, developing stakes in the preservation of the system, and has thrived by relinquishing its prerogatives in a number of economic sectors. This can be corroborated by looking at the privatization of state-owned enterprises in both China and India—as everywhere else—on the insistence of the international capitalist system (Xu, 2012: 9). The core of the capitalist world-system, which is controlled by the transnational capitalist class, feels no hesitation in welcoming a socialist state in its orbit if it agrees to accept the dictations about the liberalization of its economy and ensures facilitating capital accumulation.

The postcolonial state of India also followed the similar path. For more than four decades after independence, the political landscape was dominated by the Indian National Congress with deep influence from the Nehruvian philosophy of national autonomy and independence because of prolonged colonial exploitation. According to Kohli (2004), the state of India led economic growth from the front but had a mixed outcome. It was able to develop infrastructure and an egalitarian socio-economic outlook of the country. However, India could not modernize its economy until it willingly integrated into the global capitalist system. Kohli's comparative analysis of India, Brazil, and South Korea shows that South Korea was more able to integrate into the capitalist world economic system and consequently develop more than the other two countries due to their peculiar socio-economic backgrounds. After initial hesitation to embrace the neoliberal economic system, economic policymakers in India agreed "to the view that an open trading environment can help catalyze and sustain faster growth" (Bhagwati and Panagariya, 2013: 96). India, therefore, introduced a series of economic reforms by the start of the 1990s whereby the dominant role of the state started to give way to the private sector. In order to lure FDI, India relaxed its legal requirements. While the federation withdrew a number of its prerogatives for greater regional and state autonomy in the economic sector, it ensured its monopolistic and deterministic say in national economic policies. According to Nirvikar Singh and T. N. Srinivasan, the federation adopted a role of what they call "market-preserving federalism" whereby it enforced a common national market over the regions (Singh and Srinivasan, 2013: 35).

India's aspirations to shine brighter than other regional economies have not materialized. It is still regarded as a "low-income" developing country with a gross national income much lower than that of China. It is still largely an agricultural economy, though rapid industrialization and technological and service-sector growth have taken place. It is majorly because of the very nature of the polity of the state of India whereby a multiethnic and multicultural social structure, regional diversity, and conflicting ecological demands led the federation to grapple with numerous issues. Kohli, arguing before the liberalization of economic policies took place, stated, "The failure to mitigate even the worst of India's poverty is a consequence of the institutionalized patterns of domination within India" whereby "an alliance of a nationalist political elite with entrepreneurial classes" was able to grab most of the benefits resulting from economic incentives devised by the political class. For Kohli, this was one of the major reasons that India observed a modest economic growth while the income and regional inequalities started widening (Kohli, 1989: 8). Three decades after this observation, Kohli has come to believe that this alliance "is now so well entrenched that many observers do not shy away from characterizing India as "India incorporated." Kohli argues that "a close alliance between the state and big business is responsible both for releasing economic dynamism and for limiting the spread of the resulting gains" (Kohli, 2012: 3). In its pursuit of "economic growth," the state of India embraced the capitalist economic structure, facilitated an alliance between the national political and economic class and the transnational capitalist class, and received mixed results of faster growth in industrial and service sectors with ever-widening economic and regional inequalities. Expressing satisfaction with India's successful transition from import substitute industrialization to economic liberalization, Piya Mahtaney (2007) admits to the divergent priorities of "two distinctly disparate socio-economic strata in India." The first consisted of an alliance among urban class and international donors and investors, while the other is comprised of individuals and organizations from the nationalist outlook with vested material interests in anti-reform agenda. He argues, "It is the perceptible conflict of interests between these two realms that stokes the country's political economy of underdevelopment and enables it to rear its head from time to time" (p. 32).

The case of the postcolonial state of Pakistan provides another opportunity to show the interplay between the system and the state whereby maldevelopment is adopted because it serves the national politico-strategic interests as well as the strategic interests of the system. The position and role of Pakistan in the world-system has been minute and of a parochial nature. While the interplay between the state and the system resulted in the economic growth of the former for the broader benefit of the latter, "strategic growth" in Pakistan was conceived as a befitting approach by both the state and the system. While the system facilitated and embraced both China and India to develop in order to serve its economic interests, it left Pakistan maldeveloped in order to serve its strategic interests.

A comparative analysis of India and Pakistan shows that while India had to face the "bread question" before anything else, the postcolonial state of Pakistan was mired with strategic questions. Historically and during the colonial period, the areas that formed India had witnessed some form of economic and industrial development, while the colonizers kept areas of future Pakistan producing crops, including, most importantly, wheat and cotton. These areas were considered sufficient to feed not only the whole population of the Sub-Continent but also the colonial requirements in Europe as well. When partition took place, India faced a food crisis as the first and most important issue to deal with. In case of Pakistan, it was a new state whose two parts were separated by a geographic distance of more than 1,100 kilometers. The 1948 Indo-Pak war engraved survival as the top preference in the list of national interests. Ayesha Jalal provides an excellent analysis comparing how different national needs led both nations toward different ends. India adopted a developmental state model whereby the state supervised the process of economic and industrial development, while Pakistan went on developing its military capabilities. During the initial years, "the annual budgets of the Pakistani central government were essentially defense budgets with practically nothing available for developmental purposes" (Jalal, 1995b: 22). It led the state centralize administrative and financial powers at the domestic level and adopt a foreign policy led by defense considerations, resulting in the formation of various alliances with the Western powers of the world, particularly the United States.

Both Pakistan and India carried different geostrategic features. While India had emerged as the major power in the Indian Ocean, Pakistan, being in the vicinity of the then USSR, turned out to be serving crucial global strategic interests in the wake of the Cold War. Throughout the Cold War, Pakistan was assigned the role as a frontline state against Russian communism. The peculiar nature of its independence, defense needs, and strategic culture led the country to overdevelop its military at the cost of civil governing institutions. The capitalist world-system encouraged these developments because they served its own interests in the region.

Thus, while India saw modest socio-economic development before it liberalized its policies, Pakistan adopted national policies that led to economic growth guaranteed to serve not social stabilization but defense development. Finding its economic power in the budgetary allotments duly supported by international powers keeping in view their respective strategic interests, military establishment in Pakistan was able to capitalize on these powers more compared to other state and political institutions, such as judiciary and political parties, and carried out four coups against the civilian governments in the first fifty-two years of the country's history. Ayesha Siddiqa (2017), Hasan Askari Rizvi (2003), and Ejaz Hussain (2013), among others, argue that it is in the economic interests of the military in Pakistan—budgetary prerogatives, international direct aid to the military, and its economic ventures ranging from agricultural farms to educational institutions to banking to industry—that the military finds an incentive to occupy the reins of decision-making in Pakistan.

The economic consequences of the military's role in the politics of Pakistan are significantly important to look at. During the predisintegration period (1947–1971), economic development in eastern Pakistan was mired at the cost of development in the western part. During the 1960s, the era of development—as it was named due to impressive overall growth rates—the manufacturing industry grew at a higher rate in western Pakistan (8.4 percent per annum on average) than in eastern Pakistan (6.3 percent per annum on average) despite that more than half of the population lived in eastern part (Khan, 1999). Overall economic growth was recorded higher in the western part of the country (Zaidi, 2005). More importantly, the people of eastern Pakistan were denied a fair share of power by suppressing their quest to enter into any of the three sections of the elite class in Pakistan: the civil-military establishment, an emerging industrial class, and the landowning feudal class (Amin-Khan, 2013: 171). While the military regime delivered higher growth rates compared to civilian governments, the long-term consequences of military rule in Pakistan were increasingly evident in the form of institutional breakdown. The founding party of Pakistan, the Muslim League, collapsed due to the bureaucratization of politics whereby the military picked civil bureaucracy as its junior partner in negating the development of political institutions. It became the partner of the West in the Cold War by being a signatory to the US-led defense alliances called the Southeast Asian Treaty

Organization (SEATO) and the Central Treaty Organization (CENTO) (Jalal, 1990; Khan-Amin, 2013). The impressive growth rates during the 1960s were mostly sponsored by the influx of foreign aid and investment as the country, under the hegemonic influence of modernization theorists, was quick to liberalize its economic policies. The so-called "era of development," however, was made possible on two crucial costs. One, the "development" was made possible due to "aid" in the form of interest-bearing loans from international financial and development institutions dominated by modernization theorists. The flow of aid, which was $455.5 million from 1950 to 1955, increased to $3.4 billion during 1960–1968. The crux of this approach was the US determination "in configuring Pakistan's economic policy to make it subservient to American economic and global interests" (Amin-Khan, 2013: 173). These policies resulted in socio-political inequalities, leading to widespread discontentment with government affairs. At the regional level, the whole approach alienated the people of the eastern part and led to civil war in 1970, which turned into the Indo-Pak war of 1971 and resulted in the disintegration of Pakistan and independence for Bangladesh.

While the 1970s were dominated by populist politics led by Zulfikar Ali Bhutto, the first elected prime minister of Pakistan, the military was able to reinvigorate itself in the wake of historic defeat in the 1971 war. Bhutto adopted nationalist socialist policies that led to the nationalization of a number of industries and educational institutions. Considering another defeat at the hands of buoyant India as unthinkable, the military establishment recommended a nuclear program as the only option. In Pakistan, Bhutto is recognized as the first statesman after Muhammad Ali Jinnah, the founder of Pakistan, to give to the nation its first unanimously approved constitution—and nuclear program. In 1977, when he was dethroned—he was eventually hanged in 18981 by the third martial law of the country—he argued that it was because the "international establishment," the major powers of the West, were angry with him over initiating the nuclear program. The United States was not happy over Bhutto's decision to buy a uranium enrichment reprocessing plant from France and threatened to "make a horrible example of Pakistan" (F. H. Khan, 2012: 137).

The 1970s were considered a "decade lost" due to nationalist socialist policies leading to slow economic growth, international sanctions, and political instability. The martial law administration of Muhammad Zia-ul-Haq took a different route: Islamization of the country's social, political, and economic systems. More importantly, the 1979 USSR invasion of Afghanistan allowed him to stay in power, burgeon military strength, and keep building nuclear capability because the international capitalist system required Pakistan to become its frontline soldier in the war against the Soviet Union. For about a decade, Pakistan served the global interests of the international capitalist system in three ways. First, it was the principal backyard of the capitalist fight against communism. It established recruitment centers across the country for “Jihad” in Afghanistan and invited Islamist fighters from all over the world to join the centers, thereby incubating forces that established global terrorist organizations about a decade later. Second, the war in Afghanistan led to the establishment of direct relations between the national defense establishment of Pakistan and the global military-industrial complex led by the Pentagon. The state of Pakistan was bypassed and “military aid” was delivered directly to the Pakistan military, thus not only burgeoning its domestic political significance but also facilitating it to develop transnational client-patron relationships. Third, in order to mitigate domestic skepticism, the international military establishment agreed to condone nuclearization activities of Pakistan.

Average economic growth in the 1980s under military and quasi-democratic rule remained at more than 6 percent, higher than the average growth rate of the 1970s, which was 4.42. The major reasons cited for this economic growth were, again, the influx of foreign aid because the country had become the frontline soldier in the war against the Soviet Union in Afghanistan. As the war ended through the Geneva Accords in 1988 and the withdrawal of Soviet soldiers in 1989, the strategic utility of Pakistan diminished. The immediate effect was a number of international sanctions pertaining to the nuclear program of the country. One of the major consequences was slower economic growth. The country progressed with an average GDP growth rate of 4.48, with 1.97 being the lowest in the year when it tested nuclear weapons in the wake of Indian nuclear tests.

The fourth military coup took place in 1999. General Pervez Musharraf took power by establishing military governments in the country and dissolving national and provincial assemblies. The international capitalist system adopted the same approach as it had been adopting in the previous cases: denial, acceptance, and warm reception. President Clinton refused to shake hands with General Musharraf in public. All that changed when the September 11, 2001, attacks took place. The international system required Pakistan again, in a similar manner as in the 1980s. This time the target was the element once produced by the international system: Islamist terrorists. Sanctions were removed, aid poured in, the military dictatorship was able to stabilize for about a decade, economic growth took place, and the system collapsed under a multidimensional crisis once the military was compelled to leave political affairs to the civilians.

Alavi (1983) argues that the state of Pakistan, being a peripheral capitalist state, was able to develop an authoritarian outlook and produce military dictatorships because it “overdeveloped” and turned out to be “relatively autonomous” from society and economic classes, including the elite class, by extending its regulatory and controlling powers “far beyond the logic of what is necessary in the interests of the orderly functioning of the peripheral capitalist economies over which the state presides, and specific needs of each of the dominant classes." Alavi argues that the "overdevelopment" enables the state to mediate among the competing interests of various elite economic classes such as the metropolitan capitalist, indigenous bourgeoisie, and landowning classes. In intra-elite wrangling, the mediating state has been controlled by a "military bureaucratic oligarchy" since its independence in 1947 (pp. 42–43). The underdevelopment in the state of Pakistan was mainly an outcome of the unequal relationship between the competing entities of the national capitalist class, on the one hand, and advanced capitalist class in the developed world on the other (Gardezi and Rashid, 1983). The "dependency" factor is beneficial to both entities; it helps them survive in a structure whereby the capitalist class in the core allows the peripheral capitalist class, controlled by the military in the case of Pakistan, to continue ruling in order to keep serving the interests of the core. The capitalist system accrued every benefit—including the adoption of the Western modernization model in the 1960s to create a consumer market of "experts" and "products" from the West to the slogan of "Jihad" in Afghanistan to serve global politico-strategic interests—at the cost of the virtual collapse of the state and its institutions. This has been evident from the fact that, since its independence, what Pakistan has received in the form of "aid" has been either interest-bearing loans or "finished consumer goods" (Amin-Khan, 2013: 185).

Pakistan is one of the failing economies. In the wake of the debilitating tax-GDP ratio since the early 1980s, and thereby the widening imbalance between government earnings and expenditures, Pakistan joined the International Monetary Fund's Structural Adjustment Program in 1988. The immediate consequences were, among others, a depreciation in the value of currency, thereby increasing the volume of national debt, a reduction in the magnitude of a number of public services, a complete ban on government employment opportunities, a *decline* in the GDP growth rate, and a rise in inflation and poverty levels due to increases in direct taxation (Anwar and Iqbal, 1996). A consistent pattern of "stop-go" can be seen in the influx of aid and loans from both the United States and the international monetary and development institutions, thus reinforcing my argument that the capitalist world-system determines the nature and outlook of economic development or underdevelopment by creating needs in the states and compelling them comply with the dictates. Pakistan's public debt has crossed $150 billion, which is about 61 percent of the total GDP of the country (*Economic Survey of Pakistan, 2013–2014*).

The Third Phase: The Rise of the Semi-Core in the Twenty-First Century

Starting the 1980s, in the case of China, and the 1990s, in the case of India, the global economic system reflected unequal economic growth and modernization of production relations in the semi-periphery. Post-Mao China introduced structural reforms meant to enable the state to align its interests with the interests of the world-system. Similarly, in the case of India, the 1991 financial crisis led to the liberalization of the national economy and an effective end to the state-led economic growth model. In 1995, the World Trade Organization (WTO) replaced GATT (General Agreement on Tariffs and Trade) as the global trade agreement, thus starting a new era of global economic relations. In 2000, China joined WTO and quickly redefined the outlook of global economic relations. Since then, the nature of the world-system has been transforming in a rapid manner. For the first time in history, a mosaic of tangible changes—communication and transportation revolution, human movement, compartmentalized industrialization, particularly in the global South, and unavailability of any alternative powerful economic system, to mention a few—are on the scene in order to let the forces of global capitalism unleash unprecedented endeavors to take their ultimate interest of capital accumulation to new heights. Globalized forces of capitalism are reaching every corner of the planet and ushering far-reaching implications for local communities by absorbing them into global production and consumption processes and connecting them with other parts of the world in an increasingly complicated and interdependent manner. I have named it "complexification" of the production and consumption system. I will explain in the next pages as to why complexification of the world-system enables the core to maintain the status quo for a prolonged period. The spread of capital is also on the rise, though of greater magnitude is its accumulation in the core. Through a variety of manners, including but not limited to the communication revolution and digitization of capital, the whole planet is increasingly turning into a virtual one market whereby the patterns of production and consumption are being determined while keeping in view the maximization of accumulation of capital in the core. The emergence of a virtual economy featuring "the exchange of symbols: primarily money in the context of global financial markets; but also, information in the context of a 'postindustrial,' 'informational,' or 'service economy'; and 'signs' in the context of postmodern aesthetics, consumption, meaning, and culture" (Peterson, 2003: 113–14) leads the contemporary global outlook of the capitalist system.

Historically, the Western-centered capitalist system remained the only dominant economic structure for a long time; only since the last half of the twentieth century has its transformation been so comprehensive, multifaceted, and multidimensional that Alaine Touraine (2014) calls it a post-social system where "events of such gravity [such as capitalist transformation, crisis, and its looming collapse] would not only call into question the management of the economy; they would affect the entire organization of our society" (p.11). Though we can argue about the "failure" of the neoliberal project, it is difficult to argue against the claim that the transnational capitalist class continuously yearns for new methodologies of accumulation since its every endeavor fails to sustain for a longer period. Certainly, the transformation of the production and consumption processes is being used as a strategy to protract the looming collapse of the system; capitalist forces are endeavoring to ensure the continuity of the system through placation of the revisionist forces by incorporating them into the management mechanism of the capitalist system. In this process, the functioning of the globalized world-system has been complexified. As I explain in the following pages, the emergence of the semi-core is one of most significant strategies that is being utilized to co-opt the fast-growing economies of the global South and to minimize any chances of reaction from the dispossessed communities. Since the idea of the semi-core is a subjective claim, though it is based on data and may be untraceable for some experts, I am arguing about its emergence because I am arguing about the dynamism in the system, a creative ability to find (temporary) solutions ensuring the accumulation of capital in the core and deferring the eventual and inevitable destruction of the whole world-system. I agree that the semi-core as a relatively new concept is arguable because of the strong arguments in favor of the trilateral structure of the world-system. I, however, will cite various experts indicating its presence. Using a long-term historical reference I will show in the next chapters how, as the world-system transformed from world-empires to world economy, European powers forcefully integrated Asian lands into the capitalist system, impoverished them through colonial policies of plunder, denied development there during postwar years when it did not suit their interests, insisted on the greater inclusion of these countries in the world economy on their own terms and conditions, and are now facilitating the emergence of this new tier in the system. The semi-core is a structural arrangement that facilitates the impeding of technological transfer, compartmentalizes production and reproduction processes, and creates a new kind of dependency accrued through cooperation from these newly emerging economies.

Political economists throughout the world cite, perceive, and name the nature of transformation and consequences in a variety of manners. A number of theories have been presented. Most of the scholars belonging to the leading streamlines of critical political economy argue about the looming nature of the inevitable collapse of capitalism from the status of being the only economic system of the world. Accordingly, the contradictions within capitalism—such as faster technological change versus declining rates of profit, borderless movement of the capital versus an ever-increasing requirement of maintaining a quasi-monopolistic status of the state and its taxation powers, a desire to ensure flow of the capital toward the core versus a compulsion to share it with new stakeholders in the global South, and an assumption of limitless natural resources versus an increasingly powerful ecological restriction—have been exposed in a vivid manner. As the capitalist forces accumulate increasingly through dispossession, dependency theorists refer to the rising alienation and impatience on the part of the masses of the developing world. "The central paradox of our time," according to John Gray (1998), is that "economic globalization—the worldwide spread of industrial production and new technologies that is promoted by unrestricted mobility of capital and unfretted freedom of trade—actually threatens the stability of the single global market that is being constructed by American-led transnational organizations." He argues that "there is nothing in today's global market that buffers it against the social strains arising from highly uneven economic development within and between the world's diverse societies" (pp. 6–7).

World-systems theorists, the most prominent being Wallerstein himself, have claimed the eventual demise of global capitalism because of the increasing levels of acute contradictions such as those within the system. According to him, the naturalization of the concept of the capitalist system as the only viable evolutionary "development" occurring at a particular stage of human history resulted in increasing difficulties for the alternative concepts or ideas to penetrate or make ground within the intellectual discourse (Wallerstein, 1992). The notion that capitalism rose derives from the concept of its material growth as invented and imposed using cultural force. For more than five hundred years, the notion of "development" equated with the concept of material growth resulted in an inexorable quest of limitless production engulfing the whole globe into a monstrous capitalist machine. The critical economists, sooner than later, questioned the sustainability of the drive, leading many, including world-systems theorists, to argue about the eventual fall of the whole system.

There is widespread consensus among critical political economists that the system is in crisis. Theories of the crisis of capitalism agree on a number of points. The jolts have become more frequent, severe, and disruptive. A broader generalized environment of distrust, fear, and collapse is widespread. According to Zygmunt Bauman and Carlo Bordoni (2014), the contemporary crisis in the capitalist system is "characterized by the simultaneous combination of an economic gamble on an international level (the causes) and the measures taken locally to deal with it (the effects)" (p. 4). In this crisis, they argue, the effect is profound because of two simultaneous developments: the neoliberal success in weakening the institution of the state by separating politics from economics, and the renege of modernity from its promises such as enlightenment and security. According to Bill Lucarelli (2004), the crisis multiplies itself as monopoly capitalism is stagnating. According to Nobuharu Yokokawa (2013), one of the main reasons why the capitalist world-system faces stagnation is what he calls the loss of the "dynamic comparative advantage." Leading industries in the developed world are always in need of maintaining an unbridgeable gap between the products being produced and the levels of sophistication of the products when compared to the developing or "catching" countries. This challenge has become difficult to meet because technological spread and its diffusion in the global capital management system has reduced the margin of capital accumulation; the volume of surplus is increasingly being reduced to a level where it may equal wages and recurrent expenses of production. According to him, at such a stage, failure in the accumulation of capital destroys existing structures with an intention to develop a new cycle. Yokokawa argues that we are fast reaching such a stage.

Various scholars, such as Henk Overbeek and Bastiaan van Apeldoorn (2012), Ernesto Screpanti (2014), and John Smith (2016), argue that globalization is resulting in the loss of the margin of profit due to an overaccumulation of capital. According to Walden Bello (2006), contrary to the expectations of globalists, the project of globalization in the first place was no "mirage" because "rather than being a new, higher phase of capitalism, it was in fact a reaction to the underlying structural crisis of capitalism" and "a desperate effort by global capital to escape the stagnation and disequilibria overtaking the global economy in the 1970s and 1980s" (p. 1346). He argues that the trifold nature of capital accumulation can be explained by analyzing the overaccumulation of capital, the overextension of US military power, and the legitimacy crisis of liberal democracy. In terms of my research questions, Bello's framework is helpful to emphasize the role of military power in organizing production and consumption processes in the global capitalism. Agreeing with Wallerstein (2004), technology has brought "complete" information of the market to consumers and enabled them to compel the producers to minimize the margin of profit to an infinitesimal level, thus causing unrest among the capitalist class. In other words, the changes in the operational mechanisms of global capitalism during the last three decades have been enormous and "have occurred against the background of a lengthy period of stagnation and crisis" (Postone, 2010: 7).

There are three unprecedented dimensions of contemporary capitalist crisis: financial, ecological, and political. One can say that while the global financial system has never been a stable mechanism since World War II, its fault lines and wreckages have become more apparent during the last quarter of the twentieth century, while the real blow to the whole system has been witnessed since the sub-prime mortgage crisis in the United States and its spread over Europe, known as the Euro Crisis (Zestos, 2016). Among the main reasons cited by various recent studies include a risky mortgage loan system, excessive deregulation and digitization of the capital coupled with overaccumulation, delinking of gold, the rise of "fictitious capital," and declining profitability (McNally, 2009; Nayak, 2015). Among critical political economists, contradictions within the capitalist system are found to be so glaring that it can truly be termed a system in crisis that can survive while in the crisis unless some unnatural death kills it (Fumagali and Mezeddra, 2010). Analyzing the postwar history of the US-led project of globalizing capitalism, Yanis Varoufakis (2011), former finance minister of crisis-ridden Greece, argues that an interplay between the US desire to dominate and control global capitalist developments, on the one hand, and its failure to restrain itself in the face of financial challenges, on the other, have led to a new level of crisis. According to him, the crisis does not seem to be ending since he perceives that the transnational capitalist class now is looking to liberate itself from the constraints of the money supply.

Leading world-systems theorists argue that the financial crisis in the global capitalism is not a surprise at all. In a lecture, Wallerstein (2009) explained it in detail. According to him, the looming crisis of capitalism was triggered by the worldwide revolution of 1968 and subsequent developments whereby producers have been unable to meet the incessant demand for ever-new products. Simultaneously, the hegemonic position of the United States also declined due to its self-liquidating monopoly and the overstretching of military power to maintain the monopoly, and the rise of competitive producers such as China. Arrighi's (2010) argument, known as the cyclic theory of accumulation, is somewhat similar. Looking at the rise and fall of hegemonies in the history of global capitalism, he argues that the crisis of accumulation results in the fall of the hegemons. In other words, one can find an overwhelming consensus among critical political economists that while hegemonies endeavor to keep their status intact, they decline due to increasing competition, loss of the competitive advantage, rise of competitors, and overstretching of military capacities. Since they all place excessive pressure on the accumulation capacities and the volume of accumulated resources within the center, dethroning of the hegemon stands to be an inevitable outcome. World-systems theory assumes that the current hegemonic structure is going to face the same fate, though the time and exact nature of the fate are contentious. By "naturalizing" the rise and fall of powers, especially hegemonic powers, and emphasizing the hierarchical structure of interstate global politics, world-systems analysis comes closer to other theories such as hegemonic decline (Gilpin, 2012) and power transition theory (Organski, 1968). The main differences between these theories and world-systems analysis as represented in "systemic cycles of accumulation" by Arrighi (2010), then, are the relative significance of the unit of analysis, the role of the transnational class, and the historicity of finance capital, or *haute finance*, creating, in the end, the core in Europe and North America and the periphery in the rest of the world.

The second dimension of the contemporary crisis is ecological. Since the Industrial Revolution, fossil fuels proved to be the lifeline for burgeoning industrialization and capitalist development. While over one trillion barrels of crude oil have been extracted since the discovery of fossil fuels, and about four to eighteen trillion are estimated to still be in the reserves, the global climate has been polluted to such an extent that it is increasingly causing irreparable costs to global capitalism. It leads some scholars to argue that "extracting, refining, combusting, and dispersing the by-products of another trillion or more will only compound those effects (not just add to them or continue them) and will almost certainly be catastrophic" (Princen, Manno, and Martin, 2015: 4). Historically, American capitalism's addiction to oil has been one of the most basic reasons for violence, war, occupation, and subjugation of socio-political rights in the Middle East (Rees, 2006). While there is evidence referring to the increasingly unbearable ecological effects of fossil-fuel-based industrial processes of production, transportation, and consumption (Foster, 2013), the insatiable drive of capital accumulation is sustained by "a pattern of production and consumption which builds intensively on the nearly limitless availability of matter and energy, sophisticated technology, and the existence of natural 'sinks' in which solids, liquids and gas-emissions can be dumped" (Altvater, 2006: 37). The crisis is exacerbated by the fact that the dominant understanding of the ecological crisis and its governance structure, called by Bernstein (2002) a "compromise of liberal environmentalism," promotes a peculiar version, the result of which is that "the institutions that have developed in response to global environmental problems support particular kinds of values and goals, with important implications for the constraints and opportunities to combat the world's most serious environmental problems" (p. 2). According to Peter Newell (2012), some of these solutions are "marketization of environmental governance, the preference for market-based over so-called command and control solutions, the rise of payments for ecosystem services approaches to conservation, or the commodification of water, forests and carbon as responses to environmental problems." These so-called remedies and solutions, then, "serve to entrench capitalism rather than respond to the need for structural reform in advanced capitalist economies demanded by environmental crises" (pp. 26–27). In other words, it means that global capitalism has come to dominate the agendas of global environmental crises through a two-pronged strategy; it has reshaped the ontology of crisis, and it has redesigned the response in order to implement the most fit solution in accordance with its own interests.

From the ecological perspective, however, it means that the deteriorating conditions of the global environment will be dealt with through solutions that are least threatening to revise the established pattern of accumulation of capital. Foster, Clark, and York (2010) argue that the contradictions within capitalism—such as limited ecological capacities versus the desire for limitless accumulation the capital—are the real reasons for ecological crises; environmental destruction is inevitable under a capitalist system. The very kind of "progress" as required by the capitalist system is inherently contradictory. "Capitalism is incapable of regulating its social metabolism with nature in an environmentally sustainable manner. The constant drive to renew the capital accumulation process intensifies its destructive social metabolism, imposing the needs of capital on nature, regardless of the consequences to natural systems" (p. 86). A variety of consequences are in the offing and can be considered as the single most credible reason leading to the collapse of the system.

The political crisis of global capitalism pertains to the interplay between the transnational capitalist class, the capitalist state, and the rise of socio-political anti-globalization movements across the globe. Contrary to the claims made in the "new world-order" and the "end of history" theses, global capitalism is claimed to be imploding in the wake of the rise of BRICS, financial crisis in the core, and the rise of political Islamist movements in the Middle East (Amin, 2014). The magnitude of the crisis is unprecedented and likely to increase further in the near future. Despite the spread of the capitalist mode of production across the globe, world-systems theorists such as Giovanni Arrighi (2007) and Jonathan Friedman and Christopher Chase-Dunn (2005) refer to a number of signs to infer a decline in the American hegemonic position in the global-system. Three of the five "linked crises," as chalked out by Chase-Dunn (2013)—namely, hegemony and global governance, inequality and democracy, and the crisis in the global Left—are essentially political. According to Leslie Sklair (1997), David Harvey (2005), and Thomas Volscho (2015), socio-political movements during the 1970s posed serious challenges to capitalism in the form of a significant reduction in the margin of profit and the pace of capital accumulation, resulting in the conscious effort on the part of the transnational capitalist class to take "revenge" by launching a neoliberalism project and transnationalizing production and consumption processes. However, the neoliberal project resulted in the rise of anti-systemic movements that, according to Wallerstein (1990), are meant "to argue that neither liberty nor equality is possible under the existing system and that both are possible only in a transformed world" (p. 36). Given the basic premise that capitalism is unsustainable, Amin, Arrighi, Frank, and Wallerstein (1990) consider these movements as the harbinger of change that would eventually transform into "a more democratic and more egalitarian world-system" (p. 11). Globalization of conflict between the capitalist class and the working class is becoming a recurrent phenomenon in the wake of the foiling of democratization and the mushroom growth of ultra-terrorist networks throughout the Middle East, North Africa, and Southwest Asia (Heydarian, 2014). Historically, the working class could reap the benefits of democratization throughout the world, and democratic states have been found enforcing relatively justifiable socio-economic contracts between working and elite classes (Przeworski, 1991; Rueschemeyer, Huber, and Stephens, 1992). The pattern changed in the wake of the fall of the Berlin Wall. The transnational capitalist class pushed for greater market access without ensuring or catalyzing proportionate transformation on social and political accounts. Some of the consequences, arguably, are that since the end of the Cold War, not only has the democratization project met abysmal failure, but it also gave rise to "crony capitalism" in these societies, resulting in the clash between the bourgeoisie and the working class and paving the way for a new rise of social movements (Pei, 2016). The desperate quest to terminate endeavors to limit the otherwise limitless and continuous expansion of capitalism and the violent resistance against accumulation by dispossession are reaching new levels.

There has been more than one occasion when the collapse of global capitalism felt imminent but somehow was avoided. The protraction of the inevitable collapse of capitalism is thus one of the primary questions that critical theorists, particularly of Marxist tradition, have tried to deal with. From Gramsci and Habermas to Schumpeter, Samir Amin, Andre Gunder Frank, and Wallerstein, the explanations rested on a variety of arguments. Many of these often cited theories—the third face of power, false consciousness, manufacture of consent, development of underdevelopment, and accumulation by dispossession, among many others—grasp the complexities involved in the functioning and crisis-survival-crisis movement of capitalism to a greater extent. A review of the literature produced by Marxist and critical political economists reflects a number of probable reasons. According to Michael Lebowitz (2004), there are four primary reasons that help capitalism—"a relationship in which the separation of working people from the means of work and the organization of the economy by those who own those means of work has as its result that, in order to survive, people must engage in a transaction-they must sell their ability to work, to those owners"—keep going. First, that the exploitation is not *obvious*. Contrarily, the contract shows that the worker is being paid in return for the time he is selling to the capitalist. Second, the generation of capital must remain mysterious, at least to the working class, because the workers are asked to sell their ability to work, while in effect they are selling their ability to produce capital; the ability of productivity must be assigned to the capitalist. Third, since the working class is dependent on the capitalist to buy its ability to work, it needs the capitalist class to buy these abilities; "the real tragedy is not the sale of her labor-power; it is the inability to sell it" (p.

22). Fourth, it is the capitalist class that determines the kind of abilities that are in demand in the market. It, therefore, creates a dependency of the working class to look for "particular capitals." In the long-run, it creates animosity and competition within the working class.

In capitalism, crisis is the norm. The magnitude of these crises, however, has been too weak to convulse the whole system. Simon Stander (2009) theorizes that the real reason for the survival of capitalism can be found in what he calls "a class of shock absorbers." The absorptive class, he argues, is "the shock of the absorbers of the title" with a primary function "to absorb the commodities that are overproduced by the capitalist system" and "to absorb the economic crises" through the continued consumption of these commodities. Stander argues that this new class has been used as a guarantor to let the capitalist accumulate capital in an endless manner. John Weeks (2014) argues that there has been no "general" crisis, except the Great Depression and the recent Great Recession, that could have jolted the very foundation of the system. Many other scholars agree on the notion that the steep decline in the share of profits is one of the most important factors determining the spread of capital in markets. More importantly, in a recent and very important collective work, Wallerstein and other leading world-systems theorists argue about the Great Recession as the "prologue" of the final crisis featuring "deeper troubles and transformations" (Yagi et al., 2013). Wallerstein (2013), in particular, argues that all "systems" have a "life"; they are meant to die one day. Capitalism, like any other system or civilization in history, has a life that is coming to an end sooner rather than later. The primary reason why this may happen sooner is that the primary interest of the capitalist system, the "endless accumulation of capital," is increasingly getting tough to secure. The institution of the state and the interstate system were created to "quasi-monopolize" production and consumption processes. However, the core is losing its exclusive control over the "leading quasi-monopolized" products since the spread and trickling down of technology has become rapid enough that the profitability of invention is losing its attraction for the capitalist class. Wallerstein feels that abject disappointment may eventually lead the capitalist class to seek to develop an alternative system, something that may be the last nail in the coffin of capitalism. While I have not disagreed in principle with the Wallersteinian conclusion, I have argued that in an endeavor to prolong this inevitable fate, the core has now come to complexify the hierarchical structure of the world-system through the creation of the semi-core.

Like any other theory, world-systems analysis is not free from criticism. A number of assumptions made by Wallerstein, as the pioneer of the intellectual tradition, and his subsequent works received critical evaluations across the spectrum. It has been argued that there is a lot missing from many of the theories popping up in contemporary discourse about capitalism and its crisis.

I consider that these criticisms can be classified into four main arguments. They include epistemological questions (unit of analysis and economic reductionism), stagnant trimodal structure, and an intra-neo-Marxist challenge. My theory of the transformation of the trimodal structure argues that in response to recurring crises being the norm, capitalism has been creative in bringing new mechanisms to prolong its eventual death. By acknowledging structural dynamism in capitalist enterprises, it becomes easier to see the complexification of the production and consumption processes at the global scale and its interplay with military power as a stabilizing force. The semi-core, I argue, is a new strategy through which capitalism is not only slowing down the transfer of skills and technologies from the core to the periphery; it is also winning over to its side societies that could have challenged the system by now.

The first criticism against world-systems analysis pertains to epistemological grounds. The theory claims that the state is an incompatible unit of analysis to study the evolution of world history and its economy and politics. Wallerstein (2004) substituted "world-system" for the standard unit of analysis, the nation-state. To Wallerstein, it was an expression of the "concern with social temporalities, and concern with the barriers that had been erected between different social science disciplines" (p. 16). According to Wallerstein (2002), the development of the concept of a "world-system" as the unit of analysis was actually the result of his dissatisfaction with the nation-state being the standard unit of analysis, as urged by Marian Malowist's work on colonial expansion and the trade of gold between the west coast of Africa and North Africa, as well as by Fernand Braudel's *The Mediterranean*. He combined these scholars with Karl Polanyi's concept of three modes of economic behavior: reciprocity, redistribution, and exchange. Wallerstein argues that Polanyi's reciprocity was actually "mini-systems," while his redistribution and exchange modes turned out to be "the two varieties of world-systems: world-empires, and world-economies" (p. 361). The ontological understanding that the whole world was in fact one system led to the epistemological endeavor to broaden the unit of analysis by taking it above the social groups, the nation-state, and even the region. The endeavor, however, did not go unnoticed. The unit of analysis objection is common and continues to be reposed by referring to some of the eminent criticisms, such as that from Robert Brenner (1977) in his *New Left Review* article. Philip McMichael (2000) acknowledges that the terms and currency used in the theory received a number of criticisms. Theda Skocpol's (1977) critical review of the first volume in Wallerstein's multivolume work is particularly remarkable. She makes two important objections. First, she argues that while Wallerstein makes a remarkable contribution by broadening the unit of analysis, it is done at the cost of relegating the status of the nation-state in favor of (transnational) class interests. Second, Wallerstein places immense significance over economic factors but condones other avenues of state power, especially the military. According to her, "Unfortunately, the independent reality and effects of a system of militarily competing states cannot be comprehended by a theory that reduces politics to the expression of market situation and class interest" (p. 1086). At another place, she categorically rejects world-systems theory, as it is, according to her, essentially comprised of economic reductionism, preference of the "world-system" over the state as the unit of analysis, and condoning of military power with an overwhelming emphasis on economics (Skocpol, 1994). For my purpose in this book, Skocpol's criticism is significant for two reasons. First, like her, I am discontented with the "economic reductionist" approach espoused by Wallerstein. As I discussed in brief in the introduction, a world-system, even when it is an interstate system, is not comprised of economic activities only; nation-states are hierarchized in the realm of hard power as well. The tiers of the system are not merely so because of differences in their economic power; they are different also because of the differences in their military power. Second, while there is no doubt that the state remains an effective "sub-unit" of analysis in the world-system, Skocpol is correct in mentioning that its position is nevertheless relegated. The difference in the two arguments should be seen in the difference between the two ontological positions; Skocpol belongs to the statist school, while Wallerstein is one of the pioneers who perceive that the state is an extension of a transnational economic system, and that it has essentially been established to serve the interest of capital accumulation. With the rise of globalization, however, the neoliberal economic system has surpassed the power of the state. In fact, Malcolm Waters (2009) argues that "globalization theory only appears genuinely to be prefigured by the work of Wallerstein" because its understanding "appears to argue for an economic determination of the process." Contrary to Skocpol, who laments Wallerstein for ignoring the state as the unit of analysis, in Wallersteinian framework, according to Waters, "nation-states play a key structural role in stabilizing the system" despite that "under current conditions the integrity of the nation-state is being called into question" (p. 11). While some world-systems theorists, such as Amin (2006), rightly consider that globalization, capitalism, and transnationalization of the capitalist class are inseparable realities of the times of transition, Ernesto Screpanti (2014) argues that capitalism in fact has turned into global imperialism whereby the manufacturing and business corporations are transnationalizing their operations and processes. Overall, a dominant understanding within the contemporary critical political economy acknowledges that although the state has not been made totally irrelevant (since it cannot be), it nevertheless has been sidelined in terms of the conduct of economic activities. The methodological implications of this reality are enormous; they neutralize, if not nullify, the objections raised by Skocpol, at least within the context of the analysis of contemporary developments.

Economic reductionism is one of the most-cited criticisms leveled against the Marxist tradition. It is argued that Marxism and its various versions concentrate on economic factors as the most significant reason for development across the globe; this significance is stressed to such an extent that other factors, such as society and culture, are either ignored or termed as auxiliary causes influencing the patterns of development. The Marxist emphasis on economics, then, is justified by the argument that economics determines the reproductions of social relations. Since the principal objective of the capitalist system is economic—the accumulation of resources for the accumulation of capital—because of the fungibility of economic and capital power into any other currency of influence, the Marxist tradition asks us to concentrate on this driving force as the principal reason for development in the world. As Polanyi (2001) explains, since one of the primary purposes of the capitalist (class) is to disembed society from the rules of the market, instead wanting society to be subjected to the rules of the free market economic structure, it becomes necessary to look at the development of any society primarily from an economic perspective.

This, however, does not mean that world-systems theory ignores other factors, particularly when looking at macro-level development from a long-term perspective. One can argue that global capitalism does not depend merely on economic power to exploit various societies and nation-states. Military power is one of the most destructive capacities that has historically enabled imperial states to not only survive in competitive environments but also maintain their positions in global affairs for longer periods (Modelski and Thompson, 1988). Even Wallerstein (1974) agrees that one of the three factors ensuring the continuity and survival of the modern world-system is "the concentration of military strength in the hands of the dominant forces" (p. 404). While it is true that, in the words of Boswell and Chase-Dunn (2000), "military hegemony is dependent upon economic hegemony because military is widely expensive" and declining economic hegemony eventually results in military decline, it is difficult to reject the argument that the mismatch between economic power vis-à-vis military power is a common phenomenon in international politics. One of the central questions this book is trying to answer is how to bring together the economic *and* military power of a nation-state to determine its positional standing in the system. I argue that in order to become a member of the core club in the world-system, a country needs a combination of both economic and military power. I argue that a country can sustain its positional standing in the system as long as it succeeds in maintaining a rough balance between its economic power and its military power. This is not an easy task, however. One of the reasons is that military technology is essentially a zero-sum game and the transfer of technology from the core countries to the developing, semi-peripheral, and peripheral countries is blocked whenever doing so seems fit to the interests of the transnational capitalist class. The transnational capitalist class does not allow the release of technologies to developing and semi-peripheral countries. As we will see in the next three chapters, while the political elite of the core countries was less reluctant to extend economic cooperation, far more restrictions were put in place to ensure control of military technology. It is because war is a reality, and peace through suppression and deprivation is a desire. As argued by Mills (1958), "Imperialism by definition involves the interplay of economic, political and military institutions and men. No event of significance can be understood without understanding how these interests come to points of clash or of coincidence. 'The international system' of the world today cannot be understood without understanding the changing forms of their interplay" (p. 63).

World-systems theorists disagree about the nature and role of military power in global capitalism. Writing in 1998, Chase-Dunn argues that although "real capitalism" relies on "a mix of both competitive production of commodities and political-military power," it is in fact "commodity production [that] has the greater weight in the determination of outcomes in the system as a whole" (p. 43). He, however, agrees that the hierarchical structure of the capitalist world-system is maintained through frequent use of political and military power by the core countries (p. 77). Amin (2006), on the other hand, argues that "the main instrument in the current US drive for hegemony is military" and that "the ruling class of the United States freely proclaims that it will not 'tolerate' the reconstitution of any economic or military power capable of challenging its global domination" (p. 10). Arguing that the Wallersteinian world-system presents "an inadequate or historically misspecified model of development" by treating "militarization as a mere consequence of the capitalist mode of production," Muhammed Asadi (2012) argues that "development and underdevelopment within a global social structure is pervaded by militarism and continuous (global) war, in which nation states are positioned based upon a militarized division of labor" (p. 1). Incorporating the military as one of the dimensions of power to determine the position of a country in the hierarchical structure is a necessary step forward since it will expand the theoretical capacity of world-systems analysis when responding to the question of the rise of fall of global and regional hegemonic powers. I stated in the introduction that there are two parallel and highly convoluted but still different world-orders within the world-system; whereas economic world-order enables global capitalism to expand and penetrate through trade and commerce, and the positional standing of a country is determined based on its utility to promote accumulation of capital in the core, military order is maintained to extend security guarantees to those states that fulfill the economic objectives of the core and penalize others that resist. A better analysis of the world-system, therefore, must incorporate both realms of power in its calculations.

Broadening the world-system perspective to inculcate military power as an independent and equally significant factor influencing the rise and fall of powers within the world-system allows me to respond to yet another criticism: the stagnant outlook of the hierarchal structure of the world-system based on its *economic* division of labor. According to Stephen Sanderson (2005), world-systems theory assumes that the shift in the position of a state in the hierarchy of the world-system is "limited." Although it is possible that a state may decline or elevate its position within the structure, such a shift is more probable and of relatively short distance. In other words, in the absence of any hegemonic shift, the world-system should behave as a stable structure. Sanderson agrees with the assumption that the trimodal structure—the core, the semi-periphery, and the periphery—is based on the relations of exploitation driven through the global division of labor. However, he strongly rejects the stagnant nature of this structure, arguing that "the evidence is now rather strong that much of the capitalist periphery has been gradually disappearing." He is optimistic that "with the exception of Africa, other peripheral countries will move into the semi-periphery and some semi-peripheral countries will move into the core" (p. 186). The debate about the changing position of countries and the emergence of a new tier in the world-system, as well as other theoretical issues that the world-system perspective is facing, as mentioned in a debate between Sanderson and Chase-Dunn (2010), are of crucial importance since they have been raised by different scholars belonging to the same tradition, as well as by outside critics, for a considerable time. A number of scholars have empirically argued about the existence of more than three tiers. This is the central focus of this study and will be explained in the next pages, but at the moment it is necessary to look at yet another criticism emerging from within the Marxist tradition.

Within Marxist circles, according to Sklair (1991), world-systems theory has been criticized for two important shortcomings. One, it neglects class struggle. Two, it obfuscates the progressive role of capitalism. Central to this criticism is Brenner's (1977) critical evaluation of the Wallersteinian theory. Besides a number of other disagreements, Benner particularly hits hard when he disagrees with Wallerstein over the factors causing underdevelopment in the periphery. He argues that Wallerstein's immense stress on structural world-level factors obscures the exploitative nature of state-level factors where development is influenced more by class-based exploitations. Similarly, the process of accumulating capital depends more on the relative surplus value, which, in turn, is dependent on the process of innovation. An important evaluation of both works shows that while Brenner falls short on some points, his criticism of the Wallersteinian perspective holds ground that the world-system as a unit of analysis condones the role of class interactions in the development of capitalism (Denemark and Thomas, 1988).

Current theoretical explanations for the capitalist crisis and its eventual collapse, particularly as forwarded by world-systems theorists, neglect some other factors at play as well. One can argue that the generalization of arguments leading to an oversimplified conclusion of the collapse of capitalism is based on the premise that any financial and economic earthquake in the core—essentially the United States—should lead to the collapse of the whole system. Historically, the United States has outperformed all of the previous imperial powers dominating the capitalist system. Technological and communication revolutions also provided prompt access of the capitalist forces to remote areas of the world. Since capitalism has historically been housed in the West, and it has turned into an unprecedented monstrous form, *its* shift of the core from its traditional geographic location—Europe and North America—is mistakenly perceived to be the destruction of the system itself. The rise and fall of imperial powers throughout history, such as Dutch, British, and American power, to the apex level in the global economic system should be considered more as a paradigm shift in the system rather than its imminent collapse.

THE RISE OF THE SEMI-CORE: A FOUR-TIER WORLD-SYSTEM

Wallerstein emphasizes that the system is eventually going to collapse; simultaneously, we do not find him willing to consider the various ways that it could be delayed. Though I agree that the system will eventually collapse, I do not agree that it is *as imminent as anticipated* by Wallerstein and others. The theory of the semi-core helps me explain why the capitalist world-system will survive *longer* before it eventually collapses. I agree with the many of the theoretical postulates adhered to by leading scholars of world-systems theory, as explained very clearly and succinctly by Sanderson (2005). I agree that the world-system as a whole is the basic and appropriate unit of analysis. Before this capitalist world-system was born during the sixteenth century, world trade was facilitated by world-empires under a tributary system. As the capitalist world-system emerged in Europe and expanded under mercantilism and colonialism, it coerced the non-European empires, occupied them, redefined the concept of economic relations, and enriched its core by enforcing new roles on these territories in the world-system. I also agree that the capitalist world economic structure is hierarchical with a global division of labor. The domination in the world economy is of the upper tier over the lower tier.

The capitalist system expands, deepens, and evolves and will eventually collapse. In the long run, the descendance and ascendance of powers present at the various tiers is a fair possibility following Kondratieff waves; the modern capitalist system has seen three hegemonies: Dutch, British, and American. The modern capitalist system, like other systems of the past, has a life and will come to an end.

Though capitalism emerged in the sixteenth century and expanded during the next three centuries thereafter, the transformational changes during the second half of the twentieth century redefined the whole outlook of the system. An unprecedented proliferation of nation-states, the rise of global institutions, and other changes mentioned above require world-systems theory to relook at the contemporary system and define its complexities using contemporary data while contextualizing it in global economic history. More importantly, as I have mentioned earlier, world-systems theory needs to accommodate the aspect of military power in its approach since it is an undeniable aspect of national power, behavior, and conduct in the global political system. The world-system, in simple words, is not so because of its economic nature; only its contemporary structure is defined by unequal and unbridgeable military power as well.

The Cold War arrangement between the then USSR and the United States, in the words of Wallerstein (2000), had "enabled both countries to present their relationship as an unlimited ideological confrontation, with the important proviso that no changes in the East-West line were to occur and no actual military confrontations were to ensue, especially in Europe" (p. 356). At the end of this arrangement with the demise of the USSR, while neoliberals found it a jubilant moment and declared it "the end of history" and the initiation of a "new world-order," Wallerstein (1991) took it as the end of institutionalized hegemony for the United States, and a reawakening of the challenges to its economic supremacy and advantage of benevolence. He argued, "The world-system is in mutation now. This is no longer a moment of the minor, constant cumulation of cycles and trends. 1989 is probably a door closed on the past. We have perhaps arrived now in the true realm of uncertainty" (p. 15). Post–Cold War developments showed the launching of the imperial project of restructuring the world-system whereby new roles were defined and assigned to the actors, particularly the developing economies. In more than one place, Wallerstein emphasizes the term "peripheralization" in order to argue that there is a "world production structure," an ongoing process of reproduction of global inequalities, defined primarily by the institutionalization of endless accumulation of capital in the core. This process defines and allocates the core processes of production centered in fewer places, while other residual and labor-intensive tasks of production are assigned to the peripheral areas (Hopkins and Wallerstein, 1996). This process continued throughout the post–Cold War years, and the twenty-first century has seen its growth at unprecedented levels. The end of the bipolar structure led to a new phase in the evolution of the world-system that ushered a set of transformations by defining and magnifying the role of new complexities in the system.

Beside many other deleterious consequences, one of the effects of the unleashing of already introduced neoliberalism and structural adjustment programs was that the interrelationship between the state and the national economy changed. Kohli (2004) presents the case of India where the concept of a developmental state met the challenge of pressures from global financial and economic institutions led by the transnational capitalist class, resulting in the opening of the economy and the penetration of neoliberal economic policies in the country. Global capitalism, however, ensured that this development remained uneven. Global economic and financial institutions were moved to finance projects promoting technological gaps and supporting unequal exchange; territorial disputes were kept unresolved; violence was let to prevail so that drug and weapon markets remained functional. The outflow of capital from the global South to the global North reached unprecedented levels in the postwar period. While it is not the case that the countries in the global South witnessed this all with an abject sense of disempowerment since they were the principal and unavoidable actors in the mayhem, it was, however, the ultimate decisive power of the core countries institutionalized in the global capitalist structure that left little, if any, space to maneuver. The capitalist system, as argued by James Petras and Henry Veltmeyer (2013), is intended to maintain peace and order at one place through the spread of chaos and violence at some other places. The developing state, therefore, had to follow opportunities in the system to seek development. Such a development, ultimately, required that the core would maintain an edge over the decision-making power in the system. Simultaneously, neoliberal projects failed to resolve the issues of development and underdevelopment in a number of developing countries; as expected, the capitalist mode of production widened income inequalities within and between states. Something that Graham Hancock (1994) famously called "Development Inc." led to "the poor man's burden." Uneven development, "the hallmark of bourgeoisie ideology" (Smith and Harvey, 2008), reached new levels. Uneven development, therefore, turned out to be "a function of the contemporary universality of capitalism" (Mandel, 1975).

Some of the developing countries, however, managed to survive and excel in economic development. Japan, China, Taiwan, Singapore, South Korea, and later on India and Malaysia showed remarkable progress on economic development through industrialization, higher foreign direct investment, growth in international trade, and an increase in per capita incomes. It was, however, more of an expansion of global capitalism. Though this study concentrates on China, India, and Pakistan, and I will try to show that these countries grew modestly under the control of a developmental state, global capitalism patronized the regions where it could do its business peacefully and by winning the support of the host countries. The penetration of the neo-liberal model represented by global financial and economic institutions and transnational corporations intensified as these countries gradually submitted to the system. In the case of countries where peace prevailed, the capitalist class didn't need to initiate a conflict on its own. As mentioned, war, chaos, and violence have always been policy options when peace failed to prevail and serve the interest of capital accumulation, such as in the Middle East (Hinnebusch, 2011). The fast-developing countries were clutched in a mechanism where their dependence on the core was inevitable. Keeping aside the consequences of such an integration into the modern world-system, which has been considered "conducive to the establishment of the new world economic order and the modern world system" (Deming, 2010: 13), it is important to emphasize that it happened only when the countries showed a willingness to accept the domination of global capitalism by reversing the policies and agenda of the developmental state, opening national economies to foreign direct investment determined by transnational corporations and the capitalist class, and accepting externalities emerging out of the penetration of the market economic structure.

The growth lag within the semi-periphery has complicated the structure of the world-system. It has raised certain questions about the ability of the world-system to remain a powerful theory diagnosing the nature of global development and prescribing to a particular interpretation in its own manner. The stagnant nature of the trimodal structure is a particular impediment in thinking about dynamic change within the semi-periphery, and since theory does not include military power as a source of division of strategic labor defined and imposed by the core, we are blinded from seeing strategic power as more than an extension of economic power. The trimodal structure of the capitalist world-system, as explained by Wallerstein (2011b) and other leading scholars of the theoretical tradition, refers to the concept of hierarchy based on division of labor across the system. According to Wallerstein (2011a), "semiperipheral areas . . . are in between the core and the periphery on a series of dimensions, such as the complexity of economic activities, strength of the state machinery, cultural integrity, etc. . . . The semiperiphery is a necessary structural element in a world-economy" (p. 349). In the same year in another famous article, Wallerstein (1974) explains semi-periphery as "not the result merely of establishing arbitrary cutting-points on a continuum of characteristics," as well as "not merely inductive, sensing the presence of a third category from a comparison of indicator curves" but a deductive category that "is needed to make a capitalist world-economy run smoothly" because it is assigned a specific economic-cum-political role to ensure "that the upper stratum is not faced with the unified opposition of all the others because the middle stratum is both exploited and exploiter" (pp. 403–5). A few years later, he set two criteria for a country to be included in the semi-periphery. First, "in a system of unequal exchange, the semi-peripheral country stands in between in terms of the products it exports and in terms of the wage levels and profit margins it knows." Second, "the direct and immediate interest of the state as a political machinery in the control of the market (internal and international) is greater than in either the core or the peripheral states" (Wallerstein, 1979: 72–73). According to Chase-Dunn and Hall (1997), while the concept of the semi-periphery is controversial, it can be explained through four different but interlinked perspectives. They include "mixed forms of organization," "spatial locations," "a place mediating activities between the core and the periphery," and a group of countries possessing and exhibiting "intermediate institutional features" (p. 37). Historically, there have been different ways—chiefdoms, city-states, European hegemonies, the fall of the hegemonic core, and revolutionized peripheral capitalism—that semi-peripheries developed and sustained themselves in the world-system (p. 83). At another place, Boswell and Chase-Dunn (2000) mention the following characteristics of semi-peripheral countries: They are politically more stable, economically more developed, have been independent for a long period, possess powerful militaries that can act "regionally either as core surrogates or as the largest country in the region," and exhibit greater diversity in trade and productivity compared to the peripheral countries. According to them, a main defining feature is that "while they are still dependent upon the core," they are able to exploit the peripheral countries politically and economically (p. 27).

However, far from being accepted as a stable definition of the hierarchical structure of the modern world-system, the trimodal structure has been a controversial concept. Among the frontline critics of this structure are the status, role, and significance of the semi-periphery. The criticism can be grouped in two categories. One is from a group of scholars who criticize the structure mainly because of the blurred and vague nature of conditions advanced from time to time by Wallerstein, Arrighi, Chase-Dunn, Amin, and others. The second group of scholars are those who have challenged the very concept of three tiers and instead gone ahead to corroborate that there are more than three groups of countries in the world-system. Far more important is that neither of the two groups of scholars pay attention to the strategic world-order within the world-system. So far, there has been less focus, if any, to explain that the core relies on both sources of power: economic and military. It organizes the global division of labor keeping in view countries' relative significance and utilitarian value in these both roles. As I show in the next pages, despite a decline in the economic growth rate of the core countries, their military capacity, and its collective version in the form of NATO, has remained far more powerful than that of other countries, including the fast-emerging economies in the world.

Among the first group, Cornelius (Kees) Terlouw (2002) is a prominent figure. He argues:

> Semiperipheral states have no distinct features that separate them from core and periphery. The boundaries towards the core and the periphery are vague, and the foundations of the semiperipheral position are diverse. The semiperiphery is not a clearly delimited zone that can be fixed on a map. The semiperiphery appears as an amorphous group overlapping with the more distinct core and periphery when one compares characteristics of members of the semiperiphery. The social structure within each semiperiphery is much clearer. The average position in the world-system results in an extremely stressed social structure in the semiperiphery creating strong differences in development. (p. 6)

In another research paper, Terlouw (1993) tries to quantitatively identify the semi-peripheral concept by using six indicators—surplus flow from the developing world to the core countries, national participation in global trade, real GDP, military manpower, military expenditure, and diplomatic strength (number of embassies and diplomats each state sends and receives)—that in turn allow him to develop a single indicator called the "degree of the core-ness of the state." The research led him to conclude that "the diversity of states which are thus classified as semiperipheral is striking. They are not only scattered all over the world, but the similarities . . . are hardly apparent" (p. 89). However, Terlouw was able to reclassify the semi-peripheral states into two distinctive groups, which he named "political" and "economic," based on their stronger standing in the respective areas.

Carl Strikwerda (2000) argues that Wallerstein's "semi-periphery" is a "frustrating concept" because of the large variations within this group of states. This very reason, however, pushed Gilles Van Hamme and Geoffrey Pion (2012) to look at the hierarchical structure at the interstate level through two variables: the intensity of trade and investment links, and the country's position based on the international division of labor. Based on their findings, they classify semi-peripheral countries into two subgroups. Semi-periphery I includes the countries "specialized in manufacturing goods but in a less massive way than the core countries," and semi-periphery II is defined as "the exporters of light manufacturing goods and agricultural products." However, in classifying countries, Van Hamme and Pion miss the element of exploitation; it is in fact the scale and magnitude of exploitation that enables countries to elevate their positional standing in the hierarchy of the global capitalist system. Terlouw (1992) and Minqi Li (2008) also mention that the semi-periphery is exploited by the core while it exploits the periphery. In this sense, it is both an exploiter as well as the exploited. Since this exploitation is primarily screwed through pulling both the economic and political-military muscles together, Giovanni Arrighi and Jessica Drangel (1986) criticize Wallerstein for neglecting the interrelationship between economic and political-military dimensions, and those within the structural mechanism of the world-system (pp. 13–14).

The interplay between the economic and political-military dimensions of national power and their relative positional standing in the world-system has pushed some other scholars to inquire about the nature of the semi-periphery. More importantly, the stable-cum-stagnant nature has been criticized. Wallerstein (2011a) argues that while it is not impossible for a state to change its position in the trimodal structure, it is nothing less than a challenge. This stance is criticized particularly by those who consider world-systems theory as failing to incorporate and reflect the real effects of globalization. William Robinson (2011) and Stephen Sanderson (2005), for instance, argue that a shift in the positional standing of any given state has been the norm, except that the United States and Western Europe have always been included in the core, while almost all of Africa has continuously been labeled as the part of the periphery. Sanderson shows his discontent with this approach. He argues that "much of the capitalist periphery has been gradually disappearing"; most countries of Asia and South America were at the periphery at the start of the twentieth century, but by 1980, most of them had elevated themselves to the semi-periphery. In order to address the complex processes of uneven development, he introduces another category within the world-system, namely "the lower-core." One can infer that the transformation of the world-system since the last quarter of the twentieth century needs to be incorporated into and reflected by world-systems theory.

Among the critics, some other scholars, such as David Snyder and Edward Kick (1979), Wil Hout and Frits Meijerink (1996), Steven Sherman (2009), and Matthew Stephen (2014), have tried to introduce different new tiers into the trimodal structure of the world-system as proposed by Wallerstein and others. They have named it in different contexts depending on the factors they took into account while determining the suitability of any state for its placement at a particular tier. Edward Kick and Byron Davis (2001) use the term "the semi-core" to differentiate between the uneven pace of economic development and the rise and decline of some powers within the core and the semi-periphery. Arguing that the semi-periphery is an extremely heterogeneous group, they state:

> Our position here is that theory is best served by distinctions among these semi-peripheral countries, based on the more nuanced nature of their international

> ties as they relate to international power and dependency. These positional differences lead us to identify what traditionally might be called an upper semiperiphery, which we feel is more properly conceived as the semicore of the world system, and a lower semiperiphery, which we feel is the true semiperiphery of the system. (p. 1563)

"True semiperiphery," then, "comprises nations that, during most of the last half-century, have been strongly tied to the capitalist core and semicore, or the socialist semicore, or weakly tied to both" (p. 1563). By looking at the world economic status of states during 1945–1975, one can safely argue that a stable two-tier structure of the global economy, comprised of the developed and developing worlds, remained effectively in place. The unequal exchange of resources between the developed and the developing world, between the developing and the underdeveloped world, and between the developed and the underdeveloped world resulted in the accumulation of capital in the core, on the one hand, and intensification of the stratification within the developing world, on the other. Moreover, the end of the Cold War opened Eastern Europe to integration into the world-system in a reinvigorated manner. The consequent patterns of uneven growth resulted in increasing incompatibility of the trimodal structure when one wants to explain why and how, within the developing countries, some are progressing at faster growth.

The reinterpretation of the position of some of the semi-peripheral countries, as well as some of the countries of the core, is important because it allows me to develop a long-term perspective and explain the fall and rise in positional standing of various countries, in general, and of China and India, in particular. In the buzz of discourse, it is important to ask about the dynamic nature of the status of fast-developing countries in the capitalist world-system. While these developing countries have come a long way to develop themselves, even after they have been co-opted into the global capitalist system, the core remains intact, strong, unmoved, and the epicenter of business around the world. On the other hand, a combination of co-option and coercion has led these fast-developing countries to associate their stakes with the functioning and survival of global capitalism. I argue that the complexification of the functioning of the capitalist world-system can better be explained through the creation of another tier in its hierarchal structure. As mentioned above, various scholars have pointed to emerging complications within the trimodal structure and offered their own interpretation and corroboration about the newer realities. They do not argue that these complexities are a challenge to the global capitalist system. Instead, they argue that the developing countries with a development level higher than that of the rest of the developing countries and lower than that of the core countries have allied their policies in favor of the sustenance of global capitalism. My position is closer to this argument.

Discourse about uneven the development of semi-periphery and its effects on the system misses one important thing, however: It does not incorporate the changing dynamics of political-military power within the Wallersteinian semi-periphery. More importantly, the research shared here fails to provide a quantifiable idea about the shift in positions of countries. It does not offer a plausible explanation as to when a country should be expected to shift from one tier to another. It should be admitted, as I will explain in the next pages of this chapter, that world history lacks robust, regressive, universally acceptable, and reliable quantitative data of global economic history that we can access in the manner we have since the 1950s when specialized global institutions started defining, collecting, and processing various indicators of economic growth and development. However, that does not mean we are devoid of data altogether. The problem is with its health, verifiability, acceptability, and, more importantly, universality.

This study, therefore, tries to provide a definition of these concepts in as comprehensible a manner as possible so that the growth and elevation, and the decline and fall, of countries within the system should not become a matter of great shift. As a matter of fact, one should expect fewer threats to the survival of the world-system as long as the core remains intact, strong, and effective. A peaceful pluralization within the world-system structure or a transformation within the core should also be less threatening to the existence of the system per se. Conversely, the system should expect challenges to its survival if the status quo states of the core refuse to acknowledge the shifts in power of the aspirants and contender-hegemons. In such cases, a lack of concentration of political-military power will aggravate the challenge of explicability for world-systems analysis. This study, therefore, tries to reflect on this dimension of transition within the world-system by focusing on China and India during the last two and half centuries.

My definition of the semi-core countries relies on historical data. I develop criteria in order to differentiate between economic *and* military power and economic *or* military power. These criteria are parsimonious and rely on recognized factors, and the operational definition of these factors depends on measurable facts. I argue that a nation-state candidate being considered as a part of any tier in the hierarchy of global capitalism must meet a maximum number of the conditions laid down. From an economic point of view, for the core tier, these conditions include the following: (1) The country must be among the top thirty economies of the world, based on GDP and per capita income, for at least fifty years since 1950. (2) The share of industrial production in its national economy should outweigh its agricultural production. (3) The share of the service sector in its national economy should have been greater than the share of the industrial sector for at least the last twenty-five years. The powers in the core should also possess credible military power. The definition of credibility asks that such a country (1) since 1900, has successfully participated in at least one regional war or a world war *or* has credible international institutional guarantees for its national security; (2) has naval and aerial power to navigate globally and respond to any threats coming any part of the world *or* has credible international institutional guarantees for its naval and aerial security; and (3) individually, is one of the top thirty countries in terms of expenditures on acquiring military power as ranked by the Stockholm International Peace Research Institute. These conditions help me define the nature of the core.

The focus of attention for this book is the semi-core. I argue that a country that lacks military *or* economic power of the level of the core but has stronger economic and national defense capacities falls in this category. A country is in the semi-core if it meets the following conditions: (1) The country has been one among the fastest/highest top thirty economies of the world, excluding the core, for at least thirty years since World War II; and (2) *on average*, the growth in the country's service sector is larger than that of the industrial sector for at least last twenty-five years. From military perspective, a country is a semi-core if it (1) has successfully defended itself in a regional or world war, and (2) excluding the core, is one of the top thirty military powers in terms of national military power as ranked by expenditures on acquiring military power as ranked by the Stockholm International Peace Research Institute.

This book argues that a country falls within the semi-periphery if it has been growing in an uneven manner, and the fluctuations in its economic growth are noticeable. Fluctuations means the rise and fall of 2 or more percent in GDP growth rate in a decade, with five or more such fluctuations happening in the last fifty years, *or* during the postwar period, the GDP growth rate has not been more than 6 percent *continuously* for more than a decade. The military power of these countries is evaluated according to the following criteria: (1) The countries are weaker in military power compared to their neighbors. (2) They need international support to defend their territorial integrity. (3) They have been defeated in one or more wars during the last fifty years. (4) They have faced one or more civil wars. To me, the peripheral countries are those ranked by the United Nations Development Programme as least developed countries.

Given the nature of the argument that this study proposes, it is less acrimonious to label a large number of countries as developing or belonging to the semi-periphery tier. During the modern history of global development, starting with the rise of imperialism and the rise of Europe, the Western countries were able to take over global sources of wealth. It let the conquered or colonized areas become underdeveloped and remain so even after their so-called political independence during the second half of the twentieth century. The debate about fast-developing economies and some European countries failing to maintain the gap between themselves and newly rising countries attracts arguments of every kind. The term "semi-core" pertains to this debate. The countries coming within range of this circle can be claimed to be the aspirants of global recognition and as playing a visible role in the functioning of the global capitalist system.

Sources and Nature of the Data

At the start of the debate, it is pertinent to accept the deficiency of verifiable data. While there is no doubt that world-systems theorists take a long-term perspective to argue about the development processes in the world, this study still finds it difficult to defend the validity of the data collected by leading historians such as Angus Maddison and Brian Mitchell. The World Bank database does not provide any historical data. The most important hurdle, however, has been the geographical changes; states and empires disintegrated, and a proliferation of new postcolonial states emerged throughout the world. The recent admittance of this deficiency by the Maddison Project in this context corroborates the inability of its widespread use as well (Bolt and Zanden, 2014). Similar conditions pertain to almost all the datasets researched for this study. An example can be cited in the Eastern European states and the states emerging in the wake of the disintegration of the Soviet Union. There is no data that may accommodate the long-term perspective of the economic growth and military power of these newly emerging states in a verifiable manner. Though this study avoids the geographical problem by neutralizing it, comparative analysis still faces credible questions of long-term analysis. Instead of taking regional statistics, this study takes into account only that much data that it can defend with a certain level of confidence. It also makes sense because the issue of the semi-core is a new trend in global capitalism; this study accepts that before the last quarter of the twentieth century, the world-system was based on three tiers, and it is only in this latest phase of globalization that we see uneven development within the semi-periphery, which is causing the emergence of a new tier.

Data Analysis

A simple graphic and statistical analysis of economic and military indicators has been used to corroborate the claims. In terms of economic performance, relying on available data, the tables that follow show the uneven pace of development. In developing these tables, two criteria have been kept in context. First, the countries should meet all the requirements mentioned except two. Most of these conditions were met by the top thirty countries in the respective indicators. The table below is a list of countries meeting the criteria mentioned above along with their rank of economic power.

A number of important observations can be made. First and most important is that none of these countries belong to the "traditional core." In about sixty years, no European or North American country could remain in the top thirty fastest growing economies at least fourteen years. Instead, Southeast Asian

Table 1.1. Fastest Growing Economies since 1950.

No.	*Country*	*Years among the Top 30*	*Economic Ranking*
1	China	42	1
2	Singapore	31	2
3	South Korea	30	3
4	Botswana	28	4
5	Malaysia	25	5
6	Rwanda	22	6
7	Thailand	22	6
8	Oman	20	8
9	Panama	20	8
10	Seychelles	20	8
11	Iran	19	11
12	Iraq	19	11
13	Syria	18	13
14	Dominican Republic	18	13
15	Congo, Rep.	17	15
16	Ethiopia	17	15
17	Cote d'Ivoire	16	17
18	Equatorial Guinea	16	17
19	Hong Kong	16	17
20	Indonesia	16	17
21	Myanmar	16	17
22	Zimbabwe	16	17
23	Chad	15	23
24	Bahamas	15	23
25	India	15	23
26	Kuwait	15	23
27	Macao	15	23
28	Cabo Verde	14	28
29	Morocco	14	28
30	Mozambique	14	28
31	Papua New Guinea	14	28
32	Sudan	14	28
33	Turkmenistan	14	28
34	Turkey	14	28

Source: IMF and the World Bank.

and African countries have been making remarkable progress in securing higher growth rates. Second, this ranking also shows a long-term trend: A number of countries such as Iraq and Syria have fallen but still place in the list above India because of their performance in the twentieth century. Third, with some exceptions, most of these economies are not experiencing stable economic growth, so they meet the conditions of fluctuation in their GDP growth rate. Almost all these economies have touched higher, and sometimes lower, growth rates due to various reasons. China, for example, experienced a record -27.3 percent growth rate in 1961, according to data available from the World Bank used for the graph below. The reason noted was the devastating effect of the so-called "Great Leap Forward" program by the Mao administration. In 1965, Oman reported an unprecedented 189 percent growth rate. A look at the GDP per capita of countries, or the richest countries in the world, shows a different picture.

It is important to note the variation between the mode and the average. While the mode shows the recurrent highest number of ranking a country received since 1950, the average contextualizes the whole story of per capita income. Two examples clarify the argument further. The countries falling in the traditional core have kept their positions intact; there is little variation between their recurrent positional standing and average positional standing. In case of some others—United Arab Emirates, Hong Kong, Venezuela, Taiwan, and South Korea—there is a huge gap between their recurrent positional standing and their average positional standing.

Either of the two factors made this possible. They fell from a higher position in an unprecedented manner, or they rose to the higher ranks in a faster-than-usual manner. Since the first situation is not the case, we can see that these countries made enormous economic gains to become among the top per capita income-earning countries in the world. In the cases of Qatar

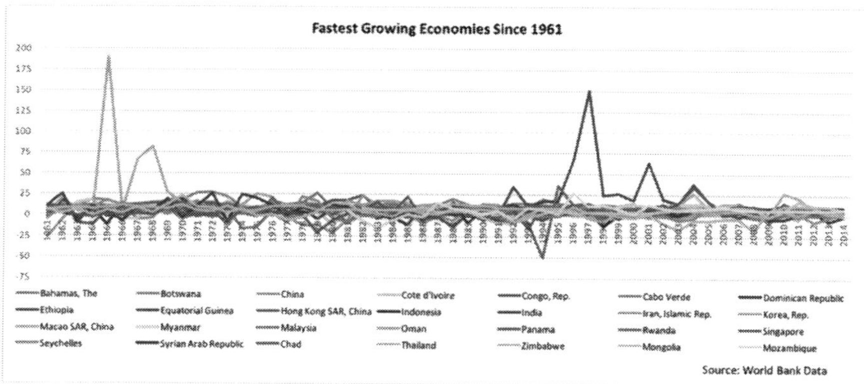

Figure 1.1 Fastest Growing Economies since 1961. ***Source*****: IMF and the World Bank**

Table 1.2. The Top GDP PC Countries since 1950.

	Country	*Mode*	*Average*
1	United States	1	3.016949153
2	Qatar	1	16.66101695
3	Norway	2	9.423728814
4	Kuwait	2	17.01694915
5	United Arab Emirates	3	11.11864407
6	Hong Kong	3	22.54237288
7	Switzerland	4	4.220338983
8	Denmark	6	6.728813559
9	Venezuela	6	23.88135593
10	Canada	8	6.491525424
11	Australia	9	9.627118644
12	United Kingdom	10	12.86440678
13	Sweden	11	9.474576271
14	Netherlands	13	10.40677966
15	Belgium	13	13.71186441
16	Germany	14	15.45762712
17	France	15	12.57627119
18	Japan	16	18.98305085
19	Austria	18	15.72881356
20	New Zealand	19	14.47457627
21	Finland	19	17.50847458
22	Argentina	21	31.52542373
23	Taiwan	21	52.69491525
24	T. and Tobago	22	23.94915254
25	Spain	22	27.52542373
26	South Korea	23	59.22033898
27	Israel	24	22.49152542
28	Slovenia	26	25.36842105
29	Ireland	27	23.08474576
30	Greece	29	31.98305085
31	Saudi Arabia	30	29.67796611

Source: IMF and World Bank

and Kuwait, the richest position in the late 1960s and the early 1970s should be contextualized in line with their petroleum economies. Almost all of these countries are outside the orbit of the traditional core. A closer look at this graph provides two important insights. First, the relative gap in income of the richest countries of the world is increasing; the range of per capita income has widened over time. Second, the uneven patterns of economic gains are increasingly glaring; one can identify that the rise and fall in the per capita income of the leading economic powers of the world is resulting in the emergence of new centers of power. Yet another important observation is that although China, India, and other Southeast Asian and African countries showed commendable economic growth by achieving the highest GDP

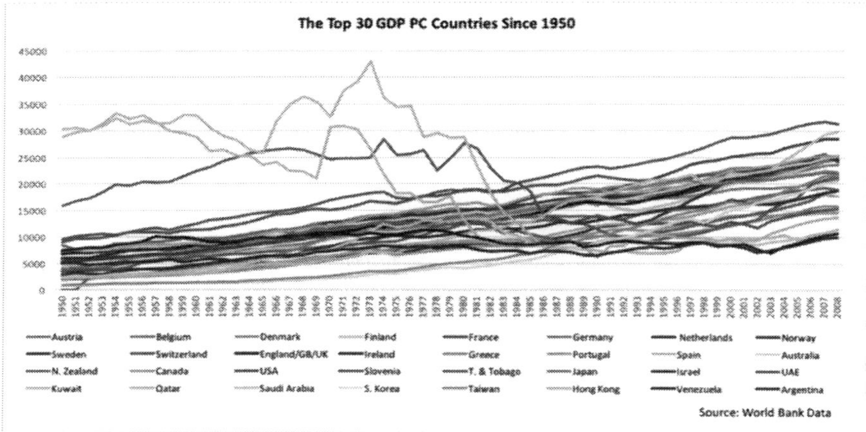

Figure 1.2 The Top 30 GDP Per Capita Countries since 1950. *Source*: IMF and the World Bank

growth rates, and though they are still behind in the race to enter the club of richest countries in the world, they are on their way. China and India are not among the top thirty richest countries in the world when we look at per capita income mainly because they are the most populated countries on earth and together cater to more than 35 percent of the world population, yet there is still rampant poverty in the countryside.

This study asks that in order to become a candidate for the semi-core tier, developing countries must also meet some other conditions. It asks that a country's economic outlook be dominated by the service sector, with the industrial sector having surpassed the agriculture sector. Data from the World Bank shows that out of the leading GDP per capita countries, China is the only country whose national economy is dominated by industrial growth instead of service. It was only in 2013 that the service sector started taking over the industrial sector, showing a much-awaited shift in the weight of the leading sectors of the Chinese economy.

In terms of continuous economic growth rate, the condition that a country should have experienced a continuous GDP growth rate of above 6 percent for at least a decade is mostly accomplished by the fastest growing economies. Yet many of them experience huge fluctuations in their growth rate. The graph below shows that these countries remain exposed to a number of factors, including foreign direct investment, as well as political and social conditions within their borders. It verifies the claim that countries are dependent on factors inside and outside their territorial jurisdiction, and the core is still capable of shaking economic foundations. Unusual changes in growth rates also show that the economies are in a transition phase. It does not affect

Figure 1.3 Comparison of China's Leading Sectors of Economy (1960–2013). *Source*: IMF and the World Bank

the claim of the semi-core since the tier is limited only to a few countries. The other important indicator, national foreign exchange reserves, reflects the health of the national economy. Looking at the top thirty countries of the world since 1960, as shown in the graph below, reflects another way to define the positional standing of countries in the global capitalist system.

A glance at the graph shows that, excluding China and Japan, there are still new economies beyond the traditional core that possess sizeable foreign exchange reserves and are thus capable of supporting their international political and economic policy interests. However, the picture changes completely when we look at the graph including China and Japan.

The "monetary geography," as coined by Benjamin Cohen (1998), shows that the rule of few internationalized currencies has been widely accepted, thus pushing countries to accumulate sizeable foreign exchange reserves in order to maintain economic resilience of the state in international society. China, however, has pushed this resilience to unparalleled levels. Since the start of the twenty-first century, China has accumulated more than $3 trillion, mostly in the form of the US treasury securities. Beijing has played a vital role in interfering with the dynamics of US-China bilateral business in order "to execute its exchange rate policy of pegged RMB against the US dollar" and ensuring that it maintains the largest chunk of long-term US treasury securities (J. Li and Wang, 2014). In terms of political economy, one can claim that the trade surplus in favor of Beijing and the expansion of US treasury securities above $1.4 trillion provide China an exclusive edge to enforce the terms of bilateral trade.

In terms of military power, reliable data has been scant. Since this study focuses on a relatively long-term progression and military powers have been

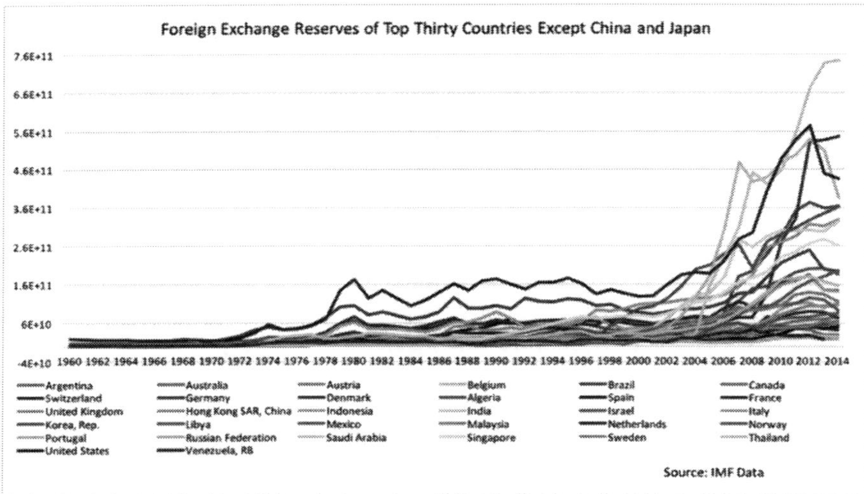

Figure 1.4 Foreign Exchange Reserves of the Top Thirty Countries Except China and Japan. *Source*: IMF and the World Bank

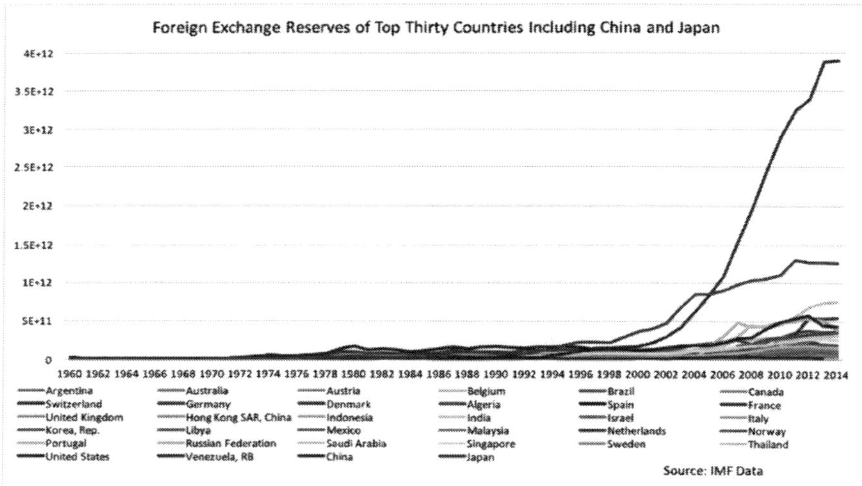

Figure 1.5 Foreign Exchange Reserves of Top Thirty Countries Including Chia and Japan. *Source*: IMF and the World Bank

in the realm of national security, there has not been enough data to develop a new scale of its own. Instead, I use an existing dataset to meet some of the requirements laid down in the criteria for the four-tier system. For other conditions, I have collected the data whenever it was available. The "Correlates of War (COW) Project" provides a number of datasets related to the military power and capabilities that countries have possessed since 1816. One such dataset, named "national material capabilities," deals with the military and military-related features that countries possess. Six indicators have been used to measure and prepare the index: iron and steel production, military expenditures, military personnel, primary energy consumption, total population, and the share of urban population. Together, these indicators help in preparing the "composite index of national capability (CINC) score." A long-term trend of this index shows the following countries appearing at the top of the list.

There is little variation between the recurring positional standing of countries and their average positional standing in terms of their rank in the index as prepared by the COW Project. Beyond these countries, the semi-peripheral

Table 1.3. Ranking of Military Powers According to the CINC.

No.	*Country*	*Average CINC Score*	*Mode of Ranking*	*Average Ranking*
1	United States	0.176650169	2	1.517241379
2	Russia	0.135482455	2	2.448275862
3	China	0.122277517	3	2.5
4	India	0.056010041	4	4.103448276
5	Japan	0.048593561	4	5
6	Germany	0.038798924	6	7.055555556
7	United Kingdom	0.031319136	7	7.137931034
8	France	0.025010031	8	8.431034483
9	Italy	0.019466929	9	9.793103448
10	Brazil	0.020591902	10	9.086206897
11	Poland	0.012506505	11	15.34482759
12	Ukraine	0.015841865	12	13.05882353
13	Indonesia	0.013075005	13	12.82758621
14	Canada	0.012177395	13	14.67241379
15	Spain	0.011203771	14	16.03448276
16	Mexico	0.010314143	15	17.96551724
17	Pakistan	0.010908248	16	16.89655172
18	Iran	0.008887447	17	22.46551724
19	South Korea	0.014949859	18	13.87931034
20	Turkey	0.010779857	20	17.06896552
21	Romania	0.006786757	22	28.20689655
22	Australia	0.007103338	23	25.89655172
23	Saudi Arabia	0.005781703	23	35.06896552
24	Egypt	0.007550581	24	25.24137931
25	Vietnam	0.0073953	25	26.7037037
26	Netherlands	0.006794348	26	27.24137931
27	Nigeria	0.006328956	27	30
28	Taiwan	0.007616703	28	25.24137931
29	South Africa	0.00634014	28	29.06896552
30	North Korea	0.007946698	31	25.51724138

Source: IMF and World Bank

countries are weaker military powers and rely mostly on international guarantees provided through the UN charter and international conventions.

It is important to mention that, according to the CINC, in 1997 China surpassed the United States as the most powerful country. However, if we take a number of other factors into account, this claim appears to be weaker. The military expenditure of the United States is higher than that of any other country in the world, and if we put together the highest military spending of NATO within the top thirty countries in the world, it is inconceivable to put a plausible challenge to the military might of the traditional core.

The graph below shows the relative share of each of the top thirty countries mentioned in the list above. As it can be observed, the United States has an unbridgeable gap with the rest of the powers. Adding that most of the powers in the list are members of NATO confirms that while the traditional core has lost some of its economic power, it still remains intact primarily because of its undeniable military power.

Discussion on Data Results

Taken together, the facts presented above and studied at length for the writing of this study support a number of claims made earlier. As a matter of fact, it has become evident that the traditional core—Western Europe and North America—remains strong and intact. Within the given data, the United States remains the top power and can be claimed as "the core of the core." In terms of technology, the United States is the most developed country and the hub of research and development. It is the final destination of the top business corporations and the transnational capitalist class of the world. What we are

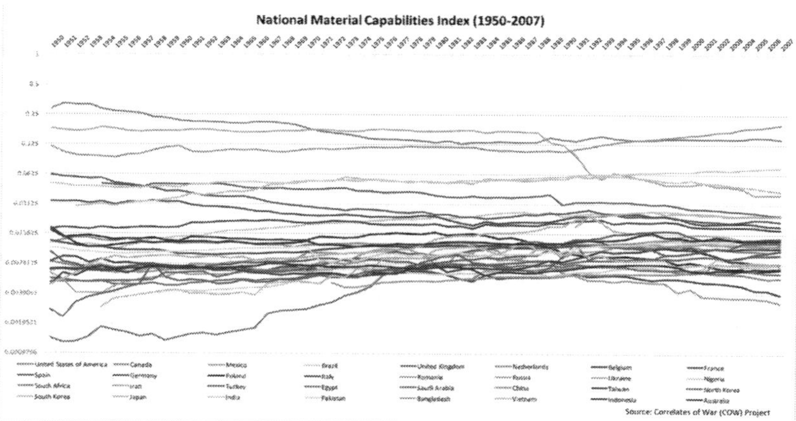

Figure 1.6 National Material Capabilities Index (1950–2007). ***Source*****: IMF and the World Bank**

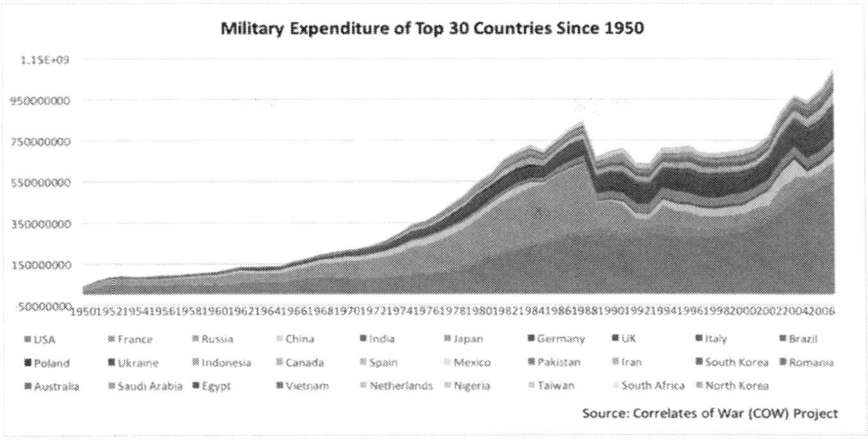

Figure 1.7 Military Expenditures of the Top 30 Countries since 1950. *Source*: IMF and the World Bank

witnessing in terms of transition in the world is not the decline of American power as such since its mode of production remains developed and advanced. It is, in fact, the rapid rise of other powers, particularly those situated outside the geography of the traditional core. According to Tom Kemp (2013), "The decline of the American economy is a relative, not an absolute decline, at any rate so far. Other countries have grown more swiftly and have been more successful in raising income levels and carving out a larger share of the international trade in manufactured goods" (p. 228). This fact supports the argument made earlier that the transnational capitalist class has spread across the world and is investing in places where it finds the highest margin of profit and thus capital accumulation. The contemporary phase of the long-term impact of this horizontal globalization must be understood as a harbinger of transformation in the global capitalist system whereby the geographical location of the traditional core may turn out to be inclusive by including new contenders in the power club.

The faster rates of growth are important only in the sense that they show a trend of the shift in the preference of nonmilitary investment being made by the transnational capitalist class across the globe. Beyond this, these growth rates do not carry a lot of significance since they do not invite any technological development in the defense sector. Two important points should contextualize the whole picture here. First, the faster rates of GDP growth may not enable the countries to reach the level of the "core of the core" because the technological gap between them and the traditional core in terms of military and war technology, and thus the difference in the mode of production, will continue to grow. Second, while the non-Western fastest developing economies are doing very well in terms of economic gains, it is actually their lack of military power that relegates their positional standing in the global capitalist system. In other words, despite that the United States and the traditional core of Western European and North American countries have not demonstrated impressive economic growth (with a few very rare exceptions, none of them have been within the top thirty fastest growing economies since 1950), they maintained, and are maintaining, their positional standing because of their mammoth military might. The defense budget (including research and development) of the United States is greater than those of the next top twenty-five countries of the world put together. That most of the top thirty countries with the highest defense budgets are allies under the umbrella of NATO provides stronger control to the core. The alliance has used its power whenever and wherever it found its economic interests to be under threat. The noncore economic powers are unable to compete against this magnitude, not because they consider defeat inevitable, but because they calculate their interests in a rational manner.

The semi-core countries, therefore, are the ones with the fast growing economies, have made their position felt in the top thirty countries of the world, and possess sufficient military power but are unable to compete, at least theoretically, against the collective might of military alliances such as NATO. The data and its results show that these countries are concentrating more on their economic growth than military advancement. The flow of global capital directed by the transnational capitalist class is one of the driving forces pushing these countries toward parochial industrialization. Taking from the both lists, and excluding economic and military power, I can say that *at least* the following countries can safely be argued to be part of the emerging semi-core in the world-system: Russia, China, India, Brazil, Switzerland, Austria, Israel, Sweden, Iran, Poland, Ukraine, Indonesia, Mexico, South Korea, Turkey, Australia, Taiwan, and South Africa.

While the neoliberal forces of globalization have been aggressive in subverting the erstwhile position of the state in terms of its ability to direct non-military businesses, trade, and commerce, they let the state claim jurisdiction over the legitimacy of violence. In other words, while economic globalization progressed aggressively, we do not see a similar decentralization of the production, assembly, and consumption of military technology. States have been spending huge amounts on research and development, and it is in fact the ability of the core to keep the defense industry globalized at the minimum possible level that it has been able to control political developments across the globe. In particular, the scale of globalization of the military-industrial complex, if any, has not been allowed to exist and burgeon beyond the territorial boundaries of the core.

Looking at the data, it can also be suggested that the route to development, particularly for late developers and countries falling at the semi-core level, is determined first and foremost by the transnational capitalist class. The flow of capital in these states is directed to only a few sectors of industry, thus creating an interdependence at the global level. To an extent, states have accepted the route and concentrate only on those sectors that it is allowed to progress. India, for example, is offering services in information technology, while China has practically turned into a global assembly line where parts are brought from all over the world for the final products. China has higher percentage of input in its national economy from the industrial sector compared to the service sector. Its military budget and status are far smaller compared to its economic status. India, Brazil, and other countries have a relatively higher ration of service sector than industrial sector, yet they still rely on agriculture as an important sector of sustainable economic growth. In other words, these countries lag in terms of development; they have solid economic growth with little or slower military advancement. When we look at advancement in military technology, research, and development, it becomes evident that the semi-core countries have still been unable to relinquish their dependency on the core.

The quest of the core to maintain the discrepant levels of technological advancement and modes of production will be crucial to define the future course of action. Keeping in view the notion of Kondratieff waves, this study covers one wave within the context of Asia and Europe. In the context of a theoretical framework of world-systems analysis, then, one needs to understand the *transformative ability* of a global capitalist system controlled by the transnational capitalist class. For three basic reasons, one can argue that the core will continue to maintain its grip over the global capitalist system, while the semi-core countries will continue to grow economically in a simultaneous manner. One, despite an increase in the margin of profit, the transnational capitalist class has been able to improve in terms of volume because of horizontal and vertical globalization. In an article, Kema Irogbe (2013) makes it clear that multinational corporations have been able to keep up with the pace of capital accumulation despite the increase in resistance from the developing world. The contemporary wave of economic growth in the global South is primarily funded, directed, and controlled by the transnational capitalist class located in the West. Two, since almost all of the leading multinational corporations are housed in the core and mostly owned by individuals and entities located in the same region, they use the military muscles of these states to push forward the material interest of capital accumulation. The state and these corporations spend huge amounts of money on military buildup in order to coerce resistant forces. This compels countries in the developing world to submit to the demands of these corporations. Three, the semi-core countries find no other plausible alternative system at the moment and, therefore, rationally calculate that it is better to cooperate than confront. China, for an example, is as capitalist as any other nation in the world because the state, controlled by the Communist Party, considers it to be serving its national interests. More importantly, semi-core status shows that they have been given some privileges, as compared to many other developing countries in the global South. The fact that the semi-core states find no alternative but to align their interests with the interests of the core countries makes it difficult for revisionist forces to challenge and bring an end to the capitalist system. The contemporary trend will continue. Given that the transnational capitalist class finds it suitable to its interests, China will return to its status of being the super accumulator of global capital over the next decades. India will also progress and compete for its share in this reverse flow of global trade. It may lead, eventually, to the relocation, or at least the expansion, of the geography of the core. Yet, unless we see a paradigm shift in the military capabilities of these semi-core countries equitable enough to restrain the existing core from challenging the loss of its central position in global capitalism, and also by bringing the economic conflict within the transnational capitalist class to a stage where a rational calculation of the cost and benefit analysis informs the parties to go to war, this study does not anticipate any *looming* credible threat to the global capitalist system per se *in the near future*.

The magnitude of uncertainty and unrest will reach new heights. The scope of chaos and unrest will also reach new levels. A paradigm shift will also take place, thereby causing an expansion and then a relocation of the core. Eventually the system may collapse in such a manner that it may transform itself into something different. In this sense, there is a higher level of uncertainty and confusion. One of the reasons for this uncertainty that is so prevalent is that for the first time we are witnessing a shift of huge magnitude in the core. The earlier shift in the core within the modern world-system—when China and India lost their positional standing in the world-system some four centuries ago—was swift, relatively less implicating toward other continents, and characterized by physical occupation of the areas. This time, the nature of shift is different and the interests at stake are far higher. As mentioned, last time China and India lost their positional standing because they were outgrown and eventually occupied by the rising powers. This time, global capitalism is witnessing another rapid rise of these powers in terms of economic growth. Once this transformation is complete, and we do not know when and how it will be, or whether or not it will be violent, uncertainty characterized by an unprecedented rush to accumulate capital will remain prevalent throughout the system. In order to analyze the whole picture, therefore, it is necessary to look into historical development of the Indian Sub-Continent and China from the time when European forces colonized them. The next chapters take on this task.

CONCLUSION

This introductory chapter lays out the nature, main arguments, and methodological understanding of the study. It provides a theoretical framework of the study that argues in favor of revisiting world-systems analysis as proposed by Wallerstein by suggesting a new tier in the system. It argues that the contemporary theoretical understanding of world-systems analysis is increasingly becoming incompatible because of a horizontal and vertical complexification process in the system. Various state and nonstate actors shuffle their positions. The varying pace of development and technological growth in developing countries is redefining the nature of production process and being facilitated by the globalization process. While a paradigm shift has not taken place yet, it is in the offing. The traditional core is facing increasing pressure from fast-growing developing countries to expand their share of global economic power. This study argues that the core is responding to this pressure by facilitating the creation of another tier in the system, which this study calls the semi-core. The shift in the positional standing of countries is not a unique phenomenon and has happened more than once. The study applies the argument to the Indian Sub-Continent and China by analyzing their fall from global economic epitomes in the eighteenth and nineteenth centuries to peripheral areas in the twentieth century. Over the last four decades, China and India have shown remarkable growth by redefining their role in global production processes. Simultaneously, Pakistan and Bangladesh have been less successful in catching the development train. This study argues that the world-system is headed by the global capitalist class, which assigns the pace of economic or military development keeping in view the utilitarian perspective of the country. It means that Pakistan could grow militarily but not economically because the system needed it grow in that very dimension. The study also argues that countries observe higher rates of growth only when they submit to the demands of the capitalist world-system headed by the transnational capitalist class. This study introduces operational definitions for core, semi-core, semi-periphery, and periphery. The model has been applied to study China, India, Pakistan, and Bangladesh over the last two hundred and fifty years.

Chapter Two

China

From the Periphery to the Semi-Core (1757–2014)

The history of China is a classic case of the fall and rise of powers in the world. Few other countries in the world have such an astonishing history. This chapter applies the theoretical framework developed in the previous chapters to study China's positional standing as a regional hegemon and "super accumulator" in the tributary trade system before the emergence of the capitalist world-system in Europe, its decline from the mid-eighteenth century onward, and its recent rise in the globalized world-system. This chapter looks at the status of Chinese-European trade before the arrival and imposition of European military power over Asia, the consequences of Chinese defeat in the face of the superior military-fiscal power of the European imperial powers, and the shift in global economic and political power from the East to the West. Starting 1757, the Qing dynasty (1643–1911) was unable to face the challenge of imposing the conditions of trade set by the British and then other European powers. The decline was slow, continuous, and embarrassing; China was eventually occupied by all the leading Western powers and Japan simultaneously, and its economy was redefined according to the needs of the capitalist world-system. Only in the last decade of the nineteenth century has China started resisting Western imperial presence on its soil. From a monarchic structure, China witnessed the rise of communism and achieved independence in 1948. Maoist policies, as long as they remained at odds with the interests of the world-system, could not deliver China noticeable material development and economic growth. It was only after Mao that China could integrate itself into the world economy primarily by accepting the terms and conditions of Western economic institutions. Though the country maintained its one-party rule and communist political system, it has adopted virtually everything from the market economic structure. It is only through its acceptance of the market economy that China is re-emerging as a global capital accumulator, a position it held some three centuries earlier in a tribute-trade world-system. China's rise, however, is partial, faulty, and parochial. Even after having become the second largest economy in the world, China still lacks the formidable military capacity to maintain and extend its own worldview in global politics. In a four-tier world-system structure, China is a semi-core country and can become a core country in future. It can do so only by competing against the collective strategic strength of the status-quo core powers, either by immensely developing itself strategically or developing a military alliance outweighing, essentially, NATO.

CHINA, EUROPE, THE GREAT DIVERGENCE, AND ITS CONSEQUENCES

To understand China's contemporary re-emergence in the world economy, it is necessary to discuss the origins of the fall of China from its status as a super accumulator. The whole array of theories, ranging from ultra-Eurocentric perspectives to ultra-Asian arguments, agree on two essential points that are very relevant to the central argument I am trying to make here. First, that China was the hub of a premodern trade system based, primarily, on a tributary structure wherein the conduct of trade inside its territory was dependent on conditional permission of the Chinese empire requiring payment of a tribute, recognition of the sovereign status of the empire, voluntary participation, and agreeing to ensure mutual benefit. Scholars agree that the introduction and penetration of opium in Chinese society was the main reason that brought a paradigm shift in the balance and nature of trade between China and Europe. For Europeans, the discovery of silver and other metals in the Americas had already eased the terms of trade, resulting in the accumulation of precious metals in China. It is important to mention that although China was the first country in the world to introduce and use paper currency, it abandoned using it in the wake of the great influx of American silver that reached the mainland through European traders. Second, and more importantly, these theories agree that by the time British forces attacked Canton in 1757, they were superior in observing, planning, and implementing strategies of war. The element of comparative military superiority is, however, either relegated or condoned altogether in the face of an obsession with economic factors. The real question these theories disagree about is the role of military capabilities and technologies facilitating the conception and execution of war strategies. European military superiority, as the next pages will show, was established when Dutch companies were trading with China. Such an edge, though it was acknowledged in Qing dynasty, did not result in provoking any strong desire in the empire to develop military power along modern and European lines. One can make a convincing argument that had China been able to develop militarily, it would not have submitted to European imperialism, and the course of the nineteenth- and twentieth-century history could have been different.

Discussing the reasons for the "Rise of the West" is beyond the scope of this study. So is an evaluation of Eurocentric or Asian-centric reasons for modern global development and underdevelopment. I am confining myself to the central thematic argument that I developed in the previous chapter, and I am trying to apply it here in the case of China: In order to join the core in the hierarchy of a world-system comprised of the states, it is imperative that a state must possess both kinds of power—economic and military. A country, I reiterate here, that is unable to expend its economic supremacy in military power is unable to elevate itself within the structure of the world-system. As I mentioned in the first chapter, the period being covered in this study can easily be defined as comprised of three phases: the premodern world, in which China maintained a regional hegemonic and super accumulator position in a global tributary-trade system; the emergence of the colonial capitalist world-system, in which Western, and particularly the British, imperial rule governed much of the world; and the postwar period, in which the United States leads the core. It was only in the first phase that China was a regional hegemon; China lost its positional standing in world trade as Western empires, particularly the British, overpowered the Qing empire militarily. Qing China failed to develop itself, particularly regarding its military power, during the time when it was a super economic accumulator. Keeping all other variables constant, had China converted its economic power into military power, it could have become a real regional hegemon and a contender in the global hegemonic competition of the nineteenth century. It was, therefore, less the rise of the West than the fall of China that changed the geopolitical landscape of the world for the next three centuries.

A debate about the rise and fall of empires is also beyond the scope of this study. I am not entering into a debate defending or rejecting leading theories of international relations ranging from realism, where military is so essential that life without it is "solitary, poor, nasty, brutish, and short" (Hobbes, 1985 [1651]), or liberalism, where possessing such a capacity or its utility is considered as "a cancer of the body politic." My argument aims to assess the role of the presence or absence of national military capability in the survival of empires, and now nation-states, particularly since the rise of the modern capitalist system. Moreover, this assessment rests on a particular theoretical approach—the parameters of which have been defined by world-systems analysis—and concentrates on the historic fall and contemporary rise of China and India only, though I aim to develop it into a theoretical framework capable of looking at the rise and fall of other states in the long run. As explained in the previous chapter, one of the main deficiencies in the theories of critical political economy, in general, and in world-systems analysis, in particular, is that they fall short of balancing their focus when analyzing the avenues of power primarily because they are descendants of the Marxist tradition. Since nation-states are essential pillars of the modern capitalist system because they quasi-monopolize modes of production, and since they are controlled by the elite class, it is necessary to assess how these states are made capable of defending and maintaining their utility for the transnational capitalist class eager to maximize the accumulation of capital. Arguing that such a maintenance depends *only* on economic power may not be true when one looks at developments in history. It is, therefore, important to see that the role of states in the nineteenth and twentieth centuries was defined by front-line economic and military actors serving capital accumulation in the West.

Theories about the fall of China and the rise of Europe, particularly Great Britain, in the eighteenth and nineteenth centuries have been a matter of considerable controversy. Named as "the great divergence" by Samuel Huntington (1996) and popularized by Kenneth Pomeranz (2000), this controversy is primarily about searching for and defending the causes of the fall of China from super accumulator status to a country distributed as booty among, and occupied by, all the imperial powers of the time, and the rise of European countries, especially Great Britain, from the periphery to being dominant powers in the world. These explanations, in principle, can be divided into two major categories. On the one hand are the explanations that curiously peer into otherwise trivial causes leading to the fall of vast areas that later on were converted into colonies. Pomeranz (2000) has been at the front of this argument. According to him, while China and Europe looked very similar in the sixteenth century, it was primarily the discovery of English coal and the New World and its resources, particularly its minerals, that created favorable circumstances for European countries to develop industrially. According to him, "It was through creating the preconditions for those flows that European capitalism and military fiscalism—as part of a large global conjuncture—really mattered" (Pomeranz, 2000: 207). Many other economic historians have also used the discovery of coal as a plausible explanation for the divergence that followed between the West and China. Whereas China had abundant fuel resources such as wood, Europe lacked any such and therefore had to find some. The competition for survival, or to get out of the Malthusian trap, was a challenge for Europeans and therefore provided a compelling reason for them to innovate (Parthasarathi, 2011). This, coupled with the trade links and the influx of metals from the Americas, laid down the foundation of the Industrial Revolution, which eventually diverted into the paths the two regions went along. It is important to mention that *both* India and China were leading exporters of cotton and textiles at the global level. Analyzing the rise and fall of China's cotton cloth industry from 1300 to 1830, Harriet Zurndorfer (2011) argues that while the rapid growth of the cotton industry was due to state patronage under the Yuan regime and its successors, it was eventually the paradigm shift in global trade led by the British and the lack of innovation in China that brought a complete decline to China's once second top export.

The second category of the arguments offered to explain the phenomenon of the great divergence between China and Europe can be brought under the broader umbrella term of *evolution*. These explanations include the pattern of global trade during the last one thousand years and beyond, the state-society relationship that evolved along different lines, and the physical conquest of the non-Western world at the hands of Europeans and their economic consequences. The first sub-category of explanation—namely, the centrality of Asia in global trade before the "recent" rise of Europe—has been forwarded by no one else but a group of world-systems analysists led by Andre Gunder Frank. In his famous *ReOrient: Global Economy in the Asian Age* (1998), he forwards a case to claim the central position of China (and India) in international political order for a larger part of the history and before the relatively recent rise of the European capitalist system. From 1400 to 1800, a time when the scale and magnitude of global trade increased immensely, Europe was unable to claim any economic advantage since it lacked a competitive edge over its competitor regions, particularly India and China. It lacked population and the mineral resources, agricultural products, and industrial products that had demand in the rest of the world. Its primary source of income, therefore, was the profit earned while sailing around the world. It was, according to Frank, through the discovery of the New World and its minerals that Europe was able to bring a shift in the balance of trade with its Asian competitors. The role of American silver in bringing a paradigm shift in the balance of European trade with Asia has been corroborated by some scholars, including, perhaps more importantly, Dennis Owen Flynn and Arturo Giraldez (2010). The centrality of China and India in global trade in precapitalist society has been established, among numerous others, by Janet Abu-Lughod (1989),who considers it "the most extensive, populous, and technologically advanced region of the medieval world," and despite that China was the central actor in global trade during thirteenth and fourteenth centuries, she corroborates her statement that the "Chinese were not interested in trade" but "tolerated it only as a form of tribute" (pp. 316–17). It was a tributary system of free trade featuring voluntary participation. Only with the arrival of capitalism in the eighteenth century did China find itself being coerced to accept the Western demands for newer terms of trade primarily serving the interests of the latter.

Perhaps a more substantial part of the literature on the discourse of the great divergence deals with the different nature of the state-society relationship in Europe and China. Those who apply this framework are essentially Eurocentric. Erik Reinert (2010) argues that "emulation," defined as "the endeavor to equal or surpass others in any achievement or quality," was "the basic strategy that made Europe so evenly rich." He cites state patronage as the most important element in ensuring the movement of wealth into Europe. Daron Acemoglu and James Robinson (2012) consider the economic institutions of the European states to be superior in the deliverance of material growth and promoting innovation during the early years of capitalism. Peer Vries (2015) argues that while compared to Britain, Qing China was agriculturally more productive, economically more capitalist, immensely engaged in global trade, and with almost a similar level of social dynamism, it was the role of the state in economic management that eventually laid down the foundation for their divergent paths of development; state institutions started playing active role in Britain from 1500 to 1700, while such activism was missing in China. Under state patronage, the society produced and promoted innovative ideas defining new uses of minerals and technologies, thus promoting industrial production. Putting the temporal factor aside, a peculiar Eurocentric case of the role of the state-society relationship and its impact on economic management has been forwarded as one of the causes of the great divergence by some other scholars as well. David Landes (2015) argues that European culture during the early modern period was nurtured by the fact that no single political power was able to direct social processes. The stiff and violent competition for resources and survival led to the Europe that "had always thought of itself as different from the societies to the east" based on its dichotomous worldview of Europe as free city, popular sovereignty, and democracy and wisdom, versus the East, representing aristocratic empires and despotism (p. 31). European cultural superiority was based on three essential items, Landes argues. He cites three sources that led to European modernization and the Industrial Revolution, something that enabled Europe to establish an unbridgeable gap between itself and the rest of the world. They include "the growing *autonomy* of intellectual inquiry; the development of unity in disunity in the form of a common, implicitly adversarial *method*, that is, the creation of a language of proof recognized, used, and understood across national and cultural boundaries [scientific research method]; and, the invention of invention, that is, the *routinization* of research and its diffusion" (p. 201, emphasis original). A similar kind of European uniqueness is found in scholars such as Jack Goldstone (2009), Joel Mokyr (2002), Eric Jones (2003), and Jean-Laurent Rosenthal and Roy Wong (2011), among others.

Another explanation of the great divergence talks about the role and consequences of the so-called "military revolution" that took place in Europe somewhere during the fifteenth and sixteenth centuries. In 1955, Michael Roberts presented his theory of military revolution in Europe having taken place from

1560 to 1660. According to him, European military modernization during this period was based on four important developments: revolution in tactics and battle procedures; huge financial investments resulting in standing professional armies and the expansion of military strength, such as in the ability to fight multiple fronts; increase in the scale of warfare; and the impact of war on society that led to newer military inventions. According to Geoffrey Parker (1976), though there is concern about the exact timing of the initiation of the revolution being the year 1560, the thesis that Europe went through revolutionary military changes during the sixteenth and seventeenth centuries has stood the test in studies since the claim was made in 1955. In his well-known book on the subject, *The Military Revolution: Military Innovation and the Rise of the West, 1500–1800*, Parker claims that the revolution was in full swing during the Thirty Years' War and though by 1600 almost all the leading powers in Europe had standing armies of more than 150,000 personnel each, the long war on the continent engulfed even those smaller areas that had been least affected by the transformation in planning, weapons being used, and style of fighting the war. These changes were not limited to land warfare only; they affected the way naval adventures were planned and implemented. According to Michael Duffy (1980), naval developments in the fifteenth and sixteenth centuries enabled the European powers, especially and most prominently Great Britain, to sail in an imperial manner across the globe. A famous military historian of our times, Jeremy Black (1991), is critical of the thesis by Michael Roberts on two grounds: first, "the extent to which stress on the period 1560–1660 minimizes the role of change in earlier centuries," and second, "the role of change in earlier centuries; in the second place that the situation in the last decades of the century 1560–1660 scarcely suggests that a revolution was nearly complete" (p. 8). In other words, he accepts that a military revolution did take place in Europe, and he agrees with Parker that it was a critical factor in expanding the political and economic control that the Western imperial powers had gained across the globe. Giovanni Arrighi (2009) argues that the victory the Europeans, particularly the British, enjoyed in the Opium Wars of the nineteenth century was the outcome of the "fundamental difference between the dynamics of the European and East Asian interstate systems during the preceding five centuries" whereby "the dynamic of the European system was characterized by an incessant military competition among its main components and by a tendency toward the geographical expansion both of the system and of its shifting center," and the interstate system in East Asia "stood out for the near absence of intra-systemic military competition and extra-systemic geographical expansion." The states in East Asia, particularly China, contrary to the Europeans, "showed no tendency to build overseas empires in competition with one another and to engage in an armament race in any way comparable to the Europeans" (p. 25). The primary result of this difference was that the dynamics of a strategic balance of power pushed the Europeans to seek newer technologies and methodologies of war, while the prevalence of peace in East Asia pushed capital accumulation in its epicenter, China.

The most important question related to this is how the military revolution in Europe affected the dynamics of the then-contemporary world-system. Keeping in view the debate on the great divergence, it is perhaps the most significant question that has been the least scrutinized. World-systems theorists recognized the role and the use of the military in bringing a shift in the balance of economic power in favor of the West to a marginal and relegated significance only. In his seminal multivolume work on the history of the modern capitalist world-system, Immanuel Wallerstein (2011a) considers military and other political factors significant only to such an extent that they facilitated the global spread of imperialism at the end of the eighteenth century. According to him, at the end of the Napoleonic Wars, "Great Britain ultimately prevailed globally in military terms." Thus, it can indeed be said that "within a *conjuncture* that was generally favorable, Great Britain created politically, sometimes militarily, its own *conjuncture*." It was these political-military victories that critically increased the economic gaps—in agriculture, in industry, in trade, and in finance" (pp. 112–13, emphasis original). It is important to note that world-systems theorists concentrate on the military only, or at least mostly, as an outcome of economic superiority. It is a relegated source of the shift in balance of economic power within inter-imperial competition. The rise and fall of powers in the world-system, therefore, is caused more by economic reasons, something I challenge in this study. The hegemonic power actually spends more money, world-systems theorists like Wallerstein (2004) argue, on military buildup, which they use to accrue economic benefits. Beyond that, eventually military strength becomes a burden and causes the breakdown of hegemons.

A focus on economic reasons at the cost of ignoring strategic and military factors, however, deprives us of explaining the roots of Western imperialism in Asia and Africa, particularly since the emergence of capitalism in Europe about five hundred years ago. Though there is no doubt that Europe was able to accrue unique benefits from the discovery of the New World and its minerals, it certainly is a weaker case if we concentrate *only* on the role of economics in ensuring the colonial occupation of regions in Asia and Africa. On the one hand, Parker (1996) mentions the benefits of military revolution that the British were able to receive in their quest dealing with China and India in the eighteenth and nineteenth centuries. Duffy (1980), however, argues that the royal navy grew immensely in the wake of the Anglo-Dutch and Anglo-Spanish wars of the 1650s. Victories in these wars led to the monopolization of the English royal navy over the maritime trade routes. The increasing costs of the military and warfare and their very viable source of income through global trade were some of the causes of colonial occupation. It was the result of a long inter-imperial competition seeking a monopoly in commercial activities between the East and the West in the wake of the discovery of the Cape of Good Hope and a new route to the Indian Sub-Continent in the 1490s.

Military revolution, naval buildup, and an expansion of global trade all took place almost simultaneously during the long sixteenth century leading to the introduction of Western imperialism in the Americas, Asia, and Africa. A global world-system was coming into being during these times. It is necessary to see what enabled the Europeans—first as entrepreneurs and then as state officials—to dictate the terms and conditions of this new world-system. The answer cannot become a sufficient explanation if we merely rely on Andre Gunder Frank and other world-systems analysts, including Wallerstein, who concentrate on economic and commercial practices. As a matter of fact, the Europeans were doing so for a long time in precapitalist centuries. They faced the persistent issue of having a trade deficit until the discovery of silver in the Americas. The control of the Americas by the Spanish empire enabled the transfer of these precious commodities to Europe and from there to Asia, thus helping European traders balance the deficit with China. Still, however, the Europeans needed to control the terms of trade and develop a competitive advantage over Asian products and manufactured goods and their pricing so as to convert the trade deficit into a trade surplus. This would not have been possible without physical occupation of these lands, and in order to take over vast areas of fertile land and subjugate millions of people, trade alone was not an effective answer; the Europeans applied the superior military technology and war skills that they developed, learned, and practiced over at least two hundred years to ensure that they got whatever they wanted. Even after they had occupied these lands by defeating local rulers and the Chinese imperial system on the battleground, they faced the persistent challenge of mutinies across the colonies. Physical control enabled them to enrich their homelands, develop military technology, and launch oppressive bureaucratic practices to establish a dreadful awe of imperial rule. It would never have been possible for them to keep doing so for two and a half centuries without policing capabilities and military superiority. It is difficult, if not impossible, to explain the economic pillage the Europeans unleashed in Asia and Africa and the consequent global inequalities without taking into account the role of the military revolution and its use by the imperial powers in Asia and Africa. In a remarkable contribution on the topic covering a long history of the development of gunpowder technology, Philip Hoffman (2015) argues:

> With [gunpowder technology], handfuls of Portuguese could intimidate South Asia and then profit by muscling in on the spice trade and selling protection to

> Asian merchants. And it allowed small numbers of Europeans to seize the rulers of the Aztec and Inca Empires and eventually take their place at the top. From that apex of political power, the Europeans could extract resources from native tribute and forced labor, without ever having many colonists or any sort of an army of occupation. (p. 12)

A concentration on merely economic activities, leaving aside the military revolution and its implications for global trade, leaves us devoid of a convincing explanation for the historical roots of the global inequality that continues even today. As explained in the previous chapter, the absence of military power as a variable in the calculation of the national power of countries to determine their positional standing in the hierarchical structure of the world-system weakens our ability to explain the chances of shifting the overall macro-structural outlook of the whole system. More importantly, we need a comprehensive context to argue about the looming paradigm shift in the twenty-first century's world-system in the wake of the rise of Asia.

As argued, the military revolution brought meaningful changes in the nature and conception of national power in Europe. Comparatively, China did not progress regarding its military ability and defense capabilities. China was the inventor of gunpowder. It manufactured naval ships bigger than ever built in medieval or early modern Europe. The compass was also invented China, thus facilitating commercial voyage to distant ports such as Africa. "But," as E. L. Dreyer (2012) argues, "these capabilities did not add up to a navy; in the latter part of the Ming and the Qing, China's seagoing forces consisted of small ships and boats tethered to the military organizations of specific provinces" (p. 28). Vries (2015) argues that "from the second half of the eighteenth century onwards, the balance of power between the fiscal-military states of the West and the big 'Eastern' empires was beginning to shift so clearly that, even without the additional advantages of industrialization, the West was already making huge inroads into what we would now call 'India,' the Ottoman Empire, . . . and finally, from the 1830s onwards, China" (p. 300). He argues that military revolution, or more specifically fiscal-militarism, had happened "*before* Britain evolved into an *industrial* superpower" (p. 301, emphasis original). According to Hoffman (2015), by the end of the eighteenth century, while France was spending more than 7 percent of its GDP, and Britain more than 12 percent of its GDP, on military equipment and armies, China was spending less than half that amount despite that it was a continent-like and populous state, a regional hegemon, and the most important actor in global trade.

Part of the reason was that whereas the Europeans lacked any regional order established by one hegemonic power, spent many resources developing military technology, and gained real war experience during the sixteenth and seventeenth centuries, China remained contended with its so-called civilizational, spiritual status. After 1683, when it subjugated today's Taiwan, China did not fight any major war in the region. It did not express any desire to colonize Asia. It did not realize the paradigmatic changes taking place in Europe during the sixteenth and seventeenth centuries. The Qing empire failed to realize that global trade was no longer a tributary system; rather, it had turned into the most important tool of Western imperialism. The Qing rulers, who belonged to Manchuria and had overtaken China by defeating Ming rulers in 1644, deepened the idea of a king possessing heavenly powers. The mysticism worked to dissuade the local rebels only. The perils of a relatively long peace included a minimal requirement of military expenditure. Whereas tributary order worked well in Southeast Asia for a considerable time, anarchy brought long-term benefits to the European powers in the end. They kept fighting for more than five hundred years, first with the Arabs and Muslims during the Crusades, and then with each other. It was only in 1840 after defeat in the Opium Wars that China started understanding the consequences of a weak defense. The long peace and pride in civilization led to a century of humiliation.

CHINA AND THE GREAT POWER COMPETITION IN ASIA IN THE SEVENTEENTH AND EIGHTEENTH CENTURIES

I have already mentioned that China was the most important actor in global trade before the rise of capitalism in Europe. Various scholars have supported this fact. According to Angus Maddison (2007), China's economic growth from the ninth century to the eighteenth century had been impressive and the country witnessed a complete shift in the composition of its economic policy on the mainland. At the start of the ninth century, about 75 percent of the population lived in the northern part of the country and relied on agriculture to survive by growing wheat and millet. However, there took place a massive migration; by the end of the thirteenth century, more than three-quarters of the population lived in the southern part of the country, relied on rice, and grew cotton. Since the southern part has better productivity and ample irrigation, as well as access to the market because of denser population reduced transport expenses, Chinese industrial and economic growth provided a "modest" rise in income and a reasonable elevation in living standards. According to Abu-Lughod (1989), during the twelfth and thirteenth centuries, Chinese technology was not stagnant, "nor were Chinese ships and navigational techniques in any way inferior to those of the Europeans" (p. 326). However, more importantly, according to her, technological growth gave China an unprecedented edge over the rest of the world, particularly East Asia, in terms of two high-demand products: silk and porcelain. According to John M. Hobson (2015), by 1100, China had undergone "the first industrial miracle," which he defines as "many of the characteristics that we associate with the eighteenth-century British industrial revolution" (p. 50). From the ninth century to the eighteenth century, it produced more iron and steel than all of Europe put together. It was only after 1700 that Europe surpassed China in iron and steel production and manufacturing. By the thirteenth century, China had a commercialized economic system; due to the Chinese invention and widespread use of paper, it had a cash-based taxation system in place, leading to the development of a market-based economy before the introduction of the same in Europe. By the fourteenth century, China had reached an industrial technological level where it was able to use water-powered spinning machines for the production of silk. Hobson provides a detailed account of how revolutions in every dimension of national life elevated the living standards of the people of China. On the eve of 1800, the global economy was "Sino-centric," and China was "the first among equals" in terms of industrial and technological development.

The national character developed under the Ming dynasty (1368–1644) was that of self-sufficiency and civilizational pride. Though international trade had extended regarding scope and magnitude since China witnessed an increase in European maritime traffic at its ports, it is pertinent to mention that China avoided dominating global naval trade. In 1434, a combination of multiple factors led China to announce its withdrawal from international trade. As mentioned, China had participated in trade as a form of tribute since the country did not need anything from the outside world. The commercial nature of trade at that time required state patronage. But under the influence of Confucianism, the Ming dynasty was hesitant to adopt a mercantilist approach to trade with the outside world.

Due to its status as a regional hegemon, Beijing was receiving tributes, and the king and the government at that time were of the view that the world needed them more than they needed the world. Hong Wu, the first emperor (1368–1398) of the Ming dynasty, imposed heavy taxes on the trading class, believing that agriculture was the backbone of the empire's wealth. Chinese sailors led by Zhang He sailed in seven of the most significant voyages of the time reaching African coasts, and according to Gavin Menzies (2008), he led and, in 1421, the Chinese reached and discovered America and well before Christopher Columbus did. According to Giovanni Arrighi (2010) and Pierre Dimaculangan (2014), when Zhang died on his last voyage to India in 1433, the fleet, comprised of three hundred ships, was recalled. The old king had died, and the new king asked to leave these ships tied with their moorings to either rot or be burned down. According to Dimaculangan (2014), "the cancellation of the naval voyages was considered to be one of the biggest blunders and major turning points in world history" (p. 107). Over the next one hundred years, the lack of any naval development, both commercial and military, led to the vanishing of Chinese presence on the seas. Dimaculangan forwards four main reasons for this otherwise inexplicable decision. First, these voyages were increasingly expensive and a huge burden on state resources. Second, the state was busy defending itself against raids by Mongols and other rebellious forces. Third, Japanese pirates had become a source of permanent tension since they were plundering the coastal areas. Fourth, and perhaps more importantly, neo-Confucianism was "conservative and indeed inward-looking, having a general neglect of foreign affairs, and an emphasis on internal matters to promote self-improvement" (p. 108). Mark Elvin (1973) maintains that the main reason for the decline and abandonment of naval power lies in the reconstruction of the Great Canal to Beijing in 1411, which made navy "for the first time a luxury rather than a necessity" (p. 220). Given that China was producing surplus grain, it was quite understandable and logical for the rulers in Beijing to promote domestic trade instead of selling the bread to the outside world for things they might not need as much. The impact of this self-abandonment of global leadership left a vacuum that was filled by increasingly advancing European countries in the following centuries.

Since the economic decline of China is related and claimed to have preceded the rise of the West, it is necessary to put in perspective the probable causes of the fall of China in the last phase of the early modern world-system. Placing developments chronologically, one can argue that the last two decades of the fifteenth century were the years of exploration; though European traders had reached China, India, and the Caribbean islands in previous centuries, the scale and magnitude of trade and inter-imperial competition in oceans grew immensely following the discovery of the Cape of Good Hope and the Atlantic Ocean route to the New World. China, however, lagged behind due to various reasons cited by authors such as Elvin. According to Elvin (1973), "During the period of the medieval economic revolution, economic growth had been accompanied by the invention of new techniques of production; but between 1500 and 1800, when there was a renewal of vigorous economic growth, invention was almost entirely absent" (p. 203). One feels surprised to think why it did not happen in China, a country that invented machines and chemicals claimed to be the foundational stones of the cumulative process leading to the Industrial Revolution. Elvin (1973, 1996) tries to answer this mystery by developing a theory of "the high-level equilibrium trap." According to him, China did not need technological developments because it was doing far better with traditional and premodern means.

Therefore, I can argue that two interrelated issues led to the absence of modern industrial revolution in China. First, China had resources that society found sufficient to survive as well as thrive. In terms of land transportation, for example, it did not require railways because there were men (population) and animals to transport goods from one place to another. It also had a domestic water transport system for which ships were required, and China had sufficient domestic supplies of expertise and wood to build such ships. In agriculture, China's per-acre production of grains was far better than that of European lands even by the 1920s. In terms of economic activities, China invented paper money but abandoned it due to the excessive supply of silver and copper from Asia and, later on, Europe. The large spinning machines used in textile mills were deemed sufficient after considering the economies of scale. The same was the case with the silk-reeling machine that was invented during the medieval economic revolution of the tenth and the eleventh centuries. Second, I am not arguing that China had an abundance of natural, physical, and economic resources. It did fall short on a number of items. However, what is important to mention is that China preferred to find domestic solutions to such issues. China faced a liquidity crisis in the eighteenth and nineteenth centuries when the flight of capital in the form of silver took place due to the opium trade. However, much before the invasion of imperial powers such as Portugal and Britain, China tried to address every local issue with a domestic solution. The growing population needed hemp for cloth, and cotton (and later on textile mills using a modified version of the silk-reeling machine) did meet the needs. When cotton became the primary raw material of textile mills, these textile mills were relocated from the north to the Yangzi delta, a region where excessive human labor eased the pressure on fuel. In order to ensure a supply of cotton as well as grains, China expanded the cultivable area instead of inventing a modern style of cultivation and scientific inputs such as fertilizers or importing cotton to meet the needs of these mills. Since the official ban on travel, trade, and interaction with the outside world persisted for a long time, China had reasons to be disinterested in the quest for technological advancement and the promotion of new ideas about the functioning of the economy. Instead of finding technological solutions to the problems Chinese society faced from the sixteenth to eighteenth century, it looked for organizational, societal, and spiritual ones. According to Willia, Rowe (2012):

> The HLET argued that late imperial China's pre-industrial economy operated at such a peak of efficiency that all possible surplus had already been squeezed out of the existing technology and expended on population growth. Consequently, there was an active disincentive to move to a higher level of technology (industrialization) because the dislocation cost would be too great. This step could be introduced only from outside the system, in other words from the West, and even

> then it would be resisted so long as it operated at a lower level of efficiency than had the earlier technology. (pp. 217–18)

The decline of the Chinese economy and social resilience, however, did not come in decades; it took a longer time of more than two centuries for China to see the nadir moments in national life. During this time, China did not completely shut down its trade relations with the outside world, as the violators of national policy continued to operate within Asia. However, during the fifteenth century, Europe started dominating global trade for a variety of reasons. From the 1430s to 1500, China relinquished its desire, if it had any, to expand beyond its mainland territory, while European powers, especially Portuguese and Spanish maritime activities, started dominating global trade. China gradually stopped using paper currency due to the inconvenience of fungibility and inflation because of internal wars. Its domestic, tributary, and contraband regional maritime trade started using silver as the most dominant medium of exchange. On the other side, the Europeans reached the Americas by the end of the fifteenth century. The initial signs of the great divergence were emerging.

According to Abu-Lughod (1989), the power vacuum created by China's withdrawal from sea trade could not be fulfilled easily because neither East Asians nor Arab Muslim merchants were ready to jump in; it took Europe about seventy years to fill this power vacuum. However, if we look closely, we can see that a classic fall-and-rise case, particularly in commerce and trade, emerges. As I will explain in the next chapter, there existed three main routes of intercontinental trade. In addition to the all-land Silk Route, there were also maritime Silk Routes and a mix of both using the Indian Ocean, the Arabian Peninsula, and the Mediterranean Sea. Europeans had started increasing their presence in Indian Ocean even before the discovery of the Cape of Good Hope. According to David Nicholas (1999), the trade of African slaves to Europe was in full swing by 1443 with at least one thousand slaves being brought to Europe every year. By 1474, the Portuguese had reached the Bight of Biafra in search of slaves and pepper. After they defeated the kingdom of Castile in 1479, the latter withdrew its claim of influence on the continent, thereby making it convenient for the Portuguese to trade in an unchallenged manner across the Indian Ocean. They discovered new routes to India and the Americas, reached the Chinese court in 1504, and started large-scale trade with Moghul empire vigorously. They built forts, factories, and appointed military forces to safeguard the routes of trade from Asia and Africa to Europe. In 1509, they symbolically colonized Goa by erecting a fort there. In less than ten years, they had done the same in Malacca (South China Sea), Hormuz, Aden (Persian Gulf), Madagascar, Mauritius, Cape of Good Hope (Africa), and Socotra (entrance of the Red Sea) (Gungwu, 1998). World trade had made a paradigm shift: China had voluntarily receded, and the Europeans advanced enthusiastically to fill in the gap. They found items of trade quite beneficial to them—silver in the Americas, and grains, sugar, salt, and spices in Asia and Africa. Patronized by their respective governments, they mastered trade. Simultaneously, Europe started witnessing the tangible consequences of the Renaissance. The age of revolution had begun; the world witnessed a whole new set of the rules in the game of global dominance set by the Europeans. Though world-systems analysts disagree about the exact date the Europeans had become dominant in global trade and politics, there is a broader agreement that by the middle of the eighteenth century, a multilateral transformation in the form of a number of so-called "revolutions" had taken place that, coupled with the power vacuum in Asia and Africa, enabled the Europeans to start dominating global politics and commerce. It was not the case that China was unable to checkmate these European advancements; it decided to stand aloof of these developments. It did not bother Beijing since the mainland was the prime concern; China was willing to defend the suzerainty over the areas it had once claimed and did so whenever this claim was challenged by the Europeans, at least during its initial encounters.

However, there were three significant impediments in the way of European merchants: comparative advantage of China in trade, the military power of China, and the comparative advantage of India. The last of the three impediments is the topic of the next chapter, where I am going to explain the fall and recent rise of the Indian Sub-Continent. In this chapter, I am concentrating on the fall of Chinese military and economic power compared to that of the Europeans. As mentioned, China could have dominated global politics and trade had it been vigorous in honing and exhibiting its economic and military power to the powers that be in Asia and Europe. During the seventeenth and eighteen centuries, the world trade transformed from world-empires to the world economy. China, the epicenter and most prominent actor of world commerce in the precapitalist world-system, lost its position due to its ineffective military capabilities and inability to resist new terms of trade. If we accept the timeline as suggested by various economic historians and world-systems analysts, it becomes evident that the European rise followed some decades after the decline of Chinese interaction in regional and world commercial trade. However, it would be misleading to assume that China and its regional merchants left everything once the Ming dynasty ordered in the fifteenth century. Contrarily, it is rather plausible to assume that although the orders of withdrawal immensely affected China's participation in global trade networks, this step and subsequent implementing mechanisms could not eradicate the concept of interaction. This view is dominant in the multivolume *Cambridge History of China*, particularly in volumes 8 and 9, which discuss the Ming dynasty's overseas trade. The strongest support for this view is provided by the fact that although the Ming government had discouraged official commercial overseas contacts, it "tolerated" private contacts and other contracts by opening a few ports for trade.

However, Europeans were far more eager to accelerate commercial relations with China. Their aggressive pursuit of commercial interaction with mainland China gave birth to a true global modern world-system covering "all the continents except Antarctica and Australia in exchanges of trade goods, food plants, diseases, people, and ideas" (Twitchett and Mote, 1998: 333). China lagged far behind in realizing the long-term consequences of the arrival of European nations in the Indian Ocean. After they had occupied Malacca, the Portuguese tried to appease the Ming emperor through a delegation but failed. In 1521 and 1522, China and Portugal fought two wars and China defended its sovereignty quite effectively. It is important to mention that by this time Europe had not entered the military revolution, nor had China dwindled regarding military power. The phenomenon of the great divergence, therefore, occurred much later. There were two main consequences of these wars. First, Portuguese had to return the fort of Malacca to its rightful sovereigns. It checkmated their ambitions and advancements in the Indian Ocean. Second, the wars resulted in promoting individualized and violent trade between Chines, Japanese, Southeast Asian, Indian, and European traders. Portugal, instead of securing governmental patronage, decided to deal with the traders directly. The Chinese government knew about this development but decided to condone it. The European traders, nevertheless, were determined to trade with China because of the high demand for Chinese products in Europe. It was only in 1557 that the Chinese accepted and agreed to trade with the Portuguese. Since 1557, we have seen an influx of European traders in Asia and Africa (Wills, 1998). By the start of the seventeenth century, the Portuguese were overcome by the Dutch empire, whose East India Company, established in 1602, started dominating the trade routes in the Indian Ocean. Quickly, they were followed by French traders, who subsequently were followed by the British and then the Americans. China's military power had started dwindling while Europe went through a military revolution. The fall of China precipitated; the rise of Europe accelerated. Some reasons have been forwarded to explain the fall of the military power of China, even in the traditional sense. It has been mentioned that contrary to previous dynasties, there was no great emperor during the long three-hundred-year rule of the Ming dynasty. While it faced the Mongol challenge in the first half of its time, its second half was characterized by the multiple sources of power that deprived its ruler(s) of the ability to decide in a prompt, proactive, and effective manner about the issues of security and war. Second, Chinese military power had actually started to decline by the middle of the sixteenth century (Chaliand, 2014: 181). One of the indications is provided by the Imjin War (1592–1598), in which Japan invaded the Korean Peninsula, and China defended the territory by declaring it to be under its protection through the tributary system. Though Japan was unable to win, China was also unable to defeat Japan and its local allies on the peninsula in a conclusive manner. It was only after the death of the Toyotomi Hideyoshi that Japan withdrew from the peninsula. In 1661, Koxinga, the Ming loyalist warrior, attacked what is today's Taiwan and, after about a year of fighting, took it away from the Dutch. Two important facts of this war are that both sides used European "superior technology" and the Dutch were defeated not because of a lack of anything, but because Koxinga was able to put in place a tight blockage and the Dutch could not get reinforcements from the nearby posts in due time (Andrade, 2011). The dwindling of military power was evident in 1757 when, under pressure from European traders, China had to sanction the Canton system to streamline trade relations with the outside world; China's weakness was proved in the Opium Wars when the Europeans were able to coerce China to accept the discriminatory terms and conditions of trade.

In addition, the social standing of the military during the Ming dynasty was low; it had a centralized structure controlled by the civil bureaucracy. The perks and privileges of civil bureaucracy attracted intelligent people, while socially impoverished people joined the army (Chan, 1982). The decline of Chinese control in inner and Far East Asia gradually became a reality in 1557 when China accepted the Portuguese takeover of Macao as the port of trade. According to John Wills (1974), before the Portuguese could fail in their quest of dominating the Indian Ocean by 1620s in the face of a resistance to expansion by not only China but also Japan and the rival imperial powers in the area, the Dutch East India Company had risen to challenge Chinese military power in the region. During the 1622–1624 conflicts in which the Portuguese defeated the Dutch in their quest to control Macao, the latter captured today's Taiwan as the hotbed of their regional trade. China, where Qing ended the Ming dynasty in 1644, could spare Taiwan only for the time being. In 1660, Qing forces attacked Taiwan and leashed an unforgettable defeat on the Dutch forces there. The Dutch were shrewd enough to reconcile with the new emperor and tried to develop an alliance, which would not succeed, though they were allowed to trade for decades to come until the end of the seventeenth century.

In this context, we see a revival of military power based on alliances within China and with little input from the Portuguese and the Dutch through which the Qing dynasty was able to take over and consolidate its rule of the country. This revival, however, was short-lived as Europe was transforming into a capitalist society based on political, cultural, economic, and scientific revolutions. The arrival of the Portuguese—and then the Dutch, Spanish, French, and British—in the Indian Ocean should have been an eye-opener for the dynastic emperors. China, however, could not realize the possible superior position and dominant role in the fast-approaching "trade revolution" of the world economy. It took the Europeans at least four decades to formally get Beijing on board to install a system of customs and taxes. Europeans used this crucial time to strengthen their presence in Southeast and South Asia. China was nearly at the verge of losing its dominant position by the end of the sixteenth century. When the Qing dynasty took over the reign of power in 1644, China was virtually out of the race for dominance in Asia and elsewhere. According to R. J. Barendse (2002), the initial signs of the "development of underdevelopment" in the world economic system were evident by the middle of the seventeenth century.

Regarding bilateral trade, however, the Europeans faced a very crucial hurdle: China had the comparative economic advantage. For the Europeans, the items of attraction from China included spices, food grains, porcelain, tea, silk, wax, dyes, cotton and cotton cloth, leather, lacquerware, metalwork, and ivory, among many others. In the wake of the discovery of new sea trade routes, an influx of these items in Europe was reported. In exchange, however, they had little to offer except luxury items, for which there was little appetite in China. Historically, China had been more connected to Southeast Asia since the Zhou dynasty. During that time, there was a strong sea network of trade and commerce between Southeast Asia, southern India, including the Bay of Bengal, and China. Southeast Asia, therefore, was influenced by both the Chinese Confucius as well as Indian civilization (Stuart-Fox, 2003). The spiritual, political, geographic, economic, and civilizational interdependence between Southeast Asians and the Chinese was totally absent in the case of Europeans and affected their quest for commercial relations in the region. The Dutch, for example, tried to force China by attacking its ships in the sea, but the policy proved counterproductive as the Chinese refused to trade with them. The demand for Chinese products in European markets and the absence of any European products of the same demand meant that Europe faced the persistent problem of a trade deficit. To deal with the trade deficit, the Europeans found three options and adopted them all simultaneously.

The first problem was the supply of exchangeable items. In European-Chinese bilateral trade, the answer was silver. Since the time when the Europeans started trading with the Chinese, first through the famous land-based Silk Route and then through sea trade, the Europeans had to produce and present silver to Chinese traders and the government to purchase items of their liking. European silver mining grew during the second half of the fifteenth century and reached its maximum level of production during the first half of the sixteenth century. Trade between Europe and the rest of the world was supported by this silver mining and coinage during 1450–1540 as silver production in central Europe rose. Production went from a few hundred marks in 1450 to more than 100,000 marks by the end of the 1480s and early 1490s due to mining notably at Schwaz, Schneeberg, Mansfeld, and Annaberg, and the Eastern Alps, Erz Gebirge, and the Sudetic Mountains (Nef, 1941). Most of this silver was used to trade with the Chinese and other trading partners in Southeast Asia and India. This "silver boom" gave the Europeans the economic tool they needed most to trade with the rest of the world (Miskimin, 1977). China, on the other hand, was known for using paper money, but the lack of fungibility in precious metals or silk threads led to inflation that was exacerbated to uncontrollable levels in the wake of military expeditions, natural disasters, and epidemic diseases in the first half of the Ming dynasty. In the second half of the dynasty years, when external trade policy was less constrained, the monetary system had to be "silverized" since paper currency was virtually worthless outside China (Atwell, 1998). The Ming emperors allowed only limited mining inside China, thus virtually raising the value of silver throughout the country. Since the official policy was shutting the doors to world trade, trade activities were conducted between Chinese and Europeans traders on the sea. Chinese traders preferred silver whenever dealing with Asian or European traders.

During the second decade of the sixteenth century, when European mines were losing their level of productivity, silver from the Americas started coming in and enabled Europeans to increase the scope and magnitude of trade with China, East Asia, India, and Africa. According to William Atwell (1998), American silver traveled to China through three routes. First, starting in the early 1570s, the Spanish empire promoted Sino-American trade by making Manila, Philippines, the trade center. Though one cannot negate the element of miscalculation and misrepresentation, and also one should keep in mind the nature of fluctuation in the quantity and scope of trade items traveling between Mexico and China, it is still a conservative estimate that from the early 1570s to the end of the sixteenth century more than 150,000 kilograms of American silver were shipped every year from Mexico to China through Manila (Atwell, 1998: 392). Second, silver was shipped from Mexico to Spain. According to Harry Miskimin (1977), from 1503 to 1660, about 16.88 million kilograms of silver and about 180,000 kilograms of gold were shipped to Spain using this route only (p. 33). These treasures helped the Spanish empire convert its deficits into surpluses and modernize its military forces for various expeditions. A significant amount of these payments in silver traveled to Western and Central Europe, notably Portugal, and eventually much of that ended up in China and India. Third, some of the silver and gold reaching Spain was shipped to London and Amsterdam, which promoted the rise of the Dutch and English East Indian Companies in the first decade of the seventeenth century. Besides these three routes, the Portuguese and the Dutch used smuggled Japanese silver produced from the Iwami Ginzan mine. From

1560 to 1610, about one-fifth of the world's silver, or about 200,000 kilograms of silver per year, was produced through mining in Japan (Subrahmanyam, 2012). Moreover, the Portuguese and the Dutch were also able to get a handsome amount of gold from Africa (da Silva, 2011: 248). According to Om Prakash (2004) "It was indeed a critically important coincidence that the discovery of the Cape route and of the New World took place almost simultaneously. For without the enormous quantities of American silver reaching Europe through the sixteenth century, the enhanced trading opportunities between Europe and Asia opened up by the Cape route would essentially have been frustrated" (p. 29). What happened to such huge volumes of precious metals in China and India is a sad story. According to Wallerstein, while these bullions were used for hoarding and ornament in China and India, Europeans used them to develop a capitalist system (Wallerstein, 1974: 46). Such huge amounts of precious metals enabled the Europeans to accumulate capital in the West, develop infrastructure, industrialize the economy, modernize the military, and eventually occupy most of Asia and Africa. Andre Gunder Frank (1998) argues that "the West first bought itself a third-class seat on the Asian economic train, then leased a whole railway carriage, and only in the nineteenth century managed to displace Asians from the locomotive" (p. 37). Even so, the Europeans were able to actually accumulate more capital than they were able to produce using precious minerals from the Americas, Africa, and Asia.

The Europeans had yet another option to dislodge China from its position as the epicenter of world trade, particularly during the transition phase from premodern world-empires to the world economy following the capitalist system. Contrary to the Ming policy of shutting down China for international trade, particularly during 1433–1557, European monarchs encouraged their traders to develop networks of trade and commerce in the Indian Ocean and the South China Sea. There were two particular patterns in this development of networks. First, Europeans were quick to fill in the vacuum left by Chinese strict foreign trade policies by sensing and creating the demand for various products in different areas. They took Chinese porcelain to Africa, India, and Europe and received precious metals to pay back the Chinese traders. While they bought spices from Southeast Asian islands, they were able to bring things of interest to these areas, thus developing a pool of "commonly accepted forms of money." Given that silver and other metals had greater acceptability, they needed them most to pay the traders. To generate higher levels of liquidity, these companies adopted a bills of exchange system whereby companies were able to purchase goods on credit to be paid later, including in London or Amsterdam. by interlinking the trade routes from one place to another, the Europeans were virtually able to produce and accumulate capital in the West. Second, the use of silver and gold as a form of money and their massive availability in the Americas enabled them to provide Chinese traders with what they preferred the most. The fungibility of silver and other metals was exploited by the Europeans for commercial purposes, while China monetized it. Because China was a far more significant country possessing a far more substantial population than Europe, it required more and more silver to meet its monetary needs.

However, it was not all good to have so much silver piled in one place such as Europe or China. Throughout history, China had been a super accumulator of capital and a regional hegemon because it needed less of anything from the outside world than the world needed from it. The Europeans, therefore, faced the persistent issue of a trade deficit in Asia, particularly in the case of China. Networks of trade and American silver resolved the problem of the medium of exchange, but it led to other problems. The perils of the huge influx of silver and gold resulted in a so-called price revolution in Europe and elsewhere. Silver and gold lost their value compared to other products, and the rise of inflation resulted in the collapse of the monetary system on the European continent. Contrary to dominant understanding, Dennis Flynn and Arturo Giraldez (1995) seem to be more convincing when they argue that the price revolution was a global phenomenon. Silver lost its value compared to other products not only in Europe but also in China and elsewhere. This led the Europeans to rethink their strategy of using precious minerals such as silver and gold for coinage and commercial commodities.

An overview of the possible benefits China could have received from its trade with the West tells us about the magnitude of loss China had to face in the following decades. Far more important is that China failed to transform from its superior position in world trade into a formidable and dependable military power *before* the rise of capitalism in Europe. When Europe went through a military revolution, we did not see China advancing regarding military technology. China could have utilized its economic bargain power and the precious minerals it was accumulating from the trade surplus with Europe to improve industrially and militarily. Notably, it could have asked for industrial technology and military hardware from Europe. Though Qing rebel leaders tried to inculcate European-made canons and in fact had established artillery corps by the end of 1634, they were never able to meet the pace of technological growth taking momentum in Europe, even after having come to power in 1644. While it is true that during the sixteenth, seventeenth, and even eighteenth centuries China was still ahead of Europe regarding industrial production and quality, we must keep in mind that during 1500–1800, Europe had transformed a lot. Using its trade networks throughout the world and having undergone various revolutions, the continent developed a capitalist system whose modes of production received blatant patronage by the state, and society was subjected to fit the demands of this system. It saw a military revolution, an agricultural revolution (mainly in England), a bourgeoisie revolution, the scientific revolution, and the Industrial Revolution, and expanded its global commercial linkage to unprecedented levels during these centuries. During these 250 years, Europe saw the rise and fall of various empires—Portuguese, Dutch, Spanish—thereby making new imperial states fall prey to an excessive consciousness of the same fate. This consciousness pushed them to strengthen both kinds of their fangs: economic and military. Anarchy and war were the norm in Europe. For a more significant part of these years, it lacked excessive and hegemonic control of any one empire claiming the whole continent under its suzerainty. Inter-imperial wars led European states to look outward for greater resources of material worth, and they were able to find them through trade, exploitation, and occupation. On the other side, throughout the Ming and Qing dynasties, we see very little and rare occasions of China's aggressive foreign policy behavior and the exhibition of its military power beyond its traditional sphere of influence. China saw the world transforming but stood aloof, immersed into the mirage of its civilizational superiority (Waley-Cohen, 2014: 5). By the start of the nineteenth century, when capitalism had become a global system of trade requiring a new division of labor, the technological gap between China and Europe was a reality. China had lost more than three centuries at the crucial juncture of human history. It had virtually been ousted from the race for domination of the world, and it rapidly lost its traditional geographical sphere of influence in the Far East and Southeast Asia. The great divergence had become a reality. According to Yi Dai (2011), China could survive as an independent country for a long time after Western powers had introduced imperialism in Asia and Africa simply because of its geographical location and for historical reasons. Geographically, China was located far from Western Europe, and the imperial powers lacked the logistical support to occupy it. Historically, China had been a civilization and a unified country. Also, China as an idea remained quite dominant and could not be subjugated by any other rival idea. While the Europeans were able to overcome the first obstacle after they had occupied India, they faced resistance in China because of its mammoth size and civilizational legacy. The Europeans, therefore, had to come together to inflict a new division of labor on the former epicenter of world trade.

The fundamental principle under which the trade policy in the second half of the Ming dynasty was crafted continued with some changes during the Qing dynasty as well. China interacted with the world through ports, with limited entry of the foreigners to the mainland. Overall, the Chinese economic outlook during the Qing dynasty can be defined in three categories: domestic growth of the market economic structure, domestic economic policy and government intervention, and foreign trade policy. During the eighteenth century, China's domestic market was growing rapidly. The influx of silver through foreign trade was helpful in resolving the liquidity question, as silver and copper coins were being used to buy and sell commodities. The reconstruction and expansion of the Grand Canal connecting Beijing with Hangzhou province was meant to promote domestic trade. As Peer Vries (2015) explains in detail, contrary to a general misconception about the intervening role of Qing rule in China, the government was least interfering in domestic trade; it facilitated the development of a free market economic system with least interference in the functioning of the development of markets. Some restrictions in domestic trade, however, were posed, and the interference was meant "to 'correct' the market" (Vries, 2015: 349). This intervention was apparent in terms of the movement of grains and the consequent fluctuation in their prices. The Qing emperors were more concerned with the welfare of their own people and less interested in developing foreign commercial trade. However, the Europeans had been consistent in their approach to benefit from China.

The development of regional networks to accumulate as much capital as possible and to address the question of the medium of exchange worked well, and American silver enabled Europe to continue trading with China with greater ease. Two broader issues were matters of concern for the Europeans, particularly the English East India Company, which had almost ousted its European imperial rivals from the Indian Ocean by 1760. First, the British wanted to keep as much silver as they could under their own control since they had realized the value of the mineral in the global economy and the potential effects of inflation. The changing geo-economic and geostrategic dimensions of inter-imperial relations in Europe were also demanding the control of such minerals. The declining production of silver in the Americas was also a sign suggesting the frugal use of the commodity, particularly when there was no apparent sign of any shift in the balance of trade. Second, the occupation and control of India set a precedent for the East India Company; if it could somehow screw China to accept its terms of trade, the question of the increasing trade deficit could be addressed. the British were willing to sell their own products in China and elsewhere if a trading party could be agreed on. However, because of various reasons, including cultural factors, Chinese traders kept refusing and insisted on silver (Wallerstein, 2011a: 167). Moreover, the number of items and their quantity to be purchased from China because of their huge demand in Europe increased; Europe showed a higher appetite for Chinese tea. In 1757, when the British East India Company started trading tea from China, the silver question resurfaced. It is important to keep in mind that the expansion of imperialism in Asia and Africa during the seventeenth and eighteenth centuries had enabled European imperial powers to expand and deepen their stronghold on the region. As Wallerstein (2011a) mentions, with every new area incorporated into a capitalist division of labor, the adjacent areas were considered the new "external arena" expected to fall into the expanding realm of global capitalism; the British considered China in the same way.

The nature of trade that the British had with China was a trade of commodities, with the deficit being met through silver and other metals. During the first half of the eighteenth century, the European East India Companies competed against each other in a quest to dominate the patterns of trade in the region and expand the networks of trade between Southeast Asia, India, China, and Europe. The inter-imperial clash intensified as the flow and kinds of goods from one region to another increased. The English East India Company had quashed French aspirations to control India and its trade through a series of conflicts known as the Carnatic Wars. In 1757, the British took over the governance of Bengal. It was the formal start of British Raj in India, though through the company. Among the most promising goods going from China to Europe and elsewhere included tea. It is important to mention that while Wallerstein (2011a: 167) considers the tea trade from China to India and then to Europe to have been under the auspices of the East India Company as early as 1757, Kirti Chaudhuri (1978) cites official figures to corroborate that tea was being purchased indirectly by the company as early as 1660 and "the first substantial imports occurred in 1678" (p. 386). During 1716–1732 only, the sale value of tea and porcelain purchased from China by the East India Company was more than £4.6 million (Chaudhuri, 1978: 389). One can assume that the flow of silver from the Americas to Asia and Europe was taking multiple routes to reach India and China. Such an influx of silver in China did not favor the company, which was increasingly concerned about the chronic nature of the trade deficit with China. The company had aspirations to turn its operation of trade into a complex globalization of barter trade featuring imperial occupation, coercive exploitation, and war. While British imperialism in the first half of the eighteenth century had become a reality, it still could not impose its terms of trade on China.

From 1755, when the control of Chinese trade by the Dutch East India Company was taken over by the Gentlemen Seventeen, until 1784, when the Netherlands was finally defeated in the fourth Anglo-Dutch war by the Paris Peace Treaty, the tea trade from China to Europe increased immensely. Until the middle of the nineteenth century, China was the only major supplier of tea in the world (Y. Liu, 2007). In 1786 alone, the British purchased directly and indirectly about eight million pounds of tea from China, which does not include the unaccounted for volume of tea smuggled into Britain from China and Asia by smaller traders (Y. Liu, 2007: 142). It was only by the middle of the nineteenth century that the British had started spreading tea in other parts of the world (Rose, 2010). As the British gained control of the Indian Ocean, they eagerly became involved in the tea trade. By the end of the 1790s, the Chinese tea trade was thoroughly dominated by the English East India

Company. The company's official documents are highly obscure and vague in explaining the volume of the tea traded, however.

THE POLITICAL ECONOMY OF CHINA IN 1750 AND THE MODERN WORLD-SYSTEM

In 1757, China established the Canton system, whereby all of its foreign trade had to be regulated through the Canton port only. A tiny group of traders, called "the Cohong," was licensed by Beijing to do business with the outside world, including foreign traders arriving at Canton. This group was placed under the supervision of a customs officer known as "the hoppo." Thus, while China was willing to do business with the world, it was still resistant to open its doors to let foreign traders and companies penetrate deep into its territory. Since China was adamant to sell and not to buy, and Chinese produce and products were in demand in Europe and elsewhere, the Europeans, particularly the British, had no other choice but to pay in silver, thus facing the consequences of the trade deficit. Though tea was promised to increase trade volume between various regions, and with it provide a capital benefit to the company, it nevertheless augmented the money crisis in the trade with China.

In order to establish its rule in the world, British imperialism had to convert its trade deficit with China into a surplus. Imperial policies had virtually penetrated throughout most of Asia and Africa. The company was able to exercise direct control over many areas in India and Africa. Merchant capitalism had penetrated deep into state politics; during its expansion in the second half of the eighteenth century, a large number of directors and key officials in the company were members of British parliament as well (Barber, 1975: 101). The company, therefore, was fully confident to receive economic, political, and military patronage from the Crown in case of an occurrence of the looming conflict with China. The company, however, found an item that could address the chronic trade deficit problem with China: opium.

The Chinese people already had a history of using opium for pain killing. Introduced by Arabs and other merchants from India in the sixth and seventh centuries, opium was already in use in China, and the Portuguese had also traded opium from India to China since Bengal was a prime area of opium cultivation. The British knew about the trade, yet it took them some time to indulge in it. Hosea Morse (1926), an American citizen who served as the Chinese customs service commissioner at Canton for about thirty-three years and later wrote about China, its international relations, and foreign trade, cited official reports stating that in 1729 only Chinese traders purchased 3,744 British pounds of opium (p. 73). In the same year, the Qing emperor Yongzheng banned the import of opium into China. China also asked the company to refrain from promoting the penetration of opium into China. However, imperialist forces had found the answer to the long-standing trade deficit and currency question in their bilateral trade. According to Patricia Ebrey, Anne Walthall, and James Palais (2009), after Britain had slipped into a deficit since, by the middle of the eighteenth century, it was importing over two million pounds of tea from China every year, the reverse started taking place in 1761 when the company was able to sponsor, patronize, and later on become a dominant trader in the business of opium between India and China. With the first armed defeat of local ruler Siraj ud-Daulah in 1757, the company started colonizing Bengal. In 1773, it acquired monopoly control over the production of opium in Bengal. By 1797, it had become a source producing one-seventh of the revenue the company earned in the region (Greenberg, 1969: 105). Two crucial policy approaches explain, at least partially, the political economy of imperialism in Asia with particular reference to the opium trade. First, because the Chinese emperor had banned the trade of opium in 1729 and the company was afraid of losing its commercial privileges at Canton, the company concentrated on the production of opium in India and did not get involved officially in its distribution in China. Instead, it relied on private traders who purchased it from the company in India and sold it throughout various spots across the coastal areas of the South China Sea. The company's officers also carried out the opium trade in their personal capacities and earned a lot. The company was able to recoin the silver obtained from the traders and used it to buy tea, porcelain, spices, and other items in demand in Europe. Second, the company ensured punitive action aimed at discouraging the consumption of opium inside India. Both these steps ensured a continuous flow of bullion from China to India, eventually in the hands of the Company, as well as in London.

Opium was an appropriate commodity that the British could trade to get tea and other products. Though the company also tried to sell Indian cotton to China, its demand was low because of two reasons. First, Indian cotton was not of the same quality as Chinese cotton, particularly at the price that the company had to sell, keeping in view its revenue and shipping costs. However, a more important reason was that China itself had been growing cotton in large quantities. Its Nanking province was known for cotton production. In the wake of an increasing number of opium addicts in China, cotton lost its economic significance and was soon replaced by opium. Gradually, as English textile mills grew at the cost of de-industrialization in India, the company was able to take Indian raw cotton to England. In China, to develop an oligopoly over the tea trade, the company used a "credit" system. It extended credits to the wholesale dealers of tea, and that money eventually reached farmers as advances to guarantee next year's supply. According to Frederic Wakeman (1978), by 1783 the company had extended so much that it could not afford for these traders to go bankrupt because it would mean a loss in capital extended to the wholesalers and traders. The company had higher stakes of survival in the region—before the opium trade could flourish, the company was facing a trade deficit of $3.5 million every year, something that only opium could reverse—and used a credit system to monopolize trade with China. Wakeman argues that "the most basic, the most fundamental, the most constant reason for this was simply that the English could find nothing manufactured in Europe which the Chinese would consume in quantities proportional to the gigantic English demand for tea" (p. 168). The consequences of trade were evident sooner rather than later.

Opium proved a blessing for Britain and its imperial designs in the Indian Ocean and beyond since it not only provided economic benefits to first balance trade with China and then accumulate capital in London, but because it also strengthened British Raj in India through the coffers earned. The company supervised its cultivation on a larger scale in Bengal. In 1729, when the Chinese government outlawed the import of opium, the recorded per-year sale has been mentioned as 200 chests, with one chest weighing roughly 160 pounds or 72.57 kilograms (Farooqui, 2005: 29). In 1767, annual opium imported in China reached 1,000 chests. In 1820, it reached 5,000 chests; in 1830 and 1835 it was reported to have reached 16,550, and 30,000 chests, respectively, while in 1838 it was 40,000 chests per annum. Trade kept growing despite that Chinese defeat in the first Opium War (1840–1842) did not result in fulfillment of the long-standing demand of Britain to legalize opium in China in the name of free trade. The second Opium War (1856–1860), however, forced Qing China to legalize it, resulting in the annual import reaching at 60,000 chests per year (Greenberg, 1969: 112–14). The worth of this trade can be estimated by the fact that in 1838, when the price of opium was lowered in India to unprecedented levels, one chest was valued at $485. One year before, in 1837, the price of one chest was reported at $620 (Beeching, 1975: 68). During 1821–1830, the company was able to earn 74 million rupees of revenue from opium sold only through Malwa (Farooqui, 2005: 221). The company devised various policies to ensure maximum profit from this trade. It had four important sources of capital gain: a monopoly over opium production in India, tax at the time of auctioning, higher taxes for inland sale in India, and tax on the export of opium through Malwa, Calcutta, and Bombay (Deming, 2011). It was the most devastating slow-poisoning of China; opium's widespread consumption throughout the country crippled the economy and enabled Britain to strengthen its imperial control in the region for an extended period. Wakeman (1978) states:

> During the first decade of the nineteenth century, China had gained about $26,000,000 in her world balance of payments. From 1828 to 1836,

> $38,000,000 flowed out of the Middle Kingdom. It was opium that turned the balance and ended by financing much of England's further colonization of India. In 1830, the auditor-general of the East India Company declared that every year at least £4,000,000 had to be carried back from India to England. Most of this surplus territorial revenue was transferred first in the form of opium, which was sold in Canton, and then sent home as teas, which in turn added another £3,300,000 in tariffs for the British government. After centuries of trade, the West had finally found something the Chinese would buy in large quantities. (p. 173)

On the eve of the first Opium War (1839–1942), China witnessed a shattering of the hoax of its worldview. According to Q. E. Wang (1999), the Chinese worldview was based on the empire being "the cultural center of the world," and "its claim of universalism was based on a moral and cultural order rather than on an ever-victorious military" (p. 289). Following this perception, the Chinese considered their Confucianist civilization as far superior to European or any other civilization. The hierarchical structure adopted following the sinicization thesis defines affinity of the world cultures with China and included "sinic zone" comprised of Korea, Vietnam, and Japan; an "inner-Asian zone" comprised of "most non-Han ethnic groups of nomadic tribes"; and and "outer zone" comprised of "regions in Southeast and South Asia, as well as Europe in later age" (p. 290). The Europeans' arrival and their resistance to the concept of the ultimate authority of the emperor shattered the cornerstone of Chinese world-order. In particular, there were three crucial paradigm shifts that China had long refused to acknowledge. First, its status as the super accumulator in the world-system had been taken away by rising Western imperialism in the world. Britain had brought a paradigm shift in its bilateral trade with China, ensuring capital flight from the country in the form of nothing else but precious metals. On the eve of the war, British imperialism had complete state patronage asking for so-called "free trade" because (1) it ensured that the Chinese had lost the competitive advantage not only in the spice and tea trade but also in industrial and textile production, and (2) the coercive, exploitative policies of occupation and imperialism ensured unilateral determination of pricing in the region, thus making it virtually impossible for any resistant entity to rise and oppose the word of the British empire. On the one hand, the company had developed complete monopolistic control over bilateral trade with China, and inter-imperial clashes in the region confirm that empires were fighting to control the maximum prize of occupation. On the other hand, the British desire to go for free trade was paradoxically expressed with an explicit policy of de-industrialization in India. The paradoxical link between imperialism and free trade could not have been exposed any better anywhere in the world but in the case of Sino-British bilateral trade (Celikkol,

2011: 126). Indian opium played an essential role in letting imperialism penetrate in the region, and it pushed China further down the divergent path by ensuring the development of its underdevelopment by dumping opium and taking away the coffers. China had to face the consequences of the divergent path it (and Asia overall) took some three hundred years ago.

Second, Britain could not have sustained its imperial advancement and penetration in the region had its empirical project been not supported by a plethora of political power, the most important being military superiority. For over three hundred years, China did not reach any remarkable milestone in increasing its naval power except that the Qing dynasty invested in the four fleets. A landmark study of the abortive Chinese attempt to construct a robust navy capable of defending the country against Western imperial intrusion argues that in the wake of the first Opium War, the Qing dynasty could not develop a national navy despite spending much money and importing military hardware from Europe, particularly Germany. John Rawlinson (1967) argues that a combination of conventionalism, civilizational superiority, private rather than national interests, and the unbridgeable gap between the technologies of the intruding powers and China left the latter at the mercy of imperial policies. Peter Lorge (2012) mentions that after the Qing emperor conquered Taiwan in 1683, they did not find any valuable use for the Chinese military until they faced the Europeans intruding into the mainland (p. 94). However, the war history of China shows that victory over Taiwan was the last remarkable glory the Qing emperor could enjoy. Though the Qing army won a few other wars too, by 1750 the Qing emperor had ceased to be a regional military hegemon. The royal military was defeated in almost all wars after 1750. One can see that the fall of Chinese economic power coincided with the fall of its military power. Though China was considered a super accumulator and an economic powerhouse of the world before the rise of modern capitalism in the Indian Ocean and the South China Sea, it failed to convert its economic supremacy into military power, mainly because the imperial world-system did not allow it to happen. For this book, it is appropriate to state here and corroborate that the failure to develop fungibility of economic power into military power brought the fall of imperial China when it was an external arena of the modern world-system. When China entered into the geography of the modern world-system, its lack of military power disabled it from acquiring any dominant economic position; the Europeans made it a periphery of the core. China, in other words, could have maintained its position in the developing world-system had it been able to defend its economic interests and, more importantly, convert them into adequate military power. Since China failed on both accounts, it fell from its positional standing as it was coerced to enter into the modern world-system.

Regarding China's fall and chronic lack of military power, particularly that it was not enough to defend Chinese sovereignty in 1840, inference from three critical points guides us logically. First, there is no comprehensive data available delineating the nature and magnitude of the import of Western military technology into China during the Qing rule, at least before the first Opium War. Second, two arguments nevertheless are prominent in the discourse about the nature of the great divergence by that time: (1) Before China was brought into the realm of the modern capitalist world-system, it was the economic powerhouse of the world and able to attract huge amounts of silver and other precious metals from all over the world. (2) Before the Europeans inflicted on China their will to coerce it into the world-system, the Europeans had witnessed growth in military technology and were able to sail all over the seas of the world backed by imperial military powers. They were able to display superior military technology and war skills in the Opium Wars, after which the Qing emperor was forced to legalize opium. From a Frankian perspective, two critical facts support our understanding. First, before and during the times of Dutch and Portuguese dominance in sea trade, European naval power and, in particular, terrestrial military power were in no way superior to Asian powers. More important, however, is that the Europeans did not need to engage in an economic-based military conflict in Asia during that time (Frank, 2007: 38). In other words, we can say that since mercantilism could grow, the Europeans did not require using coercive powers to enforce their own terms and conditions of trade over Asian powers. However, as economic conflict grew, they were able to demonstrate the superior military power to let their say prevail.

The logical conclusion of these two points leads us to a third important point, logical inference. Although China remained an economic superpower in the premodern world-system, it could not develop itself into a military power (Thomas, 1984: 74). It was, therefore, China's lack of formidable defenses that relegated its positional standing when it was brought into the modern world-system. It was actually its failure to develop militarily that cost China to lose its positional standing in the world-system. Realizing that the Chinese were immersed in the notion of civilizational superiority, and perhaps calculating the zero-sum effect of the transfer of military equipment and technology to China, it was logical for the so-called "red barbarians" not to pursue the Chinese decision-makers enthusiastically offering them military technology and hardware in return of goods of trade such as tea, porcelain, silk, and cotton. Even if we ignore and put aside the factors that contributed to the denial of the Chinese to develop their military power and those of the West that led it to develop an economic system to accumulate material benefits (such as its military-imperial reach beyond its land borders), we still fall short of explaining any logical reason for the Sino-European great divergence except that China failed to defend its economic interests by developing and exercising its military muscles. Philip Hoffman (2015), Peter Lorge (2005), Tonio Andrade (2011, 2016), and many other scholars emphasizing the significance of shifts and transformations in military technology and capability and the style and culture of war in Europe argue that the lack of military power made it difficult for China to defend its economic interests in the region and beyond. Geoffrey Parker (1996) argues that during the extended period between the discovery of the Americas in 1492 and the Opium Wars in China in 1840, Europe was able to sail over and rule the sea routes of the world and display a successful strife to accumulate as much capital as it could. During this time, China was also able to gain a lion's share of the global distribution of silver through trade. However, Europe witnessed a military revolution, invested in military technology, and applied its strategic power to expand its capitalist system in the world. It had also gained experience from wars in India and elsewhere by the time it invaded China. It is important to ask whether Europe could have been successful in establishing the largest imperial project in the history of mankind had it lacked adequate military power.

The first Opium War (1839–1842) was the outcome of an inherent incompatibility between competing British and Chinese economic interests. In 1832, the Qing emperor disallowed the sale of opium in China, with least effect because of corruption in the Canton port system. In 1833, the British government abolished its monopoly of the company over trade with China, thus opening the way for the influential business class in Britain to transnationalize its commercial operations. The British government, agreeing to the demands of its elite class, insisted on free trade, legalization and taxability of the opium trade, and recognition of extraterritoriality for British officials, citizens, and traders. The Chinese found lethal economic and social consequences of the influx of opium. Two important long-standing issues—the free trade of opium through its legalization, and the implementation of extraterritoriality for British traders—led to the event causing the start of the war. In order to eradicate opium trade from Canton, newly appointed imperial commissioner Lin Tse-Hsu ordered the arrest of Chinese offenders involved in opium trade, seized and burned 20,283 chests of opium, and ordered British traders to leave the area (Wakeman, 1978: 188). Though British were left with no other choice but to accept these orders, it was the start of the war that later on ended with the occupation of British imperial forces defeating Chinese forces.

The first Opium War was the first of a series of wars in which imperial China was defeated, and its civilizational pride was decimated in an unprecedented humiliating manner. Though Qing emperor did not cede to the demand for the establishment of free trade regime and the legalization of opium, the concessions British, and later on other Western powers were able to accrue, were enormous. Under the Treaty of Nanking signed at the culmination of the war on August 29, 1842, China had to surrender Hong Kong to the British government; it accepted extraterritoriality for British citizens and traders; it accepted opening of five ports—Shanghai, Canton, Ningpo, Foochow, and Emoy—for international (read British) trade; it also accepted abolition of the Cohong system and allowed presence of British counsel for commercial affairs coordination at every port; it also accepted to pay $21 million in indemnity to the British government (Wakeman, 1978: 212). Following this treaty, China was exposed to unprecedented international competition of occupation. Western powers and Japan rushed to get their share of the hot cake. In a series of "unequal treaties" that led to the establishment of a "treaty system" and the start of "the century of humiliation," China conceded to the incoming powers almost everything they demanded. From 1840 to about the third decade of the twentieth century, every leading power of the world took part in demanding concessions from China. Starting with Britain's Treaty of Nanking in 1842 and, before that, the Bogue Treaty in 1843, the United States, France, Sweden, Norway, Portugal, and even Japan signed unequal treaties since they all were almost victors at the time when these treaties were signed. In other words, starting with the first Opium War, imperial China lost almost every war it fought against Western powers. And with each defeat, new unequal treaties containing discriminatory and humiliating terms and conditions were imposed on China.

China lost to Western imperial forces again in the second Opium War (1856–1860), which resulted in the signing of the Treaty of Tientsin on June 26, 1858, with China on the one side and Britain, France (allied in the war), Russia, and the United States on the other. The final form of this treaty, which took some time to take effect and emerged only a month later, "levied indemnities totaling about 16 million taels, roughly tripled the number of treaty ports, confirmed the unusual right of foreign participation in China's coastal and riverine carrying trade, permitted foreign travel in the interior under passports, opened the Yangtze as far as Hankow, provided for tariff duties of 5 percent ad valorem (except as otherwise enumerated) and a single transit duty payment of half that amount, urged the extension of a unified foreign inspectorate of customs to all the ports, and finally, legalized the opium trade" (Fairbank, 1978: 251). Beside such sweeping concessions, the British wanted the Qing emperor to accept the appointment of a permanent minister representing Britain to ensure implementation of these treaties in letter and spirit. Two important consequences of these treaties were in the offing. First, China was forced to enter into a modern world-system in which its positional standing was determined based on its status not as an economic powerhouse but as a supplier of the raw materials and consumers of end product(s) produced elsewhere. In other words, it was the implementation of a new world-order in which the international division of labor was implemented by relegating China's positional standing in the hierarchy of the world-system. Second, through opium and subsequent wars between Western empires on the one hand and China on the other, the latter lost its political and economic sovereignty to the imperial powers. Once under imperialism and semi-colonialism, China had neither "low levels of foreign intervention" nor "high levels of domestic defense capabilities," two important conditions that S. C. Thomas (1984) considers significant to ensure industrial growth in any country; contrarily, it faced a well-coordinated effort on the part of Western countries and Japan to ensure that the Qing government had little room to maneuver. Thomas argues that because of a lack of sovereignty, a drain of resources was imposed on China; between 1870 and 1897 it lost about 1.347 billion taels (three taels equal one British pound) due to foreign intervention, the freedom it conceded to foreign traders in terms of the choice of trade items, and the constraints imposed by imperial countries on its capability to industrialize, resulting in the bankruptcy of the Chinese government in 1897.

Following its defeat in 1840, the Qing government lost almost all the wars it fought against Western powers. The second Opium War legalized opium. In 1884, French forces defeated the Qing imperial army. In 1895–1896, Japanese imperial forces defeated the Qing imperial army for the first time in history. During the last phase of the Qing dynasty, the imperial force was able to defeat its opponents on the battleground only occasionally. It could defeat and suppress the Taiping rebellion only after it had been defeated more than once and, more importantly, only after it was aided by British and French forces since this civil war affected trade growth, particularly at the port of Shanghai (Michael and Chang, 1966: 170). The defeat at the hands of Japanese imperial army, however, was an essential setback because of two reasons. First, it assured Chinese leaders of the paradigm shift in the strategic balance of power in the region maintained for over a millennium at least. While they knew the designs and interests of Western powers on mainland China, Japanese victory over China confirmed to them the leap Japan had taken ahead of the rest of the regional contenders despite that it had been subjected to a port treaty system led by the Americans that was almost identical to that of China led by British. It was a reformist agenda initiated in the wake of the Meiji revolution that had in fact brought widespread change and strengthened the economic and military power of Japan. The defeat left a lesson for a growing number of Chinese intellectuals to refer to the outcome as an acceptance of new ideas in the world and embrace economic and defense development. Second, it was the worst kind of humiliation China could face to its regional status because it had always maintained its suzerainty, not over the mainland, but in Taiwan, the Korean Peninsula, and many other areas in the region. The war resulted in not only the destruction of whatever conventional and "old" naval force it had but also the occupation of Taiwan, Port Arthur, the Liaodong Peninsula, and the Pescadores Islands by Japan. In the words of Sarah Paine (2003), "Japan's miracle became China's great tragedy. Its triumph was China's humiliation. In a reversal of the millennia-old Far Eastern balance of power, Japan replaced China as the dominant power in Asia" (p. 293). With the signing of the Treaty of Shimonoseki on April 17, 1895, China reaffirmed to itself the failure of its "self-strengthening" policy. The verdict of the day was clear: China had lost the status of a great power.

However, the most important effect of Chinese defeat in wars against Western imperial and Japanese forces was the birth and rise of the modern sense of nationalism in the country. China has been a civilization, an economic hegemon, and the home of Confucianism. Its influence has been visible throughout Southeast Asia. However, the concept of China as a "nation" could develop only through experiences of humiliation since the first Opium War. The disrespect the imperial forces leashed was less on the Chinese state than on Chinese culture. Therefore, the idea of a "nation" in the modern Westphalian sense was a product less of the "state" and more of the culture (Zhao, 2004: 16). National politics in China in the wake of its defeat in the first Sino-Japanese War can satisfactorily be called an interplay between republican, communist, local imperial, and foreign imperial forces. The most prominent feature of national politics during 1900–1949 is the controversial claim of legitimacy of representation of nationalist aspirations; Kuomintang and the Communist Party of China fought a protracted civil war to prove their legitimacy. However, before we reach this stage, we still have to look at one of the most important nadir moments of Chinese history: the Boxer rebellion.

For China, the period of disgrace and humiliation was not over with the end of the Sino-Japanese War; the worst yet had to come. By the end of the nineteenth century, there was another effort on the part of the Qing dynasty and some nationalist forces to overturn the penetration of imperialism and semi-colonial structure in the country that had plagued its economic and social life. The Boxer rebellion was an effort on the part of the nationalist forces to "overthrow the Qing, destroy the foreigner" (Cohen, 1978: 573). Two basic reasons ushered the Boxer rebellion. First, in the wake of the second Opium War, Britain was able to triple the number of ports under its exclusive control, and after having benefited a lot by resource extraction from the southern and southwestern coasts, particularly Shanghai, and took over the ports of Tianjin, Yantai, and Zhenjiang on the Shandong peninsula, the peasants of the North China region felt the deleterious effects of the exploitative expansionism of British traders aimed at redefining the division of labor. Before the war, the region was able to maintain some industrial activities, particularly of textiles, and trade using the Grand Canal network and Shandong port at the intersection of the Grand Canal and Yangzi River. However, the growth of trade at Tianjin and Zhenjiang halted the process. Consequently, the Yantai port had but one thing to import: Indian cotton. Historically, Indian cotton was never imported into China, at least not before 1770, while since then it has been a relatively "low-scale" affair because of the market uncertainties involved (Wallerstein, 2011a: 140, 168). The situation, however, changed in the wake of Chinese defeat in wars against the Western empires. Before the effects of the opening of other ports could implicate, the Yantai port was able to import textile goods only modestly. However, to meet the growing local demand of foreign textile mills and machine spinning mills installed in the region, the British started importing huge quantities of cotton yarns through this port. In 1882, the Yantai port imported only 11,288 piculs of cotton yarn. In 1886, it went up to 56,726. In 1895, 101,035 piculs were imported only through this port. In 1899, it had reached an unprecedented level of 155,894 piculs. The import of cotton yarn through the Tianjin port also increased from 66,946 piculs in 1889 to 269,221 piculs in 1899. A similar kind of increase was witnessed at the Zhenjiang port, and by 1900, collectively 40 percent of the activities on all three ports were related only to the import of cotton yarns (Esherick, 1987: 69–70). Regarding worth, the scale of cotton imports into China went up to 231 percent from 1870 to 1900, while its cotton exports increased by 188 percent, increasing the trade deficit and capital flight from the country (Hsiao, 1974: 22–23). After having diverged from the path of modernization during the eighteenth century, China went through a "little divergence" in the region; it lost to Japan because the latter could grow and modernize its textile production mechanism at least twenty years before China. This "little divergence" between the two proved "to be fatal for [China's] industry" as "it eventually ordains totally different development patterns for the textile industry in the two countries, which ultimately led to different growth patterns for the overall economy" (Dong et al., 2015: 776). Once technologically advanced textile production was installed in China, the imperial powers sought a new kind of division of labor in the regions traditionally known for cotton and textile production. Since these Western-controlled textiles destroyed the weaving market by offering a price about two-thirds less than that of a similar product, the weaving business collapsed. It caused a depressant effect on cotton production, and imperial traders started importing cotton from India (Myers, 1965). This was particularly problematic for the cotton-growing areas where imported cotton destroyed agricultural growth.

Second, the traditional Chinese textile industry could not compete against the technologically advanced textile mills of the Western countries installed on Chinese soil, particularly because under the "Most Favored Nation" status obtained by all the Western powers and imperial Japan, these textiles were free of any in-land taxation and levy. Since 1840, with defeat on every battleground, the Chinese government had to sign a new treaty making various concessions to the victors. In many of these treaties signed from 1840 to 1899, almost all the leading imperial powers present in China were able to carve out their own "spheres of influence"—the leased areas with the almost sovereign rights of resource exploitation, construction of railway networks and factories, and management of their own judicial-administrative structure. Thus, by 1899, Britain, Russia, Germany, the United States, France, and Japan were able to "slice up" China "like a melon" to be divided among the voracious coyotes (Bailey, 2001: 29). As China was too big to be handled by any single Western power, they united to ensure that everyone gets some share in the booty. Instead of disintegrating territorially, they partitioned it economically. Moreover, even so, whenever any power felt that it was being deprived, all it needed was an "excuse" to claim indemnity and compensation. Once one imperial power obtained any concession, almost every other imperial power was also granted a similar kind of privilege (Darby, 1987: 71). During the whole occupation of imperial power (1842–1919), China signed 709 unequal treaties. It signed 163 such treaties with Britain, 153 with Japan, 104 with Russia, 73 with France, 47 with Germany, 41 with the United States, 26 with Belgium, 13 with Portugal, 7 with Italy, 5 with the Netherlands, 5 with Austria, 4 with Spain, and another 68 with other powers around the world (Zhao, 2004: 47). The Qing rulers were too feeble to annoy anyone at the cost of widespread and simmering resentment among the masses.

More importantly, however, the rise of nationalism was a response to the politico-economic-cultural onslaught on Chinese life and society. Western imperial forces, as they penetrated deep into Chinese society and economy, unleashed a force of missionaries advocating and spreading Christian religion in China. For social conservatives, it was a challenge to their socio-religious system, leading to implicate their political power in the country. However, to compete against the multifaceted onslaught, they needed to develop and organize themselves against Western patterns. China was the home of Confucianism, yet it was true that it could aspire to grow under a world-system whose rules and desired behaviors had already been defined and set by the imperial powers occupying China. With the arrival of these missionaries, China moved forward in the direction of modern notions of society, state, politics, and economics. Since the European nation-states patronized imperialism in China, they ushered a new understanding of the relationship between society, the state, and their institutions. In the words of Arendt (1945), "Wherever the nation-state appeared as a conqueror, it aroused national consciousness and the desire for sovereignty among conquered people, thereby defeating all genuine attempts at empire-building" (p. 127). There is clear evidence that the first Sino-Japanese War led to the momentum for and empowerment of the reformist movement in the country.

Chinese intellectuals developed organizations exposing the effects of Western imperialism in the country and urging the masses to resist economic exploitation. New kinds of newspapers, dedicated mostly to political ideologies and reformist agendas, started appearing. There started emerging "a new class of cultural entrepreneurs"—"editorialists, women's instructors, translators, and fiction writers"—with an objective to meet the new needs of the masses seeking a restoration of the civilizational pride that China had lost at the hands of imperialism (Judge, 1997: 20–23). Pressure from Western economic, cultural, and religious activities in the country and the spread of the new ideas pushed Empress Dowager Cixi and her conservative supporters in the royal court to take a bold step to restore the public image of the dynasty. The economic consequences of the second Opium War and the territorial concessions to imperial powers had caused widespread alienation of the masses, particularly in Shandong province.

A trilateral combination of economic loss, religious-civilizational insult, and military defeat at the hands of those who had been subordinate for a long time led a group of peasantry to initiate armed resistance against local Chinese converts as well as foreigners. In 1898, in one such attack, the killing of two German missionaries resulted in the demand of the leasing of additional territories, which was granted. However, the concessions alienated the peasantry further, and they increased their attacks on foreign installations in the country. In 1899, the Boxer rebellion reached Beijing, and Empress Dowager Cixi decided to patronize the group against Western forces. As attacks on foreigners increased, legation officers of the Diplomatic Body (a representative ministerial made up of imperial powers in China) asked for the guards from Taku to be relocated to Beijing. The calling of guards, however, was contrary to the treaties and arguably "added fuel to the fire of anti-foreignism and thus endangered the very individuals it aimed to protect" (Purcell, 1963: 248). The first attack by Western imperial forces faced combined resistance from the government and the Boxers. The declaration of war by the Qing government on the powers on June 21, 1899, resulted in the siege of the legation officers in Beijing. In a clash with the offices, 66 foreigners were killed and more than 150 wounded (Purcell, 1963: 252). More importantly, however, the Western forces took over Taku and Tientsin, reached Beijing, and occupied it after a fierce battle against the combined Chinese forces and Boxers. After the legation officials were approached and the Chinese forces defeated, with the Empress Dowager having fled the city, a great massacre and looting began and continued for a few days (Preston, 2000: 262–95). The wrath of the imperial forces was at its peak. Indiscriminate killings of Chinese civilians and unarmed military men became common in some other parts of the country as well.

While the allied forces of the Western powers were the victors in this rebellion, they took over neither the government nor the mission of dividing China into more than one country to rule. Instead, they shrewdly put forward their most important task in the country: maximization of economic gains. They let the Qing dynasty continue ruling the country but deprived it of any of the moral right and grace it could command in the eyes of its own people. China had to offer an official apology to Germany and Japan and erect monuments in honor of the foreign "martyrs." Some members of the royal family were either imprisoned or asked to commit suicide (Purcell, 1963: 260; Preston, 2000: 310–11). The most punitive measures were, however, fiscal; the allied forces imposed an indemnity of about $335 million on the Qing government to be paid over thirty-nine years with an annual interest of 4 percent on the principal amount left. The division of this money among the allied powers was determined to take into account the loss of lives and property destroyed, thus awarding Russia 29 percent, Germany 20 percent, France 15.75 percent, Britain 11.25 percent, Japan 7.7 percent, and the United States 7.3 percent (Bailey, 2001: 40–41). The total amount of indemnity, with interest taken into account, was almost double the principal amount (Purcell, 1963: 261). In today's value, this amount, including interest, would be about $8.6 billion (Preston, 2000: 310). Moreover, to eradicate any other armed resistance in the way of economic pillage, the powers razed some forts to the ground. More than two hundred Boxer leaders were executed in public in the presence of the units of allied forces. An aborted Boxer rebellion, along with the first Sino-Japanese War, was the nadir moment in Chinese history. From there we see the first credible signs of the rise of China.

RE-EMERGENCE OF CHINA IN THE WORLD-SYSTEM

Before I trace the first signs of the rise of China, it is necessary to reflect on the changing nature of China's positional standing in the world-system as it developed in the nineteenth century. Wallerstein (2011a) had argued that the second episode of expansionism in the capitalist world-economy took place when some new areas of Asia and Africa were made "external arenas" adjacent to the areas that erstwhile were external arenas but had been integrated into world economic system. He defines "external arenas" as "a zone from which the capitalist world-economy wanted goods but which was resistant (perhaps culturally) to importing manufactured goods in return and strong enough politically to maintain its preferences" (p. 167). If we agree with Wallerstein's understanding of the origins of the modern capitalist system in Europe in post-1500 development, we can still find China dominating the system for at least the first half of the last five centuries. It was only China's own traditionalism and the opium influx that caused it to succumb to the redefined terms and conditions of global trade. European economic development was embedded in its military superiority, which it indiscriminately and shrewdly displayed throughout its imperial rule in the Americas, Asia, and Africa. The positional standing of China outside the modern world-system was regional hegemon; as an "external arena," it existed for quite a while, but it was forcefully incorporated into the world-system as a periphery only after it had been defeated militarily. Its involuntary entry into the modern world-system was abrupt, and its positional standing was certainly that of a peripheral, semi-colonized country whose economic significance was used to strengthen the status quo in world trade. When it resisted economic subjugation, it could not succeed, as its military power was no match for the Western imperial powers. Historically, to become a regional hegemon, China relied more, not on military power, but on Confucianism, a tributary system, and economic centrality. Except for civil wars, China never fought in any international war beyond Southeast Asia. In other words, it had no experience fighting the "red barbarians." Before the Europeans' arrival and penetration, China's political system did not allow any cross-pollination of ideas and methods about realpolitik. The Europeans could outpace China and deprive it of its erstwhile economic positional standing by incorporating it into the modern world-system primarily because of their military superiority and the political decline of China. By 1900, China was a periphery providing the core with raw materials and consuming the goods manufactured outside of its territory. It was either consuming opium, cotton, cotton products, and numerous other items that it did not want or preparing itself for the arrival of the core powers.

Before it could liberate itself from the physical occupation and economic exploitation of the Western powers, China faced domestic challenges, which led to violent civil wars and transformations. The 1895–1949 era, therefore, is one of rapid change where we see China rediscovering itself with new identities. Since 1840, when it was defeated in the first Opium War, some intellectuals in China reflected on the misgivings about the ability of contemporary political structure. The movement initially aimed at reforming the bureaucratic structure and its foundational civil service examination. However, as defeats in wars against the imperial powers increased, the debate about reforming the interrelationship between the state and society gained momentum. The military defeats in the Sino-Western wars were important catalysts for this movement; the Sino-Japanese War nevertheless proved to be a milestone. Civilizational legacy, Confucianism, imperial occupation, and economic exploitation with consequent underdevelopment and impoverishment pushed Chinese thinkers to develop what was later called the "Self-Strengthening Movement." The Opium Wars produced public intellectuals such as Ma Jianzhang, who spent some time in Europe and, on return, stressed on the Qing government in the 1870s to retrieve its economic sovereignty from the imperial powers, invest in infrastructural development such as railroads, and exploit mineral resources (Bailey, 1998). Some scholars point out the long-term consequences of the Qing government's overwhelming closed policy with no allowing of modern Western knowledge to be taught in its educational institutions, particularly in the wake of Japan's imperial rise in the region (Chang, 1980). Feng Guifen, a scholar and former public official, "a key figure in adapting late Qing statecraft to changing conditions," "argued for self-strengthening industrialization by borrowing from the West" by mentioning that "China is the largest country on earth with ample, fertile plains and marshes, numerous people, and abundant resources. Naturally, the mouths of all nations are watering with desire" (Rowe, 2012: 208; quoted in Scott, 2009: 54). Wang Tao, another scholar, spent time in Europe and stressed learning from the organizational structure of Western governments with remarkable results (Cohen, 1974). However, the most important impact was on Kang Youwei. As a young individual living in Canton during the Sino-French War in 1884, he "personally experienced all the tensions and fears that attended the immanence of foreign attack." One of the consequences was that "direct experience of the power and militancy of Western nations lent a special urgency to his study of Western learning" (Chang, 1980: 284). His extensive reading of ancient as well as contemporary philosophy and politics led him to develop a universalistic, moralistic worldview of peace and harmony. Simultaneously, however, his overwhelming concern for Chinese national questions, particularly in the wake of Chinese defeat at the hands of Japan, led him to argue that imperialism in China was harming Chinese national character and identity. The Qing government was unresponsive to the changing nature of the relationship between the state and society as being practiced elsewhere in the world, something that could have been accommodated within Chinese national character (Bailey, 2001: 29). His reform agenda asked for a "revolution from above" by establishing a Bureau of Government Reorganization under the emperor, with the stated objectives of "building of a modern navy and army, economic development, and the rationalization of public finance." He also asked for "promoting industry, commerce, agriculture, mining and modern transportation" (Chang, 1980: 285). His influence was acknowledged when the emperor asked him to present his ideas to him in person and later announced reforming the system.

The initial signs of reform were not visible before the signing of the Protocol of Beijing in September 1901. It led nationalists to resist attacks on economic sovereignty. In some provinces, the Chinese "commercial gentry" came forward to claim the right to construct infrastructure and industries and establish production companies by relying on the Chinese industrial workers produced by the European industries established in the wake of the Opium Wars. By the end of the Sino-Japanese War, there were more than six hundred thousand modern industrial workers, including more than one hundred thousand highly skilled workers. They were mostly employed in more than six hundred industrial units established by the commercial gentry of China during 1895–1911 (Esherick, 1976: 70–71). Once the Qing government tried to hand over various territories to German and American companies for railroad development, there were uprisings and revolts.

One of the most popular demands of what was known as the "Rights Recovery Movement" was the revocation of the concept of extraterritoriality. It was against the backdrop of discriminatory treatment that the Chinese people experienced in mixed courts or Cantonese areas. The movement also demanded the revocation of British rights to import and dump Indian opium in China (Wright, 1968: 11–19). In 1906, Britain agreed to end opium imports into China within the next decade provided China itself eradicated opium cultivation in the mainland within next three years. The challenge was accepted and met successfully, compelling Britain to fulfill its part of the agreement (Des Forges, 1973: 93–102). Germany's mining rights in the Qingdao and Jinan provinces were also abolished in 1911 (Bailey, 2001: 47). Though the Qing government wanted to avoid the wrath of rising nationalism "born in the wreckage of culturalism and nurtured on imperialism's threat to China's territorial, cultural, and, in the opinion of some, even racial survival" (Zhao, 2004: 49), this approach could not succeed as the rising tide of nationalism took everything away from the Qing government. The government agreed to launch constitutional reforms, particularly in the wake of the Russo-Japanese War 1904–1905, in which for the first time an Asian power defeated a European power. In China, this defeat was viewed as a difference between constitutionalism and autocracy. If China had to grow and find an honorable place in the fast-changing world, the rationale argued, it had to abolish dynastic rule in favor of a constitutional government (Ichiko, 1980; Fincher, 1981; Bailey, 2001). In an endeavor to defend the rights of the Chinese people to govern and develop their own economy, the Railway Protection Movement was launched in the backdrop of the Qing government's decision to first nationalize locally owned infrastructural projects and then hand them to the imperial powers in lieu of the debts it owed in the Beijing Protocol of the Boxer Rebellion. Protesting against the decision, units of "New Armies" in Wuchang city rebelled against their own officers. New Armies were established at provincial bases as part of the military modernization process launched by the Qing government in the wake of defeat in the Sino-Japanese War of 1895–1996 (Hatano, 1968). Since many of the soldiers in these units were prepared to serve on different lines and used different weapons, they internalized revolutionary ideas and took it upon themselves to overthrow Manchu rule in the country. They conceived the Qing government to be a traitor and puppet put in front of the masses to let the Western powers carry on their economic pillage (V. P. Dutt, 1968).The Wuchang uprising led to the successful ouster of the Qing government with the announcement of independence for some provinces from the Qing dynasty on October 10, 1911. It ended the political system of China that had been in place for over two millennia (Bailey, 2001: 65–67). The announcement of the new republic, however, could not result in economic independence for China, as the imperial powers retained control over the areas they had leased. It was only after the end of World War II that China could liberate itself from the occupation of the imperial powers.

There is no way we can precisely assess the full range of the consequences of Western and Japanese imperialism in China. From 1757, when China established the Canton system in order to systemize its commercial relations with the outside world, to 1949, when it declared its independence in the wake of the decolonization process and the victory of the Communist Party of China (CPC) in the long civil war, China remained under the worst kind of economic control by the Western powers. Almost all the empires of Europe took a share in the booty they looted from China. They dumped their products in China through a forceful imposition of treaties that the Chinese regarded as unequal and humiliating. Europe inculcated China in its capitalist world-system using terms and conditions suitable only to itself. The perils of imperialism in Asia and, in the context of this chapter, China were overwhelming. From Andre Gunder Frank to Samir Amin, Immanuel Wallerstein, Hamza Alavi, K. N. Chaudhuri, and Sushil Chaudhury, all the leading economic historians and world-systems analysts agree that before the arrival of imperialism in Asia, China was the epicenter of global trade. While a detailed analysis of what caused India to fail despite being another economic powerhouse in global trade will be provided in the next chapter, suffice it to say that imperialism brought far-reaching consequences for both the regions. Because its military superiority developed an unbridgeable gap during the sixteenth and seventeenth centuries and onward, Europe was able to inflict plunder on Asia (and Africa and the Americas) and could introduce a new global division of labor. This new division of labor deprived China of its position and redefined it based on the imbalance between its economic significance and military backwardness.

By 1750, all empires, except India and China, were embracing economic imperialism and expansionism throughout the world. Of most significance was the naval dimension of military superiority that enabled Europe to reach and occupy Asia and Africa. The decline of China, therefore, was not economic but strategic, in particular, naval. China was subjected to a century of humiliation because it lost to the invading powers militarily. China, when it entered the capitalist world-system, had to accept a relegated positional standing because of its inability to defend its political sovereignty and economic integrity against the imperial onslaught. The capitalist world-system grew on imperial grounds; Europe was able to enrich itself and become the core of the system not because it could outpace China and other powers in industrial-technological development. On the contrary, Europe could grow only when it was able to dominate, occupy, and exploit the vast agricultural and mineral resources of the colonized areas. The colonization, then, could not have been possible had Europe not possessed superior military technology.

The gap between European and Chinese military technology started emerging in the wake of the military revolution in Europe. Even then, it took considerable time for Europe to let the Chinese and others realize that the gap had become unbridgeable. Europe's quest for world domination was supported by the rise of its military and naval power growing in response to the incessant happening of wars and anarchic structure of the political landscape on the continent. A combination of the need for Asian handicrafts and spices and superior military power enabled the Europeans to occupy Asia and Africa. They were able to destroy Asian industries and build their own economies based on the capital they were able to take away due to the discriminatory economic policies they had adopted in the colonies. The history of capitalism during the last four to five centuries validates the argument that countries in the modern world-system fall prey to economic exploitation because of fragile national defenses and meager economic abilities to survive in odd times. In the seventeenth century, China possessed the status of global economic powerhouse and a regional hegemon. It could defeat the Portuguese and the Dutch because of prevailing parity among the competitors. China, however, lost the pace of technological development in military affairs and faced the consequences in the nineteenth century. Europeans defeated it more than once on its own soil and coerced it to sign unequal treaties. From 1757 to 1919, the Europeans took away more than enough; the plunder was of such great significance that on the eve of independence in 1949, China was one of the poorest countries in the world. According to Angus Maddison's data available online through the Maddison Project, by the end of the sixteenth century, China produced more than one-fourth of world GDP (with India producing another one-fourth). The Chinese share of world GDP increased to one-third by 1820. Part of the reason was an increase in foreign trade through the Canton system. However, as opium was legalized, China's share of world GDP faced a steep decrease; in 1870, its share fell to 18 percent, and in 1913 to 9 percent. In 1950, China was producing less than 5 percent of world GDP.

Before China could rise again and free itself from economic imperialism, its intellectual landscape faced the incredible challenge of defining itself as a nation-state. While there was a greater consensus about the destructive role of

Western imperialism in the polity and economy of China and the corrupt role of the Qing dynasty in it, there were some questions that China faced during the first two decades of the twentieth century. Prominent among them include the role of Confucianism, feudalism, and Westernization. Chinese nationalism before the formation and rise of the CPC, therefore, was anti-imperial, pro-Confucius, and feudalistic. Since imperialism in China had become an integral part of national politics, it was more convenient for the CPC to take an ideological stand against the powerful odds. The origins of communism in China, therefore, can only be understood if we take into account the legacy of regional hegemony and the blatant realities of humiliation spanned over a century. Vohra (1974) argues that "fear of the West is an underlying theme of the [Chinese] revolution" because the communist leaders, including Mao Tse-Tung, referred to the "coercive policies of imperialists" to "highlight national weaknesses and need for change" (p. vi). Though it is not difficult to deny the impact of the Russian Bolshevik Revolution in 1917 as attractive to Chinese radical leaders as a possible strategy to get rid of both foreign economic imperialism and domestic traditionalism (Schwartz, 1951; Whiting, 1953), Dirlik (1989) in an important study stressed the significance of the "readiness" of these radicals to embrace communist ideology in a tautological manner. Given the peculiarity of domestic circumstances, global conflict among empires made the acceptance of communism in China "inevitable"; the rise of communism in China during 1917–1921 took place in the backdrop of increasing interconnectedness of the domestic problems of China and that of international politics. It "blurred" distinctions "between the problems of China and those of other societies around the globe." One of the consequences of this development was that "global problems were China's national problems, and China's national problems were global problems, *all of them rooted in the capitalist world system*" (Dirlik, 1989: 8–9, emphasis added). The rise of communist ideas in Beijing University, for example, was reactionary as students radicalized against the submission of the Chinese republican government to Japanese demands and other conditions laid down in the Treaty of Versailles at the end of World War I. It became clear to the youth of China that their country had become precious booty and a cause of imperial envy. The consequent rise of radical nationalism in China led to the formation of the Communist Party. China's radical leadership turned to communism because the ideology enabled it to declare the existing system and its ingredients as the core of their national problem.

The perils of colonialism and imperialism are not the focus of this study. However, it is important to briefly overview such consequences in the context of the shift they brought to the positional standing of China. At independence in 1949, China had lost the unique central position in the world economy that it had before 1757. It was no longer the epicenter of global trade. China had fallen from the position of regional hegemon of a premodern tributary-trade world-system to a semi-peripheral country in an increasingly globalizing capitalist world-system. It was meeting most of the conditions I have laid down in the theoretical framework in the first chapter of this study. As mentioned above, the Chinese contribution of world GDP fell from 24 percent in 1757 to 4–5 percent in 1950. Though we do not have any credible facts to claim the GDP growth rate over this period, we can infer quite confidently that Chinese economic performance under imperialism went from bad to worse, thus meeting the condition of fluctuation in economic performance as laid down. First, China was a weaker military power compared to its neighbors, especially the USSR, and before the US nuclear attack in 1945, Japan. Second, Japan was able to occupy Manchuria from 1931 to 1945, and China could reclaim its sovereignty over the region only after Japan had capitulated to the allied forces in World War II and the USSR had announced abandoning the area under international pressure. China, without explicit international support, could have found it extremely difficult, if not impossible, to regain sovereign control over the region. Third, although China claimed victory in World War II, that it had been unable to defend its sovereignty against imperialism, both economic and strategic, meets the conditions laid out in this study. Fourth, China went into one of the longest and bloodiest civil wars in human history, and it ended with the victory of the Communist Party. Thus, we can argue that China had become a peripheral country at the time of its independence.

However, it is crucial to contextualize China's positional standing in the world-system by taking into account the transformation that the capitalist world-system had gone through by the end of World War II. The imperial conflict resulted in two great wars, or one long war fought during1914–1945. By the end of the intra-imperial conflict in 1945, a more precise form of the global capitalist system had come into being. The United States was about to take over Great Britain as the leading imperial power of the world, with Europe ensuring that the shifts within the core, and the decolonization process, remained least disruptive to the international division of labor. The "new" countries in the world, thus, remained "semi-sovereign"; they lacked economic independence, political sovereignty, and an effective role in offering any shift in determining pattern of progress within their own territories. The patterns of unequal development, and thus the structure of the world-system, had emerged vividly. Led by the United States, the core countries were able to refine the global division of labor; the United States introduced the Marshall Plan in Europe and reconciled with the USSR to implement a long-term truce and peace treaty in the core while stressing the "development" of raw materials—the so-called Green Revolution—in the semi-peripheral and peripheral countries (Wallerstein, 2004; Jo, 2011). The noncore countries faced a tough choice. The capitalist world economy required that they surrender their politico-economic independence and let the core determine the pattern of development there. In case of denial, the countries were at least allowed to enter the capitalist world-system. While some of these were under the direct "backyard" of the USSR and could not afford any other option, China followed the Maoist principles of development, including, most importantly, self-sufficiency. From 1949 to 1976, China's quest to regain its lost status in global trade met failure; China could grow only modestly.

CHINA AND THE WORLD-SYSTEM: COMMUNISM IN ACTION

At the time of independence in 1949, China's positional standing in the international system was marked by two contrasting features. First, Maoist China had a precarious, difficult, and inevitable international alliance with the USSR. Since 1917, CPC leadership conceived the Soviet model of development as being a role model that could usher rapid industrial development not only by recovering the losses received during Western economic imperialism and the long civil war but also due to the effect of industrialism on the USSR's economic status in the world. Chinese leadership, however, was shrewd enough to keep in mind the gap in economic status between the USSR and China, and the difference in the objective geographical conditions. Therefore, a selective adoption of the Russian economic model was followed (Teiwes, 1987). The Mao-led government also kept in mind three special issues that it had to take care of while dealing with the quest for domestic economic development: regional economic inequality and unequal development, hyperinflation, and the economic effects of the Korean War.

Among the most important consequences of economic imperialism in China were unequal regional development and urban-rural inequality. Regional inequality was vivid in three perspectives. First, treaty ports and adjacent areas were developed mainly due to textile industrialization sponsored by imperial powers in the country. Though imperial intervention resulted in the implementation of the most exploitative policies to extract the maximum resources, the areas nevertheless developed due to infrastructural development, such as railroads, and, perhaps more importantly, the emergence of the industrial urban working class that later on was co-opted into the Communist Party structure. Before the Japanese War in Manchuria, industrial growth in Shanghai, Tientsin, Tsingtao, Hankow, and other treaty port cities was estimated to be far higher than in the rest of the country; during 1895–1930, industry in these areas grew at the rate of 7.4 to 9.3 percent per annum (Chang, 1969: 71). Manchuria under Japan observed swift material progress. When Japan established a banana republic in the area, it wanted to turn the region into a model for its expansion into China. During 1932–1941, 85 percent of Japan's foreign direct investment went to China, and 80 percent only in Manchuria. This massive investment, in terms of volume and magnitude, was the highest by any colonial empire in any of its respective colonies. By 1945, Japan had invested more in Manchuria than in the Korean Peninsula, Taiwan, and the rest of China put together. Transportation, education, and public health received the largest chunks of this investment. The war with Japan during 1937–1945 proved to be a disaster and destroyed much of what had been constructed. It "both made and unmade" China as its political consequences pushed for greater centralization under the new communist movement while affecting the agricultural growth in the region and adjacent areas (Westad, 2012: 250–71). This all took place in the backdrop of Manchuria as an already a relatively developed region that had been receiving international investment since the 1860s, and by 1930 its per capita income was almost 50 percent higher than that of the rest of the country. Manchuria, however, represented less than 15 percent of the total industry of the country, and since most of the Chinese industry faced immense problems during the violence of 1931–1949, the inequality in development was evident to the communist government in Beijing. The violence also affected the modernization process, and by 1949 most of the industries were lagging behind Western technologies.

Second, hyperinflation was a big problem for Chinese economic recovery. One of the corollaries of the long civil war, it reflected the inability of the nationalist government to restructure the taxation system to provide financial resources for the war against Japan and, after 1945, against the Communist Party. Instead, an overwhelming reliance on monetary expansion resulted in inflation about 1,632 times higher than prewar levels. The national deficit rose to 80 percent. The wholesale price index in Shanghai skyrocketed 6.6 million times compared to 1937, leading to an inevitable collapse of the currency in August 1948. When the CPC took over, it was initially unable to control inflation; during the first six months of its rule, inflation went up further by one and a half times (Lardy, 1987b: 150). However, some new measures, such as the expansion of the tax base through the introduction of an agriculture tax, commodity tax, and a new commercial and industrial tax helped to control the situation. With these measurements, the government was able to strengthen its fiscal position.

The real issues China faced were, however, in international relations. The postwar years had set the fault lines of conflict. Among others, two were important outcomes of the so-called bipolarity in international relations. First, it brought "long peace and order" to Europe after a "long war" featured with anarchy and chaos. In Europe, the United States and the USSR agreed to limit themselves within the boundaries of their respective spheres of influence. However, the rest of the world, particularly Asia, turned out to be the home of a new wave of imperial confrontation. Second, when the United States took over as the new imperial leader of the capitalist world-system, the exclusion of Eastern Europe, China, and some other parts of the world increased the severity of competition for the inevitable expansionism of global capitalism. There were three options that the United States worked on: "reconstruction" of Europe; Latin America to become the backyard of capitalist-imperial experiments; and the opening of South Asia, the Middle East, and Africa through decolonization (Wallerstein, 2000). To "contain" the "domino effect" of communist revolutions in the postcolonial world, the United States launched a variety of institutional mechanisms, such as that China had to accept an "unequal relationship" with the USSR due to preordained ideological, economic, and strategic reasons. Leaving aside its legacy of being the regional hegemon, China had to content itself to a relegated position in the international system; it was left to accept the USSR as the leader, though Mao endeavored to keep a maneuvering space open (Zhao, 2004).

During the first phase of Mao's government in China, the country worked on two simultaneous fronts. It had to strengthen its economic base and challenge the rise of neo-imperialism in East Asia. On the Korean Peninsula, the result of the Korean War (1950–1953) was that China had successfully checkmated the advancement of the US designs by virtually creating a stalemate by dividing the peninsula into two states. It boosted China's standing in international politics. In Indochina, as France abandoned its colonial occupation in the wake of the disastrous Dien Bien Phu massacre of its forces, the United States took on the responsibility of keeping the region out of communist influence, but it failed and faced humiliating defeat in 1972. In 1962, China fought a short but remarkable war against India and defeated it decisively (Keylor, 1996). Beyond the historical region of influence in East Asia, however, we see China least reactive to international politics. The return of military power, however, did cost a lot for China. During the First Five-Year Plan, the country spent about one-third of its total state expenditure on the purchase of weapons and the expansion of military capabilities.

The years 1949–1957 mark an integrated approach that the CPC developed under Mao. It was the outcome of long-term development of Mao's thoughts on China's economic conditions and a conservative strategy to address the problems. Mao argued that though China, being a feudal society and economy for a long time, could nevertheless have developed into a capitalist society, it was an incomplete penetration of foreign imperialism that accelerated the process and exacerbated the repercussions of socio-economic inequality. Mao compared it with the European social structure that war overturned through bourgeoisie revolutions (Gurley, 1976: 54–58). China's "new-democratic revolution," as he called it

> strives for the joint dictatorship of the revolutionary classes over the imperialists, traitors, and reactionaries, and opposes the transformation of Chinese society into a society under bourgeois dictatorship. Economically, it aims at the nationalization of all the big enterprises and capital of the imperialists, traitors and reactionaries, and the distribution among the peasants of the land held by the landlords, while preserving private capitalist enterprise in general and not eliminating the rich-peasant economy. Thus, the new type of democratic revolution clears the way for capitalism on the one hand and creates the prerequisites for socialism on the other. (Mao, 1965: 327)

Economic transformation, therefore, required that China should become a socialist society before it could aim at any restoration of its status in the world-system. Mao was able to lead the party and the government since he took over in 1936. He made his lieutenants admire his shrewd insight and credible cognizance at decisive moments, such as going into Manchuria against the nationalists and the Japanese, indulging in the Korean War, and accepting the USSR as the leader by providing territorial and ideological concessions to Moscow. By accepting the USSR as rightful to hold and lead the apex level of confrontation against Western neocolonial imperialism in the world, China was able to not only find a space in international politics but also spend its remnant energy on domestic reconstruction efforts. The results of concentration and reconstruction were terrific. With the signing of a thirty-year Friendship Treaty with the Soviet Union, China was provided the much needed financial support of millions of dollars. During the First Five-Year Plan (1953–1957), the USSR provided investment to rebuild the dead industrial units and a hundred new industrial plants for machine-building, coal, iron, and steel (Bailey, 2001: 161). Despite that Sino-Soviet relations remained strained and issues kept affecting the growth of China's international standing, the country made immense progress in the first decade under communist rule. Land reforms led to the formation and growth of Agricultural Producers' Cooperatives (APCs), a target achieved in 1957. The First Five-Year Plan witnessed the growth of national income at 8.9 percent per annum. The biggest contribution was caused by industrialization, which grew by 18.7 percent, while the agricultural sector could grow at a modest rate of only 3.8 percent. Income for the working class increased by 40 percent compared to the cost of living, which could jump by only 10 percent. Income for the rural population and agricultural working class grew by one-third during the plan years. Indices of human development were also impressive; average life expectancy was 36 years in 1950, but it went up to 57 in 1957. Urbanization increased from 57 million in 1949 to 100 million in 1957. The number of children attending school rose from 25 percent to 50 percent during these five years. This is significant because Maoism placed a higher emphasis on education and the transformation of ideas as the prerequisite of social transformation aimed at "the making of the communist human being" (Gurley, 1976: 6). There were two important consequences of these developments. First, the first decade laid down the foundations that China could develop on quickly and firmly. It could have been a significant development in the international economic system because China's growth would have provided an alternative model to the semi-peripheral countries in the capitalist world-system. During the times when there were fewer countries to be placed on the semi-peripheral ladder in the hierarchy of the world-system, China was truly inspired to provide not only an alternative source of "development" but a challenge to the US-centric system as well. Second, they supported the personality cult of Mao. He was once again recognized as a genuinely cognizant and visionary leader of the country.

These achievements faced a serious setback in the following years, however. As mentioned, though Mao had no other choice but to accept the USSR's leadership in international politics and economics, he was least willing to submit to the relegated positional standing of China in the world-system dominated by bipolar global politics. As early as 1956, Mao was reportedly expressing his alienation and distrust of the Soviet model of economic development. The principal differences between Soviet and Chinese conditions such as agriculture and colossal population required, in Mao's view, that China should concentrate on light industry, agricultural modernization, industrialization in the countryside, installation of labor-intensive projects, and strict adherence to Maoist communist principles in order to deepen communism as the ideology of life (Bailey, 2001). Collectively, these founding ideas were espoused to be the guiding objectives of the Second Five-Year Plan, also known as the Great Leap Forward. More importantly, in his speech titled "On the Ten Great Relationships," Mao outlined what he believed to be the future direction of the party, politics, and national economic development. In particular, he stressed on bridging the inequality gap between various sectors of the economy and synchronizing them with the ideological position of the party (Mao, 1977: 284–307). It is important to mention that by the time the Second Five-Year Plan went into the implementation phase, the cleavages among the top leadership of the party were quite open. Mao, keeping in view the criticism of Stalin and his policies in the Politburo of the Soviet Union, proclaimed to "let a hundred flowers bloom, and a hundred schools of thought contend." It was a deliberate attempt to bypass pressure from top leadership in the party and insist on the mass-based reinvigoration of the revolution.

The origins of the Great Leap Forward and its catastrophic repercussions, however, are both domestic and international. Domestically, cleavages within the top cadre of the CPC appeared as one group, led by vice chairman of the CPC Liu Shaoqi, wanted to influence the direction of economic development, while Mao was least willing to lose his grip on the party, politics, economy, and foreign affairs. As the Great Leap Forward was the brainchild of Mao, he made a futile attempt to control the damage from unintended consequences. Though Mao accepted the criticism, he was particularly impatient to the critical appraisals of those belonging to the group led by Shaoqi. Defense minister Peng Dehuai criticized Mao for his approach in the Great Leap Forward and its disastrous consequences in 1959 after his return from the USSR, resulting in his ouster from the position (Lieberthal, 1987). The intra-party politics pushed Mao to reinitiate the Great Leap Forward in 1960 with even more disastrous consequences, the most important being the Great Famine, which killed 45 million people due to starvation "coercion, terror, and systematic violence" (Dikotter, 2010). During 1958–1966, three factors could be considered responsible for the lower-than-possible economic performance in China: competing interpretations of the motivations, processes, and consequences of the Great Leap Forward; second-tier party leadership squabbling for the looming replacement of Mao; and Mao's personal understanding of bureaucratic rule within the polity of the country (Lieberthal, 1987). More importantly, however, the withdrawal of Soviet aid in the wake of sidelining officials closer to Moscow and Mao's criticism of Soviet leader Nikita Khrushchev played a vital role in foiling the plans of economic growth. The economic consequences of the wrangling were horrific. Yearning to achieve higher growth rates, the policymakers kept revising the production targets by inflating them to unprecedented levels. It put pressure on the urban resources, and a higher number of workers were put into the factories to produce more. It also drained human resources from the countryside and brought the agricultural sector under stress, therefore increasing the gap between the facts reported to the Politburo and the realities on the ground. Grain production actually fell by 13 percent in 1959 compared to the previous two years. It fell further in 1960 when an additional loss of about 11 percent in the production of grains was found, thus making 1960 the lowest grain production year since independence. Production of other crops also met the same fate. Mass mobilization toward industries also could not produce what Mao and his associates wanted. During 1958–1962, industrial growth faced a setback as the production of coal declined from 230 million tons to 180 million tons. Production in the light industry, the focus of Mao's plan, declined by about 30 percent. The heavy industry, however, faced a huge setback of a 65 percent in production during these years. Mortality rates increased as well; the ratio went up from 11.1 per thousand in 1956 to 25.4 in 1960, though it fell back to 14.2 per thousand in 1961. The year 1960 proved unprecedented in Chinese history as it reduced the country's population by at least 10 million in one year, the highest number in Chinese history (Lardy, 1987b: 372–77). It is quite appropriate to state that 1958–1962 and then 1966–1976 were the lowest years of Chinese economic growth by any standards. As the GDP growth record shows, Chinese performance during 1949–1957 and then 1962–1966 had been better. Most of the economic gains in these two periods were undone by the following years of violence and political wrangling inside the CPC.

The international dimension of China's low economic performance is very significant for the corroboration of my main arguments in this book. When China signed the thirty-year Friendship Treaty with the Soviet Union, Mao knew that China was agreeing to a relegated positional standing in the world-system by allowing the USSR to lead the communist bloc in global politics. For Mao, it was acceptable, as the USSR was ready to confront the capitalist world for its imperialist policies and establish an egalitarian structure in the regions under communism. Strained Sino-Soviet relations, even before the CPC came to power in 1949, however, solidified Mao's impression of the USSR's inability to effectively counter the economic and political onslaught of Western capitalism. In particular, Mao was mindful of the withdrawal of Soviet aid to China in the midst of the economic crisis of the Great Leap Forward. The USSR was also least willing to provide China with nuclear weapon technology, something Mao publicly yearned to get. The USSR's role in the Sino-Indian War of 1962 deepened his suspicions about the Soviet role in the foreign policy behavior of China. In 1961, Mao went public to lament Khrushchev for his policy of "peaceful coexistence." In Mao's opinion, it was equal to abandoning the endeavor to establish a socialist world economic system and instead joining the capitalist world-system (Cuming, 1996: 31). The Cuban Missile Crisis and subsequent succumb of the USSR to US pressure confirmed to Mao the inability of Khrushchev to put up credible resistance against US imperialism (Mark, 2013: 45–51). In response, Mao adopted two visible patterns of foreign policy behavior. First, instead of claiming leadership of anti-imperial states and powers in the world, China focused on saving its own economic autonomy while trying to control the damage in its relations with the Soviet Union. Second, it tried to preserve its influence in its traditional areas of interest: East and Southeast Asia. It supported the North Korean communist regime in the war against South Korea aided by the United States. It also supported communist forces in Vietnam both politically and militarily. In Indonesia, it attempted to aid and promote the spread of communism through the Communist Party of Indonesia (PKI) but failed, resulting in the large-scale massacre of communist supporters in the country during the initial years (1965–1966) of Suharto rule (Mortimer, 1974). In the international economic system, however, there was far less left for China compared to its pre-1840 positional standing in global economic hegemony. Chinese products found the least space in international markets. Bipolar global politics affected diplomatic space for China, as the Republic of China occupied a permanent seat on the United Nations Security Council until 1971.

> The quest for economic autonomy and political independence was main reason for the reduction in China's positional standing in the global economic system. Mao had a clear anti-imperial approach. He was least willing to submit to the demands of the capitalist countries due to his ideological orientation, historical experiences, and political compulsions in the global system. In September 1949, at the opening of the proceedings of the Chinese People's Political Consultative Conference, the gathering where he was inaugurated as head of the People's Republic of China, Mao stated: "The Chinese have always been a great, courageous and industrious nation; it is only in modern times that they have fallen behind. And that was due entirely to oppression and exploitation by foreign imperialism and domestic reactionary governments. . . . Ours will no longer be a nation subject to insult and humiliation. We have stood up. (Mao, 1977: 17)

Simultaneously, he was sure that China could outpace Britain in less than two decades if it could grow according to its potential (Lardy, 1987a: 362). The strategy he picked stressed mass mobilization more than financial and material investment. He initiated and did far better in collectivizing the land and developing APCs, thus virtually meeting the condition of modernization that requires "a revolutionary break with the past" (Moore, 1966: 431). Mao shut the Shanghai Stock Exchange down and nationalized all the banks and other financial institutions. During the Cultural Revolution, all banks and financial institutions were merged into the People's Bank of China and all pension funds were liquidated. Foreign investors of European and Japanese origin were harassed to abandon their industrial enterprises. Foreign trade was redirected from the Western countries and Japan to the communist bloc. To carry on the process of industrialization, particularly at times when China had little than the required capacity of foreign exchange reserves and capital to import technology and machinery from the capitalist world, he had to rely on autarkic policies such as mass mobilization and indigenous production. Since China was at odds with the status quo powers of the world-system, it had little, if any, influence to determine the processes for expanding its commercial relations with the core. China and the capitalist system were the antonyms of each other. In tough times, Mao bargained with the USSR and, in the 1970s, allowed the establishment of diplomatic relations with the core of the world-system, including the United States. Mao, however, did not let any country influence China's international anti-imperialist posture, foreign policy in its backyard, and economic policies. Mao defined foreign policy when he stated, "Internationally, we belong to the side of the anti-imperialist front headed by the Soviet Union, and so we can turn only to this side for genuine and friendly help, not to the side of the imperialist front" (Mao, 1975: 417).

China lacked capital and was least willing to submit to the demands of capitalism to borrow financial tools from the institutional mechanism set by the core in the capitalist system. In 1974, when the Mao government rejected the World Bank's offer to join the platform, one of the two reasons it cited was that there were some inherent contradictions between the nature, scope, and powers of these international organizations and the socialist economy of China (Jacobson and Oksenberg, 1990: 64). China's capacity to integrate and gain advantages from Bretton Woods institutions, even if it wanted, was curtailed due to a variety of sanctions imposed on it by the core countries in the wake of the Korean War and support provided to the Viet Minh in Vietnam. Given its "excessive obsession" with the notion of sovereignty, "Beijing insisted on the one hand that China be accorded due respect by other politically powerful countries, and demanding on the other hand special privileges due to China's economic underdevelopment and past victimization." Since it did not receive an ideal treatment, Beijing struggled "to gain the benefits of global economic exchange while maintaining its sovereignty" (Roy, 1998: 4, 77). China, as long as it remained outside the orbit of capitalism, could grow only modestly and had to rely on indigenous resources. By the end of the Mao era, China was a semi-peripheral country by the standards widely accepted across the spectrum of theoretical approaches to world-systems analysis.

As one of the three countries being looked at in this book, Chinese post-1949 geo-economic and politico-economic choices and conditions seem to be unique to an extent and can arguably be labeled as nongeneralizable. One can argue that China had a self-imposed style of foreign economic policy whose one corollary was that it was unable to integrate into an economic system that remained not only alive but had expanded and penetrated in numerous other areas of the world before 1978. One may also argue that China's denial to become part of the world in terms of the capitalist division of labor pushed it to lag further behind other countries in economic and technological development. This is true. However, truer is that China (and other countries) redefined its identity in the light of ideological confrontation and positioned itself against Western imperial designs. Instead of submitting to the procrustean bed of the capitalist system, China preferred to lag behind in the global competition for economic development by acquiring foreign technology. While there was disagreement about the possible role of advanced Western technology in the country's industrialization process, the Maoist perspective did prevail that "political purity was more important than technical expertise and efficiency" and that "even if Western practices seemed to be more productive, they came at the cost of exploiting workers and other kinds of social injustice" (Roy, 1998: 83). The fact that the paraphernalia of global economic development, as they were defined in the 1960s and 1970s, contradicted the ideological posture the CCP had adopted under Mao pushed China to lower the scale of its commercial contact with the West and instead focus on its own indigenous development.

However, this does not mean to say that China shut itself down regarding foreign trade; it did trade with Japan, Hong Kong, and the nonaligned world. Despite that the United States posed a highly consequential economic embargo against Beijing and the USSR withdrew its vital economic assistance in the wake of the Sino-Soviet split, Beijing did import the technology and machinery it required to carry on its industrialization process. China's foreign economic policy was successful in exploiting the shifts in international diplomacy. In the first instance, the Eisenhower administration failed to convince its allies in Europe and Asia to shut down trade relations with China. After the CPC took over and made many foreign investors leave the country by abandoning their businesses, which were later on nationalized, British traders managed to survive in some sectors by following the burdensome rules and regulations. Though the British government followed a coordinated policy devised with the United States in the wake of the Korean War, it removed a number of the sanctions in 1956–1957 (Shao, 1991: 109). In the second half of the 1950s, other Western European countries, Japan, and Canada also relaxed some of their trade sanctions. Instead, there took place a kind of "credit race" within the capitalist bloc to promote commercial relations, primarily grain trade, with China. During the first half of the 1960s, there emerged a virtual "Japanese/Western race for commercial relations with China as trade relations expanded from agricultural to heavy machinery, technology, and aircrafts" (Mitcham, 2005). However, it is significant to keep in mind that these relations did not lead China to compromise its international anti-imperial posture, support for communist movements in and beyond Asia, and overwhelming emphasis on self-reliance. China lacked foreign direct investment, which had virtually come to a standstill during the Cultural Revolution.

CHINA: POST-MAO ASCENDANCE IN THE WORLD-SYSTEM

The year 1976 proved to be a turning point in the political-economic history of China. The most significant development was the natural removal of the top leadership of the country. In January, Zhou Enlai, the country's premier since 1949, died. In July, Zhou De, co-founder of the CPC and commander of the People's Liberation Army (PLA) for over two decades, died. In September that year, Mao himself died. The period 1976–1980 is truly a transitional phase during which China moved from a Marxist-Leninist-Maoist ideological identity to a capitalist form of economic system muffled in socialist slogans. The death of Mao and his associates enabled the reformers to overcome and control the ideological faction within the CPC and elevate those who had been purged by Mao and his Gang of Four. Ideologically, the reformers bowed to Mao and his services for the country; practically, he was gradually scrapped away from the economic policies and China's moved toward integration into the capitalist world-system. The real change in the direction and orientation of the country's economic system took place in December 1978. In the Third Plenum of the Eleventh Central Committee of the Communist Party meeting, reformers backed by Deng Xiaoping prevailed over Maoist elements led by Hua Guofeng not only ideologically but also from the perspective of economic and foreign policies. The re-evaluation of the ideological stance of the party—accepting the role of market forces in the modernization process of the country—contradicted with the teachings and policies of Mao. The fact that Mao had been resisting the intrusion of "rightists" in the party and government machinery needed to be adjusted in the records of history. These two questions were debated and in the Sixth Plenum of the Eleventh Central Committee Party meeting in June 1981 when the CPC passed a resolution commending Mao for his great services to the country with "some errors" having been committed by him, particularly during the "bad ten years." His services, the resolution announced, were far heavier than his mistakes, and his principles would remain the crystallizing force for the collective wisdom of the party.

The resolution eased the task of creating a space for the reformers to keep Mao's name on paper while in fact accepting capitalism as their de-facto economic policy. The three-decade-long resistance on the part of communists in China against the introduction or practice of market principles in domestic and foreign economic policies eventually met an abysmal failure. During 1949–1977, China had a very intolerant attitude toward any role of the foreign capital. It became the most prominent feature of economic policies even before Deng became the most powerful person, but without any official designator of the country. Though China started borrowing foreign capital in little amounts, it did start integrating into the capitalist economic system. China declared 1978 "the year of diplomacy" as Chinese state officials visited Western countries and met officials and investors to encourage them to invest in China. A delegate of the ministerial level was sent to visit Western European cities, industries, and higher education institutions and, on its return, required to write reports and present its findings before the top leadership of the country. Deng himself made more than a dozen visits to foreign capitals and economic hubs such as Japan, Singapore, Burma, and the United States. The Chinese, and particularly Deng himself, were interested in knowing the role of foreign direct investment in the economic development of these countries. The effect of these visits was that China "learned" about modern capitalism and adopted an "open-door" policy.

With only $14 billion in foreign trade in 1977, China went up to $21 billion in 1978 (Coase and Wang, 2012: 35). Foreign direct investment (FDI) took some time, however. Following the models of other Southeast Asian countries, China started establishing "Special Economic Zones" in coastal provinces and signed contracts with European and American companies to invest in China. According to International Monetary Fund (IMF) data, China received $430 million in FDI in 1982, which climbed to $11.156 billion in 1992, $44.237 billion in 1997, $53.074 billion in 2002, $171.535 billion in 2008, and $290.928 billion in 2013. Hong Kong (before its eventual emergence into China), Taiwan, the United States, and Japan have been the largest source of foreign direct investment in the country. In 2020, at the peak of COVID-19 crisis, China was the top recipient of foreign direct investment: $163 billion. However, in 2023, as business disputes between China and the United States intensified, the FEDI went down to only $15 billion. According to the same statistical data source, China's exports were $9.75 in 1978 but then grew to $30.94 billion in 1987, $91.74 billion in 1993, $182.79 billion in 1997, $325.6 billion in 2002, $ 593.33 in 2004, $1,220.46 billion in 2007, $1,898.38 billion in 2011, $2,342.75 billion in 2014, and $2,589.098 billion in 2020. China's imports also grew, but the gap between exports and imports kept growing in an unprecedented manner. Since 1990, China's international trade has been at a surplus, except in 1993, when China had a trade deficit of about $12.22 billion. Since then, it has always been in trade surplus. In 2000, the volume of the surplus was $24.11 billion, which grew to $102 billion in 2005, $181.51 billion in 2010, $382.46 billion in 2014, and $535 billion in 2020. Moreover, the data used in the previous chapter show that since 1978, China's GDP has been growing with an average of about 9.82 percent per annum. Currently, China holds more than $3 trillion dollars in foreign exchange reserves. With this massive integration in the world economy and an ever-increasing surplus in world trade, China is regaining its "super accumulator" status.

Three important points should become the focus at this point. First, it is necessary to look at how the Chinese Communist Party and society transformed into a capitalist economy. In particular, it is necessary to see what "prices"—theoretical as well as practical—were paid in the process of transformation. With the argument that no nation-state can progress unless it has "submitted" to the demands of global capitalism, it is necessary to look at exactly what China has done since 1978 that made it an attractive place of investment for expansionist capitalism and caused it to redefine its position in the global division of labor. Second, China was involved in the world economy and became a member of global trade agreements and organizations, including GATT (General Agreement on Tariffs and Trade) and WTO (World Trade Organization). It is also important to see the magnitude of the impact of these developments since it is where we can see transformative changes in its economic system and a boost in its rise in the world-system. Third, whether China has been able to transform its military power with equal zeal is a question to be seen, if we want to establish an argument of its elevation in the hierarchy of the world-system. This is very significant since I have argued that to elevate its positional standing in the world-system, a country needs to progress in both dimensions of power: the economy and the military.

For China, transformation toward a capitalist economic system was not an easy fix. The current constitution of the country, adopted in 1982 and later significantly amended, reflects the impact of Deng's approach to the economy and society. In its current constitution, China de-emphasizes class struggle and has deleted references to the "dictatorship of the proletariat" while adding a reference to the "people's democratic dictatorship." The constitution explicitly stated ending the revolution and revolutionary radicalism. More importantly, it declared the country's economic system as "the socialist market economy" governed by the "people's democratic dictatorship." It, along with subsequent amendments introduced, therefore, has been labeled more as a "political" constitution than a "legal" constitution that "resorts to the constituent power of the people and their political will" and has "de-revolutionized" the state-society relationship, separating it from any international link with the revolutionary movements against imperialism (Quanxi, 2014).

Even After Deng resolved the question of Mao's status in Chinese history and politics by arguing that he was 70 percent correct and 30 percent incorrect since in later years of his life he was unable to directly contact the masses and see their miseries, the question of communism and Marxist ideas in China's economic and foreign policies loomed. Since the legitimacy of reformists under Deng relied on economic progress, they had to display their legitimacy as soon as possible. The reformists, then, could have done nothing but "open the doors" of China to let the foreign capital, investment, technology, and, in fact, the system come in and do the job (Chang, 1980). They also required generating competition in the national market by permitting greater autonomy to state-owned enterprises (SOEs) regarding both decision-making as well as selling their products in the marketplace. For the first requirement, top officials, including Deng, himself embarked on the process of establishing SOEs designed to fit the demands and requirements of global corporations willing to invest in China. Liberalization of fiscal control, particularly regarding facilities to the foreign direct investment, was also adopted. In rural areas, de-collectivization, greater autonomy to the peasants through a long-term lease of lands and the establishment of a household responsibility system, and the introduction of light industries away from the urban centers were encouraged. In other words, while the government maintained exclusive control over the direction of economic development, it adjusted to the demands of the capitalist economy by creating a space to attract domestic and foreign investment to do business in a free economic structure with the assurance of their financial security. A household responsibility system was adopted that, in plain words, was nothing but a YOYO ("You're on Your Own") economic venture. In 1978, at the time when the party under Deng's leadership was redefining the philosophy of its relationship between the state and the commune, it declared:

> Economic organizations at all levels in the People's Communes must carry out the principles of "from each according to his ability," "to each according to his work," "more pay for more work," "less pay for less work," and "equal pay for equal work between men and women," strengthen norm management, pay wages according to quantity and quality of work, establish necessary reward-penalty systems and criticize egalitarianism. (Quoted in Chossudovsky, 1986: 43)

In 1984, the CPC issued the "October Directive" introducing the so-called "Socialist Commodity Economy" and the establishment of SOEs in coastal provinces. The reform program, deletion of Maoist ideas from practical economic policies, and increase on the reliance and invasion of foreign capital in the country, for which the October Directive gave the go-ahead, needed a theoretical justification since these developments were contradictory and paradoxical to Marxist ideas and the Maoist concept of self-reliance. In order to defend the redirected party and government policy, the *People's Daily*, the mouthpiece of the Communist Party, stated in December 1984, "We cannot expect the writings of Marx and Lenin of that time to provide solutions to our all current problems" (quoted in Goldman, 1994: 137). The reformists argued that this was a partial rejection of Marxist philosophy to only the extent that "socialist countries should not sell and buy the means of production." Lin Xili, chief economist and guide of the CPC in reforms, criticized Marx by arguing that "reforms are faithful to Marxism, which is an evolving doctrine based on seeking truth from facts" (quoted in Myers, 1991: 262). It, then, was clear that the CPC had realized that to "develop," it needed to transform into a capitalist economy.

China's participation in the capitalist world economic system was not an ideological contradiction for the Chinese reformist leadership as long as it ensured development, economic growth, industrialization, and prosperity. The state, however, kept strict control over the planning and direction of economic development by arguing that "it is necessary to intensify the unified guidance of state plan or social plan and at the same time to utilize the market mechanism for ensuring the socialist orientation for economic development, for ensuring coordination in national economy, among various departments and various regions, for maintaining public interests of the whole society, and for correctly dealing with the relationship of material interests in all respects" (G.-G. Liu, Wu, and Zhao, 1979: 19). Simultaneously, the reform agenda aimed at creating compatibility with global financial institutions produced three results similar to elsewhere (Broad, 1990). First, it led the leadership of the country to change its ideological understanding of the capitalist world-system and China's own prospective economic performance in such an integrated system. Chinese isolationists—remnants of Maoism—were put out of the political spectrum by the end of the 1980s; Marxist economists were also muted. Deng and his followers were then free to use and embrace Western capitalist standards and processes of economic development. Initially though they were not ready to accept the *demands* of international financial institutions, they showed a willingness to accept their *advice* (Jacobson and Oksenberg, 1990: 18, emphasis original). On the part of these international institutions, the core countries pushed them to re-evaluate China's role in the global economy from the perspective of the strategic benefits it could extend to the core. IMF officials, at the time of negotiations with Chinese officials, were reminded of the significance that China's entry into the IMF could extend to the promotion and stability of the global liberal economic order. The terms and conditions of China's admission to these organizations and later the GATT, however, show that it was the state of China that was made to fit into the system. Despite Chinese protests, Taiwan was permitted to take the final benefit of about SDR 124.1 million, leaving for China only SDR 309 million instead of the $450 million initial tag (Jacobson and Oksenberg, 1990: 77). The demand from IMF about the introduction of economic reforms was also met through the privatization of markets, establishment of Special Economic Zones, decentralization of SOEs, introduction of floating labor, lesser taxation and control of capital movement, relinquish gold stocks to international markets, and more importantly, the agreement to share economic data, something that the Chinese had considered highly classified. China redirected its foreign trade from the communist and developing world to the capitalist West. Since its textile industry was flourishing, it had to sign and agree to the conditions of several agreements before it could formally apply for membership in the GATT. It had to shun the centralized planning system in favor of the greater flexibility awarded to the coastal provinces. In 1982, it reorganized its foreign trade administration by merging various institutions into what was named the Ministry of Foreign Economic Relations and Trade (Jacobson and Oksenberg, 1990: 83–89). China also introduced an excessive decentralization of foreign trade. In 1992, the government was controlling the foreign trade of about 112 items. In 1993, they went down to merely 16.

While the core was determined to expand burgeoning capitalism into mainland China, it ensured that the latter's access to the GATT would not infringe on its own interests. A report prepared by the Organisation for Economic Co-operation and Development (OECD) Trade Committee's Working Party on East-West Trade argues that though the member countries of the organization were excited to take China into the agreement, they were afraid that China, being a big country, would offer a number of politico-economic ramifications for them (Seats, 1987). The GATT officials, when informally talking to the Chinese, made it clear that in order to enter into an agreement, China would not only have to accept reducing and, in some cases, eliminating tariffs but also that (1) the level of imports would not be determined by the state but by the market, (2) government corporations responsible for foreign trade would not interpose between foreign sellers and domestic buyers, (3) China would either eliminate or reduce the cumbersome nature of licensing requirements for business and trade, (4) the mechanism of setting the exchange rate would be reorganized, and (5) the nonregulation of foreign exchange would be observed (Jacobson and Oksenberg, 1990: 89). The Chinese officials, however, referred to a number of transformations—reduction in the scope of centralized planning, reduction in intervention in foreign trade and commodities, reduction in the number of items requiring licenses, establishment of a stock market and foreign exchange market, and sharing of economic statistics with international organizations and institutions—as an optimistic gradualist approach aimed at complete integration of China into the world economy. The Chinese government, however, had to adjust several policies in response to objections and concerns raised by the United States, the European community, Japan, and Australia (Jacobson and Oksenberg, 1990: 92–99). In other words, the capitalist core was determined to make sure that its interests were adequately addressed before China could be granted a seat in the GATT. The Chinese were determined to accrue several benefits from this development. China submitted more to the demands of the international institutions than vice versa. It is corroborated by the fact that when asked whether the "GATT will have to make special arrangements to facilitate China's entry," three of the twelve participants in the negotiations strongly disagreed. Moreover, those who even agreed to the statement referred to a number of safeguards the United States, the European community, and other member states had put in place in the final draft of the agreement (Jacobson and Oksenberg, 1990: 103). The clandestine nature of the Chinese official mechanism, however, played an important role and persists in every new development in the international political economy with reference to China.

Second, it affected the functioning of the government by redefining the relationship between Chinese society and the revolutionary state. As mentioned above, the Chinese reform agenda in rural areas redefined the nature of agricultural production, access, and consumption. Starting with those areas where the CPC had low popularity or the consequences of the Great Leap Forward were enormous, a contract system whereby the control of a piece of land was awarded to a person or family enabled peasants to exercise greater autonomy and create the market economic system. Three kinds of contracts—contracting output to the group, contracting output to the household, and contracting everything to the household—were designed, and the government asked the contracting party to produce a certain amount of production beyond which it was up to the contracting party to sell and earn a living (Shih, 2001). In return, however, the government was eager to withdraw all kinds of support that it had laid down under Mao or even Deng Xiaoping. To "adjust" to the demands of the global capitalist system, the government let the labor "on the loose" to move from rural areas to the coastal and adjacent industrializing provinces. The paradoxical term "socialist market economy" resulted in denial of welfare rights to rural workers migrating to cities, introduction of a contract system and the removal of job security, downsizing of the SOEs, production of an unemployed pool of the workforce in order to put pressure on contractual job holders to go the extra mile to perform, increased surveillance and quantification of performance, rationalization of salaries and job benefits, introduction of flexible seasonal jobs, merging of enterprises, and "the creation of giant conglomerates and multinational companies capable of competing with international rivals." The result of these changes, many of which were designed to align the economic system along the lines recommended by global institutions in the core countries, was that the process produced a labor surplus of "more than 150–170 million people which remains after the outflow to the cities, the induction into town and village enterprises, and the revitalization (and effective privatization) of agricultural production" (O'Leary, 1998: 58–63). During the rapid growth of the market economic system, those who could not go along were considered "a dependent social group destined to disappearance" (Day, 2013: 70). The rationalization of jobs in the SOEs resulted in aggravating the deteriorating conditions of the working class, which had already been left to take care of itself. The growth of the private economy, constitutionally recognized in 2002, led to the hiring of more than half of this population on market conditions. The result is that while a large part of the population could come out of poverty through inland migration and industrialization, many people in today's China are left to struggle with no socialist patronage. The private sector now comprises more than 80 percent of China's industry, if we take into account town and village enterprises (Brown and Von Ruda, 2008). However, since agriculture still is one of the leading sectors of the national economy and currently employs the most significant percentage of the workforce while producing less of a share in the GDP, it is necessary to keep in mind the consequences of the introduction and penetration of the market economic system and the removal of socialist policies have brought to the rural working class.

Third, the state "learned" and "socialized" itself with the capitalist system. From the perspective of the CPC and government officials, this socialization was necessary to "adopt" the thought process required to develop a capitalist mentality. In order to "learn" about the technological progress the world had made during the Mao era, top officials, including Deng Xiaoping, visited the Asian and European countries. It is said that when Deng visited the manufacturing and assembly plant of Nissan in Japan, he told his host, "Now I understand what modernization means" (Coase and Wang, 2012: 33). Deng himself encouraged and sent top officials to visit European factories and financial institutions and learn about the market economy. European and American economists were invited to "train" Chinese officials about the functioning of the market economic system. In 1978 only, Chinese delegations led by vice premiers and top government officials visited more than twenty-five countries; China also hosted more than thirty state visits, mostly from the Western world (Coase and Wang, 2012: 33). To placate the domestic audience and Maoist-communist conservatives, Deng Xiaoping named the venture "socialism with Chinese characteristics," by which he meant to proceed ahead with material development in coastal cities and rural areas with a socialist character. Contrary to the conventional understanding of socialism, however, Deng labeled it "the primary stage of communism" and argued that it would seek "highly developed productive forces and an overwhelming abundance of material wealth," at the end of which "the principle of from each according to his ability and to each according to his needs will be applied" (Xiaoping, 1984). Learning from the experiences of Western capitalist development, therefore, Deng was more interested in improving China's position in the world-system and less concerned about ideological issues. He famously argued, "It does not matter if a cat is black or white, so long as it catches mice" (quoted in Naughton, 1993). The government and CPC officials resented the loss of time under Mao delaying China's integration into the capitalist world-economy and its accrual of the potential benefits. During China-IMF negotiations, Chinese officials reportedly inquired about "what China's quota would have been had the people's republic held continuous membership and its quota been regularly and proportionately increased" (Jacobson and Oksenberg, 1990: 75). Socialization enabled the Chinese to learn manipulative tactics such as currency devaluation and using cheaper labor and production costs to attract foreign direct investment to the country.

China's joining the WTO shows that the state accepted integration into global capitalism as an inevitable requirement of the process of industrialization and elevation in the global economy. The country was virtually left with no other choice but to agree to the demands of the capitalist economic system. The terms and conditions the WTO) imposed on China took away a lot of its economic sovereignty. At the conclusion of prolonged negotiations spanning over fifteen years, China agreed "to undertake a series of important commitments to open and liberalize its regime to better integrate into the world economy and offer a more predictable environment for trade and foreign investment in accordance with WTO rules." Precisely, these commitments, among many others, included the following: nondiscriminatory treatment to all WTO members; elimination of dual pricing practices and differences in treatment accorded to goods produced for sale in China in comparison to those produced for export; elimination of price controls for the purposes of affording protection to domestic industries or service providers; modification of existing domestic laws and enactment of new legislation fully in compliance with the WTO agreement; full and unrestricted access of all enterprises to import and export all goods and trade them throughout the customs territory with limited exceptions; and elimination of any export subsidies on agricultural products (WTO, 2001). The WTO also addressed the concerns of the core countries about world trade. In an unprecedented nine-hundred-page-long agreement with China, the organization put in place a number of "unfriendly" rules and regulations resulting in the initiation of an unprecedented number of trade disputes against the country. The most important discriminatory provisions were "nonmarket economy provisions." Originating in the GATT, the capitalist countries erected a barrier against communist and socialist countries by refusing to provide them full inclusion and access to the benefits of world trade on the pretext that these countries—the Eastern European countries, the Soviet Union, China, and other communist countries with the state being the charge and driving the pattern of economic development and growth—patronized economic development in a mercantilist manner. The developed world and Japan used this pretext in the WTO-China negotiations to refuse to extend the full privileges and benefits of free global trade. Since China was yearning to join global trade but unwilling to relinquish SOEs and agricultural subsidiary policies altogether, it was left with no other choice but to accept the discriminatory provisions. The European Union, the United States, and Japan were able to secure their respective "personalized" agreements with China over the WTO. According to the WTO-China agreement, Beijing accepted being labeled as a nonmarket economy country for fifteen years after joining the organization. More importantly, and contrary to WTO policy with any other member country, China was deprived of the power to claim itself as a market economy; it was left to the member countries to treat China as a nonmarket economy if they saw fit. The consequences of this status have brought huge losses to the country's exporters. Beijing has been dragged into some trade disputes involving all the major powers of the world. During 1995–2008, about one-fifth of all antidumping complaints were launched against China, of which about 70 percent were settled against Beijing (Pan, 2015). It has been observed that "China has become the leading target of antidumping and countervailing investigations worldwide over the past two decades." It has also been observed that "these measures of contingent protection are particularly damaging, have a strong chance of success, and have become the main instruments for addressing US trade concerns with China outside of the multilateral framework" (Zeng, 2013: 356, 359). Though China has used the WTO's dispute settlement mechanism to counterattack, it has also faced negative consequences from the discriminatory provisions in the China-WTO agreement. China's quest to be removed from nonmarket economy status have been foiled by both the European Union and the United States. Currently, about four thousand Chinese products are subjected to antidumping policies by the United States (Pan, 2015). The free market economy is a hoax; if and whenever needed, the West does not hesitate to take mercantilist measures to protect its status in the world economic system.

Despite the discriminatory treatment the country received, China has re-emerged on the global stage as one of the most powerful economies in the world, a status it enjoyed in the seventeenth and eighteenth centuries. During the Mao era, China was nowhere near the developed world both in terms of GDP and GDP growth rate. The reforms have brought improvement in China's positional standing in the world-system. Before it could join the WTO, China was the ninth largest economy in the world. In 2004, it became the fifth largest economy. In 2009, it surpassed Japan to become the second largest economy in the world. The rapid rise during 2009–2014 in terms of GDP shows the benefits China could accrue in terms of foreign direct investment and surplus accumulation. China currently attracts the highest share in global foreign direct investment and holds the largest foreign currency reservoir in the world. Though there is speculation that the country's economic growth could gradually calm down and stabilize, China is still poised to take over the United States as the largest economy in the world by 2030.

CHINA AS THE SEMI-CORE IN THE WORLD-SYSTEM

That China's impressive elevation as a rising power in the world-system pertains more to its economic transformation and development than anything else requires us to re-evaluate its positional standing in the world-system. To an extent, the rise of China is the reversal of the shift that took place some three hundred years ago, after the development of capitalism in Europe. European mercantile and colonial policies took the supremacy in the world economy away from China. The West developed a capitalist system and reigned over the world for more than two hundred years, during which it was able, thanks to its imperial power and exports overseas, to accumulate capital and wealth and put a huge gap between itself and the rest of the world. The dynamics of the global political economy today can be understood by contextualizing this historical development. China's growing dominance in the global economy and politics is a transitional shift, at the end of which the United States would be lagging behind and eventually lose its status in the international system. More precisely, China's rise in the complex functioning of the world economy must be seen as the expansion of global capitalism. Globalization this time is more about compartmentalization and decentralization of production and consumption in an increasingly interdependent world. With an inherent tendency to expand and accumulate to the benefit of the capitalist class, capitalism found it beneficial to exploit China's capacity and potential as the manufacturer of the world. As mentioned, the capitalist class and multinational corporations were represented in negotiations aimed at integrating China into the world economy. Consequently, China was pushed to accept the terms of the global capitalist system. China could grow because it showed its willingness to accept the dominance of the capitalist system and benefit from global capitalism. In fact, it showed its willingness to turn into "pink" from the "red." An evaluation of China's rise in the system must take into account the compromises the state made to be able to develop and become one of the actors in the world economy.

Still, there are some elements missing from the discourse. The contemporary phase in the world economy is not characterized by merely the rise of China or the fall of the West. Like any other country in the world, China had a desire to grow and develop. It would find socialism not only insufficient but, as a long-term approach, exhaustive and painstaking. The country could neither rely on Maoism-socialism nor provide any alternative indigenous path to development, one that could promise to bring China to where it finds itself today. Though the Mao era laid down the foundation on which the country could grow, the politics of economic collapse during the Cultural Revolution left socialism disgruntled and rejected in practice. The post-Mao era required Western technology, which could only be imported along with the economic system. Therefore, while for conservative socialists the arrival of Western financial institutions, multinational and transnational corporations, and foreign money was the restart of imperial trade in the eighteenth and nineteenth centuries, for reformists, it was an inevitable solution to address the rampant poverty of a growing population. The lure of development and modernization as represented by the West found its way into China mainly because the country eventually realized that ideological rhetoric could not provide the stability required without improving economic conditions and thus elevating its status in the world-system. However, China and the global capitalist system found compatible interests that could be served through the country's integration into the globalized system of production and consumption. Mutual transformation of both China and global capitalism made it possible for the country to regain its status as a super accumulator in the contemporary world and for the system to sustain, at least for the foreseeable time, expand, and ensure the preservation of the status quo—the position as the core in the world-system—for an extended period. The decline in the hegemonic power of the United States, the fall of the communist bloc, and the unleashing of capitalist forces to introduce a new global division of labor made the rise of China possible (Hung, 2009: 13).

China's elevation in the system is dependent not only on its economic rise but also its skill to use the fungibility of economic growth for military power. Historically, China has been a regional power with limited imperial designs. During the dynastic and republic periods, its military strength had mainly been meant to suppress rebellions. The rise of guerrilla warfare under Mao and the rise of the People's Liberation Army in communist China were also meant to address domestic security issues and defend Chinese strategic interests in the region, such as during the Korean and Vietnam Wars. Anti-imperialist in essence, Mao had no other choice but to depend on the Soviet Union to provide weaponry, defense technology, and international security. Conflict within the communist bloc was grounded in a realist competition whereby the USSR was least willing to allow China to become a strong military power. Therefore, the military alliance established during the early 1950s provided only outdated and obsolete weapons and fighters to China, despite that they were very costly, and China had to spend almost half of its budget on the purchase of these weapons (Garthoff, 1966). The post-Stalin USSR tried to belittle Mao's personality cult in China through the public ridicule of Stalinism in the communist world. The most significant dimension of the Sino-Soviet split, which eventually took place in the early 1960s, was due to Mao's publicly expressed desire to acquire nuclear capability, which China achieved in October 1964. However, a detailed analysis of global developments in the early 1960s shows that it was due to the abhorrence of Western imperialism and the inability of Soviet leaders to withstand diplomatic and political pressure that Mao went public to criticize Moscow, thus effectively reducing Sino-Soviet military cooperation (Luthi, 2008: 230). China's quest for military power, therefore, had to rely mostly on domestic sources. By the end of Mao's era, though China's military power was not strong in terms of technology and weaponry, the country had gained the ability to defend itself against foreign aggression, defend its strategic interests against Western imperialism, and achieve nuclear status.

Military modernization was one of the "four modernizations" announced as the cornerstone theme of reform agenda under Deng Xiaoping. Because post-Mao China was able to integrate with the world and secure fiscal surplus through this integration by improving its foreign exchange reserves, it was able to spend on defense modernization. The legacy of communist treatment of national strengths as classified information, however, has been prevalent more in national defense than any other sector. While China was willing to share economic facts, such as the total worth of currency notes in circulation and the growth rates of different sectors of the economy, it remained highly sensitive in making public information related to its defense progress and spending. This practice is prevalent even today, as various international institutes, research organizations, and departments of defense struggle to estimate the actual volume of the budget being spent on defense and the nature of weapons country is developing. Officially, since 1989, China has been spending more than 9 percent of its annual budget on national defense and its principal organization, the PLA (People's Liberation Army) (Dreyer, 2007). However, these statistics are doubted by the developed countries and their organizations, such as the US Department of Defense, the International Institute for Strategic Studies, or the Stockholm International Peace Research Institute (SIPRI). In 2008, China declared the volume of its defense budget to be \$57.2 billion, while SIPRI considered it to be \$86.4 billion and the Department of Defense estimated it to be \$105 billion (Cordesman and Lin, 2014). One of the main reasons for this noticeable difference is that several defense-related expenditures are not counted in official statistics. China does not mention foreign weapon procurements, subsidies to defense-related SOEs, paramilitary force expenditures, defense-related construction projects, and administrative costs such as payments to demobilized personnel. That China quadrupled its defense-related procurement budget from foreign suppliers during 1997–2006 tells the genesis of the differences being reported by various organizations (Dreyer, 2007: 652). According to various reports and the data on the military ranking shared in the previous chapter, China has the second highest defense budget after the United States. The difference between the two, however, is unbridgeable, as the US defense budget is more than the next twenty-six countries put together, of which twenty-three are US allies under NATO or other alliances. The offensive military capability of the PLA has been built on both the workforce and modern weaponry. However, it lags behind in terms of quality, technology, precision, and other aspects of modern warfare.

A comparison of the United States, NATO countries, and China shows that Beijing lags behind palpably. A comparison between the United States and China is in favor of China only in terms of number of active personnel, number of tanks, towed artillery, a rocket launcher system, merchant marine strength, fleets, frigates, and patrol craft. In many of these areas, statistics do not reflect the quality of weapons, an area where China lags behind significantly.

Currently, it has more than 200 fifth-generation J-20 aircrafts in operation. Additionally, its most advanced J-31 will be in final shape by the end of 2025. According to a recent report by the US Congressional Research Service, the Chinese military modernization drive concentrates more on quality than quantity. Though China reduced its number of aircraft from around 4,600 in 1990 to nearly 1,500 in 2014, the share of modern and fourth-generation and above aircraft has increased from less than 1 percent to about 50 percent. The percentage of modern forces in all four services (ground, naval, air, and missile) has increased significantly. China is reducing its standing ground force by more than 300,000 in coming years. Simultaneously, it is recruiting qualified officers and improving training quality. The percentage of its naval surface force increased from less than 3 percent in 2000 to about 26 percent in 2010; during this period, the percentage of submarine forces went up from 8 percent to 65 percent, air forces from 2 percent to 25 percent, and ground forces from 5 percent to about 24 percent. China lagged behind the United States in all of these aspects of military powers both in terms of quality and quantity. The difference between NATO and China, then, is far more significant than assumed.

A comparison of US military capability with that of China is an important factor in my calculations since it is where I see China as a partial power in the world-system. China is probably more powerful in terms of its economy than anything else. It is weaker in its military power, however. China is progressing to modernize its armed forces. It is increasing its research and development capabilities in the defense sector. The Central Military Commission, the apex control body of the armed forces of the People's Republic of China, and its four principal departments have increased their capacities, quality, and approach to the role of technological research and development in modern warfare. The General Armament Department, established in 1998 as a part of the reform and modernization agenda of the PLA, "is responsible for the weapons and equipment of the PLA, including maintenance, repair, ammunition, and research, development, testing, and procurement of major weapons, equipment, and ammunition" (Blasko, 2012: 35). Some of these research centers, such as the Academy of Military Sciences, the premier research institute of the PLA, the National University of Defense Technology, and National Defense University (NDU), have installed research and development facilities capable of redefining the concept of warfare for the entire PLA (Blasko, 2012: 36). China has also improved in modern warfare capabilities by investing in research and development and purchasing the latest equipment in nuclear, cyber, and electronic warfare. It has also developed ambitious espionage and exfiltrating networks throughout the developed world (Office of the Secretary of Defense, 2015). These improvements, however, become less significant whenever a US-China comparison is drawn.

Following the indicators used in this study, I argue that China has lagged behind in military technology. Compared to the magnitude of the economic reforms that led the country to master the capitalist style of conducting commercial and economic activities and lured foreign direct investment to the country in an unprecedented manner in human history, China could not achieve any such success in its defense sector. It has been unable to integrate as well into the global arms trade, even as a consumer, as it has in the global merchandise economy. According to a SIPRI report published in 2013, China exported weapons worth only $2.068 billion to Asian and African countries. It was the third largest exporter of weapons in the world but covered merely 6 percent of the total arms trade that year. The United States dominated the market with a 33 percent share in the global arms export, while Russia had a 25 percent share in such exports. China's share in global arms trade as an importer is even lower; according to the same report, China imports only 4.7 percent of the arms sold in the global market. While China's top consumer markets are, respectively, Pakistan, Bangladesh, and Myanmar, its top suppliers are Russia, France, and the Ukraine (Fleurant, Perlo-Freeman, and Wezeman, 2016). China, however, is still far behind in terms of becoming a strategic power of corresponding economic level. According to Michael Chase (2015), the PLA faces two broader categories of weaknesses. Its organizational weaknesses are evident through its "outdated command structures, quality of personnel, professionalism, and corruption." Its shortcomings in combat capabilities include "logistical weaknesses, insufficient strategic airlift capabilities, limited numbers of special-mission aircraft, and deficiencies in fleet air defense and antisubmarine warfare." They are "type 3 weaknesses that degrade the efficiency of the PLA to carry out its missions" (pp. ix, x, 60).

Two plausible reasons explain the Chinese lack of military power as a superpower status. Foremost is that the US-led core countries of the modern world-system are least willing to let rising powers—their economic competitors—redefine the nature of the global division of labor in terms of the manufacturing and production of defense equipment. From a realist perspective, this is a zero-sum game for the core countries. The transnational capitalist class and its global military-industrial complex, however, find it very important to enable the political class of the developed world to prepare and present to their masses a worldview of fear of the rise of China and other non-Western and less democratic countries in the world. It facilitates the war machine and the elites of military-industrial complex to receive substantial fiscal benefits in research, development, and procurement. A combination of patriotism, financial interests, globalization of strategic competition, and actual conduct of warfare in the non-Western world enables the military-industrial complex to keep accumulating capital. The portrait of an economically powerful China is less frightening because it strengthens the international division of labor and the process of capital accumulation in the core by facilitating the expansion of global capitalism through the decentralization and compartmentalization of production. The portrait of military power China, however, is disturbing because it represents a dislodging of the core countries from the top position in the hierarchy of the world-system. Second, though China is increasingly conscious about the changing matrices of strategic relations within Southeast Asia, it has relied on its domestic and regional expertise to develop its own version of modern weapon systems. It is a long-term but perhaps sustainable process of military development. Therefore, though China's strategic posture has been peaceful, it has been firm to defend its strategic interests in the region effectively. It does not portray itself as a threat to the existing global balance of power while ensuring that it is capable of defending itself in any scale of war at the regional level. It is a consistent approach that China has relied on during the last three centuries under different regimes.

There are several convolutions in reaching any conclusion about the status of China's positional standing as a military power in the world-system. Three things make my case strong to consider China as a semi-core country, however. First, China has not entered into any military conflict since its war with Vietnam in 1970. In fact, since the communist revolution, China has not fought any regional war since the Korean War of 1950–1952. Its war with India in 1962 is known as a limited border conflict. Therefore, China's military capabilities on an actual battleground have not been tested for over four decades. By taking into account the unknown volume of China's defense budget, the actual strength of its offensive military capabilities has yet to be seen. The peaceful rise of China, however, eventually will face challenges whenever the core countries of the world-system find their positional standing—the capacity to accumulate capital—under credible threat. The rise of an assertive China in the South China Sea is being observed as a credible challenge to the global political power of the United States. In the post–Cold War world, China has not challenged any military venture beyond its own traditional sphere of influence. Chinese leadership, however, is aware that the era of peaceful rise is eventually going to end. According to Chinese perceptions, by 2020 the "period of strategic opportunity"—"the relatively benign period in the first decades of the new millennia when China can grow its power without serious challenge"—will be over (Gitter, 2016). In this small period, China wants to develop a complex, interdependent system of trade by pulling in greater stakes of countries from Asia and Africa to Europe. China's aggressive economic foreign policy is, therefore, the first test of its power in the changing world-system. For the time being, Chinese leadership has not expressed any explicit desire to convert its regional and interregional economic system into a military alliance. Even if it desires so, China will face enormous challenges since several other countries being integrated into economic bloc have political and territorial conflicts.

Second, the concept that the United States or the core countries are far more powerful militarily compared to China or any other country in the world assumes a hypothetical warfare in which China (or any other country) would alone be competing against a unified front comprised of the developed world and led by the United States. In a world where there are neither permanent friends nor permanent enemies, this may seem highly improbable, or at least quite uncertain. This concept also assumes NATO as a unified body of over twenty countries. While it is true that NATO has been able to remain an effective defense alliance even after the disintegration of the communist bloc and its champion, the Soviet Union, it has been able to do so mainly because it did not face any credible severe conflicts of interest within itself or the various sections of the transnational capitalist class controlling it. In one such test—war in Iraq in 2003—NATO failed to act in a unified manner. Despite that there were several financial interests at stake in this war, such as oil and postwar construction deals, the core could not display unity. The conflicts of interest, particularly economic interests, would become a matter of great concern for the NATO member countries in any possible conflict in or beyond the South China Sea.

Third, we are also uncertain about the dynamics of any possible Chinese strategy to embrace a shift in power in global politics. So far, China has risen peacefully. Economic integration has been the most visible cornerstone of its foreign policy posture. Relying on its status as a super accumulator, it is using its power of more than $3 trillion in foreign exchange reserves to advance its commercial-cum-strategic interests throughout Asia, Africa, and Latin America. In 2013, China floated the idea of "One Belt, One Road" (OBOR) to revitalize the old Silk Route that connected Africa, Asia, and Europe and brought a number of civilizational transformations of immense significance to the regions involved. As reported by *The Economist* in its July 2016 issue, China views the OBOR project as a combination of numerous mega-projects involving more than sixty-five countries and the population of 4.4 billion people in the world—excluding Latin America and Central Africa—and comprising more than one-third of China's foreign investment since the start of the project. Once completed, the total financial investment in more than nine hundred mega projects of infrastructural development, transportation, and energy production is estimated to be more than $4 trillion, though China has not made public the timeline for these projects. The OBOR project will develop into a complex and multipurpose transnational maritime and land Silk Route connecting Western Europe with Southeast and Far East Asia and Africa through China. This is a Chinese version of capitalism characterized by a new endeavor to redefine the division of labor throughout the world by realigning the production and consumption markets revolving around Chinese capitalist interests. The transitional phase of the paradigm shift in the global capitalist structure has been relatively smooth because it hurt the interests of the transnationalized capitalist class the least. The marriage of interests between capitalist China and the transnational capitalist class has enabled the former to grow and elevate its positional standing in the world economy. That the transnational capitalist class is currently enjoying the benefits of Chinese manufacturing and production services explains how controlling the elite class of global capitalism has ensured capitalist expansion by sharing the benefits but keeping the lion's share of the profit. Global corporations are located in the core countries, no matter how they conduct business offshore. A paradigm shift in the nature and geography of capital accumulation, however, may result in the initiation of tough times for the West-dominated world-system, something that seems inevitable.

Though a peaceful transition in the world economy—the re-emergence of China as the epicenter of the world economy—has virtually taken place, the West can still be assured of receiving a more significant share of it. Any such transition in world politics, by which I mean the emergence of China as a military power or the formation of a China-led military alliance, has not taken place yet. China is the second most powerful economy; it is not a credible military power because its modernization drive has not been tested on any actual battleground and it lags behind in technology, research, and development. A partial power, China has aspired to become a member of the core club. A long-term approach looking at the history of China will dictate that China may not find it easy to achieve the status of world hegemon as has been enjoyed by the Britain in the nineteenth century and the United States in the twentieth century. China could grow economically only when it opened its doors to global corporations and provided a conducive environment for the capitalist mode of production to grow through foreign direct investment in the mainland. Nirmal Chandra (2012) argues that China could not have grown as rapidly and as immensely had it insisted on its own nationalist interests and not agreed to the terms and conditions of the corporations, such as deferring the transfer of technology, and with international institutions in terms of ensuring the security of private properties. The return of Western corporations in China after a brief period of about four decades (1949–1989) was made possible only when China concluded that it could not grow while remaining aloof to global capitalism. Though the terms and conditions of the benefits of integration are far better for China compared to its semi-colonial period, it is still important to recognize that, to grow, China allowed the exploitation of its population and resources. Simultaneously, while new powerhouses in global capitalism are emerging, they are least harmful to the interests of the transnational capitalist class. Western corporations have found new allies in Beijing, Shanghai, Hong Kong, and elsewhere. The core therefore has enabled China to grow because it found it to be in its own interests. The lack of or slower transfer of technology, particularly in weapon systems, is where China is pushed behind. SIPRI reports on the global transfer of arms since the 1950s show that China's inventory of imported weapons is not only less impressive but also considerably less advanced. China would find it difficult to rely merely on its economic power to become the credible hegemon of the world. A Chinese world-order, therefore, will take considerable time to emerge and be recognized as an established reality. It has become a semi-core power because it is rapidly redefining the division of labor in industrial production and consumption across the globe. It is still away from becoming a member of the core club in the world-system because it lacks military power. A disequilibrium in its sources of national power is what makes it a semi-core country.

CONCLUSION

In this chapter, I analyzed the fall and rise of China in world history to bring forward evidence in support of the assumptions made in the theoretical framework. At the start of this study, I mentioned a set of hypotheses that, together, laid down a theoretical structure arguing in favor of the dynamic nature of the world-system. Since this study covers a time period during which the regions under study were coerced to transition from being external arenas to become the peripheries of the capitalist world-system, the system could redefine the economic outlook of these areas. I argued that China maintained its position as a super accumulator before the rise of the modern capitalist world-system but lacked any formidable military power to defend its interests against Western imperial powers. Europeans, facing a chronic challenge of trade deficit with China, found American silver and opium to reverse the pattern. However, the Europeans could incorporate China into the world-system only after they had acquired superior military power. It was coercive military power that enabled the British and other European empires to impose unequal treaties on China. The forceful inclusion, then, redefined the economic outlook of the mainland and resulted in the rise of nationalism and communism. China was defeated in all the wars it fought from 1840 until its independence in 1949. Postindependence political realities in China affected its positional standing in the world-system. China could grow only when it accepted and acknowledged the dominance of the capitalist world-system in the world economy. Since 1978, when it started liberalizing its economy and cementing trade relations, through now, China has elevated itself again to become the second largest economy in the world, though it still lags far behind in military power. It fulfills the conditions of a semi-core country and poses credible risks to the status quo of the core powers.

Chapter Three

India

From the Periphery to the Semi-Core (1757–2014)

In the first chapter, I presented major hypotheses and provided a theoretical framework that I aimed to apply to three countries in this study. In the previous chapter, I applied that theoretical framework to China and showed that the fall of China took place when European powers were able to coerce the country into incorporation in the world-system during the eighteenth century. It redefined China's economic outlook as a peripheral country. China, after it had gained independence in 1949, remained a peripheral country until 1978. The rise of pragmatist leadership in the country changed the nature of China's relationship with global capitalism and, the mutually beneficial economic venture between China and expansionist global capitalism enabled the former to re-emerge as an economic powerhouse of the world and to the latter to become a truly global system of trade and prolong its eventual collapse. In this chapter, I look at India during the same period. This chapter will explain India's central position in the precapitalist economy of world-empires. The Europeans had developed a commercial relationship with India even before the discovery of the Cape of Good Hope and the New World. The two geographic discoveries by the end of the fifteenth century enabled the Europeans to promote commercial relations with India. The fall of Mughal empire, this chapter will show, was more political than economic; by the middle of the eighteenth century, the Europeans had found a political vacuum and, relying on their superior military capabilities and political maneuvering, could muster a formidable challenge to India. They used coercive power to, in the end, occupy the entirety of India by exploiting mutual mistrust among various native wrangling states. It was more due to superior strategic capacity than anything else that the British were able to exploit Indian resources and usher the Industrial Revolution in England by the end of the eighteenth century. Indian incorporation into the world-system, thus, redefined its positional standing from economic hegemon in the precapitalist world-system to de-industrialized and impoverished region responsible only for producing raw materials to feed English and other European industries. During this period, India's integration into the world-system depended on its economic restructuring favoring the interests of the core. India's positional standing, therefore, was reduced to that of a periphery responsible for providing raw materials and a vast market of consumable products manufactured in the core. After independence in 1947, India tried to develop an indigenous model of economic growth but found it hard to foul with the international division of labor laid out by the world-system. It was only in the wake of its abandonment of socialist egalitarianism and self-reliance that it started growing. Since one of the leading arguments of this study is that a state can grow only when and to only such an extent following the requirements of the system, I show that India, just like China, could grow only modestly for the time it remained a closed economy under the License Raj. For the first four decades, India did not liberalize its economic policy or open its various sectors to international investors. Global capitalism, thus, found little incentive to develop a mutually beneficial relationship though it desired following its inherent expansionist nature. It was only in the initial years of the 1990s that India rewrote its relationship with global capitalism and started emerging as a new, robust economy in the world. However, since India still is a weak military power, it can be regarded as a semi-core country.

INDIA, EUROPE, THE GREAT DIVERGENCE, AND CONSEQUENCES

The Indian Sub-Continent (today's India, Pakistan, and Bangladesh) was one of the most important regions in world economic history. In the premodern world, the region was an economic powerhouse linked with East Asian, African, Eastern Mediterranean, Eurasian, and European regions. Historically, the region produced food grains, spices, minerals, and metals, which led to the development of extensive trade networks both over the land and through the sea. While the discovery of the Cape of Good Hope at the end of the fifteenth century made it possible to link Europe and Asia through an all-sea route, trade between the regions had been made a fact in the premodern world. According to Pius Malekandathil (2013), before the Portuguese could become the new dominant power in Asia-Europe trade, various Indian ports, such as Bengal, Orissa, Calcutta, Gujrat, Kerala, Goa, Bombay, and Surat, among others, situated all along the long coastal belt of the Southern and Southeastern Sub-Continent had already flourishing maritime trade networks throughout Asia, the Middle East, and Africa. These networks enjoyed the patronage of all the leading powers in the Indian Ocean: the Ottomans, the Safavids, Muslim rulers in India, and China. Intra-Asia trade has been a fact and is believed to have defined the nature of Asia-Europe trade in the pre- and early modern times (Hall, 2011; Kang, 2012). India, like China, became the center of this trade. This centrality in the premodern world, however, did not enable India to maintain its positional standing when it was brought into the capitalist world economy. One of the factors, as in the case of China, was its dismaying defense capabilities. The idea of the "great divergence," as it has been applied to China in the previous chapter, is applicable here in the case of India.

As I have done in the previous chapter for China, here I put in place a clear division between the premodern world-system and the modern and capitalist world-system in the context of India. This transformation, according to Immanuel Wallerstein (1974), started taking place after 1450 and gradually solidified in the seventeenth century. By the end of 1640, Wallerstein argues, the world-system was "still only a European world-system" (p. 10). Wallerstein relies on claiming that *inside* the new European-centered world economy was the core (mainly Central and Western Europe), the semi-periphery (Russia and Eastern Europe), and the periphery (the areas dependent on the center). During this time, there was more than one world economy. However, Wallerstein tries to deal with the question of why only Europe could succeed. The is far more controversial in the case of China than that of India. In economy, India was Europe's competitor before it was brought into the capitalist world-system. This inclusion redefined India's status from the center to the periphery. In warfare, India tried to be a competitor of Europe. Once it was in orbit, its military utility was also redefined; its soldiers were used in the Napoleonic Wars and the World Wars. India became a supplier of human resources, similar to it being a supplier of economic resources.

Without any doubt, India was an economic power in the premodern world, at least before the Europeans could get there using an all-sea route in the wake of the discovery of the Cape of Good Hope. During that time, according to Wallerstein (1979), India was an "external arena" of the expansive European world economy. When the European world economy expanded during the seventeenth century, India was brought into the modern world-system and assigned a relegated positional standing as a periphery meant to serve auxiliary and agrarian needs of the European core. This forceful inclusion redefined the nature of the economic outlook of the whole Sub-Continent and Indian Ocean. India lost its economic status because the European powers succeeded in dictating a new role for it in the emerging world-system. For more than two hundred years, India was physically occupied, and its economy was depleted to serve the interests of the core and its ruling class. Among the reasons for this fall in positional standing, I reiterate here, is the fact that while India could grow when it was in the "external arena" of the expanding European world economy, it failed to defend its status as it was forcefully brought into the world-system through colonialism. The reasons for this great divergence are, therefore, both economic and strategic. To understand the recent rise of India in economic positional standing in the capitalist world-system, it is necessary to figure out why it could not defend its erstwhile position in the seventeenth and eighteenth centuries.

In this chapter, again, I am concentrating on the central argument of this study: To survive and defend their positional standings in the world-system, geographical units (empires as well as states) need to maintain sufficient and credible economic *and* military capabilities. By applying this argument to a comparative study of China, India, and Pakistan, I seek to develop a theoretical framework within the broader assumptions of world-systems analysis to expand the boundaries of focus beyond economic factors. Since this study covers the period when the tributary world-system was converted into the capitalist world-system, a distinction has to be made between the two. Theories about the fall of India and the rise of the West are, again, divided into lines similar to those we saw in the case of China. Although economically India and Europe, notably Great Britain, were similar in the sixteenth and seventeenth centuries, their paths started divergingin the eighteenth century. The debate about this divergence has received various explanations. To an extent, the argument mentioned above is uncontested—that before the invention of capitalism in Europe and the arrival of the Europeans through the Cape of Good Hope, discovered at the end of the fifteenth century, India held a superior economic position in the regional world-system. The "California Hypothesis," as forwarded by scholars such as Andre Gunder Frank (1998) and Kenneth Pomeranz (2000), argues about the superior position of China and India in the precapitalist world-system. It has been argued that the abundance of fuel materials, in case of India, and the lack thereof, in the case of Europe, pushed technological and economic development in the two regions in almost opposite directions. Prasannan Parthasarathi (2011) applies this hypothesis to India and compares it with Britain to argue that India was as efficient and productive as Britain and other European countries on the eve of the Industrial Revolution. However, the reasons for the great divergence between India and Britain were, according to him, not due to the fall of India but to the rise of Britain backed by deliberate industrial policies at home and mercantilist policies abroad. Compared to Britain, the political economy of the Indian Sub-Continent could not enjoy government patronage. Parthasarathi argues that "two pressures were critical in generating British divergence." First was "the competitive challenge of Indian cotton textiles." The British desire to compete against India resulted in "the great breakthroughs in the spinning of the late eighteenth century," "new technologies [that] transformed the world economy and shifted the center of global manufacturing from Asia to Europe." Second, he argues that a scarcity of energy resources—primarily wood since it was the primary source of fuel in the eighteenth century—also promoted divergence. Great Britain's search for a substitute for wood resulted in finding coal, which "sparked the development of the steam engine, new techniques for the smelting of iron and eventually new means of transport, including the railway and steamship" (p. 2). It was, therefore, a combination of competing for imperial power in the region and the Indian Ocean, ecological factors, and mercantilism that enabled Great Britain to become a world hegemon within the expansive world economy.

In the discourse of the "great divergence" between India and Europe, the other argument is, as in the case of China, related to the concept of evolution. These arguments rely on the divergent nature of the evolution of society, technology, and state-society relations resulting in the modernization of Europe and the absence of it elsewhere, particularly in China and India. I debated the flaws in this argument in detail in the previous chapter. The focus of the debate about the great divergence is China and Europe. However, many of the arguments mentioned in this comparative analysis are also applicable in the case of India. For example, Peer Vries (2015) argues that the role of the state in patronizing the nature, direction, and magnitude of economic and technological development, and the lack of it in China, became the most significant factor in bringing modernization to Great Britain. This argument can, arguably, be extended to India as well. Jeremy Black (2015) argues that "whatever their economic strength, non-Western states did not develop to match the West either a policy of trade-oriented development or an intellectual engagement with understanding the world as a dynamic process. There was significant economic development in India, but not an interaction between economy, technology, and state formation that was aimed at creating or fostering maritime effectiveness" (p. 408). He also argues that instead of focusing on the sea both as a source of and a challenge to their quest to control the whole Sub-Continent, the Mughals and the Marathas concentrated almost exclusively on land control as the ultimate avenue to power. As I will explain in the coming pages, compared to China, where the Ming and Qing empires had developed a centralized unified political power, India lacked a central authority, political development, and the concept of nation-state based on the rule of law, even though Mughal empire provided long-term stability, peace, and order in a greater part of the region. They, however, did not patronize the nature, direction, and magnitude of technological development and thus could not witness the dawn of modernization in the eighteenth century when it rose in Europe.

Another explanation in this regard is by Roman Studer (2015). By concentrating on the Smithian concept that market integration is a principal prerequisite in the development of a market economy because it creates "territorial expansion of the division of labor, inducing a reallocation of resources within regions or national economies, leading to an increasing division of labor" (p. 1), he concludes that markets in India, particularly the grain market, could integrate only after the mid-nineteenth century. Before then, though there was trade within the regions, it never led to the emergence of a free market economic structure at the national level. The major impediments in the way, he argues, were "transportation costs" and "political fragmentation" (pp. 145–47). India is vast geographically and in fact lacked means of mass transportation beyond human and animal means. Weather conditions, such as monsoons, and a relative lack of contact between traders linked with sea routes and land routes also affected the development of integrated networks of markets (Habib, 2014; Solar, 2013). Among the other reasons mentioned in the discourse of the great divergence, cited mostly in Europe-China comparison—including the mercantile role of the state, society, and their institutions (North and Thomas, 1973); the enlightened nature of the economic structure (Mokyr, 2009); and encouragement of experimentation and innovation in technology and autonomy of economic development (Jones, 2003; Rosenberg and Birdzell, 1986)—receive visible attention in Eurocentric arguments. Most of these comparisons either ignore India altogether or belittle its significance in the global economic transformation of the seventeenth and eighteenth centuries, though one can argue that India and China behaved similarly during the formative centuries of the European world economic system.

Three main sea routes historically facilitated the growth of Indian trade in the world market. The first route was directed to East and Southeast Asia and connected today's Indonesia and the Philippines through the Strait of Malacca. The second route headed to the Eastern Mediterranean through the Gulf of Oman and the Gulf of Eden. The third route concentrated on East Africa. Besides this, the land route through Afghanistan to Central Asia and Eastern Europe also enabled a large volume of trade. The discovery of the Cape of Good Hope allowed the Europeans to initiate a new wave of trade connecting Europe with Africa, India, and China. The discovery of the Americas and its rich treasures of gold and silver enabled traders to penetrate deep into Asia and benefit from intercontinental trade.

Historically, India was an economic powerhouse as long as it remained an "external arena" to the European world economy. As mentioned in the previous chapter on China, that Asia was the economic epicenter during that time, and China and India were the two most prominent regions in it, are accepted almost across the board. India, in the pre-1500 world, attracted maritime and land-route trade from Asia, Africa, and Europe. According to

Malekandathil (2010), maritime India in the early medieval ages had already resulted in well-defined sea route maps and trade networks connecting Persia, the Arabian Peninsula, the East Mediterranean region, and parts of Africa with Southeastern India, the Southeast Asian islands, and China. According to him, most of this trade was dominated by the Iranians, Arabs, Christians, and traders from Southeast Asia (p. 3). Persia, also known as Pharis at that time, supported the permanent settlement of its citizens in Indian areas such as central Kerala (p. 9). With the rise of Islam in the Arab world during 800–1000, Muslims started arriving at Indian ports, resulting in the arrival of foreign and qualified "managers" in southern India, particularly its seaport of Goa. Rashtrakutas, founding ruler of one of the great empires spreading from Malwa to Kanchi on the Sub-Continent, appointed in 926 a Muslim trader, Muhammad Tajjik, as governor of one of its administrative units, reflecting the politico-economic ascendance of foreigners and the significance of the maritime trade in the empire's economy (p. 20). In another work, Malekandathil (2013) argues that India's products, particularly spices and textiles, were already reaching Europe through a mixed sea and land route using the Persian Gulf, the Red Sea, and the Arabian Peninsula. Depending on their route, the Chinese, Arabs, and Indian traders shipped spices and textile products from either Goa or Kerala to either Basra or Cairo. From Cairo, the goods eventually were sent to Alexandria and then to Europe. From Basra onward, the traders had two options: the Basra-Baghdad-Aleppo-Tripoli route or the Basra-Damascus-Tripoli route. While all three routes flourished during 800–1500, the Basra-Baghdad-Aleppo-Tripoli route was declared secure and the favorite when the Ottomans took power in Egypt and other African areas in the early sixteenth century. According to James Tracy (1990), another critical route from India to the Arabian Peninsula was between northwestern Indian port of Surat and Mocha in the Red Sea, and then onward to Europe. Historically, Surat became a far more important seaport when European started colonizing India. I will explain the politico-economic and strategic significance of this port in the following pages when I discuss the impact of British imperialism on the region.

Before the discovery of the Cape of Good Hope, most of the maritime trade between India and Europe was conducted by traders interested in buying goods from one port and selling them at the next port. Two facts support this understanding. First, there was no presence of any transregional shipping company capable of shipping from India and dealing with all the regional governments and officials. Second, the element of risk was quite visible in deterring the emergence of any such significant "corporations"; pirates, dacoits, weather conditions, sea storms, and the precarious nature of political conditions in the regions involved pushed traders to maximize their margin of profit within the limited space where they were able to manage to do business. This is evident from the profit accumulation of the goods traded in the network. According to a collection of letters from Jewish traders involved in trade over the Indian Ocean, the margin of profit in some cases was 100 percent. However, in other cases, the prices of some textile products earned traders twenty-seven times more than what they paid at the source (Goitein, 1974: 110, 184). It was perhaps the margin of profit that led the Mamluk rulers to not only monopolize the trade networks but also impose taxes. Interestingly, these taxes were more against Indian than Chinese traders; however, Arab traders were taxed the least (Malekandathil, 2010: 108).

The crusades and the Mongol factor affected the direction of the routes and the scope of trade. In 1322, when the Venetians were banned from trading with the Egyptians, the port of Lajazzo or Ayas developed and redirected the spice trade there. The Mamluks, however, reacted with two brutal attacks, in 1322 and 1337, destroying the fort and imprisoning about twelve thousand Armenians (Atiya, 1962: 138). The caravan trade flourished extensively from the fourteenth century onward; caravans comprised of more than five thousand people became routine. These caravans traveled the routes mentioned above and brought immense wealth to the region. The participation of Indian traders on the Indian Ocean and at the seaports was quite evident; Arab merchants dominated the land routes.

To understand the redefinition of the role of India when it was brought under the Western-centered world economy during the eighteenth century, it is necessary to understand and contextualize the significance of Asian commercial networks in the premodern world. This necessity emerges from a need to understand why and how Asian empires, China and India in this study, could not maintain their superior positional standing once they were forcefully and involuntarily brought into the Western-invented modern capitalist system. The case of China has been explained in the previous chapter. In the case of India, its network of commerce was not limited to the Middle East or Africa. Besides these two regions, India had an extensive network of trade with Southeast Asia. As mentioned in the previous chapter, historically, the Southeast Asian region—except imperial Japan—had been a semi-sovereign part of mainland China. Throughout the Ming dynasty and during the first half of the Qing dynasty, trade, commerce, and legal-political settings in the region developed following a tributary system under the auspices of mainland Chinese monarchs. In the medieval age, regional trade flourished, benefiting all the regions: mainland China, eastern India, and the Southeast Asian islands. The benefits of trade outweighed any assumption of animosity, which was further mitigated by geographical distance and the mighty mountains separating the two regions. Seafaring between India and Southeast Asia was far more ancient, extensive, rapid, and complex since it involved island and tribal political factors. While Surat, Bombay, Kerala, Goa, and other seaports were connected with the Arabian Sea or Persian Sea and the Red Sea, Bengal, Orissa, Andhra, and Tamil Nadu were connected with the islands in the South China Sea. Most of this maritime trade had to pass through the Strait of Malacca, thus leaving irreversible cultural and religious effects in the adjacent regions (Reid, 1988: 16–17). However, India's commercial network in Southeast Asia virtually reached every part. Indian merchants carried items from Europe through the East Mediterranean route to India, and luxury items from India itself. Starting in the Bay of Bengal, these vessels carried these items to the Gulf of Thailand and Manila, eventually reaching Canton, China (Stuart-Fox, 2003: 26). In the premodern world, this route through numerous ports of trade involved thousands of merchants and was the most significant transregional commercial network outside Europe.

Besides maritime trade, India had another important trade route: the famous Silk Route starting from Xi'an (Chang'an) in China and ending in Rome, with an extensive network of smaller and interconnected trade spots, including Kashi (Kashgar) in China; Peshawar in today's Pakistan; Kabul, Mazar-e-Sharif, and Herat in Afghanistan; Shihezi, Almaty, Bishkek, Samarkand, and Buxoro (Bukhara) in Central Asia; and Mashhad, Yazd, Shiraz, and Tehran in Persia (Iran). From Tehran, there were two routes. The route lesser taken was Tabriz-Ankara-Istanbul-Rome; the far more famous route, however, was Tehran-Baghdad-Aleppo-Adana-Konya-Bursa-Istanbul-Rome, which connected with the Asian maritime route in Baghdad via Basra. Spanning over 7,000 kilometers, this ancient route remained active until the end of the sixteenth century and was the lifeline of intercontinental trade. While silk, ceramics, and other luxury items were among the most valuable items from China, Indian products such as beads, textiles, and spices were sold in Europe through this route. This connectivity strengthened as Muslim warriors from Central Asia began invading in India, starting with Mahmood Ghaznavid in 998, and eventually resulted in the establishment of the Mughal empire in 1526. The state investment in routes, roads, and market networks under pre-Mughal Muslim rule in India (1206–1526) was aimed at increasing "the safety of the caravan routes, both by suppressing predatory tribal groups and introducing policies designed to enhance the safety of travelers," and facilitated the growth of westward trade (Levi, 2016: 13). In the Mughal empire, the Grand Trunk Road (GT Road) was built when Sher Shah Suri usurped power for five years (1540–1545) by ousting Humayun—the son of Baber, founder of the Mughal empire—and forcing him into exile in Iran. The road, known as the first highway of India, comprised of more than 3,000 kilometers connecting East Bengal with Afghanistan and the Silk Route via the Chittagong-Calcutta-Jharkhand-Delhi-Lahore-Peshawar-Kabul route.

The network of these land routes was the lifeline of trade connecting India (and China) with Europe before the Portuguese could discover an all-sea route via the Cape of Good Hope in 1498. In the premodern world, it is important to mention that India, unlike China, needed various items of trade that it was unable to produce on its own. India offered the world agricultural goods, including rice, sugar, oil, cotton, and indigo. More important, however, were manufactured goods such as silk embroideries and textile products. In return, India imported various spices from Indonesia, rosewater from Central Asia, horses from the Arabian Peninsula, precious stones from Burma, tin from Malaysia, and silver from Europe through trade in the Indian Ocean or the port of Mocha in the Red Sea (Prakash, 2004: 10). India, therefore, was less in need of European and Mediterranean products, thus creating the chronic problem of balancing trade for the European traders; they had to bring silver to India to trade. For most of the time in premodern history, these trade networks flourished peacefully.

If we accept the Wallersteinian argument that the invention of capitalism took place in Europe during the long sixteenth century (1460–1640), we can argue that when Europe was undergoing a multifaceted economic, social, and strategic transformation, India was facing two kinds of invasions: warriors from Afghanistan and Central Asia, and traders from Europe. In the early medieval period, Afghan and Central Asian warriors, as mentioned, started invading India to extend their empires into the rich, fertile lands of the Sub-Continent. In the thirteenth century, Muslim expansionism annexed the northwestern part of India and established its own empire—the Delhi Sultanate—in 1206. During 1206–1526, Muslim warriors remained busy fighting local Indians and annexing the boundaries of their empire. Various families of warriors ruled India during that time. The anarchic situation ended when the Mughals defeated the Lodhis in 1526 and claimed suzerainty over Delhi. The second kind of invasion, initially economic but eventually political, brought colonialism to India. The Cape of Good Hope enabled Europeans traders, initially the Portuguese and Dutch, French and eventually the British, to enter the Indian Ocean, bypassing the all-land route of Central Asia, the Arabian Peninsula, China, and India. The land route—if we stretch it from East Bengal and take it all the way to Rome—meant huge risks in terms of time consumption, means of transportation, and volume of trade. The all-sea route also had risks but was less threatening.

The arrival of the Portuguese in the Indian Ocean during the early years of the sixteenth century enabled the Europeans to nullify the risks and the time factor to extend their trade with "the land of the riches." It is important to mention that European discovery of the all-sea route and their faster penetration affected the pattern of regional trade in a lasting manner. While India was still an "external arena" of the nascent capitalist world economy emerging in Europe, the nature of wars on the continent affected the patterns of trade in the Indian Ocean. Since the Portuguese discovered the route, they claimed a monopoly over it. These claims of monopoly were conclusively rejected by the Dutch, whose East India Company, established in 1602, used the principle of "free seas" to rapidly expand commercial activities in the Indian Ocean. They were followed by French traders, and soon thereafter by British traders. During this time, India was unable to put in place an active and aggressive maritime mercantile policy in reference to its commercial interests in the Indian Ocean represented by Indian traders. The arrival of the Europeans changed the economic organization of maritime trade in the Indian Ocean permanently. India failed on two accounts. First, it could not dictate any terms or conditions for commercial expansion of the Europeans even on its own soil. Second, it overlooked the potential significance of the associated threats involved. The Mughals and other rival forces, such as the Marathas, encouraged free trade but did not bother to see the inevitability of armed conflict.

Two important points can help us explain the nature of the great divergence between India and Europe starting in the sixteenth century. The first point pertains to the economic conditions of India before the arrival of the Europeans *as a political force.* India had had a comparative advantage over European and Southeast Asian traders for centuries before the Europeans' arrival. The interaction between Europeans and Indian merchants was a fact; as mentioned above, trade links had been established through the East Mediterranean Sea trade route and the Silk Route. It brought valuable wealth to India, the most important being silver, which was used by the sultans of Delhi to build their armies and expand their territorial control. In the case of Ala-ud-Din (r. 1296–1316), one of the most notable sultans of Delhi, "economic policies were implemented primarily so that he could support a larger military force" (Asher and Talbot, 2006: 39). Economic progress under the first Muslim rule—the Delhi Sultanate (1206–1526)—continued unabated since it was crucial to the needs of the newly established kingdom. It was further extended, deepened, and internationalized under the Mughal emperors. Since it was always a matter of surplus because India had quite a variety of products to offer to the world while requiring far little, it always earned valuable resources through this trade. However, throughout Muslim rule in India (1206–1857), agriculture remained the most significant source of income for the state. About half of the GDP of the Mughal empire was received in the form of precious metals, silver, and gold, by taxing the maritime trade (Moosvi, 2010: 2, 4). The Mughals established a whole new system of agrarian taxation—*Zabt*, or literally, confiscation—which varied according to the needs of the state and the will of the emperor. Far more important is the fact that the Mughals, and before them the sultans of Delhi, established the rule of imperial suzerainty over the land; the emperor was the owner of all the land of the state, and it was up to him to award any region, area, district, or smaller part of land to anyone he wished. This system, organized on institutional grounds under Akbar the Great, was named *Mansabdari* (Entitlement) or *Jagirdari* (Landlordship). The Mughals used agricultural and other taxes to build an army in a quest to control the whole Sub-Continent, a credible reason causing the ultimate collapse of the whole empire.

That India was an industrial and economic hub in the precapitalist world is now a fact. Though India had many commodities to purchase, the earning of silver initially through trade became a reality. By the first decade of the sixteenth century, the Portuguese were interacting with Southeast Asian and Indian traders on their source points: the seaports. Their quest for control of seaports in Southeast Asia, such as Malacca in 1511 and Macau in 1557, exhibited the signs of the stakes involved. By 1520, the Portuguese had established residential colonies in Goa and other areas, thus building a network of long-distance trade from Goa-Bengal-Malacca-Canton on the one side and Goa and Calcutta on the way to the Cape of Good Hope and then turning to Lisbon. The most important fact of this network under Portuguese and later Dutch, French, and English traders was that India accumulated huge volumes of silver. The sixteenth century was the time when the Mughals held the most expansive territory in the history of Asia; their empire stretched from Afghanistan to East Bengal, covered an area of more than three million square kilometers, and was earning an annual revenue of more than 334 million rupees by 1690 (Eraly, 2007: 288). Angus Maddison (2001) estimates the per capita GDP of India at Rs. 533 in 1820, 533 in 1870, and 673 in 1913. However, Amiya Bagchi (2010) contradicts this estimate by arguing that the highest-paid jobs and professions were denied to the Indians, and that income earned through these professions was eventually taken to Britain, meaning that India lost a lot under colonial rules. As mentioned in the previous chapter, in the case of China, Europe also had a chronic balance-of-trade problem in bilateral trade with India. According to some conservative estimates, before the War of Plassey (1757), which is considered the starting point of British colonialism on the Sub-Continent, India had received about one-third of Spanish silver (Moosvi, 2008: xxvi). Most of this import was converted into coins; in 1636, the minting factories in Surat were producing coins worth roughly Rs.9000 every day (Rs. 6000 for the English and Rs. 3000 for the Dutch). Relying on extensive calculations done through firsthand information, Moosvi calculates that in 1595, the Mughal empire had a stock of 4,550 metric tons of silver only. This stock reached 9,235 metric tons in 1645 but declined by about 525 tons during 1645–1675, after which it increased sharply and reached 10,700 metric tons in 1705 (Moosvi, 2010: chapter 2). According to Kirti Chaudhuri (1978), by 1750, the total worth of European "treasure" exported to Asia had reached more than one million pounds a year, after which there was a steady decline (p. 512). Moosvi

(2015), Bagchi (2010), and Habib (2013) argue that the import of silver by the Europeans virtually stopped as soon as they were able to take over *Diwani* (the finance) of Bengal, Orissa, and Bihar. However, Bowen (2010) argues that these scholars omit three important factors. First, they ignore private exports of silver to India by non–British East India Company and other European traders. Second, they also do not recognize that the East India Company's own imports of silver into India from Europe increased remarkably during 1785–1807. Third, silver continued being imported into India from other ports such as Malacca, Mocha, Bengkulu, and Canton. He calculates that during 1760–1820, the total export of the East India Company to Asia accounted to about £67,231,512, of which about £30,900,459 went to India. Exports of bullion to Canton (China) during this period were worth £34,129,293 while those to Bengkulu (Indonesia) were worth £2,201,760. Importantly, these volumes are for the company only; private trade is excluded. Given that British nobility, the government, and public discourse resisted intercontinental trade based on the export of bullion to Asia in return for consumable or luxury items of "dubious worth," the company had a compulsive desire to develop an intra-Asia silver trade. Territorial occupation and the usurpation of *Diwani* in Bengal, Orissa, and Bihar gave hope of this happening. However, it did not; the company had a huge volume of trade, far greater than the supply of Indian bullion that could be shipped to China or East Asia. The exports, Bowen concludes, resumed in 1772 and continued until 1820. According to him, "Indeed, between 1785 and the end of the period under review [1820], the Company dispatched rather more silver to India (£8,504,738) than it did to China (£7,618,253)" (Bowen, 2010: 458). According to Carl Trocki (1999), from 1570 to 1780, Europe shipped 590 million guilders to Asia. While many of these exports were trade-oriented, territorial control, particularly since 1750, required the investment of silver in arms build-up, military services, and administrative control. One can confidently argue that a sizeable portion of this wealth ended up in India.

The second point pertains to the political—or more precisely, military—conditions on the Sub-Continent. Given that the Mughal empire under the sixth and the most powerful emperor, Aurangzeb Alamgir (r. 1658–1707), had reached its zenith, it is important to analyze why it collapsed exactly 150 years after his death. More importantly, though the Mughal rulers survived during 1707–1857, they were neither emperors nor a force capable of challenging the rising power of rivals in and beyond the Sub-Continent. The devaluation of India's status in global commerce could take place because non-Indian forces succeeded in subduing it. This redefinition, which was in no way less than the modern IMF-led "structural adjustment" (Bagchi, 2010: xxix), could not have taken place had India had some credible military power to defend its interests. The lack of modern military power and a unified system of governance, as compared to the Europeans and particularly the British, brought de-industrialization and exploitation to India.

Historically, rare have been times when India lived as a unified country under one ruler. During the recorded history of more than three thousand years, two or, arguably, three emperors—Chandragupta Maurya (r. 321–297 BCE), Ashoka (r. 269–232 BCE), and Akbar (r. 1556–1605)—are believed to have unified India as a country and developed some rudimentary level of nationalism in the masses. However, for most of precolonial history, Indians went to war either against the invaders or one another. Contrary to the anarchic conditions in Europe that resulted in military revolution, anarchy in India did not inspire the opposing forces strive for new technology. In 1757, in the War of Plassey, many of the more than fifty-thousand soldiers of the Nawab of Bengal, Siraj-ud-Daulah, were horsemen carrying swords, shields, and arrows, whereas the company army had guns and ammunition. It was thus not a surprise that an army of three thousand company soldiers defeated them in a conclusive manner (de la Garza, 2016: 8).

The debate about the presence and role of military technology in precolonial India has received new impetus. There are two opposing views about the status of military technology in the Mughal era (1526–1857). One point of view is that the Mughals were as sharp as the Europeans in incorporating the modern military technology being invented in Europe. Arriving in India in waves, this technology and weaponry were modified according to local needs. In fact, Andrew de la Garza (2016) argues that India witnessed a "military revolution" under Babur, the founder of Mughal empire, and particularly Akbar the Great, the third and perhaps the most prominent ruler of the Mughal dynasty. According to de la Garza, pre-Mughal India was not aloof of the changes in the conduct of warfare taking place in Europe; the Lodhi rulers of India—the last of the seven dynasties during the Sultanate period—had a similar level of gunpowder technology as possessed by the forces involved in the Hundred Years' War (1337–1453). Consequences of this introduction in warfare were extensive fortification of urban areas and the use of mines and gunpowder bombs in siege warfare. The sultans of Delhi, and particularly Babur before he became ruler of India, benefited from the military modernization drive initiated by Shah Ismael Safavi, the ruler of Iran, after his defeat at the hands of the Ottoman forces in 1514. Being an ally of Shah Safavi, Babur got access to Western weaponry and utilized it in his wars in Panipat in 1526 and Khanua in early 1527, the two battles that established him as the ruler of India. During the Mughal period, and particularly under Akbar, various types of Western military weapons, such as lighter cannons, small arms, and swivel guns, were included in the Mughal army. Simultaneously, Akbar paid particular attention to modifying and developing his own models of artillery. The extensive use of rockets also continued; they were modernized, and their Indian versions prove to be more accurate, efficient, and reliable.

Akbar's army was of two kinds: a standing army under the direct control of the emperor, and a large "active" army under *Mansabdars*. A *Mansab* was a status through which the magnitude of economic and military responsibilities was defined. It was a system of ranks from *Dahbashi* (ten) to *Panjhazari* (five thousand), with *Panjhazari* being the highest nonroyal rank. It meant that the holder of the status would be responsible for contributing five thousand active soldiers on horses at any time depending on the needs of the emperor. The horses—and elephants in some cases—were branded with a stamp on their back indicating their numbers and establishing the fact that the horse belonged to the emperor (Moosvi, 2015; Habib, 2014). In many cases, this pledge was not fulfilled, and the *Mansab* was later separated from the number of horsemen required. According to Shireen Moosvi (2015), during the Akbar (r. 1556–1605), Jahangir (r. 1605–1627), and then Shah Jahan (r. 1627–1658) eras, the Mughal empire spent at least 45 percent of its income on the maintenance of the Mansabdari system; the maximum expenditure has been estimated to be about 72 percent of the total income (p. 221). In Shah Jahan's times, the *Mansabdari* system took away about 82 percent of the revenue (p. 199). This expenditure excluded the standing army of thousands of soldiers and modern weaponry system under the direct control of the emperor. Calculating everything, the total strength of the Mughal army can be estimated at least one million soldiers. Therefore, the Mughal empire was primarily a military-fiscal state meant to sustain itself only through the continuous maintenance and expansion of its defense capabilities.

The view about a militarily powerful and advanced India during the Mughal era is supported by some other valuable works as well. Kaushik Roy (2011; 2014; 2015) and Iqtidar Alam Khan (2004) are prominent in this context. The recurring themes in these works are that the maritime trade linking China and Europe and commercial links with Central Asia brought military technology—weaponry, light and heavy artillery, cavalry, and infantry—to India way before the Mughals arrived. Roy (2015) argues that by the sixteenth century, the military revolution was taking place in Deccan with the arrival of gunpowder weapons from the Ottomans and firearms from the Portuguese. "The Portuguese tradition of gun making got fused with the Ottoman method of manufacture, and the net result was the emergence of hybrid gunpowder systems which were comparable in quality with the best weapons manufactured in Germany." He argues further, "Whatever may be the origin and exact trajectory of the introduction and development of gunpowder weapons, the Delhi Sultanate and the Vijiayanagara Empire, by integrating the hand-held firearms (muskets, rockets) and artillery with cavalry, infantry, and elephants, generated a multidimensional RMA" (p. 116). According to Khan (2004), the Vijiayanagara empire (1336–1646) established in South Deccan had also acquired firearms from both the Ottomans and the Portuguese during the 1360s, while knowledge of mining reached these areas by the end of the fifteenth century. Since the sixteenth century, battles between the Portuguese (and other Europeans) and local forces included gunpowder weapons and artillery (p. 21). The destruction of the empire was also due to its inferior infantry and artillery power (Roy, 2015: 121). Military progress under the Mughals was, however, quite impressive, according to both scholars. In particular, the *Mansabdari* system provided critical support to the empire. Roy (2014) mentions that Aurangzeb also advanced the role of technology in both his defensive and offensive strategies, particularly in his wars against the sultans of Deccan. Initially concentrating on trade only, the English East India Company did not pay much attention to developing military muscles. However, in 1687, when it revised its policy in the wake of trade conflicts with rival European companies in the region and decided to "manage . . . [its] . . . commerce with . . . sword in . . . hand" (quoted in Banerjee, 2008: 1541), the company looted some of the Mughal vessels in the Indian Ocean and blockaded some ports. The Mughals retaliated with force, compelling the company to apologize to the emperor (Prabhakaran, 1990: 112–13). The event reflects two points. First, the Indian force was quite effective during the Aurangzeb era. Second, the company did not have sufficient military power to challenge Mughal might on Indian soil and in the Indian Ocean.

The other view about the role and status of technology in Mughal and Indian military affairs argues that India lagged behind Europe in technology, discipline, and the conduct of war. Marshall Hodgson (1974) coined the term "gunpowder empires" for the Ottomans, Safavids, and Mughals and argues that the emergence, ascendance, and survival of these empires owed to their access and use of gunpowder weapons. Building on his work, Douglas Streusand (2011) argues about the Turko-Persian origins of Mughal polity and warfare. However, he does not agree with Hodgson's assumption. To him, it was the penetration of the state as an institution throughout the territorial space it occupied that in the end determined the period it lived. The Ottoman empire, as compared to the Safavid and Mughal empires, lasted for an extended period because of its presence in rural areas.

Some other works also provide valuable insights to explain the decline of the Mughal military in the eighteenth century. William Irvine's (1994) *The Army of the Indian Moghuls: Its Organization and Administration*, initially published in 1903, is considered a pioneering work on the subject. In a detailed description of the military strength of the Mughal empire, it explains some of the critical reasons for the decline of Mughal army. Despite that the Mughals were able to maintain a sizeable level of the European military equipment that they acquired through Portuguese trade links and connections in the Safavid empire's Iran, the use of bows and arrows was common until at least 1894. They were used in huge numbers during the Mutiny of 1857. Irvine considers bows the most significant offensive weapon in the Mughal army, while the matchlock "up to the middle of the 18th century was looked on with less favor than the bow and arrow, which held their ground" (p. 103). Despite having acquired heavy artillery, their purpose was less for utilization on the battlefield and more for the aggrandizement of Mughal power (p. 118). Regarding the use of rockets, the Mughal army lacked training (p. 149).The Portuguese, Dutch, German, French, and English were employed and paid quite handsome amounts to train the Mughal army. However, with Aurangzeb coming to power, these trainers were not only terminated from services but also declined lucrative remunerations if they wanted to continue at all (pp. 153–54).

Jos Gommans (2002) calls the Mughal empire an "itinerant empire" and defines it as a combination of cavalry from Western India and a supply of finances from the fertile lands of eastern India such as Bengal. The inner frontier of Delhi and adjacent areas, therefore, could become the center of power. This could sustain itself through the *Mansabdari* system established by Akbar. In particular, he argues that the Mughal empire was able to survive through the process of *zamindarization* (feudalism) whereby the landed gentry was patronized, assimilated, and incorporated into the business of the defense and expansion of the state (pp. 40, 68). The system of awarding *jagirs* to some, however, annoyed others. As this process progressed, it eventually weakened the empire due to growing rivalries within the landed elite and the inability of the empire to keep everyone happy. The East India Company was able to take over the Mughals because it could distribute the land more efficiently while maintaining an ability to muster strength over the landed elite whenever required. Sekhar Bandyopadhyay (2014) also supports this argument and cites the wrangling among members of the royal court as one of the primary reasons for the fall of the Mughal empire.

In the presence of two opposing views, however, it is not difficult to construe the facts. If we look at the proponents of Mughal and Indian advancement in military technology and warfare, we find a general agreement on two important points. First, though the Mughals, Marathas, and other contenders for power in India acquired and included gunpowder technology in their armies, they still relied on conventional and local weapons and methodologies of war. Khan (2004) mentions that "throughout the seventeenth century and the first half of the eighteenth century, the nature of firearms in the Mughal armies, as well as those of the Deccan states and the Marathas, was, by and large, the same as had been evolved before the death of Akbar" (p. 103). A few exceptions, according to him, included innovations such as "the extensive use of light canons," "the addition of cast-bronze casings around the barrels," "standardization of bores," the modification of light guns to become *shaturnal* (camel barrel) used with its swivel mounted on the back of camels, dual-horse gun-carriages, and metallic cannon-balls and shells." These developments, however, do not impress him. He argues that "despite the innovations, . . . gunpowder artillery in Mughal India, during the seventeenth century became increasingly obsolete, in comparison with European artillery that had in the meantime progressed in every department" (p. 114). He wonders why those who mattered in decision-making condoned the increasing divergence between Europe and India in terms of military technology. Roy (2015) argues that by the beginning of the eighteenth century, India (and China) should have had witnessed a new military transformation. Both countries failed; in the case of India, the reasons mentioned include "interests of the *mansabdars*, political weakness of the Mughal center, the low-intensity challenge posed by Marathas, and the conventional threat posed by Persia" (p. 148). Even if we accept the argument raised by de la Garza (2016), Khan (2004), and Roy (2015) about the profound development and "military revolution" in India during Akbar's rule, all of them agree that by the time the Europeans developed political objectives in India, the regional states were against each other than any *firangi* (European).

Second, the Mughals and other regional states were used to conducting siege warfare. The construction of fortlike cities has been a significant development during the Sultanate and Mughal period. Though it was not unique to India, the Mughals excelled in developing expertise in the conduct and success of siege warfare. They built forts, deployed a sizeable force on strategic locations, and trained their armies in both defense and offense in siege warfare. However, the lack of transformation in military tactics and technologies affected the powers that be in India to develop alternative war scenarios. Since their purpose was elevating defense capabilities, and Indian forces always faced low-intensity anarchic conditions, siege warfare did not allow the Mughals to build a mobile force and sprint technologies and equipment (de la Garza, 2014). When Akbar forces excelled in offensive capabilities in siege warfare, such as the use of mines, his opponents relied on building even stronger forts (de la Garza, 2016: 49; Roy, 2014: 107). The wars by Aurangzeb in Deccan also strengthened the concept of fortification as the best possible strategy of defense. Gommans and Kolff (2001) provide an important explanation about the role of siege warfare in denying the acceptance of modern military technology in India. They argue that since the forts were constructed in such a manner that guns were unable to penetrate the outer walls, the kings, strategists, and warriors concentrated on conquering cities and forts through traditional methods.

De la Garza (2016) argues that the Mughals did not find incentive in developing multipurpose offensive capabilities based on modern military technology because "the Empire never faced a serious threat of invasion" (p. 184). This is arguable since the Mughals were constantly at war, particularly during the Aurangzeb years. The rival states also needed a strategic advantage. However, they all could not aspire for a successful military revolution initiated by the Mughal pioneers in India. It was an "unfinished military revolution," de La Garza argues, which could not be carried on when the Mughals entered Deccan terrain, a different landscape requiring different specialties of warfare. Beyond this, the Mughals also "failed at state building, at translating military success into more effective government, a more prosperous economy, and a more enlightened society. . . . The Mughal Empire was inherently and irredeemably defective—as proven by its failure to survive into the modern era—its tragedies and excesses cannot be justified. It had to be an especially corrupt and morally bankrupt state that demanded such sacrifices from its people without any prospect of reward for future generations" (pp. 188–89). What were the consequences of anarchy, precarious peace, and perpetual warfare in India? First, it did not allow the development of nationalism. Second, it took away great strategists and warriors that could have contributed meaningfully to the development of India's maritime defense policy on nationalist grounds. Third, the Mughals failed to encompass and redirect human and financial resources to lay down a stable foundation based on the concept of "Indianness."

There is no doubt that post-Akbar India diverged from modernization and advancement, particularly in military technology, which affected its defensive abilities. Economically, however, India prospered by its contacts with Europe, particularly through the Cape of Good Hope route. When Aurangzeb died in 1707, the central treasury of the empire in Agra possessed gold and silver worth 240 million rupees (Richards, 1993: 253). Apparently, Aurangzeb's wars against the Marathas did not damage the finances of the empire to a greater extent. It is also important to keep in view the developments taking place in Europe during the seventeenth and eighteenth centuries. Europe by that time had adopted mercantilism as its principal policy of global trade. East Indian companies of the leading European empires were established and encouraged to increase trade links. The lack of military technology and its use in India was, however, one of the significant reasons why India was unable to resist redefining its positional standing in the burgeoning world economy during the eighteenth century. When the region was incorporated into the European-centered capitalist system during its "second era of expansion" (1730–1840), it no longer was able to put in place any credible military resistance in the way of advancing European mercantile forces. Wallerstein (2011c) agrees with the military genesis of the India-Europe divergence and European capitalist expansion during the mid-eighteenth century, particularly on the Indian Sub-Continent. He argues:

> Of course, the process of incorporation might receive resistance. It was argued, however, that the technological development of the capitalist world-economy, itself a process internal to that system, led over time to strengthening the military capacity of strong states of the world-economy compared with the military capacity of parts of the external arena. Hence, for example, whereas in the sixteenth century pan-European military strength was perhaps insufficient to "conquer" India, by the late eighteenth century this was no longer true. (Wallerstein, 2011c: xv–xvi)

By the mid-eighteenth century, a militarily moribund India witnessed stiff competition from the successor states for domination. One of the most remarkable outcomes of intra-India military competition was the loss of human and fiscal resources. India did not lose its warriors against the British as much as it did when Indians fought against each other. With the rise of European companies, these states allied with them and against each other instead of realizing the rising threat of the Europeans and uniting against them. In history, it is named "myopia hypothesis," meaning that Indian successor states were unable to visualize the long-term consequences of their mutual animosity and alliance with the Europeans, and they could not imagine that by allying with Europeans, they, in fact, were weakening their own prospects of long-term survival (Malcolm, 1826; Ali, 1982; Roy, 2005). However, Oak and Swamy (2012) argue that the Pitt's India Act of 1784 bound the East India Company to remain peaceful. The act stated that "to pursue schemes of conquest and extension of dominion in India, are measures repugnant to the wish, the honor, and policy of this nation." They argue that it bound the company to be more "peaceable and credible," thus urging the competing states to pose a higher level of confidence in the company than in any other precarious regional and Indian state and its ruler. However, a significant reason was access to the weapons that these states needed but could not afford, except Mysore. It was therefore in the mutual interest of the Marathas and the company to destroy Tipu Sultan. However, this argument decontextualizes the fact that the company and the Marathas were soon at war after the end of the state of Mysore in 1798. For every concession, the company coerced the states to hand over control of the vast territories. Whatever the circumstances, the company's formidable military capacity and manipulative economic power remain the most convincing reasons for the establishment of British imperial rule in India. During 1757–1857, the company fought many wars and stood victorious in all. Despite being fewer in numbers, its forces were trained and disciplined, and its professional conduct of war was based on weapons and modern organization of the military. British imperial rule in India could be established *primarily* through the gun.

INDIA FALLS TO THE COMPANY: A POLITICO-ECONOMIC HISTORY, 1757–1857

By the mid-eighteenth century, European trading companies had penetrated deep into the Indian economy. Their advancement was based on a combination of assault, alliance, bribery, coercion, occupation, and exploitation. Before the English East India Company could dominate the political economy of East India, it had to compete against its rival the French East India Company. During 1746–1763, known as the Carnatic Wars years, rival companies actively patronized and exploited Indian successor states and their rulers by pitting them against each other. Influenced by the wars in Europe, by the end of third Carnatic War, the British East India Company was left with no rival European power in India. The competitors were, then, the Marathas ruling over the Deccan plateau, some other successor states, and the moribund Mughal empire. During 1777–1818, the company went against the Marathas and defeated them by exploiting their mutual grievances, pitting them against one another, and pacifying them momentarily when it went against some other states. By 1818, however, the company had conquered all coastal areas of India plus the Deccan plateau.

Economically, European traders had taken over the sea trade between India, Southeast Asia, China, and Europe long ago (Marshall, 2005: 19). During the seventeenth and first half of the eighteenth century, they successfully pursued an objective of installing their factories and warehouses on Indian soil. As the Mughals weakened and the successor states proliferated, European merchants found themselves in hot waters. The first and foremost significant objective for them was to secure their commercial interests in and beyond India, which could not be ensured without stiff, credible, and punitive action against those who threatened them. Chaudhuri (1978) termed European commercial activities in India "armed trade" (p. 139). The East India Companies, particularly the French and English, imported weapons from Europe, hired Indian soldiers, provided mercenary services to the Nawabs and lords in the coastal areas and Deccan plateau in return for economic gain, gifts, and territorial annexation. In its home country, the East India Company bribed the ruling class and secured rights and favorable commercial deals from the state (Cain and Hopkins, 2016). The economic role of the company is evident from its immensely important role in the burgeoning British imperialism in Asia and beyond.

Three motives of the East India Company have been explained. I label them the "free market argument," "Indian political dynamics argument" and "imperialist explanation." European traders had been directly involved in the Indian Ocean trade since at least the fifteenth century. They increasingly expanded their operations and reached Southeast Asia, China, and the Arabian sea. As explained in the previous chapter, their occupation of some of the areas and locations in Southeast Asia during the early sixteenth century reflected their desire for a secure and seamless passage of trade. In India, they sought the patronage of the Mughals, minted coins in their names, and pursued royal permits to install their factories in Surat Gujrat and Calicut Bengal and other coastal areas. In the wake of the decline in Mughal authority and the rise of successor states in these areas, a power vacuum emerged that led the French and British companies to develop military power. Initially, these capacities were meant to be defensive, guaranteeing the security of commercial interests. Until the early 1740s, these companies conducted their business peacefully, though they both assembled military forces comprised of Indians and headed by European officers. They had less interest in indigenous Indian political affairs that did not affect their commercial operations. However, political wrangling and wars among the successor states pushed them to involve as a strategic asset to the rival Indian forces. For example, while the French trained, equipped, and supported the state of Mysore, the British were taken on the side of the Nawab of Carnatic. In a free market manner, the Europeans found military capacity as a sellable product; they received heavy amounts of precious metals and revenue collection rights in return for their services. The local business class, such as Jagat Seth, also supported the decisive European interventions that eventually turned these states as satellites. With every victory, the English company received additional areas, rights, privileges, and prerogatives. According to Marshall (2005), "it is clear that Indians were not helpless victims in the process. They had motives of their own. In providing armed men or raising money, Europeans were rendering services that Indians wanted" (p. 23). It was, therefore, the supply and demand of military capacities that dragged the companies into Indian wars and threw on them the necessity to control the areas for their primary objectives: trade and profit.

This need was heightened by the rise of the anarchic situation, particularly in areas that had been least under Mughal control. Within thirty years after the death of Aurangzeb, Eastern India slipped into a series of wars of succession and emergences of small kingdoms. Every smaller state, therefore, strived to exist, defend, expand, and prosper at the cost of its rivals. Since almost all of them lacked resources and the access to build formidable defensive and offensive capabilities based on modern military weapons, they had to rely on the companies' power. These companies and their top brass had their own interests in weakening the kingdoms, annexing additional areas under their prerogatives of economic activities, and strengthening their own decisive strategic positions in Indian affairs as they built and exhibited their capabilities of waging war from 1746 onward. In 1757, when the British went against Siraj-ud-Daulah, the Nawab of Bengal, for he had taken over the port of Calicut, they put in place a variety of tactics to ensure they defeated the forces of Nawab. The most prominent of them was conspiracy "by promoting treason and forgery" (Nehru, 1959: 275). Mir Jafar, commander in chief of Nawab's army, conspired against Nawab and was promised his position. With less than three thousand soldiers, the British were able to overcome Nawab's army of more than fifty thousand soldiers since the actual war went on for only a few hours. It was, in fact, Mir Jafar's use of company force that enabled him to dethrone Siraj-ud-Daulah and become Nawab of Bengal himself. "The price of the use of the army on that and subsequent occasions," writes Marshall (2005), "was to be mortgaging of more and more of the revenues of Bengal to the British, until they were all made over to the Company in the grant of the *Diwani* in 1765" (p. 23). The political dynamics of post-1707 India invited the British to fill in the vacuum of power and intervene for the sake of their own benefits. In doing so, they ensured that their interests were served to their satisfaction. Within years, they replaced Mir Jafar with his son-in-law Mir Qasim and then brought Mir Jafar back only to get exclusive control of the revenue department.

Both explanations mentioned above are valid only to an extent, however. While it is true that the European companies, in their early years, had little incentive to occupy Indian territory and install their own rule there, truer is the fact that they took little time to realize the widening power vacuum in India and their potential role in domestic Indian political and economic affairs. This realization was promoted through two simultaneous initiatives. The arrival of Robert Clive in 1755 pushed the expansionist policy further. The company named it the "national agenda" and pursued the British government and decision-makers in London to consider its commercial activities in India and the Indian Ocean as "a national trade" because of the fiscal benefits it was delivering to the government and ruling elite in London, and the consequences of the loss of such revenues and resources in the absence of patronage from London (Cain and Hopkins, 2016; Frank, 1996). The British government and the masses were also informed that territorial control of East India was due to the power vacuum created by the collapse of the political order and its detrimental consequences for the commercial interests of the company (Fisher, 1994). In a briefing to the House of Commons in 1767, Secretary of the Company Robert James stated, "We do not want conquest and power; it is commercial interest only we look for" (quoted in Marshall, 1968: 17). However, the conduct of the company in India was nothing less than imperial, and coercive advancement took place through economic plunder and social destruction.

In 1757, when it defeated Siraj-ud-Daulah and his French allies in the War of Plassey, the company adopted a policy of coercive territorial expansion and financial usurpation. Contrary to the free market argument, the fact is that the company realized the immense economic benefits in these policies and, thus, acted proactively to advance its interests. It developed a patron-client relationship with the government in London and received "delegated sovereignty" from the Crown to design and implement a governance structure in the occupied areas. Moreover, it also agreed to pay £400,000 a year to the Exchequer for possession of the territories in India occupied after 1765 (Sen, 1998: 126). To meet its expenses in India and balance its trade deficit with China, the company used its mercantile powers to screw the Indian rulers and Nawabs by creating a need to hire its military services by pitting them against each other and exploiting their differences. With every victory they achieved, company officials demanded more treasure, revenue rights, and territorial control. In 1756, when the company won against Siraj-ud-Daulah with a treacherous conspiracy, Mir Jafar paid £275,000 to the company force and another £2.5 million to the company over the next four years, while Robert Clive was also gifted a *jagir* (fief) worth £37,567 (Bandyopadhyay, 2014: 44). As the company's demands increased, Mir Jafar could not pay, thus creating an opportunity to replace him in 1770 with his son-in-law Mir Qasim. The new Nawab also paid a hefty amount for this prize, but he tried to control trade and reinvigorate taxation (the company had a free trade right, as compared to the locals, who had to pay customs and other duties); he was removed and Mir Jafar was reappointed. In 1764, the combined forces of Mughal Emperor Shah Alam II, the Nawab of Awadh Shuja-ud-Daulah, and Mir Qasim fought against the company in Buxer, Bengal. The company defeated this force and captured the Mughal emperor but treated him with respect in return for the signing of the Treaty of Allahabad, whereby the emperor agreed to the company's territorial occupation and the acquisition of *Diwani* in Bengal, Bihar, and Orissa. Mir Qasim could not be captured; he reached New Delhi and died a few years after living practically as a beggar. Shuja-ud-Daulah was fined Rs. 5 million as compensation for the company's military and human losses. The company was also given the right to free trade throughout Awadh, and the Nawab also agreed to an annual payment of Rs. 1 million in return for the security of the province against any aggression. For this purpose, the company constructed a garrison in Awadh in 1773 and demanded the Nawab to pay for the stationing of the company's force (Fisher, 1991: 50, 378). The Nawab of Awadh was unable to collect the required amount because the company's officials were violating the free trade right for their private commercial activities. In 1775, after the death of Shuja-ud-Daulah, Banaras—a part of Awadh—was taken over by the company and Raja Chait Singh was appointed as its vessel on behalf of the company. For the next five years, the company coerced Raja Chait Singh to pay half a million rupees annually to finance the British-French War in Europe, in addition to the recurring expenses of the company's forces stationed in the region. When found unable to comply with the demand, the company arrested the Raja and took over administrative and financial control in 1781. The company ordered the women of the royal families of Banaras and Awadh to hand over their possessions of gold, silver, and other precious metals to company officials as a form of payment for penalties and fines. In 1801, the company annexed half of Awadh (already excluding Banaras) and took over its taxation and administrative control. It was a far more lucrative option for the company since Awadh was producing cotton and indigo, high demand in China and London, respectively (Barnett, 1980). The war of succession in Hyderabad and Carnatic provided the French and English Companies an opportunity to grab resources; the profiting military campaigns were essentially financed with Indian money and blood. Both companies received huge territories. In 1766, the Nawab of Hyderabad handed over control of the valuable and fertile areas of Southern Sarkar to the English company in return for its military support against the Marathas. During 1767–1818, the company fought against the Marathas and Mysore. The French backed Tipu Sultan of Mysore, but the company defeated him in 1799. The company brought Tipu's local opponents to power and coerced them to collect revenue to pay for the company's expenses with the state and provide an additional contribution to its treasury. Once free from Mysore and the French, the Company found the Marathas as the only remaining force in the region. The Marathas were particularly a matter of concern because they controlled the cotton-producing regions. In addition to Awadh, the company needed direct possession and control of these areas in the wake of its growing cotton trade with China and the real prospect of reducing their balance of trade. The company exploited mutual differences in the Marathas, particularly during their wars of succession, and supported one over another. In every war it fought against the Marathas, the company was able to neutralize some of their force by deterring the rulers. By the end of the third war in 1817–1818, the Marathas had been defeated, and the Company was the de facto ruler of all of Eastern India and the Deccan plateau (Gordon, 1993: 50).

After the Marathas, the only challenge left in India was the Sikh Kingdom in Punjab. In the wake of moribund Mughal empire, the Sikhs of the Punjab province had ascended and succeeded in developing a state of their own comprising, at its peak, today's Punjab of Pakistan, Punjab of India, Kashmir, Khyber Pakhtunkhwa, including the Federally Administered Tribal Areas (FATA) of Pakistan, and Tibet. After its most prominent ruler, Ranjit Singh, died in 1839, the war of succession resulted in an anarchic situation. The crisis in Afghanistan during those years also worsened the trade link between the company's empire and northern India. During 1845–1849, the company fought various small wars by exploiting the mutual differences among the contenders for the throne of the Sikh empire. By March, however, the whole Sikh kingdom was declared the property of the company, thus annexing imperial rule to the borders of Afghanistan (Gandhi, 2015: 130–86). Even before it occupied the Sikh state, by 1833, "the Company had established control over 500,000 square miles of territory in India, containing 93.7 million 'British subjects' who paid £22,718,794 a year in taxation" (quoted in Bowen, 2006: 5). Two years before India came under the suzerainty of the British Crown, the company had occupied almost all the Sub-Continent by employing war, coercion, treachery, exploitation, bribery, and plunder.

During 1757–1857, imperial rule by the Company involved a three-pronged strategy: preservation of the royal order, as long as it kept fulfilling the fiscal demands of the company, and its immediate termination at the first possible opportunity; the direct possession of valuable territories wherever and whenever required, with the introduction of new crops, industries, and economies in the areas; and the transformation of Indian economy from being an external area to its integration into the world economy as a periphery. During the hundred years (1757–1857) of the company's direct rule, India was reduced from flourishing economic hub of the continent to dependent economy. The British Raj, then, impoverished it further. By the end of colonial rule in 1947, the Sub-Continent had become one of the poorest regions in the world. From being a producer of about 23 percent of world GDP in 1750, the Sub-Continent could produce only 4 percent of world GDP by 1947. The company's policies were based on strategies that, in the words of Robert Clive, included "fighting, tricks, chicanery, intrigues, politics, and the Lord knows what" (quoted in Roberts, 1916: 142).

The British policy to Mughal suzerainty was similar to what we saw in China in the wake of the Opium Wars: preservation of the imperial order while usurping territories and the control of trade, taxation, and duties. However, while the Qing dynasty in China survived until 1912 with almost no credible attempt of succession in any area throughout the century of humiliation and imperial plunder, the Indian Mughal empire disintegrated quickly after Aurangzeb's death. However, while the company kept gaining from its commercial prerogatives, it did not extinguish the overall political order in India. Thus, when it defeated Shah Alam II in 1764, it did not kill the besieged king but took him on its side and pushed him to issue orders in the company's favor. It was on its insistence that the Mughal emperor handed over the *Diwani* of Bengal and other two provinces to the Company. However, the policymakers of the company did not enact a policy of preserving the old order for an indefinite time. In fact, the company devised a four-stage strategy called "subsidiary alliance" to entrap the successor states. Under this policy, during the first stage, the company offered security guarantees to the smaller successor states and kingdoms against their supposed enemies by stationing its own soldiers, to be financed by the ruler of the area, and in return receiving economic and commercial benefits. During the second stage, the company issued its distrust of the ruler's native force and asked for its dismantling. At the third stage, the company army instigated a crisis to launch a campaign against the identified enemies. The cost of the campaign was to be met by the ruler. At the final stage, the successful campaign resulted in demands for higher monetary compensation. Since the rulers found themselves increasingly unable to meet these demands, the company eventually took over the revenue and governance rights by retiring the ruler on a nominal pension (Prabhakaran, 1990: 133).

Before 1857, when Indian masses resisted British imperialism in an armed manner, the company paid verbal homage to the royal court at Delhi. However, it kept taking territory and accumulating treasure. As mentioned above, this treasure was used to balance trade with China. However, a mere occupation of the lands was not enough; it was necessary for the company to redefine the economic outlook of India, particularly Bengal. Relying mainly on the works of Romesh Chunder Dutt written during the first decade of the twentieth century, M. P. Prabhakaran (1990) mentions four strategies adopted to ruin India: free trade entitlement, monopolization of trade, unfair competition, and abolishing the monopoly. In the first instances, English traders were able to secure free trade privileges from Mughal emperor Jahangir (1605–1627) and exercise them during the Shah Jahan (1627–1658) and Aurangzeb (1658–1707) years. This privilege was exclusively to the company's external trade. In the wake of the company's victory in the War of Plassey, private trade by English traders and company officials was also proclaimed exempt from any duties and taxes inside India. This extension of prerogative into the private realm on Indian soil deprived Indian merchants of a chance at fair competition because they had to pay taxes, duties, annual fees, and so on. This abuse of the privilege went so far that Mir Qasim had to send a letter of protest to the company's governor and council in Calcutta. The company, however, flouted his orders. Compelled, he abolished all duties on internal trade altogether, thus nullifying the competitive edge that the company's officials had unlawfully gained in private and domestic trade. The company demanded a reinstatement of duties on Indian merchants, and on the refusal of Mir Qasim, ousted him from power and brought in Mir Jafar. After Mir Jafar's death in 1765, the company took over administrative, defense, and revenue power, enabling the Company to monopolize both internal and external trade from Indian soil. People were compelled to buy from and sell to the company only at the rates arbitrarily determined by the company. Violators were penalized in an exemplary manner to enforce deterrence. The company developed and patronized a bureaucratic structure of *Gumashatas* (Indian brokers) to suppress those who resisted. This monopoly extended to almost all necessities of life, including edibles, items of domestic use, opium, cotton, and so on. Brokers compelled local traders to buy from and sell to them only. Heavy punishments were ordered for violators or those who resisted the policies of dispossession. The arbitrary decisions about economic activities did not stop there. The company intervened in determining individual professions. With Indian-owned factories starting to close due to unavailability of raw materials, as well as the extinction of English market, the company hired weavers and other artisans. A system of mass production was invented by stretching human power to the maximum. Weavers were chained to produce as much cotton as they could, failing to do so meant severe punishments, including starvation, denial of sleep, and even the loss of life. Many of the raw products were included in the foreign trade list to ensure that the newly established factories in England could be provided with the required materials. The company pushed ahead with cultivating new crops in fertile areas, including cotton and opium, in particular. The company required the cultivators to grow the crops it chose, ignoring the needs of the local communities.

The third important strategy that the company adopted was the introduction of new crops and a shift in trade from manufactured goods such as cotton fabric to raw cotton. This strategy, known as unfair competition, was in international trade. During the seventeenth century, the company flourished in its cotton business in India to such an extent that it almost withdrew from the spice trade to concentrate on exporting textiles. Establishing its first factory in Hugli, Bengal, the company shipped 8,000 pieces of fabric to England in 1658. During the next three years, the number of pieces went up to 18,000. After receiving appreciation from its office in London, the company expanded its textile export business to such an extent that in 1678–1679 it shipped 123,000 pieces. This went up to 207,000 in 1680–1681, and 718,000 in 1683–1684 (Ray, 2014: 55). Trade after that fell due to the company's business disputes with the Mughals, including the one in 1688 when English traders tried to loot Mughal vessels, an incident that resulted in the company's free trade rights being revoked. However, exports continued to a great quantity throughout the last decade of the seventeenth century. It threatened the infant textile industry in Britain. The Indian textile question, therefore, dominated British national politics from 1680 until the 1730s (Broadberry and Gupta, 2005). During the first two decades of the eighteenth century, the British parliament passed laws prohibiting the sale and use of silk and cotton fabric manufactured in India. After it reached England, Indian cloth of far better quality cost about 50 to 60 percent less than English cloth, threatening the growth of the English cotton industry. In response to pressure, the British parliament, in 1700, passed the Calico Law to ban the importation of Calico fabric from India and China. However, import of the contraband flourished after a temporary depression because Indian cloth was cheaper and popular. In 1700–1701, the volume of textiles exported from Bengal to England was worth £196,950. During 1702–1707, it went down to £41,760 per annum. However, it went up again to £203,196 in 1710–1711 and reached £297,500 in 1719–1720 (Ray, 2014: 56). Therefore, in 1721, the British parliament passed another law prohibiting the sale and use of Indian and Chinese cotton cloth. However, this law did not affect the import of raw cotton and fustian thread. These laws affected Indian cotton fabric exports to the English market. With the loss of the English market, Indian cotton was left to be consumed in Asia, Africa, and other European countries. During the first half of the seventeenth century, when European companies were in competition, the Dutch East India Company benefited from the English trade sanction. During 1730–1735, it exported massive quantities of cotton, silk, and woven cloth from India to Southeast Asia. However, the trade gap between the English East India Company and other European companies increased after the 1740s (Chaudhury, 1995). These laws were repealed in 1774 only after the textile industry started mechanizing and developed a competitive edge against Indian textiles. It could happen only because during 1733–1774, the English textile industry survived by "drawing on cheap but good cotton imported from slave-worked plantations of Brazil and West Indies" (Habib, 2013: 47; Eacott, 2016: 327). Almost simultaneously, the company's textile exports increased exponentially in the wake of its usurpation of *Diwani* in Bengal in 1765. According to Chaudhuri (1995), while the company shipped about 390,390 pieces of cloth to England during 1751–1755, this went up to 839,905 pieces of cloth exported to England in 1793 (p. 188). Despite these enormous exports to England, Europe, and China, the company utilized its coercive monopolistic powers to reduce the price of cotton, the wages of the weavers, and the overall production cost of the fabric. It affected the weavers and their socio-economic privileges. As early as 1768, weavers throughout South India protested and demanded the pre-1757 system whereby they were able to raise credit for their work whenever they needed. The company refused to bring back any such leverage (Parthasarathi and Wendt, 2009). The whole sector of the economy and an established division of labor was uprooted to accumulate maximum capital in England. Using the company's official documents and records from factories in Dhaka, Hameeda Hossain (1988) argues that the company transformed the whole system of production, trade, and payment of textiles in a deliberate attempt to ruin the weavers who had been producing cloth for the world for centuries. According to her, by 1813, the textile industry of Bengal had died. India, an economic center of the preindustrial world, was turned into a dependent economy in the new industrializing world economy dominated by the West. The company's monopoly over Anglo-Asian trade was, however, a hurdle in the way of British traders. In 1813, the British parliament passed the Charter Act and abolished the company's monopoly on Anglo-Indian trade while maintaining its monopolistic jurisdiction in trade with China. The Chinese monopoly also ended in 1833. It opened the Indian market to English traders; India became a consumer of English products. Ironically, most of these products were made from Indian raw materials. The company turned into a ruler. It established a local administrative setup in the areas under its control and dictated the production of crops in need, particularly opium to settle the chronic trade deficit with China. It was primarily opium produced in India that the company took to China and imposed it on Chinese merchants as a fungible commodity. The Opium Wars, fought in 1840 and 1842, discussed in the previous chapter, show the nature of the commercial operations that the British imperial enterprise conducted in Asia.

The company redefined the agrarian economy of India as well, and for the worse. Under the Mughals, India had two simultaneous systems defining the relationship between the state and society. Under the *Zamindari* system, the state allotted an area to a person and made him responsible for managing its production and the collection of revenue from the small cultivators. He could keep a particular portion of the taxes to meet his administrative and socio-political expenditures. The *Mansabdari* system, enacted by Akbar, was primarily a *Zamindari* system plus military service. Under the *Ryotwari* system, the cultivators paid their taxes directly to the state. However, in both cases, ownership of the land remained with the state. Both the systems had provided social stability and order in the functioning of the state. After the company took over revenue rights in Bengal, it abolished the *Zamindari* system altogether and started auctioning the fertile land initially for three years and later for five years. It destroyed the whole social fabric; the landed elite responsible for maintaining public order and establishing the writ of the state across the country was left with financial questions, while auctioning provided the business and merchant class an opportunity to enter the agricultural sector. Since the duration of the period was limited, the ultimate purpose of these new owners was to exploit the land and gain financial benefit. Since the company was interested in securing its own share, it never bothered with the treatment of peasants and cultivators by the newly landed elite. Given that the company took away nine-tenths of the produce, and the new contractors also took some share of the produce, the cultivators were left with almost nothing. In 1770, therefore, Bengal faced the first in a series of famines killing ten million, or roughly one-third of its population, followed by other appalling numbers of deaths caused by about fifteen more famines. Shashi Tharoor (2016) mentions these famines as follows: the Great Bengal Famine (1766–1770), Madras (1782–1783), Chalsia (1783–1784), Doji Bara (1791–1792), Agra (1837–1838), Orissa (1866), Bihar (1873–1874), Southern India (1876–1877), the Indian famine (1896–1900), Bombay (1905–1906), and the most notorious of all, the Bengal famine (1943–1944). Tharoor argues that in these all famines, "between 30 and 35 million Indians needlessly died of starvation" (p. 177). In 1793, the company introduced a "permanent settlement" in India. The land became a commodity open to anyone willing to pay the company its share of the income: 90 percent of the produce. Since many could not pay, they had to relinquish the land. The new buyer was required to pay the arrears plus interest accumulated, thus making it nearly the principal cost of the land. However, the revenue rate was so enormous and unprecedented that eventually the company had to retreat. Gradually, the company's share went down to 83 percent, 75 percent, 66 percent, and then to 50 percent in 1855. It is important to mention that the highest rent recorded in England during this time was only 20 percent.

The introduction of new crops in Bengal and Bihar, particularly commercial crops such as cotton and opium, resulted in a redefinition of the outlook for Indian agriculture. The transformation was both spatial and diverse. Bengal, Awadh, and Bihar produced cotton and opium. While the expansion of cotton from Awadh and Bengal to other areas, particularly the Punjab, continued throughout British imperial rule thanks to irrigation, it was opium that solved the problem of a chronic deficit in the balance of payments in such a manner that the British empire was equated with being the "Opium Empire." According to Benoy Chowdhury (1964), the rising demand for indigo in England and opium in China pushed the company to develop coercive and exploitative measures. One of them was the deliberate lowering of prices at the production spot to maximize profit at the sale point, either at the seaports or in China. Answering a puzzle mentioned by Fernand Braudel, "if it is virtually beyond question that Europe was less rich than the worlds it was exploiting, even after the fall of Napoleon when Britain's hour of glory was dawning—we still do not really know how this position of superiority was established and above all maintained—for the gap grew steadily wider" (Braudel and Reynolds1982: 534–35), Trocki (1999) refers to opium as the principal reason. According to him, while the Dutch provided the "necessary foundation" for an expansion of the market of already-available Indian opium, the British championed in exporting unprecedented levels of opium to China. During 1702–1706, the company's import of the tea soared from 20,000 pounds to 100,000 pounds, placing it under the increasing pressure of trade deficit and bullion transfer. The level expanded further; in 1760–1766, the company's annual export of tea from China to England reached six million pounds. As mentioned above, the company was importing huge quantities of bullion from Europe to meet its exchange requirements both in India and, more importantly, China. Opium, then, stood out to be a principal commodity capable of replacing silver as a form of payment and therefore addressing the exchange question. In India, this changed the dynamics of its agricultural outlook; the company, as it won the war in 1757 and *Diwani* authority in 1765, pushed the production of opium as a cash crop. Moreover, since 1773, with the arrival of Warren Hastings as the governor-general of the company, poppy cultivation, opium production, and its trade on Indian seaports were monopolized by the company. The large-scale production and sale of opium to China started in 1781. In 1787, China received 200 chests of opium from India. This number grew to 2,000 in 1800, and 5,147 chests in 1820 (Habib, 2013: 46). The company sold opium to private "country traders," who then took it to China. An overwhelming majority of these traders were officials in the Company itself. By labeling it as private trade, the company saved itself from many complications, including competition and violence in the opium sea trade. Under its monopoly, the company appropriated opium and other tradable products to meet its trade deficit with China. In other words, India paid for the company's purchases from China. Hastings's predecessor during 1767–1769, Harry Verelst, reported that in his times, the cost of the trade was covered through the revenue collected from India "without importing a single ounce of silver from Europe" (Woodruff, 1954: 111). As reported above, new research mentions that the import of silver did not end altogether because the company expanded its military and administrative expenditures. A far as trade is concerned, it seems that Indian agriculture and revenue paid for it for quite a considerable time. By 1828, twelve years before the British fought the first Opium War against China, the company was shipping opium in such huge quantities that it alone was covering its entire tea trade with China. British monopolistic control and expansion of opium cultivation in India, however, reached its maximum level during direct British rule after 1857. During 1868–1878, more than 560,000 acres of fertile land in Bengal alone were used to cultivate poppy. During this time, the British traders earned a lucrative profit of about Rs. 1000 per chest. This trade alone provided a yearly net profit of about £4,000,000 to the British government (Janin, 1999: 39). India, therefore, was able to finance British trade and colonial occupation abroad and prosperity at home. Meanwhile, India faced famines that killed a considerable part of the population.

The consequences of this resource extraction were immense. It was massive de-industrialization that deprived India of whatever it had on the eve of the arrival of European companies in the sixteenth century. According to Bagchi (2010):

> Within sixty years of the defeat of the last independent Nawab of Bengal by the British, India was reduced to the status of an agrarian and underdeveloped economy. The process of colonialization of the Indian economy involved the extraction of a tribute from the economy at an unprecedented rate. That extraction, in turn, required the structural adjustment of the economy in the sense that

> the domestic absorption of commodities produced by India had to be squeezed so as to yield an exportable surplus that would be remitted to the ruling country. That structural adjustment involved the severe depression of investment in both agriculture and industry and also required radical alteration of the "modes" of extraction of the tribute. (p. xxvi)

It is a fact that massive de-industrialization took place during British rule in India (Clingingsmith and Williamson, 2008; Habib, 2006, 2013; T. Roy, 2002). It was on such a massive scale that India, a preindustrial manufacturing textile exporter and economic center of the world, turned into an agrarian economy dependent on the new Europe-dominated core. Indian integration into the world economy, as it expanded in Asia during the eighteenth century, deprived it of its erstwhile economic positional standing in the world-system. Clingingsmith and Williamson (2008) divide Indian economic history since 1700 into four distinct parts. The first period, marked as a high-water mark (1700–1760) during which India was "a global manufacturing powerhouse." The second period (1760–1810) is the time "during which India lost its significant share of world textile markets to Britain," though "that result can be partly explained by increasing cost competitiveness favoring Britain, superior factory technology was not yet the main force at work." During the third period, 1810–1860, "India lost much of its domestic textile market to Britain" due to "the combined influence of relatively rapid factory-based productivity advance in Britain and by increased world market integration, the latter driven by declining transport costs between the two trading partners, and to the free trade policy imposed on India by her colonial ruler." The fourth period, 1860–1914, the process of de-industrialization was reversed only to a marginal extent, resulting in partial re-industrialization (p. 223). This partial re-industrialization, then, can be observed as a process of structural adjustment through which India was integrated into the world-system as a dependent peripheral economy.

The English Industrial Revolution, a European economic miracle, was not the cause but the outcome of Indian de-industrialization. Long before it happened in England, India had been enjoying its status as the epicenter of world manufacturing. It was a developed economy, though of a preindustrial nature, whose GDP volume and growth had been far greater than all of Europe put together. As mentioned above, as the British started occupying India, they extracted invaluable capital from the Sub-Continent and accumulated it in Britain. Bagchi (2010) estimates that the extraction of the resource from Bengal to England was about 7.07 of its GDP during the initial occupying decades when India was being transformed from a manufacturing and export-oriented economy into an agrarian and dependent economy. This calculation of the extraction of resources is comprised of revenues and trade surplus managed by the arbitrary lowering of prices in India and exporting of raw materials only; it does not take into account other sources of capital accumulation such as tributes, gifts, and looting. He estimates that during 1765–1812, £122.8 million was transferred from India to England, capital or its benefits that were never returned to India. More precisely, Bagchi claims that by 1914,Great Britain had "invested" about £400 million in its colonies; about 75–95 percent of this investment was Indian capital extracted through land revenue, trade surplus, capital transfer, and so on. Most of this transfer was used to industrialize England. In today's calculations, Minhaz Merchant (2015) argues, Britain owes more than $3 trillion for the damages it inflicted on India during imperial rule. Taking into account three factors—namely, the difference between India's GDP growth rate between 1757 and 1947, pre-1757 GDP growth rate, and post-1947 GDP growth rate; the monetary value of the goods and services exported from India to Great Britain and elsewhere; and differences in social life, such as rates ofliteracy, fertility, mortality, and infant mortality—Merchant argues that "Britain's colonial rule destroyed India's industries and made India a vassal for the newly industrializing Britain in the 19th century." Tharoor (2016) reports that "India was treated as a cash cow; the revenues that flowed into London's treasury were described by the Earl of Chatham as 'the redemption of a nation . . . a kind of gift from heaven.' The British extracted from India approximately £18,000,000 each year between 1765 and 1815" (p. 11). These were the years when England witnessed an Industrial Revolution. Indian treasure enabled the monarchy, elite class, and an infant industrial class to dominate and expand the processes and patterns of production and the division of labor across the imperial world. Writing in 1897, Brooks Adams admitted it glaringly:

> Very soon after Plassey, the Bengal plunder began to arrive in London, and the effect appears to have been instantaneous, or all authorities agree that the "industrial revolution," the event which has divided the eighteenth century from all antecedent time, began with the year 1760.
>
> Plassey was fought in 1757, and probably nothing has ever equaled in rapidity of the change which followed. In 1760 the flying shuttle appeared, and coal began to replace wood in smelting. In 1764 Hargreaves invented the spinning-jenny, in 1779 Crompton contrived the mule, in 1785 Cartwright patented the power loom, and, chief of all, in 1768 Watt matured the steam-engine, the most perfect of all vents of centralizing energy. But, though these machines served as outlets for the accelerating movement of the time, they did not cause the acceleration.
>
> Before the influx of the Indian treasure, and the expansion of credit which followed, no force sufficient for this purpose existed; and had Watt lived fifty years earlier, he and his invention must have perished together.

> Possibly since the world began, no investment has ever yielded the profit reaped from the Indian plunder, because for nearly fifty years Great Britain stood without a competitor. (pp. 313–17)

It was, therefore, Indian capital and resources that were put into the foundation of the English Industrial Revolution. As the company occupied India, it contributed to the government finances used to expand the empire through conquests. Indian money, more precisely, was used to settle the British balance of payments. Britain, a debtor due to French Wars in the second half of the eighteenth century, was able not only to afford the war expenditures but also offset its debt and become a creditor nation. The magnitude of the drain of Indian capital to England varies hugely. William Digby (1901) argues that "modern England has been made great by Indian wealth, wealth never proffered, by its possessor, but always taken by the might and skill of the stronger" (p. 35). He estimates that the total wealth taken from India to England between 1757 and 1815 was probably £1,000 million (p. 4). In the other source, Hamilton (1919) calculates this wealth to be no more than £34.1 million. However, Javier Esteban (2001), after admitting to using highly conservative estimates of the *minimum* transfer of capital from India to England, argues, "Britain was nearly free from overseas indebtedness by the onset of the French Wars. In sharp contrast, without the Indian transfers, Britain could have required mounting foreign borrowing in 1772–1820, to seemingly unsustainable levels after 1809." Using a counterfactual method, he shows that in the absence of Indian wealth, Britain could have been under in debt for about £170 million by 1815; by this time, it was a creditor of about £30 million. Thanks to the company's monopoly over trade and its direct patronage by the government in London, Indian wealth not only funded the French Wars but also contributed 61 percent of the total accumulation of English government wealth during this time (pp. 64–65). The use of this money to fund infrastructural development and industrialization is a logical inference. As mentioned by Irfan Habib (2013), Indian cotton exports to England accounted for about 67 percent of the company's whole trade in 1757–1758. After the War of Plassey, cotton exports went up to 80 percent of total exports. That it was in the 1770s that English textiles started to be mechanized so England could produce fabrics cheaper than Indian fabrics so that the demand for Indian cloth could be reduced shows that mercantile policies at home joined excessive looting in India to mature the Industrial Revolution in England. In 1770, English textile mills were consuming 1,500 tons of raw cotton every year. During the 1780s, demand went up to 81,00 tons a year. In 1798–1800, the demand reached 18,500 tons a year, enabling the textile mills to not only meet the British domestic demand but also export a bulk of it to the colonies. During 1795–1804, the British exports of cotton fabric only earned the country a revenue of £5.3 million every year (Habib, 2013: 62). Joel Mokyr (2009) admits that "cotton was still a marginal industry in Britain in 1760, quite small compared to wool" (p. 82). It was after the British conquests in India that the macroeconomic indicators started booming in England. Patents, for example, started being taken out after 1757; the annual ratio went up from 9.9 in the 1750s to 22.1 in the 1770s and 51.2 in the 1780s. The number of banks increased from 10 in 1750 to about 400 in 1800. The level of public investment in mega civil engineering projects also increased disproportionately, from 12 during 1750–1759 to 47 during 1790–1799 (pp. 80–87). Given that the company had been paying £400,000 to the exchequer since 1765, it is entirely convincing to correlate the developments during the Industrial Revolution (1760–1830, as mentioned by Mokyr) with the plunder that took place in India. Even those who claim that "Plassey plunder did not fund the Industrial Revolution" argue that the primary objective of the company's drive in India was financial gain to be utilized for the purchase of military equipment, conquest consolidation, and expansion of trade operations. It was the financial strength of the Mughal empire, the successor states, and the financiers that the company targeted. "Clive's actions were not directed from London; but they cannot be understood unless they are placed in the broader context of the financial revolution, the expansionist forces that it generated, and the problems these forces experienced on distant frontiers, where credit lines were fully stretched and where the junctions made with representatives of indigenous financial and fiscal systems were a necessary precondition for commercial success" (Cain and Hopkins, 2016: 95–96). In 1825 the first major global financial crisis erupted in England, destroying the Indian agriculture and industry further. British control over trade and pricing enabled English manufacturers and traders to dump their productions of cotton fabric and yarn; during 1825–1829, this dump increased by about forty times. The made-in-Britain vessels annihilated the shipping industry in Bombay. It placed the company under pressure to maintain balance in its trade. It turned toward raw cotton, silk, and opium, the latter to be dumped in China. The Indian economy, whatever it could have been, was demised by the nature, terms, and conditions of its integration into the world economy (Wilson, 2016: 208). Had there been credible Indian resistance to any such expansion, and had no process of imperial expansion taken place, world history would have been entirely different.

Therefore, it is a fact that Industrial Revolution in Britain took place *after* the arrival of Indian treasure. By the time it expanded into other European countries, England had developed an unbridgeable gap between itself and European contenders. With expansionism being inherent in capitalism, English technologies in textile could have challenged Indian weavers and their preindustrial artisanship. It should have happened, and it did happen.

However, had the British not taken over India, and had the company not done what it did—namely, the extraction of capital and resources on arbitrary terms—India could have created an indigenous model of development based on higher tariffs, security of interest of its producers and other stakeholders, and gradual industrialization based on its own needs, constraints, and opportunities (Tharoor, 2016: 10). The British were able to occupy India because they excelled militarily and were able to exploit mutual differences among the Indians to forward their own agenda. The Indians' sense of nationalism was either nonexistent or just in a phase of incipience. The lack of military power and nationalism, coupled with mutual disagreements and the absence of a sense of unity, enabled the Europeans to penetrate deep into India and extract as many resources as they could. For there does not appear to be any other convincing reason to admit, as pointed out by Habib (2013), that an economy eight times smaller than that of India could overcome and subdue it. Therefore, in the case of India, the significant divergence was involuntary and happened primarily due to the military superiority of the company and British forces. In under two hundred years (1600–1800), the Indian economy was structurally transformed and integrated into globalizing capitalism as its periphery without any considerable indigenous input. From its status as the economic epitome of the world, India was integrated into the capitalist world economy as a dependent periphery.

INDIA UNDER BRITISH IMPERIALISM (1857–1947)

The "War of Independence" of 1857, the event that Western historians know as the Sepoy Mutiny, was a desperate expression of resistance to the plunder imposed on Indians. As mentioned, by 1856, the company's rule had expanded throughout the Sub-Continent. Though hundreds of principalities maintained their autonomous status, they were independent in a nominal sense since the company regulated their economic relations. The company's monopolistic control of trade between Asia and Europe had been revoked in 1813. Thus, it became a company controlled by the state. The events of 1857–1859 started when Indian soldiers in the British army were forced to use ammunition containing the fat of either cattle or pigs, both of which contain significant religious symbolism for Hindus and Muslims. Their refusal to use these bullets resulted in a "rebellion" that spread across northwestern, northern, and central India. Eastern India was less affected, while some areas, such as those under the Madras presidency, remained aloof (Pati, 2007, 2012). The rebellion failed because of complex intricacies intersecting the religious, social, economic, as well as political characteristics of the Indian masses. According to S. B. Chaudhuri (2007), it was a rebellion initiated by military units comprised of Indian soldiers that turned into a popular rebellion with mass participation. However, since the Mughal army, if there was any, was dissipated, demoralized, and immensely disorganized, it did not dare to attack and defend Delhi, the symbol of resistance and continuation of Mughal rule in India. Had it dared, the tired, increasingly disobedient English force could have been ousted from Delhi since it had already lost 38 percent of its force in the rebellion (Wilson, 2016: 257). However, the Mughals capitulated, and India surrendered to a new alien imperial power. Many other reasons causing the debacle of Delhi include the feudal structure of society, religious differences, lack of leadership, and the repressive carrot-and-stick policies of the British forces.

The most significant outcome of the 1857–1859 rebellion was that the company lost its ruler status in India, and the Sub-Continent was brought under the direct rule of the Great Britain. By the time Britain took over India as its colony, the Sub-Continent had already been defeated militarily, subjugated politically, and crippled economically. Through the process of integration into the burgeoning English-led capitalism, its political economy had been restructured to such an extent that it had lost its position as manufacturer, particularly of cotton fabric, and had instead become a producer of the raw cotton meant to meet the demands of the European textile industry (Dutt, 1950). The economic pillage continued after the British made India a colony and an integral part of the empire; it was institutionalized. The nature of India's deepening integration into the world-system followed from its redefined positional standing as a periphery. Resource extraction, therefore, remained the primary objective of London. The institutionalization of the perpetuation of underdevelopment took various forms, including infrastructural development, agricultural and industrial development, bureaucratic institutionalization, and social transformation. The crux of ninety-year direct colonial rule was the metamorphosis of Indian society based on terms it did not agree to.

By the time Britain took over India as a colony, a huge gap had appeared in the status of the capitalist development between the two countries; Britain had surpassed other regional industrializing nations and maintained a distinct edge in economic affluence, while India was impoverished and lacked infrastructural development, particularly the integration of domestic markets connected with the British economy. Infrastructural development—railways, bridges, and a canal irrigation system—became the focus of the colonial administration. The British believed that since India did not observe any scientific revolution per se, and its "intellectual state of affairs" was pathetically unrefined, it should ask the white men to help it to grow and develop its infrastructure. Bureaucracy was vital for this development. Oriental, or more specifically Indian intellect, according to *The Minutes of Education* written by Thomas Babington Macaulay, a British politician and servant of the company in India during 1834–1838, was of such a level that "a single shelf of a good European library was worth the whole native literature of India and Arabia." In science, "the superiority of the Europeans becomes absolutely immeasurable" to such an extent that "all the historical information which has been collected from all the books written in the Sanskrit language is less valuable than what may be found in the paltriest abridgments used at preparatory schools in England" (p. 109). Therefore, Lord Macaulay recommended to the British government that "we must at present do our best to form a class who may be interpreters between us and the millions whom we govern—a class of persons Indian in blood and color, but English in tastes, in opinions, in morals, and in intellect." Since it was going to be an elitist project, and the whole purpose of intellectual development was to serve British interests on the Sub-Continent, Oriental literature and contributions in science and preindustrial technology were relegated to nothing. Missionary schools and Oriental colleges and later universities established and administered by the company and the British government in India served three important purposes. First, the events of 1857 and subsequent steps taken by British officials created what Francis Hutchins (1967) calls an "illusion of permanence": the idea that the British were in India to rule forever, and the Indians were unable to defeat the British power. Simultaneously, the hopes that British would assimilate into Indian diversity also failed. Using these educational institutions, the Indians were pushed to cooperate with the new rulers and learn the new governance system. Second, English schools produced a class of clerks or low-rank administrative officials to facilitate the functioning of the company-state and the British administration. In 1835, the company declared English its medium of communication and instruction. Using English instead of Persian as the medium of communication, the lower Indian cadre of bureaucracy was trained in modern science, mathematics, European history and philosophy, ethics, and culture. Their role, as predicted, remained serving the colonial state through bureaucratic practices, including controlling the masses, revenue collection, political developments, law and order, the inflow of goods in India, and, of course, the outflow of capital to Britain. Third, since employment opportunities in the new administration were to be acquired through qualification in Western knowledge, the Indians developed a desire to receive a "modern" education. While the company had established some colleges—with Fort William College Calcutta, established in 1800, being the most notable—the colonial administration established universities in Calcutta, Bombay, and Madras in 1857. By 1887, about 60,000 students had graduated from these institutions. The colonial administration hired a considerable number of these graduates; by 1887, the colonial government had 21,466 employees, with 47 percent being Hindus, 7 percent Muslims,

19 percent Eurasians, and 29 percent Europeans (Moore, 1999: 431–32). The growth of knowledge, if any, and skills and abilities suitable to industrialize and modernize India and its economy was systematically denied or at least obstructed. The British government determined not only the nature and scale of infrastructural development but also the technological choices and their arrival in India with an exclusive purpose to expatriate Indian capital to England. The education system was used for the "transfer of Western ideas and artifacts, but . . . transfer of loyalties" was at the cost of destruction of India's indigenous expertise. It was a "weak market-based transfer of knowledge, and overall, the formation of an 'enclavist' industrial system" (MacLeod and Kumar, 1995; Roy, 2009).

From the start, the composition of colonial bureaucracy was such that the Indians were made to serve as minions under British officers. Emphasizing that the Indians lacked the modern and technical education required to develop and improve infrastructure, an unusual number of British "experts" were hired. It affected the country in two ways. First, with the medium of instruction being English, Indians were unable to learn the skills required for high-end and technical jobs. In the public works department, for example, there were 1,015 engineers employed, of which only 86 were Indians. It was because they had to study and pass exams in Greek, Latin, mathematics, science, English literature, and history (Tharoor, 2016: 212). Second, the induction of British (and European) nationals resulted in a drainage of capital. In the Indian Civil Service, the backbone of colonial rule, the top cadre was reserved for Europeans only. Fredrick J. Shore, a judge in the Civil Court and Criminal Sessions to the District of Furrukhabad, testified in 1857 before the House of Commons and stated that "the Indians have been excluded from every honor, dignity or office which the lowest Englishman could be prevailed upon to accept" (quoted in Dutt, 1906: 411). The result of this approach was that the number of British civil officers in India went up from two thousand in 1805 to six thousand in 1890, after which the proportion declined due to pressure from Indian nationalist forces to increase the quota of natives in the officer cadre. However, the British empire maintained a massive army and a variety of law enforcement agencies including the police. In 1805, the company had twenty-two thousand British soldiers on its payroll; the number went up to seventy thousand in 1890, after which the proportion declined, though it was never less than sixty thousand from 1890 to 1947 (Tharoor, 2016: 60–61). These Europeans were hired with salaries far higher than those of their Indian counterparts, and they were paid in sterling. Once retired, their pensions were also paid by the company and later by the imperial government in India. The service sector, therefore, proved to be one of the most important expenditures.

The bottom line of the nature of economic development in colonial India was myopic, self-centered, and partial. According to Maddison (1971), "the British were not averse to Indian economic development *if it increased their markets* but refused to help in areas where they felt there was a conflict with their own economic interests or political security" (p. 35, emphasis added). The purpose of any infrastructural or logistical development was to increase the productive capacity of India to support the industrial activities in England, Europe, and North America and become a fast-growing consumer market to absorb the products manufactured there. The colonial administration looked toward railways as a panacea to integrate Indian markets and economy with world markets. By 1908, the Indian colonial government had spent more than £274 million on a railway network, which was 80 percent of the total industrial investment made by the colonial administration by that time (Sweeney, 2011: 1). While track construction had reached about 10,000 miles by 1875, by 1947 it reached 45,000 miles and included about 136,000 bridges (Lalvani, 2016: 21). The motivation for such an enormous investment was economic in southern and eastern India but political and strategic in northern India, particularly in the regions adjacent to Afghanistan. When the company extended the Punjab by the mid-nineteenth century, it was quick to develop railways there because of the fertility of the area; the railway would be an effective way to transport agricultural products to coastal areas to be shipped to England. The primary purpose was to utilize local tax money for the government to develop monopolistic control over the commercial transportation system to the utmost benefit of British traders and commercial enterprises. According to Sweeney (2011), a memorandum prepared in 1909 informed the government in London that the system had produced a net cash surplus of about £30 million in 1908, with total benefits exceeding £100 million, mostly to the trading sector (p. 2). The principal beneficiaries of this infrastructural development, he argues, were the British industrialists. The railway linked the interior fields of cotton production with the coasts of Bombay, Karachi, and Calcutta, thus facilitating the transportation of raw cotton to the Manchester and Lancashire textile industries.

Another important development during colonial rule in India was the irrigation system. It was comparatively low performance, however. Some initial studies conclude that the irrigation system in India caused more harm than good to the agricultural and associated sectors of the economy. The most significant reason was that it affected the pattern of crop production; irrigation expanded the arable area and thus the production of crops, yet it negatively affected the proportion of food crops compared to cash crops such as cotton. Despite the increasing threat of famine, many of which did happen, the colonial government insisted on the massive production of cash crops while providing minimal subsidies to the subjects (Whitcombe, 1972). Later studies, however, refute this claim. Looking at the effects the canal irrigation system had on peasants in the Ganga-Jamna *Doab* (the fertile region between the two rivers), Stone (1984) argues that "the canal was a more appropriate technology than the traditional methods of irrigation, given the priorities normally exhibited by peasant households and the economic, institutional, and physical conditions in the Doab" (p. 18). However, the economic benefits of the irrigation system, like the benefits the colonial government accrued through the development of the railway, outweighed investments made in this sector. Given that the Indian cloth manufacturing capacity had already been destroyed, the purpose of the irrigation system, agricultural development, and some subsidies on cash crops was to deepen the redefined division of labor in the capitalist world-system; as a periphery, India's role was to provide raw materials to the industrial countries of the West. It was this approach that led the design of development in India. To refer to P. J. Cain and Antony Hopkins (2016), it was a *gentlemanly capitalism* whereby the imperial administration, influenced by the financial capitalist class based in London, shared the benefits of so-called development to align the landed elite class on its side and deepen its penetration in Indian society. The primary role in the development of British imperialism in India and beyond was to introduce a "particular type of economic development, centered on finance and commercial services, which was set in train at the close of the seventeenth century and survived until the end of empire and indeed beyond" (p. 648). This development in the center, Cain and Hopkins argue, rested more on services and commercial and financial capitalism. However, they admit that "the process of industrialization is undoubtedly central to modern British history" (p. 44). They are of the view that "increasing reliance upon the Indian market undoubtedly gave Manchester a keen interest in the development of the Sub-Continent" (p. 312). Therefore, at a time of disequilibrium in the supply and demand of raw cotton, capitalists and industrial lobbyists in Manchester and London influenced imperial policy to invest more in irrigation and railways in India. One of the consequences of the irrigation system was excessive production of crops; it also did not bring many benefits to Indian peasants. A study by George Blyn (1966) explains what exactly happened: Crop production and pricing trends during 1891–1947 show that "output [of cash crops] increased at a relatively rapid rate during the period" (p. 216). However, it brought adverse effects to the equilibrium between cash crops and food crops in two ways. First, the production of wheat, for example, increased during this period, but it was lower compared to the rapid increase in the production of cotton. Second, minor grains benefited the least. During the period (1891–1947), the per-acre output of nonfood grain crops increased by 1.08 percent, while that of food grain crops increased 0.39 percent (p. 225). Keeping in mind that the proportion of land being cultivated for cash crops increased compared to the land being cultivated for food grains, and taking into account the increase in per-acre production as reported by Blyn, it is not difficult to see the transformation colonialism brought in the composition of Indian agricultural production. The overall consequence of this transformation in agricultural production was that Indian agriculture was made to fit the needs and demands of British industries as a periphery.

As compared to investment in infrastructure and irrigation and the implementation of a British-dominated bureaucratic structure, little attention was paid to other sectors of social development. Education, for example, was meant to further the Macaulayian purpose of serving the interests of the empire. Suvobrata Sarkar (2013) argues that the purpose of education in India was training in such technical skills required most by the empire to expand the scope of its interests. It led to a "careless fusion between industrial and technical education" whereby the state preferred "the teaching of crafts and agrarian skills over academic education" while resisting "an academic education based on the higher level of science and technology rather than a training only in crafts" (pp. 100, 116). The educational system, therefore, performed two tasks. First, it provided human capital to run the administrative affairs. Second, it provided opportunities for cultural infiltration. However, one of the many important consequences of the inexorable processes initiated by imperial interests was a drive for Western education led by both Muslim and Hindu leaders. Most of them were scions of the elite class that returned to lead the masses after having studied in modern educational institutions in England. In technology transfer, the British adopted a conservative mercantilist attitude. The education of science and technology in colleges established after 1857 was devoid of any training in military technology or even railways. Instead of developing local Indian human resources to spread the benefits of investment and capital dispersion in India, the colonial administration relied on hiring British officers and engineers, particularly beyond 1870 when the railway project went into full swing; their numbers increased from 250 in 1870 to over 1,000 in 1920. Contractors, suppliers, and all other superior lucrative positions were put in the hands of British nationals (Derbyshire, 1995: 179). This and other development initiatives were "ambitious technology projects undertaken with specific aims and with imported men and material; it was a wholesale import with only negligible local input" (MacLeod and Kumar, 1995: 14).

It was, in the end, the tridimensional process that showed India a path to eventually shun colonialism and assert independence. It included the bureaucratic culture developed through the Indian Civil Services, the legislative and political organization installed by the British and its evolution as India went under direct control of the Crown, and the development of educational institutions to incubate political identities and organizations. Starting in 1858, the

British government introduced a series of constitutional and legal packages that gradually transferred power from London to New Delhi. However, the colonial administration under the viceroyalty gradually conceded budgetary power to the Indians through the constitutional reforms known as the Government of India Acts. In August 1858, the very first Government of India Act was announced in India, vesting all the administrative, financial, and political powers in the Crown. The Queen was empowered to appoint a council of fifteen members, all British, responsible for managing affairs in India. Residing in London, the council was led by the secretary of the state of India, while affairs in India were managed through the viceroy and his legislative council, initially all British, and the enactment of the Indian Civil Service. Before 1935, India was bound to pay all expenses, including the salaries of all the officers appointed by the government. According to the Government of India Act of 1935, for the first time, the salaries of the secretary of state of India and his staff were not withdrawn from the revenue of colonial India. The next big constitutional packages, the Government of India Acts of 1861, 1892, 1909, 1919, and 1935, gradually transferred political and administrative power to the Indians. However, during this long rule, the British viceroy maintained his absolute discretion in financial affairs. The control of the government in all sectors of national life allowed the colonial administration to transfer undisclosed amounts of capital, services, and resources to Britain. For example, it utilized revenue collected from Indian peasants and landlords to finance and build a sizeable Indian army primarily meant to defend Great Britain in both World Wars. As Indians started involving themselves in the business of the empire, they objected to the loss of financial and human resources, but to no avail.

The imperial government introduced the Indian Civil Service to effectively control and rule the Sub-Continent. Initially, British officers were hired to take care of administering government affairs in more than 250 districts across the region. A district was a territory—and the most important tier in the hierarchical administrative structure of the government—spread, in many cases, over 4,000 square miles, inhabiting hundreds of thousands of people, and administered by a British officer aged twenty-four to thirty. These officers possessed immensely broad judicial, administrative, financial, and policing powers. Called deputy commissioners, these officers could have experience as little as three years serving as an assistant commissioner at the sub-district level. The district administration "held the entire edifice together, set a high standard of personal integrity and dedicated service, attracted the best products of British schools and universities, and manned the higher ranks of the British-Indian government" (Mansingh, 2006: 22). As Indians, particularly those educated and trained in British universities, gradually started succeeding in the competitive exams for the Civil Service, the British started accepting them as reliable partners of lower significance. Still, there were some places where the British applied the "not for the Indian" rule in a discretionary manner. Rao Bahadur Vappala Pangunni Menon, commonly known as V. P. Menon, hailing from a humble background, served as Reforms Commissioner and Constitutional Advisor to the three last viceroys: Lord Linlithgow, Lord Wavell, and Lord Mountbatten, the highest position held by any Indian during the colonial period. However, before he could reach this position in 1943, Menon, in 1940, submitted to Viceroy Lord Linlithgow a plan for the federation of the princely states with the rest of India; his plan was confiscated, with the viceroy saying to him, "You expect me to make you Reforms Commissioner when the job comes up, don't you? You had better get it out of your mind. It is not a job for an Indian" (quoted in Mosley, 1961: 88). Indian officers were rarely appointed to important positions in important locations. The British policy was clear. After having destroyed the local institutions of governance, the British were not willing to empower Indian officers to learn the principles of self-government. Instead, their primary job was to serve British interests, such as the seamless flow of capital to the central government and the protection of British investments (Raychaudhuri, 1999: 156). With immense power in their hands, the bureaucracy became the godfather and king-making class in Pakistan after the partition of the Sub-Continent in 1947. Since they were recruited, trained, and made to rule in united India, the bureaucratic class carried a heavy and unrelinquishable burden for the postindependence development endeavors initiated by the postcolonial states of India and Pakistan.

However, to its credit, the bureaucratic system integrated the whole country under one rule. Though about 560 princely states were functioning in a relatively autonomous manner, they were deprived of some important powers, including defense and foreign affairs. British Raj (rule), as it was named, brought with it the Indian version of the Anglo-Saxon civil law system. These laws were put in place long before India was put under direct control of the Crown. In 1678, the company established a twelve-man jury to decide civil and criminal cases according to English law. In the wake of the company's 1757 victory, courts were established to adjudicate civil issues involving British businessmen or the company itself. Gradually, however, the company expanded its scope beyond commercial issues, and starting in 1772, it introduced several regulations infringing on the religio-cultural practices of the natives and introducing Western laws in India. While it kept practicing the explicit religious rules of both Hindus and Muslims, the court was supervised by an English judge who was aided by a Muslim Qazi and a Hindu Pundit. In 1773, the Supreme Court was established in Calcutta. Further reformations were introduced in Pitt's India Bill of 1784 and the Charter Act of 1793. In 1790, the company ended compulsory observing of

Muslim and Hindu sources of laws by repositioning the Qazis and Pundits from official advisors to independent counsels. In 1833, the Privy Council was established to hear appeals from the Supreme Court. In 1861, high courts were established in place of the Supreme Court and the Privy Council (Munir, 2005). British Raj brought new heights to the evolution of the English judicial system in India. Gradually, it effectively put to an end Hindu and Muslim religious practices, thus upholding the writ of the state. In 1829, for example, the company declared *Satti* (the immolation of the widow along with her deceased husband) illegal. Persian, the official language under the Mughals, was replaced with English in 1835. Anglo-Muslim and Anglo-Hindu laws, developed using sacred texts of both religions, were mindful of local customs to only such an extent as permitted by Anglo-Saxon laws; in cases of any contradiction between the two understandings, the latter prevailed over the former. By the middle of the twentieth century, when the great partition took place, India adopted Anglo-Saxon laws. The All India Act 1935 was a whole constitution adopted as a transitional legal framework in India and Pakistan. The All India Penal Code was adopted as it is in both countries; many laws enacted in the nineteenth century are still applied in original form.

As compared to China, where foreign ethical and political culture was rejected, India exhibited a great degree of assimilation. Having transformed from a manufacturing country and an economic hub in premodern times into a periphery during colonial rule, India found itself a recipient of foreign political, economic, and cultural norms. The transformation brought to it under colonial rule introduced new identities and complexities into the socio-cultural and political settings while promoting new socio-political movements (Ahmad, 1991). Among them, two movements, religious and political, deserve focus to show the response of Indian society to invasion from a foreign culture. The Muslim educational movement started with a view that a lesser share of the jobs and new economic realities in India required Muslims to learn the English language and get a modern education. Syed Ahmed Khan, the most prominent Muslim leader during 1857–1898, led the educational movement. Establishing a school in 1859 in Moradabad, another one named the Victoria School in 1863 in Ghaziabad, and a scientific society in 1864, he was determined to push Muslims to become loyal subjects of the colonial administration to gain material benefits and elevate their political significance. In 1875, impressed by his visits to Oxford and Cambridge universities in England, he established Mohammedan Anglo-Oriental College (M.A.O. College) in Aligarh to redefine the concept of education by emphasizing the learning of Western science, technology, language, and literature. In 1920, this college was converted into Aligarh Muslim University. M.A.O. College is credited with incubating a political organization called the All India Muslim League that, under the leadership of Jinnah, led the Muslim demand for a separate country and eventually became the principal factor in the partition of India. In the wake of the failure of mutiny in 1857 and a rapid penetration of Western norms, Indian society was pushed to redefine the concept of its polity. To interact with their subjects and for better management of huge country like India, the British needed some kind of representation. In 1886, following the British political structure, the Indian National Congress was established. In 1906, the All India Muslim League was established. The politics of mass representation in India was the result of Western education delivered both at home and in England to the scions of the elite class. It was a complex combination of Westernization, modernization, rising nationalism, and an increasing gulf between Hindu and Muslim communities that eventually led to the disintegration of India and the creation of two, and then three, countries.

By the time the British left in 1947, India had become a periphery in the world economy. The share of industry in its national income was far more significant during the precolonial years; in 1947, it was just 6.8 percent. Despite the introduction of colonial industries, factories, and railways, the share of labor power in the industry sector went down from 10.3 million in 1901 to 8.5 million in 1947. In 1950, India imported about 90 percent of its capital goods from abroad (Jain, 2012: 75–76). In other words, India had lost its position as an economic hub and the producer of about one-fourth of world GDP to become a periphery responsible primarily for producing raw materials and consuming products manufactured in Europe. Its share in world GDP was down to only about 4 percent because the British, such as Viceroy Lord Curzon, were proud of having conquered the country by relying on the sword and adamant to keep it under their control through the same means (Raychaudhuri, 1999: 156). A number of indicators showed India losing during colonial rule. The population growth rate, as well as death rates, had increased. Only 12 percent of its population was literate, with the literacy rate of women far lower. About 53 percent of the population was living in poverty and unable to earn two meals a day. The conditions in the countryside, where a vast majority of the population lived and relied on agriculture, were abysmal. Agricultural growth in Punjab and some other areas was better but remained stagnant, and in other areas it even declined (Raychaudhuri, 1999: 159). It is evident in that after independence, India, having lost the fertile areas of Punjab and Bengal to Pakistan in the partition process, faced faminelike situations from time to time and sought international humanitarian help to provide food to its citizens (Jalal, 1995b). India also found itself engaged in the international system; before it gained independence, it had already become a member of the United Nations, while Pakistan had to apply for a new membership.

INDIA FROM THE "LICENSE RAJ" TO LIBERALISM (1947–1991)

The partition of the Sub-Continent in August 1947 divided the country into two parts: India and Pakistan. In the next chapter, I will explain the calculations the core countries, especially the United States and Great Britain, made while partitioning united India into two countries. Suffice it here to say that these calculations took into account the possible geostrategic and geo-economic benefits that the partition promised. The "local great divergence" between India and Pakistan, therefore, can be found in structural factors.

The postwar world had many unprecedented realities that the postcolonial state of India had to accept and deal with. The world and its politico-economic conditions had been transformed. The core of the capitalist world-system observed a change as the United States took over the leadership of the system; this change, however, did not affect India's positional standing in the system. The Sub-Continent was the first region in the world to experience a modern sense of political independence. For the first time in more than one thousand years, the Indian masses experienced self-rule. Simultaneously, the postcolonial state of India carried a legacy of colonialism that influenced its economic and foreign policies for a considerable time. Domestically, it had a centralized parliamentary governance structure, bureaucracy, political institutions, armed forces, and a small base of industrial economy established in the later years of colonial rule. These institutions had a varying degree of presence in the vast area under the control of the new state. The state was powerful in its center but weak and dependent in its periphery. It had a diverse population, varying economic conditions, climate challenges, and intervening cultural factors. During the formative years of the second quarter of the twentieth century, the construction of the state as an institution relied on a tense relationship between the colonial administration and nationalist forces. The former emphasized and pursued laissez-faire economic policies, while the latter strived to augment the role of nationalism in economic decisions (Kohli, 2004). In terms of global economic relations, the Indian economy had been integrated into the world economy in such a manner that India had to be content with its role as a peripheral state with raw materials as its main export, at least for the time being. India's desire to exercise its independence in economic decisions was challenged by the prevalent global capitalist structure dominated by North America and Western Europe.

To redefine its positional standing in the world economy, India had three broad policy options to choose from. First, it had the option to become a socialist economy by integrating its economic and political interests with the USSR. Second, it had the option to become a liberal capitalist economy by deepening its dependency and already prevalent economic relations with its former colonial master and other developed economies. Third, India could become an autonomous state by adopting nationalist policies, rejecting the laissez-faire economic approach, and defining a foreign policy of nonalignment and peaceful cooperation with all the countries in the world.

There were also other imminent questions to be answered. The nature of state-led industrial development required solutions for overseeing indigenous capital, public sector capital, local private sector capital, and local but foreign-owned capital. India decided to engineer a domestic model of economic development based on the triangular concept of socialism, nationalism, and democracy, though it did not refuse any unconditional foreign help. It aspired to develop a planned capitalist economy with the state as the engine of economic growth and development. It also meant an overwhelming emphasis on excessive regulation, import substitution, technology transfer, and self-reliance through protection and promotion of indigenous industries with higher tariffs and customs duties. It was an approach consistent with Jawaharlal Nehru's ideas of socialism. Nehruvian socialism had some specific features. To him, socialism meant "the social relationship of the means of production and distribution and government intervention and control of the whole economy." Though it provided a viable space for the private sector—India hesitated to nationalize the private industries and sectors established before independence—the state monopolized most of the development during the first three decades after independence. State control was embodied by Nehru taking over the lead role in all planning forums and institutions (Silverman, 1972). India was a big country and a civilization in itself. Its social outlook included a mosaic of various religions, ethnicities, and cultures. To be a republic, it was necessary to develop a nationalist consensus based on pluralism, cultural accommodation, political and economic enfranchisement, and state-led development while maintaining independent but cordial relations with the rest of the world.

However, the decision to adopt an independent policy based on economic and political nationalism was neither easy nor workable. India found it tough to survive without either challenging but accepting in the end what it considered unjust to its status as a dominant power in the region or resisting and paying the price for such resistance. It claimed to remain a neutral country in the Cold War but was influenced by both the USSR and the United States in a variety of manners. Within a year after independence, India went to war with Pakistan over the question of Kashmir; the problem is still unresolved, and both countries claim sovereignty over the area. In 1950, China claimed sovereignty over Aksai Chin and the McMahon border; in both cases, India found Chinese incursions unjust and aggressive but had to be content with the status quo. In 1962, China launched an unprecedented attack on India at several points along the border. The attack caught the Indian government by surprise for two important reasons. First, during the 1950s, India and China had come closer and signed several agreements of bilateral cooperation. The era was named "Hindi-Chini Bhai-Bhai" (Indians and Chinese are brothers). It was a Maoist response to the resentment of Western capitalist countries claiming themselves as the great powers of the world and excluding China (and India) from the list. Second, following Nehru's theory of power, Indian foreign policy was built on moralist principles. Following the Nehruvian doctrine of international relations, India demanded respect for its self-proclaimed status as the largest and most diversified democracy and nonaligned power in the world. The Chinese attack blew off both concepts and annexed the areas it claimed as belonging to it. Though Nehru had already been seeking help from the United States, the Chinese attack pushed him to appeal to Washington in an unprecedented diplomatic manner. On November 19, 1962, he wrote two letters to President Kennedy. In the second letter, the more significant, Nehru put aside all his grace and ego and virtually begged for immediate military and air assistance to counter the Chinese attack. Referring to the developing situation as "desperate," he asked for air surveillance support of two squadrons of B-47 aircraft. Keeping in view US-Pakistan strategic relations, he assured President Kennedy that "all the assistance or equipment given to us to meet our dire need will be used entirely for resistance against the Chinese" (quoted in Coleman, 2012). Though the United States did not fulfill all the demands, it did provide some crucial help. Once the war was over, India had to withdraw its forces and accept Chinese occupation as a reality, though it still claims the regions taken over in 1962 are disputed territories. The Machiavellian lesson India learned in 1962 redefined its foreign and defense policy; India launched a nuclear program and sought to modernize its armed forces. Nehru's moralist foreign policy led to its own death by embodying the fact that to change its peripheral status in the international system, India needed both economic and military power.

On the economic front, India's desire to follow an independent policy faced numerous challenges. During the partition, the fertile areas of the Sub-Continent had become part of Pakistan. With a large population and relatively underdeveloped agricultural area, India was forced to seek foreign aid to deal with faminelike situations. In the partition, it secured a more significant share of the population and industrial base, while Pakistan took the more fertile land. India, therefore, faced an annual food shortage of about 0.5 to 0.7 million tons. The food import bill took about 60 percent of its deficit and brought its foreign exchange reserves down to half within five years of independence (Jalal, 1995b: 24). During the struggle for independence, Congress and the indigenous bourgeoisie allied, while the landed aristocracy supported British occupation. After independence, however, an unholy alliance between the three pillars of Indian society emerged. Congress, under the leadership of Nehru, sought land reforms but realized that the small peasantry was unable to produce the marketable agricultural surplus required to support and sustain industrial take-off. Though the land reforms were introduced, the government took care of the interests of the landed elite by compensating the landlords financially and ensuring no further action in this context. Simultaneously, during the first of three Five-Year Plans, the government introduced a "Package Plan" that provided huge incentives to the landed class ranging from capital supply to subsidies on technology and machinery. The process, according to Hamza Alavi (1975), eventually led to the rise of "capitalist farming" during the 1960s. Three types of farmers emerged: capitalist farmers, representing about 13 percent of the population of the agricultural sector but occupying about 65 percent of the agricultural land; family farmers, holding 18 percent of the farmland, that with the help of family members and hired labor could also produce a marketable surplus; and the smallholders, occupying only 16 percent of the land but representing about 73 percent of the population. This inequality, according to Alavi, redefined the mode of agricultural production exposed during the Green Revolution. The consequences of the reforms brought under Nehru deepened socio-political inequalities in the rural areas of India. However, beyond this, they affected the nature of India's positional standing in the world-system and reaffirmed India's peripheral role in global economic relations.

During the years Nehru remained in power, 1947–1964, India exhibited control over the nature and direction of economic development and the role of economics in its external relations. For Nehru, the Indian experience of imperialism had been a nightmare requiring the country to preserve its national independence and pride by exercising control of the state and its institutions over society. After independence, India wanted to participate in international trade and receive its due share in the development process, but it was "anxious to avoid being drawn into the whirlpool of economic imperialism" and wanted "neither to be victims of an imperialist power nor to develop such tendencies" (Nehru, 1959, 398). It was, therefore, important for the country to develop insulation to avoid exploitation. However, India defined itself as a democratic state. Its economy, therefore, was a mix of both communist and capitalist ideas. The state led economic development from the front but left much to the private sector. Even before independence, in 1938, emerged what was later known as the Nehru-Mahalanobis Strategy. In simple words, it advocated the focus of resources on the sectors that were impeding economic growth. In the postindependence period, the basic and heavy industry sector, or the "machine-making sector," was considered "the bottleneck" sector in need of reform and investment. The purpose was to get rid of or at least develop immunity against the dictates of world economic structure that,

Nehru believed, had pushed India into perpetual underdevelopment. Applied more forcefully in the second Five-Year Plan (1956–1961), it was based on the premise that international economic structure was least generous to Indian exports, meaning that India should also strive to relinquish dependency over manufactured industrial goods and that this self-reliance should start, primarily, from the machine-making sector (Patnaik, 2015). This, of course, went against neoliberal institutional economics. Evaluating India's planned and state-led progress in industrial development, as well as its external trade and commerce policies, Jagdish Bhagwati and Padma Desai (1970) conclude:

> Indian planning for industrialization suffered from excessive attention to targets down to product level, and a wasteful physical approach to setting and implementation thereof, along with a generally inefficient framework of economic policies designed to regulate the growth of industrialization. . . . India did not plan too much, in certain important ways it just planned inadequately. Physical, cost-benefit ignoring and choice-negligent planning, combined with detailed regulation of such inefficiently determined targets, really proved to be a negation of rational planning. (pp. 499–500)

Neoliberal economists argue that Congress's premise that Indian products faced harsher treatment in international markets was untrue, and since India had an edge to produce and export raw materials to the outside world, concentration on agriculture was more significant than industry. India's real challenge, however, as explained by Ashok Rudra (1964), was that while the machine-making industries (or mining industries) had either no or negligible effect on the agricultural sector, any endeavor to expand the base of industrial activity beyond machine making—such as agro-based industries—had to negatively affect agriculture given that the country was facing recurring food crises. The world economy required India to produce more jute, cotton, and tea. A further industrialization in this context would argue to attract foreign aid and foreign direct investment to establish agriculture-based industries. To the policymakers in the country, however, it meant compromising national food security. As Blyn (1966) reports, per capita food grain availability on the Sub-Continent declined during the first half of the twentieth century, from 200 kilograms in 1900 to about 136.4 kilograms in 1946–1947. The partition further aggravated the situation since the fertile areas had been awarded to Pakistan. The leadership, therefore, was convinced that India would be a victim of the Malthusian trap if it did not act aggressively to promote food production and industrialization in the machine-making sector. The state must assume a leadership role in ensuring such direction of economic development. India, therefore, reduced its interaction with the world economic powers in terms of seeking advice over the nature of industrial growth. Any industrialization, India argued, should include technology transfer and import substitution as inviolable conditions. Instead of letting the market determine the scope of its industrial activities, India took over. Named “License Raj,” or the rule of the permit, this economic development policy sought foreign direct investment on conditions that were mostly unacceptable to multinational corporations and the developed world. India was an impressive and growing market capable of mass production and providing raw materials to the core economies of the world. The government, however, put in place higher tariffs on imports to deny capital flight from the country and perpetuate dependency on foreign markets. Instead, India focused on developing indigenous products.

The Indian National Congress ruled the country until 1989 with a very brief pause of fewer than three years. Three generations of Nehrus brought an evolutionary approach to Indian economic development. Contrary to China’s communist model of economic development, where the state abhorred contacting and dealing with Western imperial institutions, the Indian government adopted a socialist model of economic development whereby the state patronized the progress. However, it did not shun the notion of foreign assistance in economic development altogether since it did not find the concept of assistance contradictory to the national policy of self-reliance. The third Five-Year Plan (1961–1966), argued that “among the principal conditions for building up a self-reliant economy, which can sustain a high rate of growth, are an adequate level of domestic capital formation, the maximum effort possible in developing exports, and availability of external assistance during the critical period of transition” (Government of India Planning Commission, 1961: 26). The plan justified foreign assistance as a temporary and facilitative phenomenon that should gradually enable India to become self-reliant, stating:

> A basic objective in the strategy of development is to create the conditions in which dependence on external assistance will disappear as early as possible. . . . In the transitional period, the effort to develop the basic and heavy industries and machine-building capacity, without which the growth of the national economy would itself be retarded, accentuates the balance of payment problem. . . . A developing economy, which for its part endeavors to mobilize its own resources to the utmost extent possible, faces the difficulty that its developmental effort may entail a large increase in import requirements for specialized capital equipment and for raw materials and components, for which, for a period, it is unable to pay from its own earnings. The need for external assistance is implicit in this situation. Such assistance has already done a great deal to hasten India’s economic growth, and its value can scarcely be over-estimated. (pp. 26–27)

India used the notion of self-reliance to shield its state-led developmental approach. By emphasizing it throughout the Five-Year Plans during the first four decades, India made sure that though it received significant foreign aid, it did not compromise its nonaligned status. By looking at the statistics, it becomes evident that India received considerable foreign bilateral and multilateral assistance even while maintaining a socialist outlook of the national economy. During the Cold War, the USSR, as well as the United States, extended financial assistance in various projects. According to Madan Mohan Tewari (1982), from 1951 to 1975, India received about Rs.120,896 million in external assistance, of which the US share stood at $10,327 million (or Rs.77,456.25 million). In addition, it also borrowed from various powers and institutions of the world. During 1955–1971, the USSR extended loans totaling about Rs.7,396 million, other world powers and institutions extended loans worth Rs.61,217 million, and the United States extended about Rs.48,506 million. Aid from Canada during 1951–1975 amounted to Canadian $1,375.7 million. Aid from the United Kingdom during this period was about Rs.14,748 million. The World Bank also provided Rs.8,899 million in aid and loans. Aid from the International Development Association (IDA) amounted to Rs.26,593 million during this period. By the end of the third Five-Year Plan, India had received about Rs.1,472,710 million in aid just from the United States. According to Tewari (1982), "This massive US aid can be seen to have played a critical role in India's resource mobilization efforts; in India's case, the US aid had also had a life-saving character" because "it made a very sizeable contribution to the development of irrigation facilities, new strategy of multiplying agricultural production capacity, power projects, transport and communication networks, and intermediate industries" (p. 44).

The picture was not all rosy, however. There were two important issues related to the apparent influx of foreign capital. First, by the end of 1975, India was paying Rs.7,000 million in servicing the loans it received during 1951–1975, which negatively affected its national capital formation strategies. Though the loans helped the country lay the foundation for stable economic growth in the long run, they did affect its claim to produce and rely on an indigenous model of economic development. More importantly, however, were the political and strategic strings attached to these loans. Domestically, the government in Delhi received huge criticism for its policy of borrowing from international powers. However, when the time came, India was resilient in maintaining a somewhat independent foreign policy, at least within the region. The generous aid from the United States, for example, was used as a tool to influence India to distance itself from the USSR. The 1962 war with China resulted in the provision of military aid and extensive economic aid. In 1971, when President Nixon—arguably the friendliest US president toward Pakistan—was in office, India went ahead and signed the Treaty of Peace, Friendship, and Cooperation with the USSR. In the wake of civil war in East Pakistan, which eventually broke into an Indo-Pakistani war and culminated in the disintegration of Pakistan and the creation of Bangladesh, Indian behavior refused to acknowledge that economic considerations could influence its strategic choices. In May 1974, India claimed to test a nuclear weapon through a "peaceful nuclear explosion," a development that caught the Nixon administration by surprise since it was not expecting India to have developed this level of technological capability.

India's economic growth during the years of state-led development (1947–1991) remained modest at best despite that regional strategic impediments and policy choices did not affect the inflow of foreign capital in the form of aid, grants, and loans from the core countries of the world and global financial institutions. During this period, India's annual GDP growth rate remained at 4.06 percent, with some years of exceptional fiscal growth and many others remaining even lower than average. During 1947–1980, growth was even slower, with the average being only 3.75 percent. Food grain production went up from 50.83 million tons in 1950–1951 to 176.39 million tons, and the population grew from 376.325 million to 888.513 million at a growth rate of about 2.25 percent a year, thus nearly reducing the GDP growth rate to less than 2 percent a year. Per Blyn (1966), as noted above, India also observed a decline in per capita food grain availability, compelling it to remain concerned about feeding its growing population despite having observed the green revolution in the 1960s. The reason, Francine Frankel (2005) argues in her now classic study of India's political economy, was the paradoxical relationship between the Nehruvian aspirations of modernization through industrial development and the Gandhian rejection of Western capitalism. Mahatma Gandhi, she argues, abhorred capitalism because of its incessant desire for capital accumulation, calling it a form of theft. Therefore, he stressed defining work as a means of living, possession as a means of serving needs only, and the drive for profit as exploitative. Though his ideas were never accepted as the principal approach of Congress, they did leave a lasting impression on modern economic thought in India. During the 1930s, Nehru himself was influenced by socialist ideology and found it more compatible with Indian circumstances. The Gandhian-socialist consensus, Frankel argues, was primarily value-oriented and went ahead only when Gandhi accommodated the place of industrialization in his vision of Indian society and the socialists agreed to accept state control of their industries. The outcome was Nehru's "third way," "the concept of a uniquely 'Indian' variety of socialism, a social pattern that could reconcile the modern goals of economic development with the traditional community values of small-scale agrarian societies" (Frankel, 2005: 17). This compromise lacked the revolutionary approaches Indian society required to untangle the chains of underdevelopment and overcome the impediments. The result was that India grew only modestly; state-led industrialization could benefit a few, and a vast majority of the population was either excluded or could not benefit from the initiatives taken by the government. These situations persist today even as rising India becomes a mantra for political economists.

Frankel's analysis is important because it shows the contradictions between Indian traditional social settings and the norms required for capitalist development. She agrees that the Indian leadership would not dare to admit that capitalist economic development could have widened social and economic inequalities. India also found it difficult to face consequential socio-political challenges—such as intercommunal relations—arising in the wake of any such development. In other words, India could not find the courage to accept that development could take place only on the terms and conditions of global capitalism led by the transnational capitalist class. The state of India insisted on terms and conditions that were unattractive to this class. India did not attract any considerable private investment while following the "third way." No economic indicators—GDP growth, industrial growth rate, or human development index—showed any remarkable progress during these years. As mentioned above, though India received a considerable inflow of foreign aid, it failed to attract business-oriented capital investment either from international financial institutions or through foreign direct investment for the time when the state kept exhausting its endeavors of indigenous industrialization and development. By the end of the 1980s, India was receiving only $165 million in foreign direct investment per year, and over half its population was living in poverty. The share of foreign trade in GDP, an important indicator reflecting the level of integration of the country in the world economy, went down from 7.3 percent to 4 percent.

Two basic reasons explain India's failure to thrive during the first three decades after independence. First, India's insistence on national self-reliance meant that it would seek minimal input from international financial forums and institutions effectively controlled by the transnational capitalist class in terms of capital availability, capacity build-up, or industrialization. Though India was not in an autarkic position, as it kept seeking aid and long-term loans from the developed countries, it did not adopt policies that could attract the transnational capitalist class to invest in the country. India sought the investment of private foreign capital on its own terms and conditions because it was afraid of losing its autonomy and economic independence to global capitalism. The Nehruvian concept of an indigenous model of development required India to invest state fiscal resources in sectors that decision-makers found crucial for establishing stronger foundations of socio-economic development. This, in principle, was a stand that could have received minimal resistance in the country. At the international level, the situation was quite different. The Nehruvian developmental state was contradictory to the principal interest of the global capitalist class: accumulation of capital in the core of the world economy. The world-system wanted India to embrace neoliberal and credit-based economic policies. Indian resistance did not matter much to the system because such investment went somewhere else, such as to Southeast Asia.

Second, the unattractiveness of global capitalism to India should be understood from the perspective of the global division of labor, which India wanted to revise. During the colonial period, India's positional standing in the world economy was reset from a manufacturing hub and an economic epicenter supplying fabric, spices, and other products to the world to an agrarian region responsible primarily for supplying raw materials to the modern developed core, performing intermediary industrial support services, accepting industries and technologies that had become unattractive to the core, and promoting further penetration of Western industrial products in its burgeoning market. It was the division of labor best suitable to the transnational capitalist class controlling the developed core. India was hesitant to accept this status. Its history created a nostalgia within the leadership that saw Indian treatment during colonial times as an unforgettable injustice meant to deprive it of the valued economic status it enjoyed in premodern times. Once India had become independent, such an approach needed to be revisited. It meant that India should receive investment in heavy industries, transportation and infrastructure, energy, and sectors producing capital goods. Following this principle, India declared investment in some specific sectors of economy as exclusive to the state. In 1965 and again in 1969, it nationalized certain private banks. It also kept control over the private banks by subjecting them to investment regulations; banks could issue loans for investment only in sectors of national preference set by the central government. To create a market of indigenous capital goods, India imposed an effective rate of protection—"the extent of tariff protection required by a domestic industry to impede imports"—and, simultaneously, lowered domestic resource cost—"the opportunity cost of saving a unit of foreign exchange" (Chandra, 2012: 98). Higher statutory liquidity, higher cash reserve ratios, restrictions on private investments, control over foreign collaborations, restrictions on the import of technology and capital goods, and discretionary control of the bureaucracy over the issuance of licenses for private investments and businesses were policies that India pursued during 1947–1980 in its quest to create an indigenous model of development.

This was an approach incompatible with global capitalism since it violated the principle of the division of labor, over which the whole structure of the world-system resided. Global financial institutions, particularly the

World Bank, were the least willing to allow India to redefine its role in the international division of labor through state intervention. India, the World Bank believed, should seek "mediation of the market forces through the predilection of foreign direct investment" if it had to change its positional standing in the system (Patnaik and Chandrasekhar, 2007: 219). In situations where a country had neither indigenous capital nor a technological base, it had no choice but to accept the dictates of the structure (Chandrasekhar, 1965: 106). However, India was unwilling to open the sectors with the most potential for profit, such as agriculture-based industries. India's insistence on the spread of heavy industries posed an unattractive posture to private investors who considered lack of business and investment opportunities without promising conditions leading to maximization of their profits. Facilitating any effort to revise the global division of labor meant threatening the long-term interests of global capitalism and the core countries. Divergent interests, therefore, were the primary reason for the lack of development in India. Global capitalism could not do much to change the situation. For example, India at first refused to devalue its currency. After facing immense pressure from foreign trade, India agreed to follow the rules, but the deal could not be materialized due to the 1965 Indo-Pakistani war. In the end, India did devalue its currency by 58 percent, but it did not open its market to foreign investment, therefore losing the trust of global capitalist institutions.

During 1951–1973, while India's average export growth rate remained at 2.7 percent per annum only, the world growth rate was recorded at 7.9 percent per annum, leading some economists to conclude that "the attempt to control market forces in the public interest and to direct the private sector to conform to priorities of the 5-year plans failed to serve the public interest and degenerated into a tool for political and other patronage dispensation" (Srinivasan and Tendulkar, 2003: 29). While the concept of "inward-oriented economic strategy" was "noble," it led to "the Hindu rate of growth," meaning "continuing dependence on foreign aid, intermittent economic crises, perennial foreign exchange scarcity and balance of payment crises, major bouts of inflation, perpetual shortage of food and other necessities, and persistently high levels of poverty, besides the marginalization of India in world economy" (Nayar, 2007: 29). The national policy of development, however, was a "planned economy within the framework of capitalism," something that was called "an exercise in futility" (Gujral, 1979: 51). In other words, India, under Nehru, wanted both: preservation of the egalitarian structure of society *and* the industrialization of the economy on capitalist lines. M. L. Gujral (1979) laments this approach by arguing that Nehru was impressed by the results of industrialization in the West and the USSR and wanted to replicate them by combining them. As Gujral argues, "He failed to realize that the circumstances under which growth had occurred in these countries were not present in the underdeveloped countries which only recently won their political independence" (p. 206). The approach to both failed miserably. After three decades of loss, India had to choose one of the two systems.

It was not the case that India, or any other country in the world, was considered static in its positional standing in the world-system. It did grow modestly. It addressed issues of governance by constitutionalizing a democratic approach, initializing industrial growth in light industries, and embarking on agricultural growth. Using state capital resources, India installed some large-scale industrial units that contributed to the manufacture of the capital goods and metals necessary for further industrialization. India also maintained an independent foreign policy, thus enabling it to receive foreign aid from both communist and capitalist blocs. The limitations of this approach, however, were evident by the end of the 1970s. India lacked the technology, capital, and skills to proceed. Without meaningful foreign contributions in all these sectors, it was somewhat impossible for India to grow. Estimates show that India would need about 254 years to reach the level of development of the United States (Desai, 1972). From the neoliberal perspective, therefore, India denied economic development at the cost of preserving its so-called national economic independence. For example, Garry Pursell (1992) observes that "import-substitution policies were followed with little or no regard to costs," the result of which was "an extremely diverse industrial structure and high degree of self-sufficiency" and "high production costs" because of "a general problem of poor quality and technological backwardness, which beset even low-cost sectors with comparative advantage such as the textiles, garment, leather goods, many light industries, and primary industries such as cotton" (pp. 433–34). With no remarkable achievement in self-reliance during the three decades after independence, it became evident that India could not grow without submitting to the demands of the international financial institutions, accepting the neoliberal economic model of growth, and allowing foreign capital to arrive and do its magic on its own conditions. It was, to an extent, a reversal of the so-called self-reliance approach dominating India's image in the international market during the Nehru years. Increasingly, the indigenous capitalist class was arguing that to grow and develop, the state had to submit a considerable part of its economic sovereignty to the global capitalist system.

India's economic policies were affected by international developments during the 1970s. In 1971, India intervened in East Pakistan's civil war, resulting in the disintegration of Pakistan, the creation of Bangladesh, and a redefinition of the geostrategic conditions in the region by restoring India's hegemonic position, which had been eroded in the wake of defeat in the 1962 Indo-China War. In 1973, the Arab-Israel War and consequent oil embargo affected India's balance of payments, and it had to seek long-term loans from the developed world and international institutions. Dependent on foreign fossil fuel resources, India's balance of payment had to be handled with foreign assistance and long-term loans from international financial institutions. The crisis was prolonged and worsened when Prime Minister Indira Gandhi nationalized the banks and other business institutions. Changing climate conditions, a drain of financial resources due to energy dependency, and a foreign exchange crisis pushed India to its limit. More importantly, self-reliance appeared to be a hoax given that India could not mature its food security and remained dependent primarily on the United States for wheat.

During the 1960s, India had increased its appetite for foreign assistance; by the end of 1960s, foreign assistance accounted for 3.11 percent of its GNP. The global financial institutions pushed in. The fourth Five-Year Plan was presented to US president Lyndon Johnson and World Bank president George Woods for approval and assurance of aid. India was guaranteed aid, provided it followed the dictates of the global financial institutions: devaluation of its currency, opening of its borders for trade and investment, and privatization of state-owned economic institutions. The promised aid, however, did not reach India as expected. The decade from 1966 to 1975 was a formative phase in India to finally submit to international pressures and integrate into the global economic system, thus accepting its lower positional standing in the world-system (Nayar, 2007).

Despite that India did not make an impressive economic recovery in the first three to four decades after independence, it did accumulate considerable military power, which helped its positional standing in the region and the global world-system. Even before 1962, when Indian foreign policy relied on the assumption of morality, India concentrated on its defense needs and designed a policy of self-reliance with considerable room for cooperation with foreign countries. If there was an iota of soft or nonmilitary political power left under the Nehruvian worldview, it received a deathblow in 1962 when India lost miserably to China in a border war. As a blessing in disguise, India received Western sympathy and military support following its cries of being under threat of Chinese communist aggression. Following its economic policies insistent on the dominant role of the state being a source of annoyance for the core countries, India adopted two broad policies in its defense sector. First, it emphasized self-reliance and pursued investing in arms production by keeping all defense production under state control. Second, it pleaded to the core from time to time for military technology, citing threats to its security from Pakistan and China. With the state being in charge of development guaranteed, all other terms and conditions from the core countries were acceptable to India. Therefore, India did not mind following the dictates of the core countries whenever it could not find an alternative while pursuing zealous investment policies whenever it found the opportunity

(Thomas, 1978: 119–25). By 1967, India was spending about 12 percent of its total federal investment in research and development on military technology only. It started developing capacity in aircraft manufacturing. In 1958, it was spending $3.2 million on research and development, but in 1970 the budget reached $24.4 million (SIPRI Yearbook, 1972). Most of this budget was spent on a nuclear research and development program that had started at the Tata Institute of Fundamental Research even before independence.

India received considerable international cooperation from the USSR and capitalist core countries such as Canada. In 1974, India shocked the world when it "successfully carried out an underground nuclear explosion." It was a disappointing development since the claim about the "peaceful" nature of explosion was labeled as "rubbish" and Canada had to suspend any further nuclear cooperation, at least for the time being. However, India continued receiving cooperation in developing its military technology from Western countries, including the Soviet Union. Its military expenditure increased from $914 million in 1957 to $2,861 million in 1976. In 1974, the defense budget was about one-fourth of total government expenditures (SIPRI Yearbook, 1978). India's total defense spending was estimated to be $2 billion in 1960. This amount skyrocketed to $9 billion in 1970 (RAND Corporation, 1989: 17). By that time, India had become "practically self-sufficient in the production of small arms, ammunition, bombs, explosives, and unguided rockets." Simultaneously, it was able to "produce advanced jet fighters under license" (SIPRI Yearbook, 1978: 196–97). The dual approach to defense needs and development enabled India to remain a lower-middle-ranked power in world affairs. A combination of economic and military power, thus, allowed India to maintain its positional standing in the world-system, with the option to elevate itself should the opportunity arise. Such an opportunity would arise only if India could compromise its economic and political (strategic) worldviews. According to Baldev Raj Nayar (2001), "India's desire to escape from the situation of lack of economic and political autonomy, which it inherited from colonialism, through its economic strategy was perfectly matched by the posture of the US, quite becoming of a hegemonic global power, to keep others dependent upon it." He argues that "India was unrealistic in expecting aid from others to rescue the strategy" of national autonomy (p. 104). India, therefore, was reminded of the consequences of the choices it made during the first three decades of independence.

By 1980, it was quite evident that India had reached a climax in terms of self-reliance and an indigenous foundation of economic growth. It could grow only modestly by relying on local sources of progress, invention, scientific discoveries, and capital formation. The state had exhausted its public resources in modernizing, but in the end, it came to realize that a collaborative endeavor was the only way possible to move ahead. After four decades of independence, India was still a peripheral country. Though it had received considerable military assistance and entered bilateral agreements, it still lacked the foreign exchange reserves to buy the weapons it desired for defense. The policy of self-reliance and self-sufficiency was challenged by colossal upfront and recurring costs, lack of developed human resources in science and technology, and the time factor (Thomas, 1978). It needed a strategy reneging its position as a developmental state to one allowing local and foreign capital to take over and with the government as a partner in growth. The policymakers realized that India could not live in isolation and do the development miracle on its own; it had to participate in, influence, and absorb the development strategies advocated by the core countries and international financial institutions. India could elevate itself from its position as a developing country and a valuable peripheral country in the world-system to a new level only if it could compromise with the demands and dictates of global capitalism. During the mid-1970s, the turbulent years of Indian politics, Indira Gandhi was ousted only to return as prime minister in 1980. The brief removal from power, however, enabled her to analyze ailments in the Indian economy and the inevitability of its integration into the world-system following guidelines from the international institutions. To achieve that, India needed a congruous approach by forming an alliance with the national political and economic elite class and asking the global capitalist class and institutions to come forward and help India grow primarily on its own terms. According to Kohli (2011):

> What eventually triggered the upward shift in the growth rate of the Indian economy around 1980 was a slow but sure adoption of a new model of development. Instead of the statist and the nationalist model of development of the Nehru era, which was then accentuated in a populist direction by Indira Gandhi during the 1970s, Indira Gandhi herself shifted India's political economy around 1980 in the direction of a state and business alliance for economic growth. This change was not heralded loudly and has often been missed by scholars, especially because Indira Gandhi remains deeply associated with the politics of *gharibi hatao* [ending poverty]. Nevertheless . . . evidence shows that the post-Emergency Indira Gandhi was a different Indira Gandhi: she downplayed redistributive concerns and prioritized economic growth; sought an alliance with big business; adopted an antilabor stance; put the brakes on the growth of public sector industries; and downgraded the significance of economic planning and of the planning commission. As suits a complex democracy, these changes emerged in fits and starts, and they were also often camouflaged, helping maintain some of Indira Gandhi's credentials as the leader of the masses. The changes were nevertheless profound; they involved a shift from left-leaning state intervention that flirted with socialism, to right-leaning state intervention in which the ruling elites recommitted themselves to a more distinctly capitalist

> path of development. And important economic actors within India, especially big capital, understood these changes pretty clearly, expressing their satisfaction by increasing investment and helping India's economy grow rapidly. (p. 152)

The dilemma of Indira Gandhi's economic policies—her nostalgia for the socialist policies adopted and recommended by her father, on the one hand, and increasingly harsher economic realities, such as economic stagnation, inflation, and disequilibrium in the balance of payments, on the other—led her to remain hesitant of fully embracing the neoliberal economic approach in the country. Therefore, she kept on moving in a "one step forward, two steps backward" manner during the 1970s when she was in power. Therefore, while during the early 1970s the central government adopted strict measures to control inflation following the advice of the World Bank and the IMF (International Monetary Fund), it refused to accept American aid of wheat on the condition that it accept certain concessions at the foreign policy level. The adoption of economic advice resulted in the improvement of industrial production and agricultural growth. However, after she returned to power in 1980, Prime Minister Gandhi was much more determined to embrace the neoliberal economic approach of growth. Before she was killed in 1984, Indira Gandhi had laid the foundations for the liberalization of the Indian economy. In 1979–1980, the hike in oil prices by OPEC (Organization of the Petroleum Exporting Countries) pushed the country to a new crisis in its balance of payments. India reached out to the international financial institutions and was bailed out with a $5 billion package from the IMF. However, it was never meant to be a free lunch. Despite resistance within the country's political class and even Congress, Indira Gandhi accepted the demands of these institutions to liberalize India's economic policies. The government relaxed the regulations imposed on expansion in the private sector. It also deregulated industries erstwhile under strict government protection. To ensure 1982 as "the year of productivity," the government expanded the list of core industries enjoying the new deregulation. It reduced the conditions imposed on foreign direct investment and the taxes on the import of raw materials and industrial and technological equipment, particularly electronics and telecommunications.

During the second half of the 1980s, when Rajiv Gandhi, son of Indira Gandhi, took over the government, India experienced the first large-scale liberalization of its economy. The Rajiv government, in principle, capitulated to a new definition of "self-reliance" meaning that India should interact with and integrate into the world economy at a larger scale, and to achieve it, the country should promote the private sector. To please the private sector, the government reduced direct taxation, lowered corporate taxes, reduced the wealth tax, and abolished the estate duty altogether. It liberalized the licensing regime by licensing several sectors and changing the conditions for government incentives, relaxing rules on capacity expansion, and removing limit controls on the import of technological equipment such as electronics and computers. To attract foreign direct investment, it reduced taxes on investment and foreign capital, cut customs duties on equipment required for some certain industries, and adopted an "open-door policy" for foreign direct investment in electronics. The leftist political parties and notable politicians inside Congress protested these measures by calling them a "surrender to imperialism." Rajiv Gandhi, however, remained committed to liberal policies even though the rhetoric of socialism continued. As India agreed to follow the policy directives of the core countries and their respective institutions, it started to grow; during the 1980s the GDP growth rate was 5.6 percent, with the second half growing at 5.8 percent (Nayar, 2001). The impact of reforms in the 1980s was impressive in some sectors. The country's imports, besides open general licensing, increased from 5 percent of the total in 1980 to 30 percent in 1989. From 1970 onward, the share of non-oil imports increased, though it kept fluctuating from 17.8 percent in one year to 7.1 percent in another year. The ratio of non-oil imports to GDP increased from 3.3 percent in 1971 to 6 percent in 1990. The ratio of exports of non-oil products to GDP increased from 3.3 percent to 5.5 percent in the same period. The country's GDP growth rate remained at 7.6 percent during 1988–1991; its export growth rate, which had been 1.2 percent during 1980–1985, went up to 14.4 percent over the next five years. In the wake of faster import growth over exports (mainly industrial and technological equipment) during the second half of the 1980s, the gap was met through foreign borrowing. International financial institutions came forward to extend India credit lines. From 1981 to 1990, India's external debt increased from $20.6 billion to $64.4 billion. The external debt-to-GDP ratio, which was 17.7 percent in 1981, rose to 24.5 percent in 1990. By 1990, India was embracing its integration into the capitalist world economic system. A crash was inevitable given that by 1990 the quality of the debt had deteriorated. The share of private borrowers in loans had risen from 26 percent in 1981 to 41 percent in 1990, whereas the share of non-concessional loans had also risen from 42 to 54 percent, while the debt maturity time span decreased from twenty-seven to twenty years (Panagariya, 2005). In other words, economic growth in the second half of the 1980s was based on heavy borrowing from external creditors. India had to pay back the loans it was taking quicker than in previous cases. Government control over currency and the exchange rate meant that the rupee was artificially overvalued. The crash, or the first great shock to the Indian economy, was imminent.

India's economic growth in the 1980s allowed it to expand its military power. With economic liberalization, the United States could entice India as a consumer of its military equipment. In 1985, India bought "advanced US military technology and weaponry" while also requesting technology transfer (SIPRI Yearbook 1986: 330). Simultaneously, however, India did not lose the trust of the Soviet Union. In April 1985, a visit to Moscow by the then Indian defense minister Narasimha Rao resulted in securing "arms production technology, including that for building nuclear-propelled submarines, modern long-range radar systems, and a coastal defense system." India at that time was the most significant nonsocialist Soviet arms buyer in the world. It was offered the MiG-29, by then the most modern Soviet aircraft, even before its production (SIPRI Yearbook, 1986: 331). Throughout the 1980s, India kept modernizing its armed forces and defense capabilities. In addition to the United States and the USSR, India also purchased weapons from the United Kingdom and France. From the United Kingdom, it purchased ten Sea Harrier fighters, while from France it purchased forty Mig-2000 to strengthen its defense capabilities. For the core countries, the division of labor in arms production worked well since India, just like Pakistan and other Third World countries, exhibited an appetite for defense products. As with industrial technology, however, the core maintained its privileged position and international division of labor.

INDIA AS A SEMI-CORE COUNTRY IN THE WORLD-SYSTEM (1991–2014)

The progress during the 1980s brought two significant changes in Indian national discourse. First, with the arrival of foreign direct investment—$79 million in 1980 and reaching $252 million in 1989—and material progress in the country, the rhetoric of socialism weakened and gave way to a new public debate about the role of foreign capital and greater integration into the world economy in national economic development. A fragmented democracy with stakeholders maintaining a mosaic of opinions about the role of the international system in the Indian economy meant that the state needed to ponder extensively, act slowly, and move forward gradually. Relatively, it had become more comfortable for the political leadership to talk about the liberalization of economic policies and open the doors to invite foreign investors to establish industrial enterprises in the country. Second, and more importantly, the lessons of the past four decades had revealed to the political leadership that to grow, India needed to listen to and balance its own interests with those of the core. During the 1960s, it faced immense pressure from the core capitalist countries to either shun or streamline its foreign policy approach of nonalignment with that of the core. Its rejection of these demands and insistence on exercising its independent posture strained relations with the West and affected its drive for industrialization and economic growth.

During the height of the Cold War, the USSR was able to extend some support to India. As the Cold War was ending with the fall of the Berlin Wall and the withdrawal of Soviet military forces from Afghanistan, India had to redefine its place in the global system. It needed to get closer to the United States and other countries to benefit economically and militarily. The policies in the 1980s and their success in economic stabilization led Indian politicians, in both the government and the opposition, to realize the potential for progress should India integrate into the world economy. However, since these results were inconsistent and macro indicators of economic growth, including foreign direct investment, fluctuated throughout the decades, it was perceived that an open and less embarrassing acceptance of neoliberalism should bring stability to the structure. By 1990–1991, therefore, a broader consensus to embrace neoliberalism as the de facto economic state ideology had emerged; India was ready to reap the benefits of investment from the core countries and transnational capitalist class.

The 1991 financial crisis allowed the political leadership to finally shift in the direction of economic liberalization. The transformative process turned out to be an inevitable choice due to the crisis that worsened by the mid-1991 for three primary reasons, according to Valerie Cerra and Sweta Saxena (2002): overvaluation of currency, current account deficits, and absence of investors' confidence. As India embarked on the path to liberalization, it took numerous steps, including, among others, devaluing rupee by 20 percent, allowing full convertibility of the rupee on the current account, introducing a dual exchange rate in early 1992 whereby exporters could sell 60 percent of their foreign exchange to the open market at higher prices, opening the foreign exchange market to exporters, abolishing the licensing regime for imports, cutting tariffs significanly, allowing foreign investors to hold 51 percent ownership of industries in a wide range of sectors, reducing state-controlled sectors to only six, introducing anti-trust laws to enable large firms to expand and diversify, rationalizing the tax structure, and and reducing taxes across the spectrum, thus enabling the wealthy sections of society to accumulate more wealth (Nayar, 2001: 130–31). These reforms were appreciated by both the core countries and the global financial institutions. Discussing the impact of these reforms, the World Bank in 1996 stated that "India has fundamentally altered its development strategy." "Over the last five years," the World Bank document explains further, "changes of the investment, exchange rate and trade regimes, the financial sector, and the tax system have ended four decades of development policies based on planning and have initiated a quiet economic revolution" (World Bank, 1996: xvii). To Arvind Panagariya (2005), while the growth rate of India's economy was 5.3 percent per annum during 1981–1991 and 5.9 percent during 1991–2002, the real difference between the two periods is that during the first period, the Indian economy remained unstable and had a fluctuating growth rate macroeconomic indicators; after 1991, the state demonstrated a firm pledge to adhere to neoliberalism and thus reaped the fruits of this commitment.

The penetration of global capital in the Indian market did not produce results different from what Indian policymakers had expected, at least during the 1990s. The exploitative nature of global capitalism based on the international division of labor not only prevailed but even strengthened in some sectors. The import of capital goods by foreign investors doubled between 1990 and 1995 mainly due to there being zero import duty. Domestic investors, however, had to pay several direct and indirect taxes (Chandra, 2012), which adversely affected manufacturing. A comparative look at the performance of the manufacturing sector during the early 1970s and after liberalization shows that the global trade system pushed India to accept its prerogative of determining the outlook of the international division of labor and, consequently, India's positional standing as a semi-peripheral country. Contrary to general perceptions, the share of manufacturing in the GDP remained constant during the transition years of the Indian economy; from 1991 to 1996, it remained at around 20 percent of the GDP. However, it failed to provide employment opportunities to the Indian people; its share in nonagricultural employment dropped from 29 percent in 1970–1971 to 24 percent in 1995–1996. At the same time, the import of manufacturing products increased; its share of the GDP rose from 2 percent in 1970–1971 to 10 percent in 1995–1996. The total share of manufacturing imports, however, is recorded to have increased from 13 percent of the manufacturing GDP in 1970–1971 to 45 percent in 1995–1996. While India's high-tech manufacturing exports declined during this period, its net manufacturing imports went up from -0.1 percent in 1970–1971 to 3.7 in 1995–1996. The composition of the manufacturing trade further reveals the nature of the international division of labor. Instead of increasing exports of capital goods, India increased exporting consumer goods, which went up from 50.6 percent in 1989–1990 to 72.5 percent in 1996–1997. The proportion of intermediate goods declined from 38.5 percent to 12.5 percent during the same period. The export of resource-intensive manufacturing goods declined from 68 percent in 1978–1979 to 37 percent in 1995–1996. India, therefore, became a consumer of capital goods manufactured in the West; the share of the import of capital goods in total manufacturing goods increased from 36.6 percent in 1978–1979 to 62 percent in 1996–1996. Similarly, India's import of high-tech manufacturing products increased from 26 percent in 1978–1979 to 61 percent in 1996. Moreover, India was pushed to develop labor-intensive production houses instead of tech-intensive or capital-intensive industrial units. The share of labor-intensive manufacturing products in total manufacturing products, therefore, increased from 9 percent in 1978–1979 to 13 percent in 1991–1992 and

34 percent in 1996–1997 (Nambiar, Mungekar, and Tadas, 1999), which makes sense given India's rising population. However, the country was deprived of becoming a stakeholder in the race for technological innovations, thus ensuring the core maintains its grip over the division of labor and the outlook of economies outside Western Europe and North America.

The argument that Indian integration into the world-system took place primarily through its acceptance of the international division of labor is evident from yet another vital sector: telecommunications manufacturing. Established in 1984, C-DOT, a public sector research and development organization, expanded immensely by connecting cities, towns, and villages and becoming an industry worth $1,000 million over five years. However, the introduction of foreign investors in the sector combined with the duty-free import of telecommunications products resulted in a massive expansion of digital communications in the country. In 1991, there were less than half a million consumers; in 2010, there were 650 million. In 2010, the government collected revenue of $35 billion from this sector. However, the domestic telecommunications manufacturing industry and C-DOT reached their nadir; in 2010, the local industry grabbed less than 20 percent of the total market worth of more than $30 billion (Chandra, 2012; Meemamsi, 1993). Discussing the role of foreign capital in India's industrial policy and economic development, Nirmal Chandra (2012) argues that "Indian reformers, prompted by Washington, deliberately abjured an industrial policy" with an "overriding objective to 'lock' India into the global financial system by moving as fast as feasible towards a free cross-border flow of capital" (p. 104). An overwhelming impression was that India had become competent enough to benefit from the global market with exports of both its raw materials and its manufacturing goods (Subramanian, 2008). As the liberalization process unfolded, various indicators show that the Indian economic system was reoriented to the serve the interests of global capitalism by reassigning Delhi the new positional standing of intermediary industrial power or a semi-peripheral status in the international division of labor.

Perhaps the most frightening consequences of the liberalization of economy were inflicted on the agricultural sector. Once again, after the departure of the British, India faced a challenge in the arrival of multinational corporations in the country. Following neoliberal promises, India should have benefited from foreign direct investments in agriculture and the subsequential growth in production of agricultural products and their export to world markets. Instead, the reverse took place; the share of agriculture in the GDP went down from 30 percent in 1991 to 14.4 percent in 2012 (Dhanagare, 2016). More importantly, the policy should have addressed India's chronic crisis of feeding its growing population. However, since the adoption of neoliberal policies, the composition of agricultural production faced a transformation similar to the one that took place in the wake of British arrival in the country. Data from 1990 to 2003 shows that in almost all the major agricultural states of India, cultivation and production of food grains declined due to the growth of nonfood grain crops, including fruits, vegetables, condiments, spices, oilseeds, and cotton (Bhalla and Singh, 2010). The transformation gave way to some new patterns: intensive cultivation; greater dependence on pesticides, fertilizers, and genetically modified seeds; diversification of crops; integration of a variety of agricultural products and processing at one place; and a shift toward the capitalist form of farming (Mohanty and Lenka, 2016). In part, these patterns were a reaction to the changing dynamics of the market influenced by the introduction of foreign capital and technology, and the consequent dispossession of Indian small landowners and peasants. Since the introduction of corporate farming, companies such as Monsanto entered into contract farming; they bound the farmers in states such as Punjab and Haryana to grow particular food and nonfood crops. Following the pattern of the British East India Company in the eighteenth and nineteenth centuries, farmers were extended loans. The crops belonged to the companies when they grew well. In the case of natural calamities or human-made crises, the crops belonged to the farmers, and they could sell them on the open market. Over the years, companies have developed a practice. As the harvest season reaches, they flood the market with their own products to negatively affect prices. The crops facing loss belonged to the farmers, who ultimately took them to the market to be sold at a lower price to the same companies. Now the losses belonged to the farmers, and they had to pay the companies for the damages. After failing to pay the loans, the interests rates bound them further for the next years. Since 1995, more than three hundred thousand small farmers in India have committed suicide (Dhanagare, 2016). Due to a combination of factors, including corporate farming and climate change, among others, suicidal rates of small farmers have gone up by 30% from 2019–2023. In areas where suicide rates increased, the union and state government announced relief packages for dependents of the deceased instead of fixing the companies. That this has happened in cotton-growing areas shows the tyranny of crony capitalism in India. The practice over the years has resulted in the accumulation of capital at the top with unprecedented dispossession of peasants across the fertile areas of the country. Therefore, while a significant majority of the 840 million people associated with agriculture in India earn less than a dollar a day, more than a dozen elites associated with corporate agricultural business are billionaires. Their alliance with the transnational capitalist class shows the intricacies of the world-system and its penetration around the globe.

The liberalization project in India was not altogether in vain, however. As India opened its economy, foreign direct investment poured in, thus helping the political leadership expand the foreign exchange reserves. Privatization during the 1990s deposited about $9 billion in the national reserves. However, because of a lack of one-party rule in the center, Indian political leadership had to adopt a policy of partial privatization whereby 26 percent of noncontrolling shares of some state-owned enterprises were sold to the private sector, including some foreign investors. The government plan since 1991 has been to reduce its ownership to 26 percent to keep some of the decision-making rights while handing over the governing rights to the private sector (Gupta, 2005). In 1991, the total national reserves controlled by the state of India was about $5.643 billion. The volume was less than its 1980 level of $12.01 billion and the 1987 level of $11.512 billion. However, after 1991, the country's national reserves skyrocketed. In 1994, the country had more than $24 billion in domestic reserves. The value of total reserves increased to $30.642 billion in 1998, $71.608 billion in 2002, $131.631 billion in 2004, $276.578 billion in 2007, $300.48 billion in 2010, $325.081 billion in 2014, and $620.441 billion in 2023 (World Bank data). This massive increase in national reserves has been a result of the investment by foreign companies, the liberal fiscal regime, and a pro-business approach. During 1991–2014, the average growth rate of the country's GDP has been reported at 6.78 percent, which is almost double the "Hindu growth rate" during the years of a closed economy. More importantly, the country allowed a liberal flow of capital, jobs, and human resources. An unprecedented level of low-skilled jobs moved from the developed world to India. Its computer software industry burgeoned. The city of Bangalore became the second Silicon Valley in the world. While the country promoted the export of semi-skilled workers in the Middle East, a large majority of its skilled workers, professionals, and developed human resources from other sectors of the economy moved to high-income countries such as the United States and the United Kingdom. India has long been the top recipient of remittances sent home by expatriates. In 1991, the country received $3.29 billion in remittances, which rose to $10.33 billion in 1997, $14.23 billion in 2001, $22.13 billion in 2005, $49.98 billion in 2008, $70.39 billion in 2014, $69.129 in 2018, and $111 billion in 2022. The level of integration of the Indian economy in the global financial system can be gauged by the fact that in 2014 foreign people working in India sent remittances of $6.22 billion from India to their respective home countries. In 2022, it went up to $8.533 billion (World Bank data).

This happened in part due to excessive, extensive liberalization of the country's economy. India left the path of controlling industrialization and economic development by initially allowing foreign business organizations to own 26 percent of the assets of private and state-owned enterprises. The policy of partial privatization of foreign companies varied from sector to sector, however; while some sectors that were less sensitive to the concept of "self-reliance" were opened to the private sector for ownership in the early stages of liberalization, other sensitive sectors, such as the insurance, mining, and, particularly, the defense industries, have been controlled by the state for a long time. For some sectors, this level was raised to 49 percent, while in others, liberalization resulted in 74 percent ownership being given to foreign companies. The industries installed by foreign companies were mostly export-oriented, produced fewer than expected jobs, and did not show stronger growth, as compared to indigenous firms. Sen (2008) calculates that "while trade and FDI have had major positive effects on efficiency in Indian manufacturing, they may not have had similar positive results with respect to equity outcomes, especially in contributing to the growth of a labor-intensive export-oriented segment of the manufacturing sector" (p. 1). In 2001, the Indian defense sector was opened to the private sector for 26 percent share.

The Modi government currently in power brought an ambitious program of rapid privatization. In 2014, the government launched a program called "Make in India" whereby twenty-five different sectors under state control, including defense industries, were opened for foreign direct investment. In the defense sector, India failed to achieve the stated policy of 70 percent indigenous production and self-reliance, thus asking Western companies to invest in India with 49 percent ownership. In a year, the limit was raised to 76 percent (Behera, 2016). The union government also indicated privatizing Air India and state-owned insurance companies. India's yearning for foreign direct investment through a pro-business approach, however, has not been as successful, as was the case in China. During 1991–2002, total foreign direct investment in the country was about $48.41 billion (Mukherji, 2008). However, after 2005 an inflow of more than $10 billion in foreign direct investment took place. India's integration into the world economy can also be gauged by its percentage of exports in its GDP: 6.93 in 1990, 10.66 in 1995, 12.78 in 2000, 19.28 in 2005, 22.59 in 2010, and 22.91 in 2014. It went a little down from 2015–2020 but bounced back in 2021 to become 21.45 percent of the GDP. Trade, both indigenous and foreign, makes up roughly half the GDP of the country.

Therefore, I argue that whereas India was a peripheral country in 1980, it transitioned into a semi-peripheral country quickly thereafter and is now a strong candidate to be labeled as a semi-core country for two reasons. First, it has grown economically. Second, it has become a heavy political (military) weight in the world-system. The share of its agricultural sector in its GDP has consistently been declining. It was about 29.02 percent in 1990 but went down to 26.26 percent in 1995, 23.022 percent in 2000, 18.81 percent in 2005, 18.53 percent in 2011, 17.39 in 2014, and 15 percent in 2023 (World Bank data). The share of the software industry in its GDP rose from zero in the 1980s to above 3.5 percent in 2007, and 7.4 percent in 2022 (Das, Mathur, and Richter, 2005, 2013; World Bank Data, 2023). Given that, according to the 2001 census, 156 million workers out of 312 million in the country's total workforce, about 56.6 percent, are associated with agriculture shows the growing inequality in income and economic dispossession in the country. Far more important is that while the female proportion of the total workforce is 27.98 percent, 78 percent of women are employed in the agricultural and cultivation sector. More than half of the 88 million in marginal workforce is also women. The flow of investment, job, and income opportunities, therefore, is in the industry and services sectors, where, put together, less than 25 percent of the total workforce of the country has been employed, and toward males, who dominate these sectors. The real victims of India's modernization are, therefore, rural women. The real income of the government, therefore, has been through the burgeoning service sector, foreign trade, remittances, and foreign direct investment.

India's integration into the world economy based on the principals of neoliberal economics resulted in the emergence of two important realities that are paving the way toward a set of contradictions in India's positional standing in the world-system. First, from the start, India's acceptance of neoliberalism and the Washington Consensus model as the new economic approach to solving its chronic underdevelopment problem was seen as a failure of the welfare state approach and the ultimate victory of domestic and global capitalist forces. During 1947–1990, the Indian bourgeoisie strengthened itself by benefiting from state patronage and policies. This indigenous strength, the bourgeoisie convinced the political leadership, could be multiplied only through cooperation with the global capitalist class. By 1990, the "revolt" of the indigenous capitalist class—a mosaic of regional industrialists, powerful and rich landed aristocrats, and an expansive upper urban middle class—overcame state resilience by aligning with the rise of Hindu militant nationalism and pushing the state to meet the demands (Corbridge and Harriss, 2008). Another related argument is that the state changed its mind based on its experiences over four decades and decided to follow the advice of the international monetary and financial institutions to develop. India, the argument goes, "had no choice"; it "had to reduce inefficiency in the industrial sector, generate exports, attract foreign investment to gain a new source of capital and technology." The policymakers "lost confidence in India's control system and supported the move toward a market-oriented policy" (Denoon, 1998: 53). This realization, then, provided an opportunity for the international capitalist class and its respective institutions to squeeze the country further and open it up to a global class of investors. Even during the 1980s when India received a major program from the IMF, these institutions were generous in appreciating the slow and gradual policy shift from statism to neoliberalism. "The 1991 reforms' resemblance to Washington Consensus prescriptions was," therefore, "the outcome of a long-term campaign of ideological dissemination and political lobbying by the Bretton Wood Institutions," and "their role was decisive in that, in their absence, the tentative liberalization of the 1960s and 1980s would not have hardened into the language, diagnosis and recommendations of the free market orthodoxy espoused by these institutions, which, for all intents and purposes, has remained India's guiding 'paradigm' since 1991" (Sengupta, 2009: 181–82). This role and leverage enabled India to accept opening its doors and inviting foreign capital into the sectors it had reserved for the state. At the domestic level, the incoming volume of capital required India to accept the whole "package" of the culture of capitalism, including, but not limited to, economic inequality, capital accumulation, economic dispossession, cultural riots, and an increasing renege of the state of its identity as being a social welfare institution. At the global level, the state had to facilitate cementing the relationship between the local and global capitalist class by inviting foreign capital, lowering taxes, and allowing free currency convertibility, capital movement, and so on. More importantly, however, was the acceptance of the division of labor. India had to be contented with intermediary industrial development, growth of the service sector, and uneven development by allowing foreign capital to be invested in areas with the optimal chances for growth and maximum profit.

Second, similar to other semi-peripheral countries, India's integration into the world economy was asymmetrical by nature through the intensification of its dependence on the system. Global capitalism and its institutions did not change their policies, the principal approach of a laissez-faire economy, or their insistence that India should accept its status in the world economy. Historically, India has been the top borrower from the World Bank, and its total borrowings from the bank, by 2009, were more than $74 billion. Notwithstanding the tautological expression that "the Bank needs India more than India needs the Bank," the fact is that Indian dependence on external creditors has increased over time. Far more important is the impact beyond the credit facility; these institutions, together, create and destroy the ambience suitable to attract global capital from the core countries. Since the interests of the global capital holders are primarily associated with their geographical origins, India's (or any other country's) dependence on global capitalism cannot be underestimated.

Given these two important realities, India's aspirations to become a core country in the world-system are mired with numerous contradictions. First, the core is least willing to reconsider the hierarchical structure, in whose survival it has invested immensely. It took global capitalism about two hundred years to peripheralize India. After 1947, India's indigenous endeavors to regain that status were curbed through a variety of tactics. India could grow to an extent only and within the scope of a subordinate position. That, too, could only be possible after the country submitted to safeguard the primary interests of the core and follow global norms. Since 1947, India showed a discontentment with this balance of power. It tried to liberate itself from the clutches of global capitalism by claiming moral power, establishing a foreign policy approach based on nonalignment, striving to secure a seat in the UN Security Council, and so on. In most of these endeavors, India could not succeed. Its economic growth, however, was acknowledged by its inclusion into the premier group of major economic powers of the world. It could happen only when the group was expanded; India did not unseat any of the core countries in the group. However, it should be considered more as an endeavor than a concession on the part of the core to produce a hierarchical structure to legitimize its existence.

Second, India's security policy is incompatible with its economic policy. Within the region, it strives to become a hegemon, something that would possibly lessen its dependence on the core, and something that the core would not allow. Contrary to what its economic interests would argue, India labels China and Pakistan as security threats, thus eliminating any chances for expansive regional economic cooperation. The core capitalizes on this alienation by intensifying its insecurity and, thus, the expansion of its own economic benefits of investment and profit opportunities in the defense sector.

Third, though India could grow impressively after 1991, as compared to its performance during 1947–1990, its record of economic growth is relatively small compared with other emerging economic powers of the world, particularly China. India was subjected to a structural adjustment program from the IMF, and as mentioned above, it had to reinterpret its role in the global economy, which was mostly influenced by the perspective of the global capitalist system. In part, India's emerging power in the world-system, as in the case of China, depends on its growing military power. During the 1980s, when northwestern South Asia was busy fighting for the survival of global capitalism, India kept developing economically and militarily. In 1989, it faced a resurgence in one of the long-disputed territories under its control, Kashmir. As we will see in the next chapter, this crucial geostrategic territory has been a real reason for war between India and Pakistan and has influenced the nature of strategic competition of the region. Starting in 1979, the Soviet invasion of Afghanistan pushed the transnational capitalist class to reorganize the global strategic order by placing Pakistan and Saudi Arabia at the center of its war against communism. India, however, remained peaceful and did not see any strategic challenge during the 1980s. A comparison of the two countries—India and Pakistan—in the conclusion of this study will show how the strategic or military division of labor at the global level influenced the nature of the contemporary political economy in the region and beyond. Starting in 1989, *jihad* in Kashmir pushed India to invest militarily and financially in the state of Kashmir. However, over the years, India demonstrated its firm commitment to controlling the region in order to avoid the inexorable process of its disintegration and to show to the world that it could withstand injuries. In 2019, in response to a public pledge by President Trump to mediate between India and Pakistan over the Kashmir Dispute, India scrapped Kashmir's special status in its constitution and integrated it into its mainland area as a province.

Separatist movements in Kashmir and other parts of the country, in turn, have developed a resilience, pushing India to utilize its economic gains of liberalization to allocate massive resources to modernize its armed forces. The concept of stronger military power is embedded in India's worldview in that it should possess a "legitimate" position of great power equal to, if not greater than, the power of the core countries. Commenting on the Indian strategy of military rise, the SIPRI Yearbook (1994) argued, "Indian military and industrial leaders have sought state of the art, not only to ensure technological advantage but also to demonstrate that India's capabilities compare favorably with those of industrialized countries." This is evident from the growth of its defense industry and budget. In 1990, India's military expenditure stood at $7.75 billion. During 1990–1995, the increase was modest. However, after 1995 there is a rapid rise in defense spending: $101.18 billion in 1996, $12.92 billion in 1998, $15.49 in 2000, $20.44 in 2005, $31.93 billion in 2010, and $37.4 billion in 2014, $51 billion in 2016, and $76.6 billion in 2021. Military expenditure is the largest expenditure of the country; roughly 40 percent of the union government's spending is now allocated to defense. Under the "Make in India" program, the country is now allowing complete foreign ownership of factories producing defense equipment.

India's military dimension of national power is unique from some perspectives. It is the only emerging great power that has maintained a functional democratic culture and civilian control of strategic affairs (Wilkinson, 2015). Outside Europe, besides China, India is the only country raising a powerful military, which it believes is required to ascend the ladder to great power status. India's rise in the global system is, therefore, both economic and military. Though it has exhibited a restrained approach in its use of power in the region, India's military growth is palpable. The changing dynamics of the region are redefining the nature of the strategic division of labor. In this context, the rise of China as a powerful semi-core country in the world-system poses credible challenges to the supremacy of the Western core countries in the global capitalist system. In opposition to the Washington Consensus, the Beijing Consensus—"a willingness to innovate, equitable growth and sustainable development, as well as a strong belief in a nation's self-determination"—is turning into a credible alternative approach to economic development, technological modernization, and elevation in the international system (Ortmann,

2014: 74). For India, the rise of China poses some tough choices, however. The quest to great power status is dependent on changing both economic and military power equations in the region in the world-system.

In its worldview, India perceives China less as an economic asset than a strategic competitor. Its approach to the region is based on this perception, which, in the long run, offers various opportunities and challenges to the country. Located in a strategically mobile area of the world where alliances and competitions are fluid, India finds it tough to adjust to the dynamic relationship between the core of the world-system and the rising Asian powers. From economic competition, where India has always been facing a deficit in bilateral trade with China, to strategic competition in the South China Sea, where India has recently shifted its position from neutrality to supporting the Philippines' claim of sovereignty over the resources, the nature of the bilateral relationship will affect numerous other powers in the region. More importantly, India's perception of China and the broader neighborhood around it is primarily dictated by its concept of the greatness of Indian civilization. There are three important obstacles in the materialization of this concept. First, The Pakistan factor will always "regionalize" Indian globalizing ambitions. Second, China is perceived as a challenge, and the Sino-Pak strategic cooperation is perceived as a threat to India's security. Third, against this threat, India sought USSR patronage and, after its disintegration, has developed a closer working relationship with the United States. India's economic conditions can improve if it becomes a favorite of the core and the transnational capitalist class by agreeing to serves the primary interest of capital accumulation in the core, serving its concept of the strategic division of labor by posing a threat to China and deepening a strategic alliance with the West, and supporting political leadership of the core in global affairs. As the West helped South Korea and Taiwan rise from nowhere to emerging economic powers, it can help India, too, by pushing the power of global capital there. However, similar to the case of the two countries mentioned, the core will not take the dependency factor out of the equation in its relations with New Delhi. Therefore, to grow, India must continue to follow the principal approach of the core, as it has been for the past three decades. Since there are fewer chances for the development of any Indian discontentment with such an outlook for the world, chances are greater that it will observe intermediary industrialization, economic development, and prosperity at home with the inflow increase of capital and outflow of developed human resource to the core countries.

CONCLUSION

In this chapter, I analyzed the political-economic history of another important country. Some conclusions supporting the claims outlined in the first chapter have been corroborated by facts and policy analyses. Before it could forcefully be brought into the realm of the capitalist world-system, India was an economic powerhouse in the premodern world. The polity of India during 1206–1707 was the result of a complex and continuous amalgamation of Central Asian and Indian cultures and worldviews. Though India did not experience a revolution in its economy and production, it did progress very well in meeting its own requirements and that of the world by entering into consensual trade agreements with the Europeans. India failed to resist the voracious European appetite for its ample resources primarily because it could not develop a sense of nationalism or institute a state army. India lacked defense capabilities when the Europeans attacked it, and its native population fought more against each other than against the Europeans. By the time India gained independence, it had become a periphery of the capitalist world-system. More importantly, India failed to develop an indigenous model of development due to the lack of resources. After four decades under the "License Raj," India submitted to the pressure of global capitalism and embraced the neoliberal Washington Consensus as the panacea of its quest of acquiring major power status in the world-system. India, therefore, could develop only when it showed its willingness to serve the interests of the core and adopt a role of intermediary industrial power responsible for providing auxiliary services to the global processes of production and consumption. Since 1991, India's drive for neoliberal growth has brought faster industrialization and integration into the world economy. It has emerged a strong economy. Simultaneously, India has concentrated on its defense capabilities and modernized its military through the continuous provision of the financial resources it has obtained through its integration in the world-system. In 1998, it conducted five nuclear tests to become the sixth nuclear power in the world. It has recently been involved in developing an advanced missile defense system, hydrogen bombs, and drones. India has also advanced its agenda of missile and nuclear delivery systems with help from the United States, Israel, and some European countries. Though India has not fought a full-fledged war since 1971 (it fought a limited war against Pakistan in Kashmir in 1998), one can confidently claim that its military modernization is in the formative phase, as compared to the core countries. India is still dependent on Western military technology, and it is the world's leading buyer of the latest weapons. India can confidently claim to be a semi-core country, though it still is not as powerful as China.

Chapter Four

Pakistan

From the Periphery to the Semi-Periphery (1947–2014)

This chapter analyzes a third country, Pakistan. I will try to argue that the significance of Pakistan in the world-system is more strategic than economic. My theoretical framework argues that the two world-orders within the world-system—the economic world-order and the strategic world-order—facilitate the core to control global economic and political developments. Whereas some countries occupy enormous economic significance, Pakistan is a country that carried more than usual strategic significance in the world-system. Its higher positional standing in strategic world-order, therefore, put in place specific restrictions; the core promoted strategic development at the cost of economic development in the country. Whereas India adopted a statist developmental framework for its national economy, Pakistan created a dependency factor that it has carried since its independence. In turn, the core has utilized the country to serve its strategic purposes, the most significant being its role in Afghanistan. Some of Pakistan's domestic problems promoted complications in its relations with the core and exposed its weaknesses to be exploited. The framework, therefore, explains what I call the "regional great divergence." Pakistan and India adopted two different postures, policy perspectives, and relations with the core, and therefore saw different outcomes.

THE "REGIONAL GREAT DIVERGENCE": ORIGINS, NATURE, CONSEQUENCES

Established in 1947 by carving out Muslim-majority areas in the northwest and southeast of the Sub-Continent, Pakistan was a product of multiple factors, thus allowing scholars to profess a variety of theories ranging from religious reasons and economic realities to imperialist designs. It has been argued, for example, that the identity of Pakistan is as old as the Indus civilization itself, five thousand years. This approach, essentially, stands as a clear challenge to the notion of India as a unified ancient civilization and argues that life on the Sub-Continent was, in fact, a mosaic of cultures, religions, and traditions. Religious and anthropological sub-narratives follow this tradition. Aitzaz Ahsan (1996), for example, counters Jawaharlal Nehru's argument that from the northwestern region bordering Afghanistan to the far eastern coastal borders of India, there was a "tremendous impress of oneness" notwithstanding diversity within the region. Ahsan claims that "Pakistan had existed for almost five and a half of the last six thousand years. Indus had seldom been a part of India" (pp. xiv–xv). Similarly, it has been argued that Pakistan's ideological origins are embedded in the religious identity of Muslims endured for more than a thousand years. According to S. M. Ikram (1989), Islam in India had spread through peaceful propagation, and though the Muslims exchanged culture with the Hindu majority, they could not compromise over their religious identity, which they pursued the British to guarantee. Ishtiaq Qureshi (1965), in a similar manner, argues that despite having ruled India for over a thousand years, the Muslims remained a distinct nation and struggled for the creation of Pakistan because they realized that the Hindus would not let them live honorably and with equal access to civil and constitutional rights.

Another narrative about the events of 1947 resulting in the partition of India relies on the politico-economic concept of "divide and rule," which argues that for over two hundred years, British imperial power ruled over India by facilitating the construction of distinctive ethnic and communal identities of Indians and deepening the faultlines of conflict between the Hindus and Muslims during the colonial period and at independence. It is not that they did not exist in the pre–British imperial period. While the Hindus were successfully incorporated into the business of the state during the period of Mughal Emperor Akbar (1556–1605), his successors, particularly Aurangzeb (1658–1707), adopted policies that alienated the majority of subjects, mainly the Hindus. However, these fault lines were extraordinarily intricate and complex. As explained in the previous chapter, the British capitalized on these differences by adopting a variety of tactics, most importantly the policy of divide and rule, to deepen the enmity. This narrative argues that while these fault lines enabled British rule for an extended period, it was necessary for global capitalism to deepen the foundations of dependency, exploitation, and hierarchical structure on the Sub-Continent. It was, therefore, considered necessary to partition the region and leave it exposed to foreign political and economic influence. A sub-narrative of this tradition supports the argument that the Indian National Congress did little to address the concerns of the Muslims in post-British India, pushing them to adopt the separatist option. The creation of Pakistan was a design of the British fully facilitated by Nehru's arrogance (Kaura, 1977; Singh, 2010). Pakistan, therefore, was a reaction to the tactical blunders of the Indian National Congress capitalized on by the British empire.

Some others look at the broader viewpoint of Muslim consciousness in India by applying the world-systems perspective. S. N. Ahmad (1991) locates the origins of discontentment between the two leading communities of India within the broader perspective where local socio-economic transformations, ushered by colonialism and shaped by the dynamic forces of the capitalist world economy, posed threats to the material interests of the local elite, mainly Muslims. Developments within the center of the world economy, such as the Great Depression and the two World Wars, Ahmad shows, left transformative changes within the Sub-Continent, including intensification of economic-cum-ideological conflicts among the elites on both sides. This resulted in the ossification of ideological stances, thus promoting divergent identities and political interests that led to the partition of India. For Hamza Alavi (1988), "the Pakistan movement was neither a millenarian ideological movement devoted to the realization of an Islamic state nor was it a movement of feudal landlords nor yet again a movement of an emergent Muslim national bourgeoisie," but rather "the central driving force behind the Muslim movement was a class that has a distinct place in colonized societies whose role needs to be recognized more fully and explicitly," named by him as "the *salariat*, the urban, educated classes who qualify for employment in the colonial state" (pp. 66–67). In other words, the educated Muslim class, capable of earning a livelihood under the colonial administration, faced stiff competition and took a refuge under the broader ideological banner of Islam, thus paving the way for the establishment of an exclusivist state.

An analysis of narratives ranging from socio-religious to politico-economic factors reveals that in the two new states, the ingredients of nation formation and the outlook of their composition were primarily different. The forces that gave birth to Pakistan—namely, Muslim separatism incubated, nurtured, and matured by imperialist designs aimed at exposing the postcolonial region to a neocolonial influence, and corroborated by Congress's falling short of addressing the Muslim question in postcolonial India—ensured a feeble state engulfed in a multipronged crisis of identity and existence and territorial disputes. Pakistan needed to be the antithesis of whatever India claimed to be. While India stood for an ancient civilization of Ganga and Jamna, Pakistan had to search for one that was different and distinctive. While the Indian National Congress, the champion political party leading the Indian movement for independence, claimed to establish a pluralistic and secular country, the Muslim League and Jinnah had to espouse for an ideological and religious state. India was a Hindu majority country; Pakistan, therefore, had to embrace being the fort of Islam. Rejecting the partition of India before 1947, the religious parties, stood firm to espouse Islamism as the foundation of constitutional development in Pakistan after its independence. In the long-run, India went on to adopt socialism and closer relations with the USSR; Pakistan jumped into an alliance with the capitalist countries. India adopted promoting economic protectionism, morality as a force in international relations, and nonalignment as its official ideology. Pakistan, on the other hand, sprinted to embrace laissez-faire as its approach to economic development soon after its creation. This divergence has brought results sooner than expected. By 2014, India had become an emerging economic power of the world, while Pakistan was facing terrorism leading to the virtual collapse of the state itself.

The question of Indian independence was to be resolved by three key players—the British, the Indian National Congress (INC), and the All India Muslim League (AIML). For their part, the Muslims accepted Western civilization roughly fifty years later than the Hindus. However, once there, they were thoroughly patronized by the British to become a distinct and vibrant socio-political force on the Sub-Continent. Over two hundred years, the British had come to realize that co-option of social forces capable of influencing regional economies had been a fruitful exercise. By extending considerable leverages to the Muslim bourgeoisie in Muslim majority areas, the colonial government extracted economic resources in a relatively peaceful manner. Some scholars, such as Leonard Mosley (1962), argue that the British colonial bureaucracy, pleased with its more significant compatibility with the Muslims and the role of the AIML during the four decades since its establishment, wanted to return the gesture with a similar kind of blessing. The AIML had adopted an appeasement policy toward the British government to secure some sympathy. The Muslim nobility, through its actions, ensured the colonial government of its full cooperation in return for considerable socio-political influence. This approach delivered some tangible benefits, such as recognition of a separate electorate, quotas in jobs, equal political weight of Muslim minority compared to the Hindu majority, and financial-administrative facilitation in the establishment of educational institutions such as Aligarh Muslim University. The cumulative effect of this approach was seeding separatist feelings among the Muslims of India. The demographic factor—the concept of absolute Hindu majority—in postindependent and united India intensified the fear of exploitation of the Muslims. Economic insecurity of the Muslims in Hindu-majority areas added justification for a new separate territory. The landed elite in Muslim-majority areas found it better to opt out of control of Congress, whose policies, under Gandhi, were more statist, egalitarian, and protectionist. Therefore, Muslim opinion-makers realized that the creation of Pakistan would save them a sovereign territory under their control that was free from competition with the Hindu bourgeoisie. Moreover, living in one of the most diversified cultural and ethnic areas of the world, the Muslim bourgeoisie could unite people based on identity. Under the leadership of Jinnah, the Muslim bourgeoisie found religious identity compounded with the fear of permanent demographic, democratic, and economic subordination to Hindus to be the only force capable of attracting people of diverse identities from all over the region under one slogan of territorial separatism. India was vivisected by exposing it to its socio-religious fault lines. The partition project capitalized on the concept—eagerly propagated by the AIML, justified by the British colonial government in New Delhi and India office in London, and accepted by the INC—that India would slip into endless bloodshed and civil war if it were not partitioned before the British left (Wolpert, 2009). The demand for Pakistan, thus, was justified as a project aimed at ensuring the economic and socio-religious interests of the Muslim minority on the Sub-Continent. This could not have happened without the active facilitation of the INC, whose president, Jawaharlal Nehru, rejected the Muslims' concerns expressed by both the AIML and the colonial government. Jinnah, who "was intensely suspicious of Congress motives and intentions," "reacted to Nehru's statement like an army leader who had come in for armistice discussions under a flag of truce and found himself looking down the barrel of a cocked revolver" (Mosley, 1962: 27–28). Jinnah, the one who "in fact, did not really want" to create Pakistan but used the slogan to maximize his bargaining power, used the treacherous tactics of Congress to justify his suspicions (Jalal, 1994).

Scholars point out several reasons for decolonization in the twentieth century. However, a vast majority of them agree on three reasons, though they name them differently (McIntyre, 1998). These reasons can be called a tridimensional transformation that took place in Britain, in the colonial areas, and in the core. They, in turn, can be reduced to two factors: transformation in the core, and transformation in the colonies. In the case of South Asia, Indian independence was the product of two principal developments in the core. First, in Britain, Prime Minister Clement Attlee, whose Labour Party professed socialist ideological perspectives and whose manifesto included independence for India, had come into power in 1945. In united colonial India, as explained in the previous chapter, the primary objectives of British imperial policy, at least during the twentieth century of colonial rule, included "the maintenance of India's imperial commitment to provide a market for British goods, supply men and materials for imperial defense, and obtain the sterling remittance needed to meet Home Charges and interest payments" (Tomlinson, 1979: 104–5). While all other objectives, including the provision of human resources to defend British imperial interests, could be compromised, Indian financial obligations were imposed in the strictest possible manner because "the Treasury was convinced that the British taxpayer would be left to foot the bill should the Government of India ever default on its sterling debt" (pp. 105). In 1931, for example, India owed about Rs. 10 billion to Britain. In 1945, its position had changed from borrower to creditor, as Britain owed at least Rs. 16 billion. After the war was over, Indian contributions declined over time, and a sagacious cost-benefit analysis would have recommended Britain abandon the colony to avoid accumulating debt. Controlling a vast area and a growing population that had tasted modern education, governance institutions, and nationalism through the blatant use of force and oppression was impossible in the long run. Given the significance of India in the world-economy as a periphery, the region needed a new form of arrangement whereby the flow of material resources to the core would be ensured even after the end of colonial rule. Such a settlement was not possible by pushing the Indians to agree to a formal institutional arrangement; it had to be supra-state in nature since the British had lost their urge to colonize India any further. It seems that the British were confident that through the partition of India, and by aligning the socio-economic forces in Pakistan to follow economic development based on a comparative advantage, they would keep the region open and integrated into the world economy as a periphery. Moreover, though the British military mind was divided over the possible strategic repercussions of united versus divided India, the perspective that reigned in the end looked at the significance of Pakistan as a buffer state between a stronger India and a belligerent USSR, thus providing a significant foothold for the Western powers to checkmate the spread of communism throughout Asia. Contradicting the argument forwarded by Field Marshal Sir Claude Auchinleck in May 1946 that "if we desire to maintain our power to move freely by sea and air in the Indian Ocean area, . . . we can do so only by keeping it being a United India," Lieutenant General Sir Francis Tucker, the General Officer Commander-in-Chief of the Easter Command, argued:

> There was much, therefore, to be said for the introduction of a new Muslim power supported by the science of Britain. If such a power could be produced and if we could orient the Muslim strip from North Africa through Islamia Desertia, Persia, Afghanistan to the Himalayas, upon a Muslim power in Northern India, then it had some chance of halting the filtration of Russia towards the Persian Gulf. These Islamic countries, even including Turkey, were not a very great strength in themselves. But with a Northern Indian Islamic state of several millions, it would be reasonable to expect that Russia would not care to provoke them too far. (Quoted in Ahmed, 2013: 30–31)

As the partition of India approached, the senior leadership of the British military prepared a memorandum to be sent to the prime minister urging him to accept Pakistan's inclusion in the British Commonwealth. The memorandum, sent on May 12, 1947, argued:

> It would be a tremendous asset if Pakistan, particularly North West, remained within the Commonwealth. The bases, airfields, and ports in North West India would be invaluable to Commonwealth defense. . . . From the strategic point of view, there were overwhelming arguments in favor of Western Pakistan remaining within the Commonwealth, namely, that we should obtain important strategic facilities, the port of Karachi, air bases and the support of the Moslem manpower in the future; be able to ensure the continued integrity of Afghanistan; and be able to increase our prestige and improve our position throughout the Muslim world. . . . There was, therefore, everything to gain by admitting Western Pakistan into the Commonwealth. A refusal of an application to this end would amount to rejecting loyal people from the British Commonwealth, and would probably lose us all chances of ever getting strategic facilities anywhere in India, and at the same time shatter our reputation in the rest of the Moslem world. From a military point of view, such a result would be catastrophic. (Quoted in Ahmed, 2013: 36)

It was, therefore, in the interest of Britain, and global capitalism at large, to ensure the continuity of this setup in the long run without actually controlling and ruling over the territory. Pakistan, from the British perspective, was a necessary territorial division whose primary purposes were to keep India away from physical connectivity with Russia and to serve as a bastion of the Western powers for influencing development in South Asia, the Persian Gulf, and beyond. The purpose remained the same when the leadership of the world-system shifted from London to Washington.

Second, far more important is the transition within the core of the capitalist world-system. Though the Allied forces had won World War II, it was too extortionate to benefit London. According to Mosley (1962), "British power and prestige, despite the victory, had been diminished by the war. The campaigns in Asia had shown up Britain's weakness. After Singapore, Burma and the sinking of her finest ships by the Japanese, Britain would never again be able to demonstrate in Asia the background of strength and influence—the *macht-politik*—which had for long enabled her to rule a million people with one-man-on-the-spot" (pp. 12–13). Following the destruction of its economy due to the war, Britain yearned to resolve the Indian question and had to be increasingly frugal to preserve diminishing financial resources to rebuild its welfare state (Garavini, 2012). A related fact is that during the transition years in the core, roughly 1942–1946, the new imperial master, the United States, an erstwhile apathetic bystander declining to interfere in the internal affairs of other countries, pursued Britain to relinquish control of its colonies to establish a new globalized division of labor through the perpetuation of dependence and exploitation in a new manner. Before 1930, the isolationist perspective dominant in the United States pushed Washington to support the United Kingdom's quest to maintain global dominance; this was no longer the case when President Roosevelt took over. Winston Churchill (1986), the then prime minister of the United Kingdom wrote, "The United States had shown an increasingly direct interest in Indian affairs as the Japanese advance into Asia spread westwards. The concern of the Americans with the strategy of a world war was bringing them into touch with political issues on which they had strong opinions and little experience. Before Pearl Harbor, India had been regarded as a lamentable example of British Imperialism, but as an exclusive British responsibility. Now that the Japanese were advancing toward its frontiers the United States Government began to express views and offer counsel on Indian affairs" (p. 185). In March 1942, while writing to Churchill about the Indian question, President Roosevelt suggested "the setting up of what might be called a temporary Government in India, headed by a small representative group, covering different castes, occupations, religions, and geographies—this group to be recognized as a temporary Dominion Government. It would, of course, represent existing Governments of the British provinces, and would also represent the Council of Princes, but my principal thought is that it would be charged with setting up a body to consider a more permanent Government for the whole country" (p. 189). As World War II ended, Britain owed $13 billion to the United States, in addition to the $3.75 billion that it had requested during the Bretton Woods talks (Clarke, 2009). The economic crisis the British faced by the end of the war was so imminent and huge that "if Washington refused a loan or other economic assistance, Britain herself would have to undergo a savage regime of austerity and international withdrawal like Russia between the wars" (Darwin, 2005: 69). Even those who disagree with the economic-deterministic approach as the primary cause of the fall of British imperial preeminence agree that the transformational changes on the European continent had intensified British economic issues substantially and Britain was in need of American help to recover (McKercher, 2006). In such a scenario, maintaining colonies, particularly that would have been more obstructive of the recovery process, was not a sagacious policy. India emerged as an important policy factor in US calculations as World War II progressed. In 1941, in response to the British proposal to establish a new office of the agent-general in its Washington embassy, the Department of the State welcomed the move with a desire for adequate reciprocity by arguing that India was "assuming a position of increasing importance as a source of materials essential to the implementation of the coordinated programs of the Government of the United States for national defense and the extension of aid to the British Empire" (quoted in Malik, 1991: 46). As the transition took place, Britain was exposed to influence from the United States and had to follow the order of Pax Americana. The British relinquished themselves of the responsibility to lead the capitalist world against communist spread in Eastern Europe, South America, and Southeast Asia. European continental security was guaranteed by the United States, to the great relief of Britain. Eastern Europe was left to the USSR, while Asia stood open to influence. In any case, the economic division of labor remained unchanged to a large extent. It was this broader territorial arrangement designed in the core that left some opportunities and constraints to the decision-makers in postcolonial states in South Asia.

During two centuries of colonial rule, divergent paths to development were adopted on the Sub-Continent. As mentioned in the previous chapter, it took British imperial forces almost a hundred years (1757–1855) to bring different areas of the region under colonial control. Depending on the need, utility, and geographical significance, divergent paths to development were adopted. The nature of economic development during the colonial period was meant to serve imperial interests based on the maximum utilization of resources. Therefore, while Bengal was impoverished by restructuring its agriculture to fit colonial requirements, Punjab and many other areas were provided a canal system to grow cash crops. In northwestern parts of the region, the workforce was recruited to defend the empire in both World Wars. Coastal areas were industrialized, and railway networks were established to bring agricultural products to these industries. Coincidently, a visible religious division took place alongside this economic division on the Sub-Continent; broadly speaking, Muslim-majority areas were both agricultural economies and essential contributors to the armed forces of India. The Hindu-majority areas, on the other hand, had an advanced industrial foundation. Any new division of labor on these lines would have benefited the core in the long run by assigning respective roles to these new territorial arrangements. From the world-systems perspective, therefore, the partition of India was a new arrangement of the globalizing division of labor. It was meant to create exclusive territories for different economic realities and their respective uses in the world-system. It was easier for the core to manage and exert its influence over two mutually wrangling countries than one big and united country. Since Pakistan was going to be more exclusive than inclusive, the chances for conflict in the region expose both the countries to international pressure and influence.

Once independent, Pakistan, more than India, had to rely on the core countries in order to develop its industrial base from scratch. Since it was a peripheral country meant to provide raw materials to the core, its economic performance depended on the requirements of the developed countries. Of greater significance is to see the role of Pakistan in the furthering of the strategic interests of global capitalism. As a periphery, Pakistan's economic role as a provider of raw materials and complementary industrial support was essential. However, far more important was the strategic role Pakistan had to play in ensuring the functioning of global capitalism. Throughout its existence, as we will see in the next pages of this chapter, Pakistan stood as the most suitable ally serving the strategic interests of the core. It played a vital role in ensuring a graceful exit of the United States from Vietnam, side-lining the USSR in Southeast Asia by providing good offices in Washington for the establishment of Sino-American bilateral relations. It also became the frontline state in the war against communism in Afghanistan. The September 11, 2001, terrorist attacks on the United States revitalized the significance of Pakistan and its role in ensuring that a stable global strategic order was acknowledged in the capitals of the core countries. From the perspective of the global division of labor, Pakistan was far more significant strategically than economically. Its discrepant positional standing in the two highly intertwined yet distinguishable world-orders—economic and strategic—pushed the country into a perpetual crisis of governance, though it never disappointed the core in doing the job it was assigned. India, on the other hand, developed a foreign policy to shield itself from the influence of the core. From 1947 to 1977, as discussed in the previous chapter, India did not succumb to the pressure of global capitalism. Even after it allowed the penetration of global capitalism and its financial institutions, India remained a protectionist state for a considerable time. It was only after 1991 that India opened its doors to global capital, developed complex interdependence and integration into the world economy, and progressed to develop a formidable defense structure against Pakistan and China. The Indian approach to economic and strategic questions, the comparative analysis in the following pages will show, was far more indigenous and realist. Pakistan, on the other hand, entered into a patron-client relationship with the core, thus deepening the crisis at home and intensifying its dependence on the system. The great divergence between the two countries was due to their different utilities in the system; the hierarchical structure of the world-system tagged divergent roles to the two countries complementing, of course, their perceptions and worldviews.

PAKISTAN: A MESSY LEGACY OF INDEPENDENCE (1947–1958)

The first decade in Pakistan history is when the state adopted a mercantilist approach toward economic development, albeit in political chaos. In September 1948, Jinnah died, leaving behind a legacy that no one was willing to carry on. He was "a symbol of Muslim pride in India," "Saladin" of his followers, and a "cultural symbol" of unity in the new state (A. S. Ahmed, 1997).

However, instead of following his constitutionalist approach to establishing an egalitarian society based on a modern interpretation of the socio-economic principals of Islam that he argued about in his speeches, the elite class of the country—the feudal lords, civil and military bureaucrats, and leading politicians of the Pakistan Muslim League, a majority of whom bandwagoned in the later years of the Pakistan movement only—immersed themselves in the opportunities for affluence and exploitation. The partition produced an unprecedented level of migration in human history; more than 12 million people were displaced and had to cross the new borders. Hindu-Muslim riots killed about 1.5 million people throughout the Sub-Continent. However, this did not affect the elite class, as they found opportunities to occupy land and properties, and even kidnapped women and children.

The new state faced an economic crisis from the start. Acute was the financial crisis. The country simply did not have the money to carry out the essential business of the state. Violating the terms of the agreements of partition, India refused to compensate Pakistan for the loss of its share of industries, including ordnance and armament factories, since most of them were located in areas that became part of India. The loss was of Rs. 600 million. At the time of partition, Pakistan was promised to receive £165 million and Rs. 750 million as part of its share out of the reserves of India. However, Pakistan could get only £28 million and Rs. 200 million, respectively, which put immense pressure on the state. Pakistan joined the British Commonwealth in October 1947, thus becoming eligible to receive loans and grants from Britain and the United States (Dar, 2014: 272). In May 1948, the United States extended a loan of $10 million to enable Pakistan to meet its defense requirements in the wake of its war in Kashmir.

During the first decade after independence, Pakistan's economic development was determined by three intertwined factors. First, Pakistan adopted a model of economic development based on protectionism, promotion of import-substitute industrialization, emphasis on foreign trade, and facilitation in the shift of financial resources from other sectors to the industry. According to Shahid Burki (1988), since the leadership of the country was primarily immigrants, and most of the refugees coming to Pakistan from India were either merchants, businessmen, or industrialists, they pulled a combination of sympathy and affiliation to pressure the government to develop financial and industrial policies that were beneficial to them. In 1949, the federal government refused to devalue its currency. The logic forwarded was that it would increase the cost of the industrial drive and import of machinery the government was committed to carrying on from the start. The import of goods that could have been manufactured in the country faced heavy tariffs. During this period, the agricultural sector faced a shortage in resource allocation, water scarcity due to India's interference in the flow of water to West Pakistan, and feudalistic control over agricultural production. Simultaneously, the transfer of resources from the agricultural sector to industry proved lethal in the long run because it divested resources from East Pakistan to West Pakistan; the foreign capital earned through agricultural exports originating in East Pakistan was used to buy machinery and fund industrialization in West Pakistan. Moreover, a lack of land reforms and resistance to the redistribution of state resources in a somewhat egalitarian manner elevated the sense of deprivation in East Pakistan. Even after these heavy price tags at an internal level, the policy of autarkic industrialization could not succeed due to several contradictions in the process. From the start, self-sufficiency turned out to be a mirage because the state found itself unable to survive without foreign aid and grants. In May 1948, less than a year after its birth, the state applied for a loan of $10 millions from the United States. In July 1950, the country joined the Bretton Woods Institutions, thus confirming its acceptance of the terms and conditions of the capitalist world-system and its positional standing as a peripheral country. Within a month, the United States approved another aid of $0.6 million. In 1951, the state received another grant of $1.6 million from the Ford Foundation and a $60 million loan from the World Bank. While these loans were not bad in themselves, as the economic restructuring of a new country requires substantial financial investment and management, the real problems were the conditions associated with these loans and their spillover effect. Most of the aid was meant to assist the country in developing institutions and building technical capacity that would lead to capitalist and interdependent economic development. Since the state was relying on agriculture, one can understand that the role of these institutions and foreign aid was to deepen that dependence, develop complementary industries, and promote residual technical development (Gardezi and Rashid, 1983; Noman, 1988). According to Hassan Gardezi and Jamil Rashid (1983):

> Soon after independence, the rulers of Pakistan began to yield to all types of inducements to enter into neocolonial economic and military alliances in order to preserve the internal systems of privilege and power and the external control of the cheap labor and raw materials of the country. Once these rulers accepted dependence on the world capitalist market economy and its prime movers, especially the transnational corporations and aid agencies either based in or sponsored by the United States of America, the impact of Western economic doctrines and development models proved to be decisive in shaping ensuing events of both national and geopolitical significance. (p. 5)

Second, compared to India, where food insecurity pushed the state to allocate considerable resources to the purchase of wheat and grains from international markets, Pakistan faced challenges in defending its national integrity and sovereignty. In less than a year, the country went to war with India over the issue of Kashmir. As one of the 562 princely states of the Sub-Continent, Kashmir had to decide which of the two new states to join. The Kashmiri Hindu ruler decided to join India, but the population, an overwhelming majority of which was Muslim, resisted the decision, providing Pakistani tribal militias an opportunity to intervene and occupy about a third of the territory. The war ended with India and Pakistan controlling two-thirds and one-third of the territory, respectively. Since then, the Kashmir dispute was capitalized on to promote the interests of the military establishment in the country. In Pakistan, Kashmir is cited by the military as a justification for its gigantic existence and resource allocation. The state, grappling with the question of its survival, prioritized national defense as the most significant factor in resource allocation and political domination, as well as the cornerstone of foreign policy. It consumed the infant state's scarce sterling reserves that it had inherited at partition. The situation was worrisome because, except for India, with whom Pakistan had a trade surplus of about £11 million, Pakistan's total trade deficit was about £34 million during 1948–1949 only, most of which was the result of huge purchases of arms and weapons, which happened at the cost of neglecting agriculture and other sectors of social and human development. During the initial years after independence, the allocation of resources to defense was almost double the total budget made available for socio-economic development. As compared to the defense sector, which consumed about two-thirds of the financial resources of the central government, the state could spend only 4 percent of its budget on health and education combined. Therefore, during the first decade, an abysmal state of affairs existed in the sectors of socio-economic development, namely, agriculture, health, education, and social development. The per capita income remained stagnant, though in rural areas it went down from Rs. 207 in 1949 to Rs. 195 in 1958 (Noman, 1988: 19). Average GDP growth rate was almost 3.1 percent, while agricultural growth was only 1.43 percent. Since the population growth rate was higher throughout the period (2.16 percent per annum during 1951–1961), economic growth was almost negligible in absolute terms, affecting the countryside immensely. However, due to protectionist policies and government interest in industrialization, the manufacturing sector showed a growth rate of 7.7 percent mainly led by large-scale industrial growth, which showed a growth rate of around 16 percent. The policy of import substitution was successful in many ways. Sugar production went up from 22 percent of domestic needs to 99.99 percent; in edible oils, the country's domestic production could meet 96.6 percent, up from 63.6 percent in 1951. The cotton and textile industry showed impressive growth; while the country was meeting only 14.5 percent of domestic needs through indigenous production in 1951, it was able to meet 97.3 percent of domestic demand by 1958 (McCartney, 2011: 41–42).

The consequences of the financial imbalance between the national defense and socio-economic development sectors were enormous and long-term. In the first place, this financial imbalance gave birth to institutional imbalance; the military became the most influential institution in the country, turning Pakistan into a security state. The national narrative of the country relied on the survival of the state primarily through force. The country's birth was claimed to have been possible only when the Muslims, a minority, "snatched it out of the jaws" of the Hindu majority; the price of remaining independent was equated to building a defense powerful enough to deter a much stronger and bigger enemy, India. The ideology of the state relied primarily on labeling India as an enemy, "the Other," and representative of an ideological opponent that could only be defeated through accumulating and exercising a credible force, come what may. Such a state strived to unify the country by force by rejecting or outlawing divergent and regional voices and identities. Over the years, as we will see in the following pages, the military, obsessed with securing the ideological narrative it built, found itself the guardian of the territorial and ideological boundaries of the state. Ironically, the state, controlled by the military, found refuge in an ideological illusion where a lethal combination of religion and finance led to the emergence of a genealogical disorder paving the way for the development of chronemic instability in politics, society, and economy.

Third, the geneses of the military's interventionist and monopolistic role in the polity of Pakistan need to be found in the peculiar conduct of the global capitalist system in the peripheral states; it supervised military domination in the country and found it congruent to its material interests. The most significant development during the first decade was the asymmetrical relationship between the state of Pakistan and the global powers. The relationship could not have been any other way given the hierarchical structure of the world-system and the positional difference between the core and a peripheral state. However, the way the state conducted itself in the process of its construction led the world-system to strengthen its utilitarian image of the former. The AIML's leadership, even before the country's independence, tried to convince the United States of the significance of Pakistan in its strategic management of the Cold War. As the country went to war with India in 1948, its defense requirements surpassed everything else, giving the military unparalleled control inside and making it the most dominant state actor in international politics. Consequently, the state entered into a patron-client relationship with the Western powers. During the initial years, the defense establishment in the country pushed the government to secure arms deals with the United States. According to Pervaiz Cheema (1990), as early as October–November 1947, the Pakistani government approached the United States with a list of requests for financial-cum-military assistance of $81 million per year spanned over five years; the request was declined. Several subsequent requests, even the one forwarded by the British for Pakistan, were rejected. This did not dishearten Pakistani leadership, however, because the policymakers, both civilians and military, had "calculated that Pakistan's needs, at the time, were so significant that only the Americans could meet them provided they were able to convince their leaders" (Cheema, 1990: 115). The Pakistani military attaché in Washington reported to military leadership the consistent efforts to develop a formal military alliance between the two countries. The United States was reminded of the significant strategic objectives it could secure by patronizing the defense capabilities of Pakistan. According to Mohammad Waseem (2007), the US concern about the weaker defense capabilities of the Middle Eastern powers and thus lack of credible defense potential against communism motivated the policymakers in Washington to develop regional alliances. It took some time for Washington to appreciate the significant role Pakistan could play in stabilizing the region. In 1953, when the US secretary of state visited Asian countries, he met with Pakistani leaders and was impressed by the scale of preparedness of the army and the eagerness of the Pakistani leadership to join the Western powers in resisting the spread of communism. In his memo to Washington, he mentioned the geostrategic significance of Pakistan by stating, "Communist China borders on northern territories held by Pakistan, and from Pakistan's northern border one can see the Soviet Union. Pakistan flanks Iran and the Middle East and guards the Khyber Pass, the historic invasion route from the north into the subcontinent" (quoted in Sattar, 2017: 43). Thus, in May 1954, the United States signed a mutual defense assistance agreement and committed "to accelerate the substantial military aid programs for Pakistan" (p. 95). In September 1954, Pakistan entered into a US-led regional military alliance, the Southeast Asia Treaty Organization (SEATO). The next year it joined a UK-led military alliance initially named the Baghdad Pact but later renamed the Central Treaty Organization (CENTO). During the initial years, these pacts increased the significance of military-to-military contact between Pakistan and the major powers of the world, especially the United States. According to Ayesha Jalal (1990), these contacts knotted the local elite of the country, primarily military generals, as junior partners together with the controllers of international economic and military order. Pakistan's defense establishment exploited these links not only to strengthen institutional imbalance but also to subvert political developments at home. "Far from being an innocent victim of plots hatched by foreign governments, Pakistan was in effect hostage to a handful of individuals nested in the highest positions of power and influence within state and society who were willing and able to use international connections to mold internal developments" (Jalal, 1990: 186). By 1957, though the US and the UK governments had removed themselves from the continuing political crisis in Pakistan, they agreed that "they would back the military and bureaucratic combination most capable of restoring a semblance of stability in a country in which they had invested so much for so little" (p. 269). It is necessary to understand that Western military and economic support could be made available to the Pakistan only when it was in the interests, particularly material, of the Western powers.

There was yet another important development in the country that laid the foundation of perpetual crisis, one that later challenged the existence of the state itself: the inconvenient but inevitable consummation of religion and politics during the pre-partition movement years that enabled the religious forces in the Pakistan to capitalize on and demand inclusion of parochial religious doctrines in constitutional frameworks. In the first place, Jinnah's understanding of religion and its relationship with the state was confusing at best. In a diverse society like India, he found Islam as a centripetal force that at least mitigated the significance of other identities, thus enabling him to develop the concept of a nation for the Muslims of India. For about twenty years (1916–1936), Jinnah endeavored to unite Muslims and Hindus to form an all-India alliance and put forward their mutually agreed-on demands to the British colonial government. However, after having been disappointed by the failure of his repeated attempts to bridge Hindu-Muslim differences through political compromises and constitutional guarantees, such as a separate electorate or the reservation of Muslim seats in a united and federated India, he went on to demand a separate state based on religious identity. Sir Muhammad Iqbal, a prominent politician and poet from the Punjab province, mentored Jinnah to look at the constitutional problem of India from a religious point of view. Though it took about eight to ten years, Jinnah ultimately followed Iqbal's understanding (Bolitho, 1954). However, since he was neither a theologian nor a staunch pan-Islamist, he nurtured a socio-economic understanding of religion while exploiting it to push his agenda for a new state. The perspective benefited British interests since it not only divided the Indian population into communal categories, but it also provided the rulers an opportunity to pressure the Congress to accept an uncomfortable competition from within the local population. In a practical sense, therefore, the ultimate creation of Pakistan was nothing more than a successful exploitation of religious slogans.

Jinnah had no other choice. The Muslim-majority provinces were not willing to subvert regionalism and accept an all-India approach. In Bengal and the Punjab, regional Muslim parties were influential, and their leaders were aspiring to elevate their political standing in the center. In North West Frontier Province, Bacha Khan allied with the Congress. Sindh also showed no serious yearning for Jinnah. The league could live and survive only because the

Muslims in Hindu-majority provinces found it impossible to live under an absolute Hindu-majority democracy. In such a situation, Jinnah, domiciled in Bombay, could only rely on Islam as a unifying platform. Therefore, while he was not keen to appreciate religion in public life, he appointed religious leaders in the party to pursue influential religious saints to promote separatism in the Muslim population and use religious verdicts tactfully to pressure the Muslims to vote for the league (Jalal, 1994). After having looked closely at Indian constitutional issues and the increasing communal tensions in Muslim-minority provinces, Jinnah realized the significance of politicizing religion as the only avenue to carve out a separate nation-state.

The consequences of religion intruding on politics proved lethal in the long run. Jinnah's confusion about religion's role in state affairs was evident from the statements he made. Speaking at the occasion of the passing of the famous Lahore Resolution in March 1940, he stated:

> The Hindus and the Muslims belong to two different religious philosophies, social customs, and literature. They neither intermarry, nor interdine together and, indeed, they belong to two different civilizations which are based mainly on conflicting ideas and conceptions. Their aspects on life and of life are different. It is quite clear that Hindus and Mussalmans derive their inspiration from different sources of history. They have different epics, their heroes are different, and they have different episodes. Very often the hero of one is a foe of the other, and likewise, their victories and defeats overlap. (Quoted in Cohen, 2004: 28)

While leading the movement to create a separate homeland for the Muslims of the Sub-Continent, Jinnah emphasized the unique understanding of Muslims as a separate nation. Once he was successful in achieving a new state for them, he declared in the first meeting of the Constituent Assembly:

> You are free; you are free to go to your temples, you are free to go to your mosques or any other place or worship in this State of Pakistan. You may belong to any religion or caste or creed that has nothing to do with the business of the State. . . . You will find that in the course of time Hindus would cease to be Hindus and Muslims would cease to be Muslims, not in the religious sense, because that is the personal faith of each individual, but in the political sense as citizens of the State. (Quoted in Jalal, 1995a; Khan, 1999: 176)

However, he did not shun the role of religion in state affairs. Speaking at the inauguration ceremony of the State Bank of Pakistan on July 1, 1948, the last official public appearance of his life, Jinnah lamented the Western capitalist economic system and emphasized Islamic economic egalitarianism as an effective alternative. He stated:

> The economic system of the West has created almost insoluble problems for humanity, and to many of us, it appears that only a miracle can save it from disaster that is not facing the world. It has failed to do justice between man and man and to eradicate friction from the international field. On the contrary, it was largely responsible for the two world wars in the last half-century. . . . The adoption of Western economic theory and practice will not help us in achieving our goal of creating a happy and contented people. We must work our destiny in our own way and present to the world an economic system based on true Islamic concept of equality of manhood and social justice. We will thereby be fulfilling our mission as Muslims and giving to humanity the message of peace which alone can save it and secure the welfare, happiness, and prosperity of mankind. (Quoted in El Tiby, 2011: 20)

According to Jalal (1990), "Jinnah's resort to religion was not an ideology to which he was ever committed or even a device to use against rival communities; it was simply a way of giving a semblance of unity and solidity to his divided Muslim constituents" (p. 18). That is why scholars like her argue that Jinnah's original position about religion and its relationship with the state was elaborated on in his August 11 speech in the Constituent Assembly. However, according to Dar (2014), Jinnah, in his official position as the head of the state and the father of the nation, emphasized time and again the role of religion in public life. The August 11 speech, Dar argues, has been "used out of context" and in fact was "not the last word delivered by Jinnah" (p. 245). These statements, however, create constant confusion and an endless debate between the religious and the secular-cum-democratic circles striving to define the ideological frontiers of the new state. While it is true that Jinnah, having been cornered in a pitiable manner, could utilize nothing but religion to outweigh the democratic principles being espoused by the Indian National Congress, such as universal enfranchisement, he could not foresee the lasting impact it would have on the political landscape of the new country. He also could not see the collective and inevitable effect of the state as an instrument of a religious, and thus exclusionist, ideology over the population. It is evident from the speeches and statements Jinnah made in his thirteen-month role as governor general of Pakistan that he was increasingly convinced about the prominent role of religious doctrines in determining national economic, security, and foreign policies. In some statements, he went so far as to consider Pakistan as serving the interests of the whole Muslim world (Dar, 2014: 244). Religious circles lamenting the movement to create a separate homeland used these statements to push their agenda of securing political influence in the decision-making process. This did happen, as we will see in the following pages, threatening the very existence of the state itself.

It was the confluence between religion and the state institutions, namely the military, that brought the country the most suitable subservient status to global capitalist interests in South, Southwestern, and Central Asia, on the one side, and the Middle East, on the other. The Western powers, following the containment doctrine, emphasized fulfilling the strategic needs of Pakistan only to utilize it as the "leader" in the Muslim world to block or impede the growth of communist ideology in the Middle East and support making strategic alliances. On the part of Pakistan, religion was a natural ally to lament communism. Pakistan, therefore, made it a central factor in its identity while allying with the West. The foundation of this relationship, whereby Pakistan committed to providing regional strategic services to the Western powers, was laid during the first decade of independence. The hierarchical structure, which only strengthened after the revolutionary changes in the region during the second half of the 1970s, was formed so that the military prepared religious parties to be its domestic allies and their seminaries as the recruiting grounds against future defense challenges in the region at the cost of muting political assemblage. Externally, shifts in regime types in the region enabled the military to capitalize on its ability to serve global capitalist interests by burgeoning its domestic alliance with radical Islam. From the core countries to these missionaries, a visible order was established and made to do its job.

A combination of these factors—contradictions in economic policies, insurmountable defense expenditures and institutional imbalance in the center, the religionizing of the political, and the development of the military-to-military hierarchical relationship between Pakistan and the world powers—resulted in the construction of a unique country in the world. In 1951, Pakistan faced the first signs of the rise of Islamic radicalism when religious clerics—while demanding an official declaration of the Ahmadis, a controversial minority sect of Islam, as infidels and non-Muslims—led anti-Ahmadi riots in Lahore, which quickly spread throughout the Punjab province and resulted in "looting, arson and murder of at least 200 Ahmadis, and eventually required three months of martial law over the city to be brought under control" (Qadir, 2014: 139; Khan, 2015). The political consequences of consummating religion with politics, as founded by Jinnah, proved harmful in later years. The country's economic and political decision-making was virtually determined in Washington, thus compelling US administrations to attend to the dire needs of the most significant Muslim country of during continued instability. This attention was mainly due to the looming uncertainty and its regional and global implications, and less about Pakistan's utility in the world-system. Since Pakistan's occupied a significantly more strategic than economic positional standing, US policymakers put the country into various regional alliances while adopting a policy of economic cooperation, trade, and commercial relations with India (Venkataramani, 1982). As compared to China, which Mao led for twenty-eight years, and India, where Nehru remained the head of the government for seventeen years, Pakistan saw seven heads of government and four heads of state during the first decade of independence. While Jinnah died in 1948 of tuberculosis and Liaquat Ali Khan was killed in 1951, the other leaders were removed unceremoniously. The country made its first constitution in 1956, only for it to be abrogated in 1958. Religious parties influenced political developments, and the military intervened in national decision-making, resource allocation, and foreign policy. The defense establishment, increasingly impatient with socio-political instability, finally took over and imposed martial law throughout the country in 1958.

PAKISTAN'S EXPERIENCE OF CAPITALIST ECONOMIC DEVELOPMENT (1959–1968)

In October 1959, the army took over by imposing martial law throughout the country. Mohammed Ayub Khan, commander in chief of the army, sacked the civilian government, banned political parties and activities, abrogated the constitution, and took over control of the country. It was not the first time the military intervened in politics; during the anti-Ahmadi riots, martial law had been imposed in Lahore, the capital of the Punjab. In 1954, Ayub Khan had become the first serving military general to become defense minister as well, though only for a brief period. The influence of the military in politics was a corollary of Pakistan's allocation of financial resources to its security needs in the 1950s, as well as the significance Pakistan was being tagged with given Cold War policy development in the United States.

Even before Ayub Khan usurped, Pakistan's economy had begun developing what was later called "the Dutch disease" (Ahmad and Mohammed, 2012). Pakistan had started developing an unreasonable level of dependence on foreign aid. Given the security threats from India on the civil-military establishment in Karachi, Pakistan did not have any other option but to ask the United States for assistance. In the 1950s, after several efforts, Pakistan succeeded in getting Washington to realize its geostrategic importance. Entering into military alliances enabled Pakistan to the receive military equipment it required and the financial support it needed to establish industries. Starting with 1952, when only 0.02 percent of its gross national product (GNP) was comprised of foreign aid, Pakistan developed a propensity to shun self-reliance and look toward the West for assistance to address its issues of development and governance. Capitalizing on its geostrategic significance in the region, Pakistan developed a rhetoric of embracing democracy as the antithesis of communism, thus claiming itself to be a legitimate candidate for financial and military support. Though Pakistan and the Western powers, particularly the United States, never agreed on a list of enemies against whom military aid was provided—Pakistan's obsession with security threats from India was not a legitimate reason for Washington to provide aid for military personnel and equipment modernization—Pakistan still received about $377 million during 1950–1958. After Ayub Khan took power, his government signed an Agreement of Co-operation with the United States in March 1959; Pakistan ensured continuity of military aid until 1965, when its war with India resulted in an aids embargo from Washington. However, aid was resumed shortly after the war; by 1969, Pakistan had received about $650.28 million in military aid from Washington (Venkataramani, 1982: 403). For economic development, dependence on aid was far more acute. In 1955–1956, when Pakistan started its first Five-Year Plan for national development, 19 percent of its imports and 35 percent of its infrastructure development projects were being financed by foreign aid. After five years, when the country started its second Five-Year Plan, the dependence of imports and development projects on aid had reached 31 percent and 38 percent, respectively. In 1962–1963, it climbed to 56 percent and 42 percent, respectively. The share of foreign aid in GNP rose from 2.1 percent in 1956 to 7.5 percent in 1964. From 1950 to 1967, Pakistan received about $4.7 billion in foreign aid, including $1.3 billion in grants and $3.4 billion in loans. The United States was the single largest donor and contributor; about three-quarters of the total aid was provided by the United States, followed by Canada contributing one-seventh. The United States was the leading lender as well; Pakistan received about half of its international loans only from Washington, with another 22 percent provided by international financial institutions under the influence of the United States (Brecher and Abbas, 1972: 23–25). According to the OECD's calculations, that Pakistan had received about $73.14 billion in foreign aid (bilateral and multilateral aid, at constant 2001 prices) by 2002 shows that the Dutch disease developed based on strategic location (Anwar and Michaelowa, 2006). During the 1960s, Pakistan exploited its role in military alliances and adopted policies following the guidelines of international institutions.

Ayub Khan's tenure (1959–1968) is considered an era of economic management having a "paradoxical combination of the biggest growth rates in Pakistani history and significant increases in income inequality, inter-regional differences, and the concentration of economic power" resulting in "a series of problems that were exacerbated in subsequent regimes" (Husain, 1999: 15). It was a time when Pakistan put aside its policy of state-sponsored economic development and self-reliance. Instead, in an era when "development" had become a new mantra for controlling the resources from the postcolonial countries, Pakistan became one of the few states embracing a capitalist mode of economic development willingly and wholeheartedly. Keeping in view the shortage of experts in economics, Pakistan sent several individuals for higher education in the United States. With the advent of the Harvard Advisory Group, which later became the Harvard Institute of

International Development, Pakistan was blessed with a new crop of economists intellectually harvested under neoclassical economics and a free market economy. They not only developed the Planning Commission of Pakistan but also designed and advised the government about the implementation of economic policies following the Smithian model of growth. Dr. Mahbub ul Haq, a famous official with the United Nations Development Program credited with the invention of the Human Development Index in the 1980s, was a postdoctoral fellow at Harvard and remained chief economist of Pakistan during the 1960s. Sartaj Aziz, Pakistan finance minister during various times in the 1990s, also graduated from Harvard. Some other graduates of US universities, such as Moeen Qureshi and Aziz Ali Mohammed, joined the Bretton Woods Institutions and excelled. They and other colleagues were the architects of Pakistan's transition from mercantilism to a free market economy in the 1960s. To them, the free market economic rationale was the only policy Pakistan needed to progress. According to Dr. Haq:

> It is well to recognize that economic growth is a brutal, sordid process. There are no shortcuts to it. The essence of it lies in making the laborer produce more than he is allowed to consume for his immediate needs, and to invest and reinvest the surplus thus obtained. What is important and intellectually honest is to admit frankly that the heart of the growth problem lies in maximizing the creation of this surplus. Either the capitalist sector should be allowed to perform the role, or if this is found inefficient because of the nature of the capitalist sector in a particular country or is distasteful, the State should undertake it. It would be wrong to dub the consequent emergence of surplus as exploitation: it is a justification of economic growth. (quoted in Gardezi and Rashid, 1983: 10)

The government followed this perspective wholeheartedly. It embarked on rapid industrialization based on the trickle-down philosophy of neoclassical economics. It did so through a two-pronged strategy. On the one hand, it empowered the civil bureaucracy to carry out the administrative control of progress. The idea of "basic democracies" was meant to facilitate effective control of civil bureaucracy over the masses and to develop a subservient political leadership at the lower level. It was during the 1960s that the sentiments of deprivation in the eastern part of the country grew, primarily, due to a lack of cultural recognition at the national level, the share in government employment opportunities, and the use of universal adult enfranchisement. On the other hand, the government promoted private industrialization by facilitating imports in technology, machinery, and technical input. This facilitation was financial, bureaucratic, and legal. Private business groups were provided credit lines, and the controlling mechanisms of technology import were dismantled altogether. The Pakistan Industrial Development Corporation was established to streamline industrialization following the directions and guidelines of the Planning Commission, removing any bureaucratic or capital hurdles in the way. Control of the licensing regime was deemed an obstruction and reduced to a considerable extent. A significant dismantling of the import licensing regime also took place. Lower taxes strengthened the business and trade class in the country. To promote export-oriented industrialization, the government introduced the Export Bonus System with the primary objective of offering multiple rates of exchange on foreign currencies; it was tailored to increase the appetite for higher growth rates. Access to capital was also designed to direct industrialization possessing a competitive edge in international markets (Husain, 1999). In this context, the textile industry was focused in the Western part of the country. Jute, the most significant agricultural product, received little attention regarding industrialization. Instead, political leadership from the eastern part of the country complained that the country earned about half of its foreign capital of exports through the sale of jute in international markets. However, the eastern part of the country, which produced it, did not benefit from this capital and the foreign exchange was utilized to finance industrialization in the western part of the country (Khan, 2005).

The result of these policies was that the country found rapid growth in its industries and exports. Agriculture grew at 4.1 percent per annum during the Ayub years, higher than its growth rate in the 1950s. The manufacturing sector grew by 9.1 percent, while the trade growth rate was recorded at 7.3 percent per annum. Exports, mainly of textiles and leather, grew at 7 percent per annum, which also meant that Pakistan's exports diversified from raw materials to manufactured products. Throughout the period, GNP grew at around 6 percent. After 1960, when Pakistan signed the Indus Water Treaty with India to establish control of the rivers in the region, Pakistan sought and secured financial support from the World Bank to implement the Indus Basin Project designed to develop substantial water reservoirs; the Mangla Dam was completed by 1967, while the Tarbela Dam was completed in 1976. Together these two dams have been the bedrock of the most extensive irrigation system in the world. During the 1960s, the government paid special attention to developing canals to irrigate the fertile areas of the country, resulting in bringing the Green Revolution in the country. During 1959–1964, growth in the agricultural sector was recorded at 3.7 percent, far higher than during the 1950s. However, during 1965–1970 this growth reached 6.3 percent, and during 1966–1968, was registered at an unprecedented rate of 11.7 percent per annum. During 1968–1970, growth was 9.6 percent per annum. The result was that food crops grew immensely. Wheat growth was recorded at 141 percent, while rice grew at 91 percent, as compared to their production levels in the 1950s (Zaidi, 2005: 29). However, since the growth of industrialization was even faster, the share of the agricultural sector in the national economy declined from 48 percent in 1959 to about 41.5 percent in 1968. Since the foreign capital earned through the export of agricultural products was utilized to import machinery for industries, there was a visible flow of capital from the countryside to urbanizing areas, resulting in widening income inequalities, regionalizing economic development, and creating rifts among the federating units. Instead of developing a robust import-substitute industrialization, Pakistan could not plan quotas, restrictions, and protections through tariff and customs duties, resulting in a chronic problem in its balance of payments.

Beneath the shining progress and "rare success story" of Pakistan's economic development during the 1960s simmered two significant crises that affected the status of Pakistan in the world-system. First, domestic disparities regarding development resulted in a widening of the gap between the two parts of the country, which were already divided by the physical distance of about 1,100 miles covering India. The economic disparity between the two regions was evident by the fact that by the time the military took the reins of the government, the unemployment rate was four times higher in East Pakistan than in West Pakistan. During the second Five-Year Plan (1955–1960), out of total Rs. 9.715 billion spent, East Pakistan could receive only Rs.3 billion despite that its balance of payments was always surplus. During 1957–1958 only, East Pakistan's exports were recorded at Rs. 988 million, while its imports were Rs. 735.6 million. West Pakistan, on the other hand, exported goods worth Rs. 433.6 million but imported goods of Rs. 1.3143 billion. The political leadership of East Pakistan complained that their remittances and foreign capital were used to develop West Pakistan (*Economic Survey of Pakistan, 1961–1962*). According to Swadesh Bose (1972), while agriculture remained stagnant during the first decade (1947–1958), its growth in the second decade was primarily concentrated in West Pakistan. Using official statistics, he concludes that "in West Pakistan during the 1960s value added in agriculture and major crops grew at 4.6 percent and 5.5 percent per annum respectively, while the corresponding growth rates in East Pakistan were 2.1 percent and 2.2 percent" (p. 70). Regional disparities, promoted by the rise of the civil-military bureaucratic alliance with the burgeoning business and industrial class situated in the western part of the country, gave rise to Bengali nationalism. Alavi (1976) argues that the Green Revolution and economic development were "the cumulative result of many independent developments and events and responses of large landholders who possess the requisite resources, to the opportunities which arose as a consequence." The pattern of economic growth during the 1960s promoted "not only a tendency toward increasing disparities of income and wealth between different strata of the rural population" but also "widening regional disparities" based on "the outcome largely of the class basis of the dynamics of agricultural development in the context of differences in the structure of the agrarian economy in the different regions" (p. 174). The reason for the simmering political crisis that erupted the very year when Pakistan witnessed the highest growth of agriculture was "the dominance of a bureaucratic-military oligarchy in Pakistan's political system and challenges from political leadership punctuated the political history of Pakistan with a series of crises" (p. 204). The role of the state institutions in promoting regional disparities was corroborated by various other scholars as well (Khan, 1981; Mahmood, 1977). Government policies promoted the accumulation of capital in fewer hands at the cost of general economic deprivation. Rehman Sobhan (1965) notes that "75 units or 2.1 percent of the total [industry] receive 43.8 percent of all value added. If we remember that these 75 units are themselves owned directly or indirectly by a much smaller nucleus of families then we can visualize the degree of concentration of corporate wealth" (p. 109). Two years later, Gustav Papanek (1967) observed that "while there were over 3,000 individual firms in Pakistan in 1959, only seven individuals, families or foreign corporations controlled one-quarter of all private industrial assets and one-fifth of all industrial assets. Twenty-four units controlled nearly half of all private industrial assets. . . . It is also reported that approximately 15 families owned about three-quarters of all the shares in banks and insurance companies" (pp. 67–68). However, most popular were the observations that Pakistan's chief economist, Dr. Haq, made in 1968 when he stated that about the two-thirds of the national industrial wealth was in the hands of twenty families; these families were also controlling about 70 percent of the federal funds and 80 percent of the bank assets in the country. Later there were twenty-two families, and they are still an essential example of income and wealth inequality in the country. Lawrence White (1976) estimates that by 1968, "43 families and groups controlled over two-fifths of all large-scale manufacturing and just under three-fifths of all private Pakistani-controlled manufacturing. The 20 largest families and groups controlled almost a third of all manufacturing and 45% of all private Pakistani-controlled manufacturing" (p. 66). Most of these industries were established in West Pakistan, and in cases when they were set in East Pakistan, they were owned by the families in West Pakistan. The inequalities were so widespread that in 1968, the very year with record crop production in the country, the masses went to the streets and compelled President Ayub to resign. Ayub's resignation in 1969 did not solve the problem. The regional inequality and unfair resource distribution at the national level led to the popular rising of East Pakistan. In 1971, the constitutional crisis led to the dismemberment of Pakistan, with East Pakistan becoming an independent nation-state of Bangladesh.

Second, the era of stability lasted for so long mainly due to the fiscal and military support Pakistan received during the 1960s (Papanek, 1967). In fact, Pakistan had become so addicted to foreign aid that when Ayub Khan took the reins of the government in October 1958 and wrote to Washington for the first time as the head of the state, he considered the US aid "a matter of life and death to Pakistan" (quoted in Kux, 2001: 101). Rashid Amjad (1982) calls the economic system of Pakistan during the first two decades a "Foreign Aid Dependent Regime . . . in which the mechanics of industrial growth were in one way or another made dependent on foreign aid inflows. Once the aid flows slowed down, the system, not being able to replace foreign aid with other forms of external finance like direct foreign investment, and without the peculiar boost to profitability associated with the local system for dispensing aid, found it difficult to sustain the earlier growth it had generated" (p. 183). As Pakistan entered into military alliances, it was awarded a five-year (1954–1959) military modernization program. By the end of this program, General Ayub Khan had taken charge of the government in the country and had put forward a request to Washington for supersonic F-104s. It remained a point of contention for some time and could only be resolved in March 1960. The Kennedy administration adopted a hesitant approach but continued military aid. However, it showed a visible tilt toward India with $1 billion per annum in economic aid. The 1962 Indo-China war resulted in providing India military aid against China. President Ayub, who was promised to be consulted if the Kennedy administration decided to provide military equipment to India, felt disgruntled when he was ignored in the 1962 Indo-China war. It was clear that the United States was starting to realize two different values of the two countries; it considered India's economic potential and the role New Delhi could play in global capitalism, while considering Pakistan mainly to be a smaller power primarily serving the strategic interests of the West. The Kennedy and, later, the Johnson administrations, however, did not deliver what Pakistan wished; frequent requests for military equipment were either ignored or declined, which pushed Pakistan to seek alternatives. The China option was the plan of Ayub's most notable young minister, Zulfiqar Ali Bhutto, which alienated Washington further and resulted in sanctions on Pakistan (Kux, 2001). Abdul Sattar (2017), former foreign minister of Pakistan, gives credit to the farsighted Chinese leadership in the 1960s that, despite Ayub's anti-Chinese stance in Washington and London aimed at securing military aid and his proposal of a common Indo-Pak defense against "foreign aggression," did not let negative feelings spoil the scope of their mutual relationship. The great power competition was evident during this period when the Soviet Union mediated between India and Pakistan to end the 1965 war. While Pakistan was successful in defending itself and resisting Indian advancement in its territory, it could not resolve the Kashmir dispute, over which it had gone to war with India in the first place. During 1965–1967, Pakistan sought support from China and Western countries; it bought Chinese weapons of Soviet origin and jets and submarines from France. After the US embargo ended in 1967, Pakistan purchased guns and other weapons from the Soviet Union worth $30 million (Jabeen and Mazhar, 2011), partly due to three visits President Ayub made to Moscow during 1965–1967. The increasing Pakistani-Soviet contacts resulted in the first-ever visit of a Soviet prime minister in April 1968 (H. A. Rizvi, 1993). However, both the Western powers and the Soviet Union extended more economic assistance and cooperation to India than Pakistan.

During the 1960s, the gap between the two powers in the region, India and Pakistan, started tilting in favor of the former. According to SIPRI Yearbook (1971), the difference between the two countries had always been present but widened significantly after the 1962 Indo-China war. In 1970, when Pakistan spent about $603.4 million on its defense, India's military expenditure was $1,511.9 million. The gap between the defense budgets of these two countries is partly responsible for the dismemberment of Pakistan in 1971, though its main reasons lie elsewhere.

A BRIEF EXPERIENCE OF PSEUDO-SOCIALISM (1972–1977)

The Ayubian era is considered when the foundation was laid for turning Pakistan into the first postcolonial country to disintegrate into two parts. Despite record economic growth, Pakistan's polity during 1968–1972 was challenged by three different developments. First, the early introduction and penetration of capitalist development brought with it income inequality, a class gap, and social disturbances, which deepened the division of labor in society by pushing the peasants to the corner and increasing the miseries of the labor. In East Pakistan, continued economic deprivation and a lack of meaningful participation of Bengali leadership in national affairs gave rise to Bengali nationalism. In West Pakistan, the middle and lower classes exhibited growing discontent with burgeoning income and wealth inequalities and a concentration of power in fewer hands. By the end of the 1960s, a movement of peasants and laborers emerged that "led to a popular mobilization that demanded democratic reform, economic redistribution, social justice and rights for different national groups against a long military rule that had deep links to industrial and feudal interests" (Ali, 2015: 1). Bengali nationalism, in particular, challenged the state and its institutionalization of regional deprivation. On the part of West Pakistan and its leadership of the independence movement belonging to either the Muslim-minority areas of India or the

Muslim-majority areas that later formed in western part of Pakistan, it was a grave and erroneous mistake to underestimate the conscience of Bengali nationalism; among all the regions of India, Bengal had always stood out as a distinct entity. Since the Mughals, and even before that, Bengal's contribution to life on the Sub-Continent was evident, whether in the form of food and clothes or language, art, and literature. In international commerce, it was the first area to face the European imperial challenge; Bengal was subjugated far earlier than any other area on the Sub-Continent. During British rule, Bengal fulfilled the role it was assigned under the global imperial division of labor. The desire for political and economic emancipation, therefore, was far more powerful in Bengal than any other area of the Sub-Continent. The Muslim leadership misunderstood the magnitude of resistance to any further subordination. Both Muslim and Hindu leaders resisted the partition of Bengal, the failure of which added insult to their injuries and gave rise to the emancipatory politics of the youth pushing the leadership to rise to the challenge of securing economic and political rights for the population of the province. Bengal encompassed about 16 percent of the territory of Pakistan and contained about 54 percent of the country's population. Political leadership in West Pakistan was determined to block this numerical strength from taking over leadership of the country. According to Zaheer (1994):

> The West-dominated ruling class of early Pakistan never really tried to understand the Bengali point of view. From the inception of Pakistan, it developed a self-righteous state of mind which ignored the objective political realities of East Pakistan. The Pakistani establishment, which was a conglomerate of the Punjab political leadership, the old League leadership of NWFP, migrant League leaders of Muslim minority provinces in India, and the senior Punjabi and *Mohajir* (migrant) civil servants, passionately believed (a) in a strong central government; (b) that Urdu, as the symbol of unity and Islamic ideology, should be the only state language of the country; (c) that the opposition groups in East Pakistan were generally subversive, influenced and instigated by the Hindus and communists; and (d) that the defence of East Pakistan depended on the strength of the armed forces in West Pakistan, for which resources should be allocated even at the cost of overall social and economic development. These narrow premises, and others in a similar vein, coupled with a sense of racial and cultural superiority in the West Pakistani elite, prevented the evolution of a dynamic and equal relationship between the two wings. The dominant ruling class suffered from a siege mentality. Any demand of East Pakistan which deviated from the dogma was regarded as a conspiracy and a threat to Islamic ideology and the integrity of the country. (p. 16)

A lack of a share in national resources, remittances, development expenditures, military leadership, and government services led to the radicalization of ethnic-nationalist elements in Bengal. Therefore, when Pakistan experienced its first national elections based on universal enfranchisement, East Pakistan practically voted for succession. After an almost year-long civil war, the killing of about one to three million civilians, and the rape of about three hundred thousand to four hundred thousand Bengali women, the country's army leadership in Dhaka surrendered to the Indian commander and signed the disintegration of the country.

Second, instead of realizing the mistakes in national affairs that led to the breakup of the country, Pakistan did not find any tangible support from the West in resolving a crisis it saw as an internal matter. Starting in July, India trained about forty thousand young Bengali refugee recruits to develop *Mukti Bahni* (Liberation Army). They crossed over and, guided by a large number of deserted policemen and military officers, attacked Pakistan army and its supporting citizen-based guerrilla forces of Jamat-e-Islami. On December 4, 1971, India formally launched an attack on East Pakistan and concluded the war in twelve days. On December 16, 1971, the Pakistani military commander in East Pakistan, General Niazi, surrendered unconditionally to the Indian commander and the country was disintegrated. About ninety-three thousand soldiers of Pakistani army were taken into Indian custody as prisoners of war. For Pakistan, no Western country moved ahead as vigorously as the USSR had when it provided political and strategic support to India. Pakistan considered the role of the international powers as that of accomplices that stood aloof to the situation. However, recent studies show that President Nixon and his national security advisor, Henry Kissinger, provided enough support and time to President Yahya to recover. According to declassified documents released by the State Department, President Nixon wanted to aid Pakistan in establishing a strategic balance in the region since India was receiving hefty amounts of aid and equipment from Moscow. The scale of US involvement in the East Pakistan crisis and a friendly posture from Washington were not enough when Pakistan looked at the magnitude of political support the USSR provided to India in the form of the Permanent Friendship Treaty signed between the two countries in September 1971. Though the United States tried to help Pakistan by pressing other countries, particularly China, to provide military equipment to Pakistan, Washington had developed an "aim for evolution that would lead to the eventual independence of East Pakistan" (Kux, 2001: 193). Once Pakistan was disintegrated, Nixon reportedly used the US embassy in New Delhi to deliver an unambiguous message to India about the security of West Pakistan. For Pakistan, these measures fell way short of what it was expecting from its allies in the West. The country felt let down due to the lack of support it received from Western countries. The disintegration of the country left a permanent dent in Pak-US relations. As in the case of India in 1962, Pakistan learned bitter lessons from its defeat in 1971. The year 1971 defines a permanent terse moment in its relations with the West. Pakistan eventually started developing nuclear weapons as the ultimate shield of its integrity in case of war with India, an indication of less trust in its partnerships and agreements with the core countries.

Despite the East Bengal crisis, Pakistan did serve US interests by providing good offices to contact and develop relations with communist China. In July 1970 as a part of a trip to several countries, President Nixon visited Pakistan and asked President Yahya to facilitate US contacts with China. President Yahya personally delivered this message to his Chinese counterpart, Mao Zedong. In December 1970, Zhou Enlai, the Chinese premier, replied to President Nixon's message by asking Pakistan's ambassador to the United States to personally deliver it to Henry Kissinger. China, through Zhou Enlai, wanted to discuss the Taiwan issue with the United States. The reply from Washington, after lengthy deliberations, was general and broad. In April 1970, the Chinese ping-pong team, participating in an international tournament in Japan, acted on orders from the apex leadership of the country and invited the American team to visit China. Eventually, in July 1970, Henry Kissinger reached Islamabad only to visit China by secretly boarding a Pakistan Airlines commercial flight. The two days of talks opened channels between the two countries. The mission was so secret that even the US diplomatic officials in the US embassy in Islamabad were unaware of it (Kissinger, 2012; Kux, 2001).

Third, the feeling of betrayal in 1971 led to the rise of leftist socialist forces, on the one hand, and religious forces, on the other. If these forces could agree on anything, it was resistance to Western imperialism and influence on the country. Pakistan found that, as a peripheral country, it lacked any leverage to influence the policies in the West and needed to grow from the inside through government-led economic policies and promote a relatively egalitarian structure of the economy. The rise of Zulfiqar Ali Bhutto in national politics was a phenomenon from any perspective. He was only thirty years old when he became a minister in the federal government. During 1963–1966, he was the foreign minister of Pakistan. In 1967, he established his own Pakistan People's Party, which in the 1970 general elections was the majority party in West Pakistan. As the country was disintegrated in 1971, Bhutto took over the government and led the country out of the crisis.

Bhutto was what he called a "democratic socialist." With few exceptions, his economic policies were meant to reverse a lot of what had been adopted in the 1960s. As a shrewd politician having worked with military dictators, he learned the tactics of exploitation and keen observation. He knew that among the reasons for the fall of Ayub Khan included the widening income gap between different strata of society. He cognized that slogans against the inequitable distribution of resources were an important factor in the rise of an anti-Ayub movement and socialism. Simultaneously, while Al-Badr and Al-Shams—the Islamist militias of Jamat-e-Islami (the Party of Islam)—failed to impede the secession of Bangladesh from Pakistan in 1971, they succeeded in laying the foundation for a stronger relationship between the security establishment of the country and the religious circles. Bhutto knew he had to maintain a precarious balance between the competing interest groups, such as the industrialists, merchants, feudal lords, the urban middle class, and the religious segments of society. The smaller provinces in the country objected to the unequal distribution of resources and political power (Burki, 1988). Internationally, Bhutto had to recover from a humiliating defeat and the release of ninety-three thousand military personnel taken as prisoners of war. He had to revitalize the geostrategic significance of (West) Pakistan in the international system. Simultaneously, Pakistan had to recover from the loss in economic advantages provided by the export of the raw materials of East Pakistan and the consumption of products from West Pakistan. This had to be done within the limits of his ideological base—the slogan of socialism—that had brought him to power in the first place.

At the domestic level, Bhutto adopted socialism to reverse a lot of the 1960s and restructure economic development according to his ideology. He was a known critic of capitalism and vowed to offer emancipatory politics to his people, the Muslim world, and beyond. Even before he came to power as the head of the government, his quintessential dependency theory appeared in the following words:

> The main purpose of imperialism was to exploit the resources of the colonies. Vast territories were divided and distributed among the imperial Powers, which then drained the resources of the subject peoples. With the end of imperialism in its classical form, only the system of exploitation underwent a transformation. As the colonial Powers withdrew from their colonies, the policy of "divide and rule" became obsolete and was replaced by that of "unite and rule" to meet the challenge of new times, although to achieve the same objective. The changed conditions necessitated a change in the method. In the past, the colonies were exploited separately by each Imperial Power. Now that these Powers have vacated their possessions, it has become necessary for them to merge the resources of the former colonies into groupings for better collective exploitation. As the position of the exploiters has changed, so also it has become necessary to change that of the exploited. Previously the Imperial Powers went separately about their missions of exploitation. Now that they have joined for their common advantage, it becomes equally necessary for them that their former colonies pool their resources to facilitate exploitation. (Bhutto, 1969: 9)

Leftist ideology had been prevalent in the country throughout the years preceding Bhutto's rise. The Communist Party of Pakistan put together leaders and intellectuals from the middle and lower-middle classes to develop an alternative narrative to the capitalist structure or religious identity of the country. Bhutto was aware of and in contact with these people. Simultaneously, however, Bhutto was also aware of the rise of religion in national politics. The role of religion maintained a low profile during the Ayub era. Ayub Khan was of the view that the role of the state should be limited only to facilitate individuals in practicing their religious affairs. Therefore, while he established the Advisory Council on Islamic Ideology and an Islamic Research Institute, he did not permit any constitutional prerogatives to these institutions (Khan, 1969). Ayub's understanding of Islam and its role in state affairs, Yasmin Saikia (2014) argues, was a three-pronged strategy. First, it was during the Ayub era that the Pakistan military received training, not as professional soldiers, but as the soldiers of Islam. Second, the history of the country was rewritten to introduce Muslim identity as disconnected from Indian civilization and oriented toward the Arab world. Third, the Bengalis were to be reformed into "good Muslims." Though Ayub's project failed, the cumulative effect of these developments was that religion found inroads into the corridors of power and national politics. During the crisis years of 1970–1971, political Islam emerged as a powerful tool that the country's establishment could potentially rely on during critical times. Sensing this, Bhutto coined the term "Islamic socialism" to adjust his economic ideology, "the highest expression of democracy," to fit on-the-ground realities. His first manifesto stated that "Islam is our faith, democracy is our polity, socialism is our economy. All power to the people." The agenda to restructure the contemporary economic system was based on representative democratic governance and Islamic principles of egalitarianism. It also meant redistribution of land resources through land reforms; introduction of the developmental state; nationalization of financial, industrial, and educational institutions; and the promotion of grassroots-level democracy.

The economic performance of the Bhutto years was a reversal of the trends set in the 1960s, which the international financial institutions considered a role model for the developing East Asian economies. Bhutto took over the government at a time when Pakistan had lost its eastern wing and was struggling with keeping economic life alive in the remaining country. According to the *Economic Survey of Pakistan 1971–1972*, while the agricultural sector in the western part of Pakistan grew by 2.8 percent, its industrial sector declined by 5.8 percent. The unavailability of resources resulted in the decline in the development budget by 13 percent. The GDP growth rate was recorded at only 1.7 percent. However, the GDP growth of the next year, 1973, showed that Bhutto's policies were gaining ground; Pakistan achieved 5.8 percent growth in that year. During the era, however, Pakistan's GDP growth remained around 5.5 percent per annum, below the average in the

1960s. Part of the reason was that, following Bhutto's vision of a socialist economy, the government redirected its approach to focus more on economic egalitarianism than growth. The *Economic Survey* of that year, 1972–1973, indicates the change in the government preference by emphasizing that "the Government has adopted a new development strategy, with the provision of employment, the satisfaction of the needs of the people and elimination of the worst forms of poverty being its major planks. In other words, the emphasis has shifted from growth to welfare" (*Economic Survey of Pakistan 1972–1973*: 2).

More importantly, Bhutto redefined the relationship between the state and society by following a socialist line for development. Though he did not negate the role of foreign assistance in economic development, he stressed self-reliance as the best approach for the country by arguing that "foreign assistance should serve to turn a dependent economy into a self-reliant one, but, if it is accompanied by foreign interference, dependence increases and the object is defeated" (Bhutto, 1969: 150). In doing so, he wanted to enable the state to lead from the front. Therefore, he curtained the burgeoning private business empires by nationalizing the leading industrial units and financial institutions. In 1972, the government issued a Nationalization and Economic Reforms Order to implement a three-stage process. In the first stage, metal and heavy industries were nationalized. In the second stage, in 1974, leading private banks were nationalized. In the last stage, in 1976, a significant number of smaller industrial units and educational institutions were nationalized. Interestingly, nationalization was limited to the firms owned by Pakistani nationals only; foreign companies were not nationalized. In line with his approach, the Bhutto government also introduced land reforms.

The consequences of nationalization were mixed. The state under Bhutto's government resisted a free market economy. It challenged private industrial empires by redefining the notion of distributive justice in society. It strengthened the rights of the poor, peasants, laborers, industrial workers, government employees, and students. In addition to land reforms and the distribution of government land among the poor farmers, the government announced higher support prices and provided subsidized fertilizers, seeds, and institutional credit for the import of agricultural machinery. From a nonexistent level in the 1960s, Bhutto government went on to spend 2 percent of the GDP on subsidies provided to the agricultural sector only (Husain, 1999). Contrary to Ayub's policy of industrialization, led by the private sector as the principal engine of economic growth, Bhutto prioritized the growth of the agricultural sector as the backbone of the country's economy. However, he did not neglect the industrial sector altogether. The output of industries such as fertilizers (from 375 metric tons in 1970 to 824 metric tons in 1977), sugar (from 519 metric tons in 1970 to 736 metric tons in 1977), steel (from 196 metric tons in 1970 to 270 metric tons in 1977), vegetable ghee (from 136 metric tons in 1970 to 326 metric tons in 1977), and cement (from 2,702 metric tons in 1970 to 3,071 metric tons in 1977), among others, showed the positive results of government policies (Raza, 1997). Simultaneously, the government carried forward its agenda of economic democracy by facilitating the unionization of laborers, both in newly nationalized government units and private industries, legislated in favor of laborers, strengthened job security for government employees, and introduced new labor policies with compulsory insurance, monetary compensation in accidents, housing allowances, and other benefits. For students, the government introduced free public transportation facilities, tuition-free education, and other benefits. It focused more on primary and secondary education than university education since it considered the spread of literacy to be more important. The government was successful to an extent in diverting resources to the countryside and the lower classes of society. Having adopted the role of developmental state, the country could secure substantial import substitution as early as in 1974; there was a clear decline in the share of capital goods imported, from 42 percent in 1972 to 34 percent in 1978, while the share of manufactured goods in country's exports rose from 28 percent to 50 percent during the same period (Raza, 1997).

However, the Bhutto government failed to redefine the positional standing of Pakistan in the regional or global capitalist division of labor. First, by emphasizing growth of the agricultural sector and nationalizing the industrial units and financial institutions, the government could only reject the growth of the capitalist economy in the country. Since independence, the successive governments had supported the industry and business class for ethnic, political, or even purely economic reasons. Ayub's government, in particular, adopted private industrialization and condoned economic inequalities following trickle-down logic. It had given rise to the twenty-two richest families or business groups of the country. Bhutto was the first head of government belonging to the feudal class and with a rural background. A traditional aristocrat, though Berkeley and Oxford educated, Bhutto understood the dynamics of economic development and its long-term consequences from the perspective of income inequality. Nationalization or deterministic governmental intervention in the economy, therefore, was his approach to reform the economy. In 1972, following the precondition of the IMF and the World Bank to reschedule debt and sanction further loans, the government drastically devalued the currency from Rs. 4.75 to Rs. 11 per $1, which immensely burdened the private industrialists, as they had to pay a lot more for the import of industrial equipment. When they protested, Bhutto argued that his actions were meant to "rid the economy of the concentration of economic power in the hands of a few to end the exploitation of the many" (Raza, 1997: 282). However, his industrial policy stagnated the development of private industries. The share of the private sector in national investment declined from 51.3 percent during the 1960s to 33.8 percent during the Bhutto years. Yearly investment fell from Rs. 700 million in 1971 to Rs. 183 million in 1975. The government, on the other hand, emerged as the most significant stakeholder in the economy; public investment rose from Rs. 58 million in 1971 to Rs. 1,085 million in 1977 (Husain, 1999).

Second, natural calamities in Pakistan and political developments in the region produced some problems as well. In 1973, Pakistan faced unprecedented levels of monsoon flooding that destroyed agricultural areas and infrastructure. The world community came forward to rescue Pakistan after this calamity by providing 1,000 metric tons of wheat, worth $24 million, and another $18 million in aid by the United States (Kux, 2001: 209). In 1973, Arab-Israel War led to the decision of Organization of the Petroleum Exporting Countries (OPEC) to impose an oil embargo. Pakistan, among other Third World countries, had to suffer due to an imbalance in the export of oil. The inflation rate rose to 16 percent, an unprecedented level given the fact that it had remained at 5 percent during the Ayub era. Following the oil crisis, Bhutto adopted a policy of exporting human resources to the gulf countries and earning remittances to cover the losses. The step further strengthened Pakistan's role in the regional and global economy of a country supplying raw materials and resources to the economic processes.

An inconvenient combination of religion and leftist economic ideology shrank the space in which Bhutto could maneuver and implement his policies effectively, though it did not cause any meaningful changes in the country's foreign economic relations. Despite using an aggressive and anti-imperial tone in his speeches and writings, Bhutto adopted a realist approach to the major powers of the world-system. Even when he was critical of the exploitative tools of the core countries, he was of the view that "the smaller states should evolve a policy to maintain normal bilateral relations with all the Global Powers, devoid of interference, in a perfectly understandable gradation based on enlightened national interest" (Bhutto, 1969: 22). Bhutto adopted a multipronged strategy to boost the role of the country in Asian affairs. In January 1972, he visited eight Muslim countries. In 1974, Pakistan hosted a second summit of the Muslim countries as a befitting response to India's leadership role in the Non-Aligned Movement. Bhutto was elected chairman of the Organization of Islamic Conference. His socialist ideology led him to develop closer relations with Iran, Egypt, Libya, Syria, Saudi Arabia, and other countries. He devised Pakistan's China policy and approached Moscow to mend grievances and provide crucial support for state-led economic development. However, he maintained an otherwise precarious balance between the two blocs of the bilateral world. Following this line, Bhutto approached the United States to emphasize the strategic significance of the country for the West, repeated requests for the lifting of sanctions imposed in the wake of 1971 war, an upgrade in military equipment, and economic assistance. The crux of this multipronged foreign relations strategy was that he gave up his socialist agenda in favor of a realist perspective.

However, two other developments proved hugely consequential for the future domestic politics of Pakistan and its positional standing in the global strategic order. First, Bhutto revitalized and capitalized on the role of religion in the policies within the country and beyond. He introduced Islamic provisions in the 1973 constitution, announced Friday as a public weekly holiday, declared wine and gambling un-Islamic and thus illegal, declared Ahmadis as non-Muslim, promoted religious symbols in national politics, vowed to develop the Islamic bloc as a response to the Western and communist blocs, and brought in the notion of Jihad as a tool of foreign policy (Fair, 2014). Whereas Ayub Khan's government did not stress the role of religion as the cornerstone of its foreign policy, Bhutto found appeal in reconnecting Pakistan with the Muslim world. In fact, the rise of Bhutto and his politico-economic philosophy since 1967 can be gauged better within the context of the transformation taking place in the Middle East and the Muslim world, on the one hand, and the quest to balance the relationship the young leadership of these countries sought with the West. It was under Bhutto that the government started interfering with the dwindling political order in Afghanistan by enabling the foreign powers, particularly the Middle Eastern kingdoms, to develop their stakes inside Pakistan. In the following years, Pakistan became a hotbed of competing intra-Islam ideologies. The "Arabist shift" initiated by Bhutto proved lethal for the otherwise tolerant mystic and Indo-Persian culture in the country (Irfani, 2004).Within six years of coming to power, Bhutto faced religious opposition to his socialist ideas and economic ideology. The mobilization of religious forces was so powerful that Bhutto was dethroned through the usurping of military power; he was hanged in 1979.

Second, the Pakistan military re-emerged as the most influential institution in the country within six years of its humiliating surrender in East Pakistan. It was Bhutto himself who strengthened a demoralized and beleaguered military in the scope of threats Pakistan faced from India. Given his legitimacy and popularity, and the opportunity in the wake of humiliation in the war, he could have transformed the defense establishment in the country had he moved in that direction. To his credit, he brought the military under civilian control by initiating constitutional, legislative, administrative, and financial reforms. However, once answerable to him, he used the institution to control his opponents (Shah, 2014). Domestically, he used the military to topple the provincial government in two provinces; in Balochistan, he launched a military operation against the tribes supporting the government, which enabled the military to develop stakes in political maneuvering. During the last days of his government, Bhutto dragged military institutions into political affairs to control his opponents (Aziz, 2008). Internationally, Bhutto pleaded to Washington for the resumption of economic and military aid suspended in the wake of 1971 war; he decided to leave the military alliances that Pakistan had joined under the Ayub government. In January 1972, just one month after the succession of Bangladesh, Bhutto toured eight Muslim countries in the Middle East and succeeded in securing crucial financial support for the rebuilding of Pakistan's defense structure.

However, Bhutto was more mindful of the broader structure in which the state had to operate. Pakistan lost its strategic position in the Indian Ocean after the war in 1971. However, given the upheaval in the Middle East and Eurasia, Pakistan maintained its strategic significance in Washington. Bhutto was determined to use this significance to elevate Pakistan's standing in global affairs. In this context, his decision to acquire nuclear weapons for Pakistan proved immensely significant. In 1955, Pakistan signed an agreement to receive US financial, technical, and technological assistance to develop the peaceful use of nuclear technology under Eisenhower's "Atom for Peace" program. In 1955, the Pakistan Atomic Energy Commission (PAEC) was established to develop infrastructure and human resources. Bhutto emerged as the most significant proponent advocating for nuclear weapons even when he was a minister in Ayub's government. Under his leadership as the minister of fuel, power, and natural resources, the PAEC was allocated a sizeable budget to construct laboratories and send aspiring scientists to the United States and Europe for training. In 1964 when China detonated its first nuclear device and India declared to follow suit, Bhutto believed that Pakistan had no other choice but to develop its own nuclear weapons program. In 1965, Ayub Khan and Bhutto visited China and sought Beijing's assistance in developing nuclear weapons. On his return, Bhutto declared, "If India builds the bomb, we will eat grass or leaves, even go hungry, but we will get one of our own. We have no alternative" (Singh, 1979). Even before the nuclear weapon would be missed in the 1971 war, Bhutto wrote about the lack of incredibility of any international assurance for the security of Pakistan by citing the example of France opting for its own nuclear weapons. He argued, "It will have to be assumed that a war waged against Pakistan is capable of becoming a total war. It would be dangerous to plan for less, and our plans should, therefore, include the nuclear deterrent. Difficult though this is to employ, it is vital for Pakistan to give the greatest possible attention to nuclear technology, rather than allow herself to be deceived by an international treaty limiting this deterrent to the present nuclear Powers" (Bhutto, 1969: 153).

The 1971 war, then, was a bitter lesson for him. Losing a war against India assured him that only a nuclear-armed Pakistan would be able to survive against triumphant India. On January 20, 1972, exactly one month after assuming power, he assembled a group of scientists in the relatively unimportant city of Multan and gave them three years to build a nuclear weapon. When the scientists asked for the financial and technical constraints, he took the responsibility to provide both. Within hours of that meeting, he went on an official multistate visit. In Libya, he met with Colonel Muammar al-Qaddafi and struck a deal with him. Libya would provide financial resources, while Pakistan would construct the nuclear weapon but hand over the first one to Libya (Armstrong and Trento, 2007). Pakistan acquired nuclear reactors, hired Western-trained young Pakistani scientists, and went on to develop its own nuclear weapons program. In 1974, India detonated its first nuclear device. Bhutto, while publicly insisting that Pakistan would not go for a nuclear weapon despite having grave concerns and India "brandishing the nuclear sword," expressed his deep commitment by saying, "Now, nobody is going to stop us from taking a similar step" (quoted in Armstrong and Trento, 2007: 40). Though Dennis Kux (2001) argues that the United States was unaware of these developments, several now-declassified documents show that the United States took into consideration the Cold War requirements to condone the Pakistani quest for nuclear weapons.

The global strategic order found it beneficial to observe and supervise the orderly spread of nuclear weapons technology. As the core countries were moving in the direction of newer military technologies, the spread of military nuclear technology was becoming neither controllable nor undesirable. For the great powers, a controlled spread of nuclear technology, such as under the supervision of the International Atomic Energy Agency (IAEA), could enhance their influence over the smaller countries. The next level of modern technology, the hydrogen bomb, and global aerial reach had already been mastered by the great powers, therefore removing the possibility of challenging the privileged positional standing in the global strategic order. With the spread of nuclear and other military technologies into the developing world came growing economic benefits in the creation of new markets offering lucrative capital returns while maintaining efficient control over the unnecessary dissemination of such technologies. After India conducted a successful test in 1974, the spread of nuclear weapons in the developing world became inevitable. By the time Bhutto could find widespread acceptance of the need to acquire military nuclear technology, six countries, including India, had already gained it. As a revisionist state, Pakistan was dissatisfied with its positional standing in the wake of defeat in the 1971 war and the loss of over half its population. It found nuclear technology to be the panacea of any strategic situation within South Asia and the global political system. A combination of international, regional, and domestic factors made it possible for Pakistan to follow the path of nuclearization.

Together, these factors prompted a redefinition of the role of Pakistan in the global system. The most significant impact of these developments during 1971–1977 was that Pakistan widened the gap between its two positional standings in the world-system. Regarding the global economic order, Pakistan remained a peripheral country reaffirming its role in the division of labor; though it nationalized private enterprises and business, it did not challenge the supremacy of the international financial institutions and the great powers in economic affairs. Contrary to developing advanced industries, the government focused on agriculture and the redistribution of national resources, thus widening the gap between government income and expenditure. Regarding the global strategic order, however, the Bhutto government looked to revise the order by seeking access to and control over the advanced military technology of nuclear weapons. The consequence was that while the country remained impoverished economically, its defense capabilities outgrew every other sector of national life. In the following years, the capitalist world sought Pakistan to lead wars at the cost of ignoring its economic revival. Pakistan quickly turned into a garrison state and a hotbed of global war in South Asia and beyond.

DEEPENING THE GREAT DIVERGENCE: ISLAM, CAPITALISM, AND SUBSERVIENCE (1979–2014)

With widespread changes in the semi-periphery and the periphery during the 1970s, the world-system started to shift. Across Asia and the Middle East, anti-imperial governments rose to resist the uncontested supremacy of the Western powers. Starting with the revolution of 1968, when the world witnessed massive crowds coming out and demanding a new global economic order, the Middle Eastern countries, including Pakistan, went through a domestic transformation. In the wake of the 1973 Arab-Israel War, OPEC took action that hurt peripheral and semi-peripheral countries more than the core countries. In 1976, Mao and Zhou Enlai both died and were replaced with the rather pragmatic leadership of Deng Xiaoping, ushering a new era of economic reforms and the rise of China in world affairs. In 1977, India witnessed the end of undisrupted Congress rule through its defeat in the 1977 elections. In 1979, Iran went through a full transformation with the Islamic revolution and the end of a thousand-year-old monarchy. Before the end of the year, Iranian students marched on the American embassy in Tehran and held fifty-two American diplomats, officers, and staff workers hostage. Within weeks, Pakistani students attacked the American embassy in Islamabad, killed four embassy officials, including two American officers, and kidnapped the auditor of the embassy. In the same year, Saudi Arabia witnessed the first armed challenge to its kingdom in the holiest city of Mecca. Since 1972, Afghanistan had become a battleground between rival communist groups; during 1973–1979, the country witnessed the dissolution of the stable monarchic order to be replaced only by various communist factions. In December 1979, Soviet forces entered Afghanistan, killed its leader, Hafiz Ullah Amin, and installed the puppet government of Babrak Karmal in Kabul.

The events in Asia pushed the core to transform the nature of its relationship with the periphery; it had to prioritize maintaining strategic order in the Middle East and South Asia and elevate Pakistan's positional standing in that order. In the wake of the Iranian Islamic Revolution, an ongoing diplomatic standoff between Tehran and Washington, and Central Asia being part of the Soviet Union, the West was left with only one place to support Afghan rebels: Pakistan. It was a time when capitalism could find an opportunity to revise the terms of postwar peace in Asia and beyond. It was in the long-term interest of the core countries to checkmate the second-wave communist advance in Asia after the first had produced mixed results in Southeast Asia and beyond; since there were dangers that Pakistan's open involvement in the Afghan crisis could lead to a Russian attack on the country, the United States and others feared that it might result in escalating the conflict in the Persian Gulf and beyond. The core needed to limit the war zone to Afghanistan to save its economic and strategic interests in the world. Soviet intervention in Afghanistan turned Pakistan, an already very significant country for global strategic order, into the most important state in the great powers' politics. The United States had to revise its policy toward Islamabad. Within two days of Soviet intervention, the basic sketch of US approach to the Afghan crisis was outlined by Zbigniew Brzezinski, national security advisor to President Carter. Though the US administration was aware that the Afghans were already resisting Soviet occupation of their country, Brzezinski was of the view that the rebels were "badly organized," "poorly led," and had "no sanctuary, no organized army, and no central government." Therefore, while it was necessary for the United States "that Afghanistan's resistance continues," meaning "more money, as well as arms shipments to the rebels and some technical advice," the real part of the policy pertained to a paradigm shift in how the United States should approach Pakistan under new circumstances. Given the fact that Pakistan's strategic significance had amplified immensely, it was necessary for the United States to put lucrative offers on the table while pulling the stick away altogether. The essential elements of the US policy toward Pakistan, Brzezinski argued, must include "more guarantees to it, more arms aid, and alas, a decision that our security policy towards Pakistan cannot be directed by our nonproliferation policy." Brzezinski also argued to mobilize China and the Islamic countries to put together a concerted effort led by Pakistan to repeat what happened to the United States in Vietnam less than a decade ago (Coll, 2004: 51).

While Soviet intervention in Afghanistan was the climax of events hurting the American interests in Asia, Washington saw it as a milestone in the approach that the core countries, under the leadership of the United States, had to take. According to Kux (2001), as the events in Afghanistan unfolded, President Carter himself had to call President Zia in Pakistan and inform him that the United States had reaffirmed the 1959 agreement with Pakistan guaranteeing its integrity against Soviet aggression. Initially, Pakistan was offered $400 million in military and economic aid, a package flatly declined by President Zia as "peanuts." However, as the Reagan administration took over, a more generous package—five-year military and economic aid of $3.2 billion, the sale of F-16 aircraft, and a generous rescheduling of the debt—was put on the table with the guarantee that the United States would condone Pakistan's nuclear program, human rights record, absence of democratic institutions, domestic political repression, and process of Islamization of the legal and political system. Kux (2001) quotes then Assistant Secretary of State for the Near East and South Asia Nicholas Veliotes when stating that the purpose was "to give Pakistan confidence in our commitment to its security and provide us reciprocated benefits in terms of our regional interests" (p. 256).

The arrangement laid the foundation of a new episode of patron-client relationship between Pakistan and the United States, or more accurately, between the core and a peripheral country. Pakistan agreed to become the "frontline" state in West's war in Afghanistan; it established training camps in the regions adjacent to Afghanistan, sheltered millions of refugees, and provided logistic support such as arms transfer from Western and allied countries to mujahideen. The US Central Intelligence Agency (CIA) and the Pakistani military Inter-Services Intelligence (ISI) entered in an alliance with the Saudi General Intelligence Directorate to put together the most powerful armed challenge the West could offer to the Soviet Union. Other Western intelligence organizations, including the MI6 of Great Britain, also joined the cause. The Reagan Doctrine, as it was named, was "the strategy of confronting and trying to reverse the rising Soviet tide in Afghanistan, Central America, Africa, and elsewhere in the Third World" (Kux, 2001: 261). To fulfill this objective in Afghanistan, the three intelligence services used American technology and money, Saudi ideological and financial support, and Pakistani logistics to "cause pain" in Moscow and "revenge after the series of US defeat in Vietnam, Angola, the Horn of Africa, etc. It was payback time" (quoted in Kux, 2001: 261). The Saudi government had agreed to match every dollar spent by the CIA with a dollar to be paid by the Saudi intelligence service through ISI. In the first months of resistance, the CIA discovered the potential for religion to increase the conflict and grow the war. With the help of Saudi patronage, a global drive for the recruitment of jihadists was organized under the umbrella of Wahabism, the official Saudi version of Islam. A secret service of the allied countries went on a drive to purchase Soviet- and Chinese-made weapons to provide to rebel groups. In 1983, at the insistence of the CIA station chief in Islamabad, the rebel groups were provided US-made Stinger missiles. For the next eight to ten years, as Afghan rebel groups organized and queued up for weapons and money and their activities became cost-effective, Pakistan's domestic political landscape transformed immensely (Coll, 2004). With American and international aid, President Zia and his parent institution, the Pakistan military, became the most notable beneficiaries of the war in Afghanistan. The Pakistan military, during the Afghan war years, developed a strong link with global military-industrial complexes to outpower any other institution in domestic politics.

From 1980 onward, the world-economy transformed into a global economy. Asian powers—Japan, South Korea, Taiwan, China, and now India—rose to dominate global production processes. Pakistan, on the other hand, turned into a garrison state primarily concerned with its own stability. Three critical trends in Pakistan's relations with the core dominated the process leading to significant regional divergence.

A Shambling Economy

President Zia's government in Pakistan performed relatively well on the economic front thanks to the war in Afghanistan. According to various *Economic Surveys*—annual reports on the performance of the country—Pakistan's GDP growth during 1977–1988 remained at 6.6 percent, higher than the socialist years of the 1970s but lower than the Ayub years. The growth in the agricultural and industrial sectors, 4 percent per annum and 9 percent per annum, respectively, was higher than in the Bhutto years. The share of the private sector in the industry grew by 9.5 percent during the Zia years in the wake of denationalization and guarantees against any future nationalization, higher subsidies on the import of heavy machinery and technology, and increased capacity of the industrial units nationalized during the Bhutto years. The conducive international political environment allowed Pakistan to expand its exports from $1.3 billion a year in 1978 to $5.6 billion a year in 1984. Due to Bhutto's policy of exporting human resources to the Middle East, remittances and consequently the GNP grew immensely; GNP growth was recorded at 6.25 percent per annum for the period.

However, these economic indicators could not overpower structural faults in the long-term economic crises, the seeds of which were planted during the period. While the West rewarded Pakistan through financial support to improve its economic development, budget deficit, and social development, the capitalist West ensured that Pakistan's real focus should remain at its role as the frontline state in the war against the Soviet Union in Afghanistan. In fact, the West needed to fight this war in a proxy manner by using non-Western human resources and limit the destruction within Afghanistan. The lure was quite impressive; while Pakistan received about $6 billion in economic and military aid during 1953–1979, the next decade saw an immense flow of foreign aid to the country in addition to the overt US package of $3.2 billion announced in 1981 (Husain, 1987), which increased Pakistan's level of aid dependency and lessened its appetite for reformation and modernization of its economy. Pakistan received far less in foreign direct investment in businesses and industries, and its national income earned through exports and remittances could not be turned into savings. Though the poverty level remained low during the period, it was not due to industrial activities or jobs created in the private sector. From 1983 onward, the debt-to-GDP ratio started rising and gradually turned into a chronic national economic problem. Similarly, in 1984–1985, Pakistan's budget surplus turned into a deficit that has been rising. The Zia government put the Pakistani currency on a float system, thus enabling market forces to determine the currency's strength as a reflection of the economy. One of the consequences was that the currency depreciated significantly—by 38.5 percent during 1982–1988—and provided a boost to exports. However, this also raised the national debt Pakistan owed to international financial institutions. Though the country grew its exports to foreign markets, it failed to change the nature of the division of labor and positional standing of the country in the world economy. While total exports grew about fourfold during 1980–1988, there was no transformation in manufacturing technology, the manufacture of new products, or the diversification of exports. Simultaneously, consumer goods grew at a far slower pace compared to exportable manufactured goods, thus creating a dependency on imports in the wake of higher population growth during the decade. At the same time, the growth of imports outpaced that of exports, thus negatively affecting the balance of payments and putting the national economy in a deficit. S. Akbar Zaidi (2005) mentions "the low contribution of Total Factor Productivity (TFP) growth to overall growth during the decade" in the fact that "as much as 82.3 percent of the overall growth was due to the growth in the capital stock, 14.5 percent of labor, and only 3.17 percent of TFP growth" (p. 112). The Zia government's ploy with the Islamization of the economy was meant to mesmerize the public and generate legitimacy for the military government. According to Anita Weiss (1991), "Attempts by the state to develop an Islamic economic system are not substantive departures from capitalist industrial culture but are instead substitutes for specific aspects of it" (p. 156). Pakistan, therefore, missed the crucial decade when global and regional economies transformed themselves. The easy money arriving in the form of aid affected the quest for domestic modernization. The government lost its vigor to increase the tax-to-GDP ratio, an important source of national income. When General Zia usurped the government, the ratio was above 16 percent, and the government could have taken it to 20 percent. However, by 1980, it had declined to 12 percent, creating a noticeable gap between income and expenditure. In addition to the growing budget deficit, the fact that the government started using its current account shows the stress developing as a result of the national economy.

A comparative analysis of China and India with Pakistan is pertinent to see the nature of this significant regional divergence. During the period when China and India started opening their domestic economies to global investment, Pakistan immersed itself in a war assigned to it by global capitalism. It was evident that the Western powers could utilize Pakistan's sense of insecurity to increase its dependency on economic and military aid. Therefore, when the West needed Pakistan's logistical and support services in Afghanistan, it provided a sizeable amount of weapons and equipment and condoned the country's record of human rights violations and political repression. By 1984, according to Coll (2004), the rebels or mujahideen (the jihadists) had become so independent that they did not need direct supervision from the ISI to train them; the gradual reduction in reliance on Islamabad reversed the leverage Pakistan had in 1980. In 1985, the Congress approved the Pressler Amendment, which applied conditions to the delivery of aid to Pakistan on the president's verification that Pakistan was not pursuing nuclear weapons. It was the start of the end of the relationship the core had had with a peripheral country. In 1990, as the Soviet withdrawal ended, the United States abandoned Pakistan. President Bush declined to confirm the nonweapon objective of Pakistan's nuclear program, thus halting the delivery of twenty-eight F-16s that were paid for. Pakistan paid $658 million for the aircrafts in 1993 but never received them. Instead, the country was charged $50,000 a month in storage fees while the aircraft eroded in the deserts of Arizona. In 1998, President Clinton returned $464 million to Pakistan.

The restitution of democracy in Pakistan in 1988 brought a new era of domestic instability, political wrangling, and the rise of the army as the most powerful institution, or "a state within the state." However, the most significant development during 1988–1999 was, in the words of Zaidi (2005), that "Pakistan's economic program has totally capitulated to the requirements of the IMF and the World Bank" (p. 111). As compared to India and China, which negotiated the opening of their economies and their integration into global markets after gaining a significant level of domestic economic strength, Pakistan had lost any such opportunity in the 1960s. As the democratic government took over in 1988, Pakistan needed support from international financial institutions more than ever. In 1988, Pakistan entered into a long-term relationship with the IMF and the World Bank to address its chronic fiscal management problems. Before 1988, Pakistan had various stand-by agreements with the IMF. But as the budget deficit started growing, Pakistan needed financial resources to meet the gap between income and expenditure. By then, the nature of the relationship between international financial institutions and the developing countries had started changing; as they moved toward the Washington Consensus, these institutions developed an overt and interventionist role in the national economies of the developing countries. According to Zaidi (2005), "It is fair to say that since 1988 Pakistan's economic policies, management, and performance have been almost totally determined by the country's adherence to IMF/World Bank-sponsored structural adjustment programs, and Pakistan's various governments have had no independent or original economic program of their own" (p. 336). This politico-economic intervention was so overt that Benazir Bhutto was pressured to accept financial and foreign policy ministers in her cabinet that had been nominated by the IMF and the State Department, respectively. In the wake of the ongoing last stage of the Soviet war in Afghanistan, the West wanted to ensure the new democratic government would follow the same policies adopted by the military dictator Zia ul Haq. Similarly, the IMF and other institutions dictated the terms and conditions of the new structural adjustment programs during the interim government and compelled Ms. Bhutto to accept them.

As the Pressler Amendment was enforced in 1990, the United States and other countries stopped providing economic and military aid to Pakistan. With the Soviet withdrawal completed in 1990, a new era of civil war started in Afghanistan, which resulted in prolonging the return of Afghan refugees from Pakistan. The United States, after having won the war against communism, claimed unilateral leadership and left the debris from the violence to be cleaned up by Pakistan. The war had cost Moscow about $45 billion to $50 billion, whereas the United States poured in about $5 billion to $6 billion, mainly thanks to Saudi money (Rashid, 2002). This very prudent investment returned unprecedented global political benefits. However, as a historic milestone, it took away several benefits that the United States had enjoyed during the Cold War. The removal of the so-called "threat" enabled European and rising Asian powers, including Japan, India, and China, to advance their economic and strategic interests in the world, many of which were contradictory to the interests of Washington. In the case of Pakistan, however, the fall of the Soviet Union re-imposed classic center-periphery relations; the United States abandoned the country after having created a long-term dependency in its policy formulation process. It had to deal with the consequences of sanctions imposed following the Pressler Amendment. During 1988–1999, Pakistan's economy grew at 4 percent. Political instability in the country during the decade denied successive governments the courage to take action under the four structural adjustment programs, resulting in the suspension of all. The difficulties were aggravated when Pakistan conducted nuclear tests in May 1998. The move restored strategic balance in South Asia but brought significant economic and military sanctions from the developed world and international financial institutions. With no or least-favorable access to foreign capital, governments borrowed from domestic banks. Pakistan's budget deficit grew and the country had to allocate considerable resources to pay its debts by 1995–1996; 3.4 percent of the country's GDP was used to pay the interest and principle on foreign debt, while 4.4 percent of the GDP was used to pay the interest and principle on domestic debt. Overall, the country had an unsustainable 3.6 percent per annum growth in foreign debt and 9.8 percent per annum growth in domestic debt (Ishfaq and Chaudhary, 1999). The tax-to-GDP ratio declined further in the 1990s. One of the main reasons for this economic crisis was the slowest growth of the industrial sector since independence; as compared to the 1980s, when the manufacturing sector grew at 8.5 percent, its growth was 3.6 percent during the 1990s. TFP growth in the manufacturing sector during the 1990s was recorded at 1.64 percent; it would grow only by 0.9 percent from 1998 to 2007. Similarly, labor productivity grew only by 1.29 percent compared to China and India, where this growth was 9 percent and 3.4 percent, respectively. Pakistan's share in global exports declined from 0.18 percent in 1990 to 0.15 percent in 2007. Despite having enjoyed international support for a considerable time, Pakistan's economic outlook could not be transformed; the agricultural sector still dominated the national economy, whereas industry could not grow beyond 25 percent of the GDP (Sanchez-Triana, Biller, and Nabi, 2014).

While Pakistan lost patronage from the West, the latter did not lose every interest in the region. The arrival of the Taliban in Kabul and its ability to control a vast part of the country furthered what Ahmed Rashid (2002) famously called "the New Great Game" in the region. During the nineteenth century, the British and Russian empires strived to control the region to strengthen their imperial control over the world, a struggle named "the Great Game." In the last decade of the twentieth century, the newly independent Central Asian states, already possessing sizeable reserves of fossil resources, discovered substantial new reservoirs, thereby inciting a global race among Western oil companies to accumulate capital by exporting these resources to the West—an objective that had unprecedented global geopolitical and geo-economic consequences and provided the core countries an opportunity to diversify their quest to extract natural resources from the periphery, accumulate capital, and develop a new patron-client relationship in the region. From the Western perspective, given the geopolitical compulsions in the region, Central Asian fossil resources could only be exported by building gas and oil pipelines from the region to Pakistan (and India) via Afghanistan. Whereas Washington ousted Bridas, an Argentinian oil company, and patronized Unocal's quest to build a TAPI (Turkmenistan-Afghanistan-Pakistan-India) pipeline, Mobil and Chevron pursued the Clinton administration to allow them to negotiate with the Taliban to strike a deal for the export of oil from Central Asia to the world. In December 1997, the Taliban delegation visited Unocal headquarters and negotiated an outline of the deal with the company and the US government. The project failed mainly due to the political terms that the Taliban was less willing to accept, including the handing over of Osama bin Laden. As the War on Terror started, China pushed its agenda of oil security. In 2013, Beijing signed multi-billion-dollar deals with the Central Asian republics, as it aspired to control and consume about half of the region's oil exports.

The loss of the chance for capital accumulation from the region through oil exports was compounded by the constellation of global jihadi forces in Afghanistan. Pakistan, one of the three states having recognized the Taliban as the legitimate government in Afghanistan, had to submit to pressure from Washington immediately after the 9/11 attack on the United States. Simultaneously, the 9/11 incident brought back the strategic significance—the perfect patron-client relationship between the core and a peripheral country—Pakistan had during the 1980s. This time, again, the military was in power in Islamabad. The killing of about three thousand American people in the attacks resulted in the initiation of the War on Terror. Afghanistan, having witnessed the stable but oppressive rule of Taliban since 1996, was to face another long war, this time launched by the American empire. The 9/11 attacks changed the nature of world politics, pushing the policymakers in Washington to respond aggressively. According to Immanuel Wallerstein (2003):

> It is this post-1989 geopolitical situation that permitted the collapse of so many states in the Third World and forced both the United States and Western Europe to engage in basically unwinnable attempts to prevent or eliminate fierce civil wars. . . . One cannot understand the politics of the U.S. hawks if one does not understand that they are not trying to save capitalism but to replace it with some other, even worse, system. The U.S. hawks believe that the U.S. world policy pursued from Nixon to Clinton is today unviable and can only lead to catastrophe. They are probably right that it is unviable. What they wish to substitute for it in the short run is a policy of premeditated interventionism by the U.S. military, as they are convinced that only the most macho aggressiveness will serve their interests.

Entering a patron-client relationship with Washington brought significant economic consequences to Pakistan. In the first place, the United States waived the sanctions it had imposed when Pakistan tested nuclear weapons in 1998 and at the time of military takeover in 1999. During 2001–2013,

Pakistan received $25.91 billion in economic and military assistance from the United States alone (Hassan, 2013). Considerable economic aid from other countries, including Japan, Canada, the United Kingdom, and other Western countries, was also promised and delivered. International financial institutions, following the policy approach of Washington and other core countries, provided Pakistan a new loan of $1.3 billion for a three-year period; the country was able to conclude the program prior its termination date. However, during 2002–2014, the average GDP growth rate remained at 4.26 percent, far less than expected. The budget deficit increased during the same period, and the country's tax-to-GDP ratio declined further, to only 11 percent. As US policies are about to take another shift, Pakistan is about to lose the strategic significance it enjoyed during the 2000s, which has led some commentators to doubt the country could survive without a patron-client relationship (Fair et al., 2010).

Accepting the inevitable patron-client relationship with the core has brought more economic harm than benefits. As a peripheral state, Pakistan was asked "to decide whether we were with America or with the terrorists, but that if we chose the terrorists, then we should be prepared to be bombed back to the Stone Age" (Musharraf, 2006: 201). Acceptance, however, has been more costly to the country than any benefit in terms of economic development. While aid from all the core countries put together, even exaggerated, could not be more than $30 billion, the country claims to have lost more than $118 billion in its economic and social sectors (AFP, 2016). To save itself from another threat after communism, global capitalism took its war to the periphery and pushed the countries into a new strategic division of labor. Pakistan had to fight the war, as some of its institutions found it beneficial to their own interests. As the War on Terror ended in 2022, Pakistan seems to have lost its military significance in global capitalist structure. With it, economic miseries are unfolding.

The next section tries to explain the conflict between domestic and regional interests in the state of Pakistan, its positional standing in the global strategic order, and the repercussions for global capitalism.

Islam, Military, and Pakistan's Position in the World-System

I mentioned in the first part of this chapter that Islam played the most significant role in creating and ossifying the theological basis for the birth of the state. The bloody partition of India solidified the role of religion in the country. In the postwar world-system, the ruling elite in the country took tangible steps to link the elements of the identity of Pakistan—religion, ethnicity, geography, and civilization—to the Middle East. I also mentioned that the quest for survival was used to prioritize defense as the most significant requirement in the national decision-making process. Humiliating defeat in 1971 convinced Bhutto to acquire nuclear weapons as the ultimate defense against the superior numerical strength of India in any calculation of conventional warfare. Bhutto also established and cemented Islam as an identity in domestic politics and a factor in foreign policy. The first overt experience of using Islam as a force in the 1971 war led the army to believe in the ability to develop a "second defense line" of nonuniformed soldiers, which was initially used in the war against anti-Pakistan forces in Afghanistan. The evolution in the 1970s led to a robust alliance between military and Islamist forces in Pakistan; the West also patronized the alliance in the 1980s.

The fall of communism and the disintegration of the Soviet Union transformed the relationship between the core and the state of Pakistan. The policy approach of the United States to Pakistan and the region made it clear that Washington did not need the missionary services of Pakistan and its military beyond a limited role in establishing security in Southwest Asia to benefit Washington's emerging economic-strategic interests in Central Asia. By the end of the Zia regime, however, Pakistan had transformed into a garrison state. Domestically, the armed forces of the country had been proselytized with a fundamentalist belief in jihad; they had been indoctrinated with superior social prestige derived from the idea of being "the guarantor of both the ideological and territorial frontiers of the state" (Fair, 2014: 41). The army was given the arbitrary right to intervene in the political and economic affairs of the country and turn into a supra-state institution aimed at controlling the very state. The rise of the army to the elitist institution was facilitated by the oligarchic social structure comprised of civil bureaucracy, the landed elite, and a burgeoning industrial class.

However, three developments mentioned by Wallerstein (2006) as the factors giving rise to the global movement of political Islam—the end of the Cold War, which resulted in untangling the strategic dependency of the developing world on the West; the collapse of the Old Left movements; and the start of the long Kondratieff B-phase since 1970—were more evident in the case of Pakistan than perhaps anywhere else. In the first place, Pakistan, being a smaller country with fewer resources available, has always been spending much less on defense than India. To meet the challenges to its national defense, Pakistan relied on aid from the core countries, primarily the United States, first through entering into military alliances and then using its status as the frontline state in the war in Afghanistan. According to Ayesha Siddiqa-Agha (2003), the arms transfer from the United States during the 1980s "was highly displeasing to the Indians who did not want its adversary to adopt any degree of offensive posture" (p. 29). However, these weapons—most importantly, the F-16 aircrafts—were insufficient to defend the country, especially since India moved ahead in the 1990s with buying advanced technologies from Russia, France, and other countries. Siddiqa-Agha (2003) argues, "Purely from a military technology standpoint, Islamabad's acquisitions after 1979 did not reverse or substantially narrow the military capabilities gap with its adversary" (p. 34). Despite that Pakistan spent 7 percent of its GDP on the military during the 1970s, 6.5 percent in the 1980s, and 5.6 percent in the 1990s, the gap between the two countries had widened significantly by the end of the twentieth century.

In response to an inescapable and credible threat from India and the loss of US economic and military aid after the collapse of the Soviet Union, decision-makers in the general headquarters developed a three-pronged strategy. First, they decided to replicate the Afghan proxy war strategy in Kashmir; they supported thousands of jihadist fighters returning to their homes from Afghanistan to instigate guerrilla warfare in Kashmir to inflict on India an unbearable loss of forces and finances leading to the implosion of the state, or at least its withdrawal from Kashmir, thus making it "India's Vietnam" (Murphy, 2013: 124). Starting in 1989 when a small-scale indigenous uprising in the Indian-occupied part of Kashmir erupted, Pakistan patronized the proliferation of Islamist militias and their training camps in the Punjab province and the Pakistani-occupied part of Kashmir. A mushroom growth of jihadi organizations throughout the country took place. They openly recruited young men, trained them to fight in desperate circumstances, and infiltrated them into Indian Kashmir using the difficult mountainous terrain across the line of control. Jihadi organizations received weapons and support to launch attacks. By 1995, according to Indian statistics, about thirteen thousand guerrillas had been killed, and Kashmiri leadership claimed that as many as fifty thousand Kashmiri youths had been killed (Wolpert, 2011: 69).

Pakistan's proxy war in Kashmir was an effort to eke out various socio-economic pressures at the national and regional policy levels. The defense establishment was able to accumulate financial resources through countrywide public donations collected by jihadi organizations. Though the total strength of these groups might have varied, their numbers stood in the thousands. They were zealots seeking paradise through violence against non-Muslims. Contrary to regular soldiers, for whom the defense establishment had responsibility for providing salary, food, shelter, ammunition, medical and educational facilities, and postretirement financial benefits, these organizations and their fighters did not need anything except access to weapons, facilitation in establishing training camps, and the establishment of donation collection centers. Hiring them for the proxy war in Kashmir was also meant to subvert any escalation of sectarian violence at home. The defense establishment urged the institutions of the state to facilitate the provision of financial support from Arab fundamentalists whose Wahhabi version of Islam these organizations desired to spread. Gradually, they established contacts with transnational Islamist groups like Al-Shabab, the Islamic Movement of Uzbekistan, Hamas, Chechen separatist fighters, and other organizations in the Middle East. As the Taliban emerged in Afghanistan, and as Al-Qaeda patronized the group, Pakistan's jihadists became part of the global Islamist struggle to challenge global capitalism. Their activities in Kashmir were publicized in Pakistan, and a whole new brand of jihadi journalism was nurtured. These organizations did a commendable job. India had to send more than seven hundred thousand soldiers from its army in the valley to quell the insurgence; during 1989–2000, about forty-five hundred of its soldiers and security officials were killed. Pakistan-based jihadists, with the patronage from Pakistan military establishment, made India bleed, both physically as well as financially. However, Indian economic performance since the early 1990s and its determination to defend its integrity at any cost made it difficult for the jihadist organizations to revise the status quo in the region. According to Coll (2004):

> *Every* Pakistani general, liberal or religious, believed in the jihadists by 1999, not from personal Islamic conviction, in most cases, but because the jihadists had proved themselves over many years as the one force able to frighten, flummox, and bog down the Hindu-dominated Indian army. About a dozen Indian divisions had been tied up in Kashmir during the late 1990s to suppress a few thousand well-trained, paradise-seeking Islamist guerrillas. What more could Pakistan ask? The jihadist guerrillas were a more practical day-to-day strategic defense against Indian hegemony than even a nuclear bomb. (p. 478, emphasis original)

The consequences for Pakistan, however, were immense. Writing in 2005, Burki penned it down succinctly:

> While Pakistan was to pay a hefty price for allowing Islamic fundamentalism penetrate society, at one point in time reliance on it had become an integral part of the country's defense strategy. India did not incur this kind of cost. India's Kashmir war fought on the conventional basis, did not affect its society or the country's political system. India was not scarred as badly by the long enduring insurrection in Kashmir. The fact that Kashmir is distant from the main population centers of the country has also kept the conflict in Kashmir at some distance from Indian society. That did not happen in Pakistan.

It was Pakistan's obsession with the issue of Kashmir that diverted its focus from economic development and societal liberalization to jihadist culture, leading it to become the epitome of global jihad. Using a "counterfactual" analytical technique, Burki (2005b) takes four indicators of national economic performance—reduced military expenditures; increase in intra-regional trade, in particular trade between India and Pakistan; a larger flow of foreign direct investment; and an investor-friendly domestic environment—into account and argues:

> If the country had not gotten embroiled in the Kashmir dispute, it would appear that the country's long-term growth rate could have been some two to two and a half percentage points higher than that achieved. A higher rate of growth of this magnitude, sustained over a period of half a century, would have increased the gross product by a factor of between 3.4 and 4.4. Pakistan's gross domestic product could have been three and a half times larger than that in 2003–04—$330 billion rather than $95 billion—and its income per capita would have been $2200 rather than $630 had the country been at peace with India.

The second strategy adopted by the defense establishment was reliance on nuclear weapons. In 1998, when India tested its nuclear weapons, Pakistan responded within two weeks with its own tests. Having lost its credibility by abandoning Pakistan in the wake of the collapse of the Soviet Union, the United States could not keep Pakistan from detonating nuclear weapons. This first tangible evidence of horizontal and vertical nuclear proliferation reflects the collapse of the hierarchical relationship between the core and the periphery and the chaotic global politics of the near future. One of the consequences of relying on nuclear weapons was that the defense establishment in Rawalpindi raised the threshold of provocation so high that it made it nearly impossible for India to pressure or blackmail Pakistan in conventional warfare. It also developed the ballistic missile system to ensure delivery of traditional and nonconventional weapons.

Third, though the defense establishment in Pakistan enjoyed a prestigious position through its alliance with domestic elites, it gradually emerged as the strongest institution in the country. Since 1979, the year of the military's Islamist indoctrination, the acquisition of nuclear weapons and victory in the proxy war in Afghanistan poised the country for conversion into a predator state looking for arbitrary intervention in the commercial activities in the country. Autarkic in its approach since independence, the Pakistan military developed and expanded what Ayesha Siddiqa (2017) calls "milbus," the "military capital used for the personal benefit of the military fraternity, especially the officer cadre, which is not recorded as part of the defence budget or does not follow the normal accountability procedures of the state, making it an independent genre of capital" (p. 5). From agriculture to farming, real estate, banking, power generation, fertilizers, education, and insurance, Pakistan's armed forces developed stakes in every dimension and sector of the national economy. Growing commercial interests, sponsored principally through public money, pushed the military to develop predatory political interests. Since "the value of such capital drawn by the military depends on the extent of its penetration into the economy and its influence on the state and society," the military ensures a policymaking process that guarantees a pleasant ambience in the market and higher economic returns (p. 2). The quest is supported and facilitated by a nexus among the ruling elite comprising civil bureaucracy, the landed elite, and the industrial class.

Since the 1980s, the defense establishment relied on a three-pronged strategy—the use of political Islam in Afghanistan and Kashmir, acquisition of nuclear weapons to ensure mutually assured destruction, and the development of military capital—to ensure it remains the real beneficiary of the global strategic order. Internationally, it was recognized as the de-facto controller of the country. After 9/11, the core countries needed Pakistan again. This time, as the dispersion of aid shows, the military received about two-thirds of the total aid provided by Washington. Compared to China, which is now consolidating its global influence in commerce and trade through the development of international networks of sea and land trade routes, and India, where transnational corporations are investing in almost every sector of the economy, including defense, Pakistan is still struggling to overcome fundamental structural issues in its economy. The division of labor at the global level has turned Pakistan into a garrison state.

CONCLUSION

In this chapter, I discussed Pakistan as the case of a periphery possessing imbalanced positional standing in the world-orders within the world-system. Pakistan's strategic significance in the capitalist world-system was recognized even before the country came into being. Once established, Pakistan yearned for strategic and economic support from the core countries to survive. As a periphery dependent on the core, Pakistan played the role it was assigned: to safeguard the strategic interests of the core in the region and perform the role of a peripheral country as a supplier of raw materials to the core. There are three moments in the history of Pakistan's nearly seven decades of existence—the establishment of defense alliances in the Middle East, the first war in Afghanistan during the 1980s, and the War on Terror in Afghanistan at the start of the twenty-first century—when the core required the country to play vital role in maintaining strategic order in the world. Pakistan used these three occasions to secure material interests from the core; these relations deepened its dependence on the core. The country remains a semi-periphery in terms of world economic order, but it maintains a far higher position in the world strategic order; this imbalance exposes it to pressure from the core.

Conclusion

This study is an effort to analyze the fall of the Asian empires in China and India at the time of their forceful inclusion into the expansive capitalist world-system during the eighteenth century and their recent rise at the turn of the twentieth century. This study, therefore, dealt with three distinct phases of economic history. First, it looked at the genesis of the fall of these empires from their pivotal position in the precapitalist tributary system to a periphery in the capitalist world-system. During the precapitalist tributary structure, world-empires facilitated the growth of free trade. I explained in detail in the first, third, and fourth chapters how world trade based on the historical Silk Route integrated Europe, China, India, Africa, and Southeast Asia into a complex network of commerce involving thousands of merchants and traders. The discovery of the Americas in 1492 and the Bay of Good Hope in 1498, the military revolution in the fourteenth and fifteenth centuries, and the emergence of capitalism during the sixteenth century enabled the mercantile states to convert their overseas trade into colonial occupation. The Industrial Revolution occurring at the end of the eighteenth century, therefore, was a result of capital accumulated from all over the world.

Second, I explained in detail the colonial mode of economic production that impoverished the Asian powers through systematic de-industrialization. Collectively, the Indian Sub-Continent and China were producing half of the world GDP before the Europeans started occupying these areas. By the middle of the twentieth century, when these countries gained independence, they had become peripheries with huge a dependency on the European core to survive. Their premodern industries had been destroyed, the competitive advantage had died, and poverty reigned throughout the region. The use of force was readily applied whenever required. Arbitrary terms and conditions of trade were applied with to benefit the burgeoning industries in Britain, provide funds for the modernization of militaries and the wars fought on the continent, and ensure the seamless provision of resources to build infrastructure in the core. The imperial vision of "development" in the colonies, therefore, was designed to enhance the capacity of the empire to divest the colonies further. I explained in detail the consequences of these policies in the chapters on China and India.

The third phase of capitalism, its postcolonial conduct, is the focus of this study. During the long period of colonization, when capitalism expanded and became the modus operandi of global economic management, the core developed a comprehensive and inescapable dependency of Asian, African, and South American countries on itself. In the postcolonial period, in the absence of any other viable model of development, development and economic growth could have been secured mainly through cooperation with the core. The Cold War, an insatiable quest for accumulation of capital in the core, and the expansive nature of capitalism to integrate the whole world in a complex structure of production and consumption ushered an uneven path of growth in the developing countries. Some of the countries, as they submitted to the demands of the capitalist system after either exhausting their indigenous models of development (such as in China and India) or having no other option available, progressed more than others in developing their economies along capitalist lines. In this phase, we see globalization becoming a global pattern of production, consumption, and reproduction and enabling multinational corporations to compartmentalize production processes in an attempt to maintain higher returns on their investments in global South. Simultaneously, and more importantly, the core could preserve its privileged position in the system by enforcing a dual strategy of military superiority and a complexification of the functioning of the world-system.

I can safely state that a combination of historical-cum-qualitative analysis supported, whenever possible, through quantitative analysis finds support for the hypotheses I presented at the start of this study. Let me restate the hypotheses. In the first chapter, I provided a set of five hypotheses that, collectively, argued about the ongoing complexification of the world-system through the rise of China and India. To put together what I have discussed at length, let me restate the arguments that I outlined in the first and second chapters of this study. I argued that the modern world-system is a dynamic structure of global economic management and, recently, has been complexifying itself by creating various institutions and spreading the share of benefits of capital accumulation. Second, I argued that the capitalist world-system is still dominated by Western economies led by the United States, and contrary to Immanuel Wallerstein and others, I argue for its continuation for the foreseeable future because of the complexification process that has given birth to another tier in the system, the semi-core. Third, I argued that an economic-reductionist approach is not helpful in understanding the dynamics of the world-system. I argued that we are unable to comprehend the dynamics of global management of the capitalist world-system if we ignore, belittle, or economize the role military power has played in the development of capitalism. In fact, as

I argued, there are two world-orders functioning under the world-system, which I named economic world-order and strategic world-order. It is a through a combination of the two highly intricate, inseparable, but distinguishable world-orders that capitalism has been maintaining itself as the only viable option for economic development. Therefore, I argued that a country's positional standing in the world-system depends on both economic and military power. Fourth, since the system is dynamic and continuously complexifying itself through a process of creative destruction—and developing countries are unable to find any alternative indigenous or exogenous model of economic development, particularly the one that may represent itself as a viable alternative to capitalism—the world-system has developed a hierarchy of the countries based, primarily, on its own needs and, secondarily, on the aspirations of the state. Fifth, the contemporary world-system has pacified any viable resistance by co-opting the developing countries into its orbit and building their stakes in the survival of global capitalism. These stakes are significant gains for the fast-developing countries, which have become major players in the world economy, enabling the system to prolong its eventual destruction.

I argued that world-systems theory falls short of acknowledging global capitalism as a dynamic force that, so far, has been able to find solutions to all the challenges in its way to becoming the most significant force in the world. From the start, global capitalism did everything it felt obligated to do to ensure that the accumulation of capital remains the primary and most critical interest. When it arrived in India and China in the wake of the establishment of transnational trade corporations, such as the East India Company, it dealt with every resistance through coercion and imposed a destructive structure of arbitrary terms and conditions of trade on the region. In case of China, under the hoax of free trade, British merchants urged the government in Britain to support military ventures and compel the Qing empire to accept opium as a fungible currency of trade. Different systems in India, China, and other parts of the world show that the imperial forces had no one-size-fits-all approach to controlling vast lands; in all these places, they ensured the transfer of capital, raw materials, and other necessary resources to the center while destroying local premodern industries. Enjoying superior military power from the start, the champion of capitalism, Europe, could impose a new division of labor on the peripheries. Historically, uneven development, therefore, was a quintessential requirement to sustain the capitalist world-system. Through income inequalities, the capitalist system ensured the positional standing of the core countries while spreading the processes of production and consumption across the global scale. During the postwar years, countries like China could be influenced by a noncapitalist development model. However, after having exhausted their indigenous models of growth, these countries accepted the capitalist model of growth by taking a due share of the core in the process. Since critical theory stresses the failures of capitalism, a lack of due acknowledgment of its successes in surviving for over five centuries while eradicating various challenges deprives us of understanding the modalities and methodologies of the system. In this study, I tried to explain the failure of indigenous models of growth in both China and India and the eventual introduction of the global capitalist approach of greater integration in the postcolonial period. For their parts, the countries accepted a more significant role of the capitalist system and its principal institutions in redefining national political economies. For its part, the core agreed to share the benefits of growth with these regions. However, in this deal, as I have explained, the core deployed two strategies. First, it showed resistance to relinquish its position; development in these countries was designed to be parochial, partial, and compartmentalized, serving the principles of comparative advantage and the prevalence of a greater politico-economic fragility to be dependent on and influenced by the core. The multipronged strategy seems to be working because, contrary to the expectations of some scholars, the BRICS countries are converting themselves into new powerful contenders interested in the survival of the capitalist world-system. The core, I have argued, is finding new allies in the developing world. These countries are facilitating the continuous process of transformation, as indicated by the five factors, to provide a renewed ability of the core to maintain its position. Second, the rise of the semi-core has slowed the transfer of technology from the core to the periphery. By adding yet another tier to the system, the core has complexified the production process by its further compartmentalization. Since production of goods and services at global scale is spread following the concept of the comparative advantage, no single semi-core country can become self-sufficient in its production and consumption processes. With these two strategies, the core is expected to maintain its positional standing for the foreseeable future.

One of the most significant findings of this study includes a critical evaluation of the economic-reductionist approach of world-systems theory and its consequences. There are two highly intricate yet distinguishable world-orders in action within the world-system; in addition to the economic world-order in which the division of labor regarding the production and consumption of resources is arranged according to the interests of the core, a parallel military order also prevails. The world strategic-order, the military power the core developed through the military revolution that took place during the fifteenth and sixteenth centuries, played a significant role in the expansion of economic power and the control of British and other European empires beyond the European continent. The significant divergence between China and Europe and the subsequent occupation of Asian and African lands could take place only because Europe had developed coercive capabilities to subdue the opposing forces in these areas. This study, therefore, acknowledged the role of the military in developing, expanding, and maintaining the ability of the capitalist core to conquer, occupy, and exploit non-European lands. It still is a valid indicator for defining the core, the semi-core, the semi-periphery, and the periphery.

I have argued that an economic-reductionist approach is unhelpful because it prevents us from understanding the full spectrum of the policies, approaches, and strategies devised by the core. In the first place, we fail to adequately cognize the factors enabling the European imperial project to succeed in Asia, Africa, and elsewhere. The element of military power is of immense significance since it is where we can see a complete picture of the history of capitalism. It was military superiority that enabled the European powers to control vast areas of Asia, Africa, and elsewhere. This argument required an analysis of the concept of the great divergence between Asia and Europe that took place during the fifteenth and sixteenth centuries. The imperial project was meant to reverse the trade deficit by depriving the regions of the competitive advantage that they had had for centuries and accumulating as much capital in the capitalist core. This paradigmatic transformation could not have been possible without either directly occupying the areas or subjugating the governing capacity of the native system. The military provided essential power to control these regions, and whenever required, the Europeans resumed coercive, punitive measures to secure their interests. I tried to argue that if China and India would have had an adequate level of military power, they could have defended themselves against the European imperial onslaught that started in 1757 simultaneously in India and China. The Europeans' superior fighting skills, improved sense of maneuvering, and ability to defend their strategic interests in these regions enabled them to control these regions for an extended period. For two hundred years, a variety of political and strategic mechanisms enabled the imperial powers to control and exploit these regions. In the postwar world, the role of the global strategic order became more evident. By considering strategic world-order along with economic world-order, I can identify the complexification of the world-system, on the one hand, and the dynamic nature of global management, on the other. A world-system based on these two world-orders shows the nature of resistance in the developing world. A country's dependence on the system tends to increase when there is a greater gap between its two positional standings. Thus, whereas India and China seem to be more integrated into the world-system, Pakistan's integration has been more strategic than economic. Therefore, whereas China's and India's positional standings in the world-system are more balanced and visible, Pakistan's positional standing is precarious, dependent, and imbalanced.

Based on qualitative and statistical data, I was able to support the idea that the semi-core is emerging. There is a visible gap between the level of integration of the fast-growing economies and other developing countries. I provided a contextual argument that by the end of colonialism, the capitalist core had developed an unbridgeable gap between itself and the rest of the world. In the postcolonial world-system, the capitalist core devised several strategies to ensure the continuation of dependency it had created during the eighteenth and nineteenth centuries. In this interstate structure of global politics, the core could maintain its central position by ensuring unparalleled military strength. The role of military power as the guarantor of the capitalist world-system meant that the core developed two parallel, indistinguishable, yet recognizable economic and strategic world-orders. The core exploited dependency and relied on economic means to ensure cooperation from the underdeveloped postcolonial regions. The developing countries had two choices. They could either reject the whole notion of dependency by turning inward and relying on indigenous models of development, or they deepen their dependency by opening their economies to the Western capitalist class for a new wave of exploitation, though with some guarantees of indigenous development as well. The global economic power the core placed little value on the first option and eventually led these countries to believe that they had exhausted the model of indigenous economic development and growth, particularly in India and China. I explained in detail the negotiations China and India had with global institutions and the core countries to ensure their legitimate share in transforming their economies from being communist and statist to essentially neoliberal capitalist. However, in addition to the economic world-order, the core ensured an efficient presence of the global strategic order based on NATO in the center and allies in the developing world. I have argued that the positional standing of a country in the world-system, therefore, is based on its ability to serve the economic and strategic interests of the core.

Since I take into account economic and military power as determinants to evaluate a country's positional standing in the system, I can make three conclusions in this context. First, the role of military power is a major factor in the history of the world-system. The great divergence, as we know it today, took place primarily because the Europeans could impose on Asia, Africa, and the Americas an economic system serving their interests. The genesis of this transformation, or the ability of the capitalist world-system to integrate these regions into its orbit, I argued, must be seen in the superior military power that the Europeans gained during the military revolution of the fifteenth and sixteenth centuries. Second, an understanding and acknowledgment of the role of military force in facilitating the functioning of the world-system and imposing a globalized division of labor on the developing world helps us understand the dynamics and strategies of the global capitalist class and the core. As a policy option, the core utilizes war, violence, and chaos whenever it is unable to secure its economic interests through peaceful means. The core identified and strengthened some of the countries to safeguard its strategic interests. I tried to explain the positional standing of Pakistan from a utilitarian perspective; Pakistan's military power grew during those times when the United States needed the country the most, primarily as a proxy in Afghanistan. Some other countries in the world—Egypt, for example—have been assigned a greater strategic utilitarian value than economic. Similarly, Turkey was accepted into NATO but not the European Union.

Third, and perhaps the most significant conclusion that I can draw from this study, is a probable answer to the question about the longevity of the core and its survival in the foreseeable future. This study supports the argument that the real strengths of the core are as follows: (1) Its ability to continuously invent at such a pace that housing the latest technologies and maintaining the gap between the rest of the world remain quite significant. (2) The emergence of the semi-core complexifies the trickling down of technology from the core to the semi-core and lower tiers. (3) The core has been controlling the spread of military technology. The outcome of the first two strategies is a wider spread of multinational organizations in the least developed areas of the world. The uneven pattern of growth in some parts of the developing world provides transnational corporations with some opportunities to compartmentalize their processes of production, thus complicating the dependency within the developing world and between the developed and the developing world. The semi-core countries, thus, are gradually becoming the core of their respective regions. The Wallersteinian model argues that the semi-periphery is an integral part of the functioning of the world-system. It is true. Truer, however, is the fact that uneven development has created stratification within the developing world, thus providing greater opportunities to the transnational corporations and class to maintain the margin of profit.

More importantly, we can see the control of military technology by the West and its very limited spread to the countries of preferred choice. Consequently, the gap between the core and semi-core countries regarding nonmilitary technology may seem far less visible than the gap between their military technologies. Multinational corporations involved in the business of military technology and arms production require consent from their respective states to sell their products to noncore countries; their services are restricted primarily within the core. Moreover, as I analyzed in the second chapter, what makes the core *the core* is its ability to mount a defense against any threat to the world economic-order aimed at challenging the supremacy of the core countries in accumulating capital from the developing countries. The post–Cold War expansion of NATO indicates the utilitarian power associated with the alliance; it helps the core to maintain the outlook of the world-system and remain at the center of it. The collective power of NATO is capable of enforcing and securing for member countries broader economic interests in any part of the world. Since I argue that chaos and violence are the norm in a capitalist structure of the global economy, and war is another way of securing economic interests, I can explicate the spread of violence in the broader Middle East. The role of Pakistan in Afghanistan and beyond can also be explicated using the same argument. For a detailed analysis, I leave it to future research.

The structuralist explanation for the fall and rise of non-European powers does not pacify the role of the state in question in allying with the core to develop. The state as a quasi-monopoly remains an important feature of the modern world-system. Whereas the system as a structure can control any capacity of individual states, particularly in the global South, it is fast liberalizing the policies and approaches for the institution of the state and its relationship with the world-system by continuously redefining its role. I hypothesized that within the primacy of the structure, the state is lured to accept the utilitarian role to develop. In the case of China and India, I analyzed this collusion at length. After remaining faithful to their respective ideological and indigenous models of growth and development for over three postindependence decades, they sought capitalist patronage to get out of the vicious cycle of rampant poverty, unemployment, and lack of industrial growth. Dialogue between these countries and the capitalist core and its respective institutions aimed at greater integration into the system led to a win-win for the parties; whereas capitalism and multinational corporations could diversify their sites of production and complicate the production processes, the developing countries could witness infrastructural development, industrialization, eradication of poverty, increase in international trade, and a rise in foreign exchange. Domestically, material progress has also justified the subservient position. The BRICS countries, particularly China and India, are reaping the benefits of integration into the system. They find more benefit in cooperating with the core than challenging it. Their semi-core status enables them to accrue higher benefits than they could have gained as semi-peripheral states only.

The core has maintained two important strategies regarding the semi-core. First, the semi-core is primarily economic and far less strategic. The core has ensured the fast-developing countries grow more economically than strategically; the pattern of growth remains core-centered, parochial, and dependent; and the accumulation of the capital remains directed toward the core, though with a considerable share going to the semi-core. Second, the emergence of the semi-core enables the core to slow down the trickling of technology from the core to the periphery. Far more important is that the complexification process suits the interests of the core because the world-system is finding new stakeholders in, and thus defenders of, global capitalism. The nature of capitalist development in the semi-core, however, is parochial, compartmentalized, and meant to deepen capitalism as the modus operandi of world trade. As developing states witness prosperity, they accrue stakes in the existence and continuity of the system. The active participation of the state in the process, therefore, seems logical from the capitalist development perspective.

While it is true that global capitalism has remained the principal mode of world trade and been able to overcome challenges during the last five hundred years, climate change is the most significant challenges it faces now. In other words, I can conclude that whereas the capitalist world-system could succeed in eradicating or neutralizing the various factors impacting its growth and spread, global warming will nevertheless be the issue most threatening to the survival of the whole structure of the global capitalist economy for three reasons. First, historically, the quest for unlimited and cheap raw materials and their manufacturing processes has relied on the fossil fuel economy to propel the production of capital and its accumulation in the core. The transnational capitalist class and its multinational corporations involved in the fossil fuel trade have invested so heavily that they are unwilling to forego huge material investments for something else that, without a doubt, may divest them of their control of resources. In other words, whereas oil wells and natural resources are controlled by the state and private business enterprises, solar and wind energy may take the production and consumption process down to basic social units, such as family, clan, or local communities. Therefore, it is not the case that the core or the global capitalist class has no resources or does not believe in the capacity of renewable energy; its rejection or hesitation to introduce or promote a paradigm shift away from the fossil fuel economy to renewable energy economy lies in the fact that it fears losing exclusive control of the global trade of fossil fuels and the patents and other rights to benefit from the energy and associated markets. Second, though there is a greater realization about the looming threat of global warming and it is understood that something has to be done to ensure the continuation of a seamless process of mass production, the costs of doing so are becoming so huge that it appears the core does not want to initiate any process of transformation, particularly one that will eventually deprive the core of its power to control the global energy market. In this context, even when the cost of sticking with the fossil fuel economy outpaces the cost of renewable energy, the fear of losing the power to accumulate capital will keep preventing the core to take decisive action. third, various scholars have argued about "climate capitalism," by which they are primarily referring to the so-called "self-correcting principle" of the market to address the issue. Using my model of the semi-core, I can say that climate capitalism will be a big problem between the core and the semi-core countries because stressing the appreciation of renewable sources of energy in the core will paradoxically violate the principle of industry trickling down from the core to the periphery. Industrialization in the global South and the global transportation revolution mean rising per capita consumption of fossil fuel energy. A paradigm shift from the fossil fuel economy to a renewable energy economy will require a faster trickling down of technology from the core to the periphery, as well as invite resistance from the countries that have invested heavily in building fossil fuel economies. Apparently, there is no escape from this trap. I consider climate degradation as the most significant challenge the capitalist system has faced since its inception, and I find no reason to believe that it can resolve this challenge using its predatory free market approach.

During this study, I came across several questions that I believe can become sources of future research. Due to certain limitations, this study could not develop a comprehensive statistical model to predict the rise and fall of the great powers. By including a wide range of variables, an endeavor can be made to explain the phenomenon. The issue of the changes across time and space can be addressed as well. As I mentioned above, the question of capitalism's unwillingness to address the looming issue of ecological collapse can be explained using theoretical and empirical data. Another important question concerns the possibility of a change in the leadership of the core. While it is widely believed that China is aspiring to become a global hegemon, which this study agrees with under certain conditions, an effort can be made to explain the rise of China and the reaction of the United States. While two erstwhile shifts in the leadership of the core—from Dutch to British, and from British to American—were relatively peaceful, we can explain why it can be violent this time. In this context, one can look at the factor of culture; since previous changes in leadership took place within Protestantism, and this time it is going to be from Protestantism to Confucianism, will culture be a source of contention? How similar or different can a Chinese global empire be? We can also explain the financial and demographic crisis in Europe and its implosive effects on the nature and composition of the core. Following Wallerstein, this study agrees in principle that capitalism is an unsustainable system that will collapse. However, we have not seen any statistical model explicating the conditions under which it may happen. An endeavor can be made to explain this phenomenon.

References

Abu-Lughod, J. L. (1989). *Before European hegemony: The world system A.D. 1250–1350*. New York: Oxford University Press.

Acemoglu, D., and Robinson, J. A. (2012). *Why nations fail: The origins of power, prosperity, and poverty*. New York: Crown.

Adams, B. (1897). *The law of civilization and decay: An essay on history*. New York: Macmillan.

AFP (2016). "War on terror" has cost Pakistan $118bn: SBP. *Dawn*, November 16. https://www.dawn.com/news/1297305.

Aglietta, M., and Bai, G. (2013). *China's development: Capitalism and empire*. London: Routledge.

Ahmad, E., and Mohammed, A. (2012). Pakistan, the United States and the IMF: Great game or a curious case of Dutch Disease without the oil? Asia Research Centre Working Paper 57.

Ahmad, S. N. (1991). *Origins of Muslim consciousness in India: A world-system perspective*. New York: Greenwood Press.

Ahmed, A. S. (1997). *Jinnah, Pakistan and Islamic identity: The search for Saladin*. London: Routledge.

Ahmed, I. (2013). *Pakistan military in politics: Origins, evolution, consequences*. New York: Oxford University Press.

Ahsan, A. (1996). *The Indus saga and the making of Pakistan*. New York: Oxford University Press.

Alavi, H. (1975). India and the colonial mode of production. *Economic and Political Weekly, 10*(33, 34, and 35), 1235–62.

Alavi, H. (1976). The rural elite and agricultural development in Pakistan. *Pakistan Economic and Social Review, 14*(1/4), 173–210.

Alavi, H. (1982). *Capitalism and colonial production*. London: Croom Helm.

Alavi, H. (1983). Class and state. In H. Gardezi and J. Rashid (Eds.), *Pakistan: The roots of dictatorship: The political economy of a praetorian state* (pp. 40–85). London: Zed Press.

Alavi, H. (1988). Pakistan and Islam: Ethnicity and ideology. In F. Halliday and H. Alavi (Eds.), *State and ideology in the Middle East and Pakistan*. Basingstoke: Macmillan Education.

Alavi, H. (1989). Nationhood and the nationalities in Pakistan. *Economic and Political Weekly, 24*(27), 1527–34.

Alavi, H., and Shanin, T. (Eds.). (1982). *Introduction to the sociology of "developing societies."* New York: Monthly Review Press.

Albritton, R., Jessop, B., and Westra, R. (2010). *Political economy and global capitalism: The 21st century, present and future.* London: Anthem Press.

Ali, B. S. (1982). *Tipu Sultan: A study in diplomacy and confrontation.* Mysore: Geetha Book House.

Ali, K. A. (2015). *Communism in Pakistan: Politics and class activism 1947–1972.* London: I.B. Tauris.

Altvater, E. (2006). The social and natural environment of fossil capitalism. In C. Leys and L. Panitch (Eds.), *Coming to terms with nature* (pp. 37–60). New York: Monthly Review Press.

Amin, S. (1974). *Accumulation on a world scale: A critique of the theory of underdevelopment.* New York: Monthly Review Press.

Amin, S. (1976). *Unequal development: An essay on the social formations of peripheral capitalism.* New York: Monthly Review Press.

Amin, S. (2006). *Beyond US Hegemony?: Assessing the prospects for a multipolar world.* Beirut: World Book Publishing.

Amin, S. (2011). *Ending the crisis of capitalism or ending capitalism?* Cape Town: Pambazuka Press.

Amin, S. (2014). *The implosion of contemporary capitalism.* New York: Monthly Review Press.

Amin, S., Arrighi, G., Frank, A. G., and Wallerstein, I. (1990). *Transforming the revolution: Social movements and the world-system.* New York: Monthly Review Press.

Amin, S., and Pearce, B. (1976). *Unequal development: An essay on the social formations of peripheral capitalism.* New York: Monthly Review Press.

Amin-Khan, T. (2012). *The post-colonial state in the era of capitalist globalization: Historical, political and theoretical approaches to state formation.* London: Routledge.

Amin-Khan, T. (2013). *The post-colonial state in the era of capitalist globalization: historical, political and theoretical approaches to state formation.* New York: Routledge.

Amjad, R. (1982). *Private industrial investment in Pakistan, 1960–1970.* Cambridge: Cambridge University Press.

Amoore, L. (2006). Invisible subject(s): Work and workers in the global political economy. In M. Davies and M. Ryner (Eds.), *Poverty and the production of world politics: Unprotected workers in the global political economy* (pp. 14–37). Basingstoke: Palgrave Macmillan.

Amsden, A. H. (2001). *The rise of "the rest": Challenges to the west from late-industrializing economies.* New York: Oxford University Press.

Andrade, T. (2011). *Lost colony: The untold story of China's first great victory over the West.* Princeton, NJ: Princeton University Press.

Andrade, T. (2016). *The gunpowder age: China, military innovation, and the rise of the West in world history.* Princeton, NJ: Princeton University Press.

Anwar, M., and Michaelowa, K. (2006). The political economy of US aid to Pakistan. *Review of Development Economics, 10*(2), 195–209.

Anwar, T., and Iqbal, Z. (1996). Structural adjustment and poverty: The case of Pakistan. *The Pakistan Development Review*, 911–26.

Arendt, H. (1945). Imperialism, Nationalism, Chauvinism. *The Review of Politics, 7*(4), 441–63.

Arendt, H. (1973). *The origins of totalitarianism*: Harcourt Brace Jovanovich.

Armstrong, D., and Trento, J. J. (2007). *America and the Islamic bomb: The deadly compromise*. Hanover, NH: Steerforth Press.

Arrighi, G. (2007). *Adam Smith in Beijing: Lineages of the twenty-first century*. London: Verso.

Arrighi, G. (2009). China's market economy in the long run. In H.-f. Hung (Ed.), *China and the transformation of global capitalism*. Baltimore: Johns Hopkins University Press.

Arrighi, G. (2010). *The long twentieth century: Money, power, and the origins of our times*. London: Verso.

Arrighi, G., and Drangel, J. (1986). The stratification of the world-economy: An exploration of the semiperipheral zone. *Review (Fernand Braudel Center)*, 9–74.

Asadi, M. A. (2012). *The military, economy and the state: A new international system analysis*. Doctoral dissertation, Southern Illinois University, Carbondale.

Asher, C. B., and Talbot, C. (2006). *India before Europe*. Cambridge: Cambridge University Press.

Atiya, A. S. (1962). *Crusade, commerce, and culture*. Bloomington: Indiana University Press.

Atwell, W. (1998). Ming China and the emerging world economy, c. 1470–1650. In D. Twitchett and F. W. Mote (Eds.), *The Cambridge history of China, Vol. 8: The Ming dynasty, 1368–1644, Part II* (pp. 376–416). Cambridge: Cambridge University Press.

Aziz, M. (2008). *Military control in Pakistan: The parallel state*. London: Routledge.

Bagchi, A. K. (2010). *Colonialism and Indian economy*. New York: Oxford University Press.

Bailey, P. J. (1998). *Strengthen the country and enrich the people: The reform writings of Ma Jianzhong (1845–1900)*. Richmond, Surrey: Curzon Press.

Bailey, P. J. (2001). *China in the twentieth century*. Oxford: Blackwell.

Bandyopadhyay, S. (2014). *From Plassey to partition and after: A history of modern India*. New Delhi: Orient Blackswan.

Banerjee, S. B. (2008). Necrocapitalism. *Organization Studies, 29*(12), 1541–63.

Barber, W. J. (1975). *British economic thought and India, 1600–1858: A study in the history of Development Economics*. Oxford: Clarendon Press.

Barendse, R. J. (2002). *The Arabian Seas: The Indian Ocean world of the seventeenth century*. Armonk, NY: M.E. Sharpe.

Barnett, R. B. (1980). *North India between empires: Awadh, the Mughals, and the British, 1720–1801*. Berkeley: University of California Press.

Barrow, C. W. (1993). *Critical theories of the state: Marxist, Neo-Marxsist, Post-Marxist*. Madison: University of Wisconsin Press.

Bauman, Z., and Bordoni, C. (2014). *State of crisis*. Cambridge: Polity Press.

Beausang, F. (2012). *Globalization and the BRICs: Why the BRICs will not rule the world for long*. Basingstoke: Palgrave Macmillan.

Beeching, J. (1975). *The Chinese Opium Wars*. New York: Harcourt Brace Jovanovich.

Behera, L. K. (2016). *Indian defence industry: An agenda for making in India*. New Delhi: Pentagon Press.

Bello, W. F. (2005). *Dilemmas of domination: The unmaking of the American empire*. New York: Metropolitan Books.

Bello, W. F. (2006). The capitalist conjuncture: Over-accumulation, financial crises, and the retreat from globalisation. *Third World Quarterly, 27*(8), 1345–67.

Bernstein, S. (2002). Liberal environmentalism and global environmental governance. *Global Environmental Politics, 2*(3), 1–16.

Bhagwati, J., and Desai, P. (1970). *India: Planning for industrialization: Industrialization and trade policies since 1951*. New York: Oxford University Press.

Bhagwati, J., and Panagariya, A. (2013). *Why growth matters: How economic growth in India reduced poverty and the lessons for other developing countries*: PublicAffairs.

Bhalla, G. S., and Singh, G. (2010). Economic liberalisation and Indian agriculture: A statewise analysis. *Economic and Political Weekly, 44*(52), 34–44.

Bhutto, Z. A. (1969). *The myth of independence*. New York: Oxford University Press.

Black, J. (1991). *A military revolution? Military change and European society 1550–1800*. Basingstoke: Macmillan Education.

Black, J. (2015). *The British empire: A history and a debate*. Burlington, VT: Ashgate.

Blasko, D. J. (2012). *Chinese Army today: Tradition and transformation for the 21st century*. 2nd edition. London: Routledge.

Blyn, G. (1966). *Agricultural trends in India, 1891–1947: Output, availability, and productivity*. Philadelphia: University of Pennsylvania Press.

Bolitho, H. (1954). *Jinnah: Creator of Pakistan*. London: John Murray.

Bolt, J., and Zanden, J. L. (2014). The Maddison Project: Collaborative research on historical national accounts. *The Economic History Review, 67*(3), 627–51.

Bornman, E., and Schoonraad, N. (2001). The many faces of globalisation. *Mousaion, 19*(1), 93–114.

Bornschier, V., and Chase-Dunn, C. K. (1985). *Transnational corporations and underdevelopment*. New York: Praeger.

Bose, S. R. (1972). East-West contrast in Pakistan's agricultural development. In K. Griffin and A. R. Khan (Eds.), *Growth and inequality in Pakistan* (pp. 69–93). Basingstoke: Palgrave Macmillan.

Boswell, T., and Chase-Dunn, C. K. (2000). *The spiral of capitalism and socialism: Toward global democracy*. Boulder: Lynne Rienner.

Bowen, H. V. (2006). *The business of empire: The East India Company and imperial Britain, 1756–1833*. Cambridge: Cambridge University Press.

Bowen, H. V. (2010). Bullion for trade, war, and debt-relief: British movements of silver to, around, and from Asia, 1760–1833. *Modern Asian Studies, 44*(3), 445–75.

Braudel, F., and Reynolds, S. (1982). *Civilization and capitalism, 15th–18th century, Vol. 1: The structures of everyday life*. New York: Harper and Row.
Brecher, I., and Abbas, S. A. (1972). *Foreign aid and industrial development in Pakistan*. Cambridge: Cambridge University Press.
Brenner, R. (1977). The origins of capitalist development: A critique of neo-Smithian Marxism. *New Left Review, 104*(1), 25–92.
Broad, R. (1990). *Unequal alliance: The World Bank, the International Monetary Fund, and the Philippines*. Berkeley: University of California Press.
Broadberry, S. N., and Gupta, B. (2005). Cotton textiles and the great divergence: Lancashire, India and shifting competitive advantage, 1600–1850. Centre for Economic Policy Research Working Paper 5183.
Brown, K., and Von Ruda, A. G. (2008). *The rise of the dragon: Inward and outward investment in China in the reform period, 1978–2000*. Oxford: Chandos.
Burki, S. J. (1988). *Pakistan under Bhutto, 1971–1977*. Basingstoke: Palgrave Macmillan.
Burki, S. J. (2005a). Cost and gain of Kashmir. *Dawn*, June 28. Available at https://www.dawn.com/news/1068013
Burki, S. J. (2005b) High cost of the conflict, *Dawn*, July 12. Available at https://www.dawn.com/news/1068069
Cain, P. J., and Hopkins, A. G. (2016). *British imperialism: 1688–2015*. London: Routledge.
Celikkol, A. (2011). *Romances of free trade: British literature, laissez-faire, and the global nineteenth century*. New York: Oxford University Press.
Cerra, V., and Saxena, S. C. (2002). What caused the 1991 currency crisis in India? *IMF staff papers, 49*, 395–425.
Chaliand, G. (2014). *A global history of war: From Assyria to the twenty-first century*. Berkeley: University of California Press.
Chan, A. (1982). *The glory and fall of the Ming dynasty*. Norman: University of Oklahoma Press.
Chandra, N. K. (2012). Appraising industrial policies of Indian and China from two perspectives: Nationalist and internationalist. In A. K. Bagchi and A. P. D'Costa (Eds.), *Transformation and development: The political economy of transition in India and China* (pp. 95–130). New York: Oxford University Press.
Chandrasekhar, S. (1965). *American aid and India's economic development*. New York: Praeger.
Chang, H. (1980). Intellectual change and the reform movement, 1890–8. In J. K. Fairbank and K-C Liu (Eds.), *The Cambridge history of China, Vol. 11: Late Ch'ing, 1800 to 1911, Part II*. Cambridge: Cambridge University Press.
Chang, J. K. (1969). *Industrial development in pre-Communist China: A quantitative analysis*. Chicago: Aldine.
Chase, M. (2015). *China's incomplete military transformation: Assessing the weaknesses of the People's Liberation Army (PLA)*. Santa Monica: RAND Corporation.
Chase-Dunn, C. (1996). Agency, structure and the world-system: Systemic transformation. *Humboldt Journal of Social Relations, 22*(2), 85–96.

Chase-Dunn, C. (1998). *Global formation: Structures of the world-economy*. Lanham, MD: Rowman and Littlefield.

Chase-Dunn, C. (2013). Five linked crises in the contemporary world-system. *Journal of world-systems research, 19*(2), 175.

Chase-Dunn, C. (2014). Crisis of what: The end of capitalism or another systemic cycle of capitalist accumulation? *Perspectives on Global Development and Technology, 13*(1–2), 13–35.

Chase-Dunn, C., and Grimes, P. (1995). World-systems analysis. *Annual review of sociology, 21*, 387–417.

Chase-Dunn, C., and Hall, T. D. (1997). *Rise and demise: Comparing world-systems*. Boulder: Westview Press.

Chase-Dunn, C., and Lawrence, K. S. (2010). Alive and well: A response to Sanderson. *International Journal of Comparative Sociology, 51*(6), 470–79.

Chase-Dunn, C., and Lerro, B. (2014). *Social change: Globalization from the Stone Age to the present*. Boulder: Paradigm.

Chaudhuri, K. N. (1978). *The trading world of Asia and the English East India Company, 1660–1760*. Cambridge: Cambridge University Press.

Chaudhuri, K. N. (1985). *Trade and civilisation in the Indian Ocean: An economic history from the rise of Islam to 1750*. Cambridge: Cambridge University Press.

Chaudhuri, S. B. (2007). Theories of the Indian Mutiny. In B. Pati (Ed.), *The 1857 Rebellion*. New York: Oxford University Press.

Chaudhuri, S. (1995). *From prosperity to decline: Eighteenth century Bengal*. New Delhi: Manohar Publishers & Distributors.

Cheema, P. I. (1990). *Pakistan's defense policy, 1947–58*. New York: St. Martin's Press.

Cheru, F. (2010). *The rise of China and India in Africa: Challenges, opportunities and critical interventions*. London: Zed Books.

Chossudovsky, M. (1986). *Towards capitalist restoration? Chinese socialism after Mao*. New York: St. Martin's Press.

Chowdhury, B. (1964). *Growth of commercial agriculture in Bengal (1757–1900), Vol. 1*. Calcutta: R.K. Maitra.

Chun, L. (2013). *China and global capitalism: Reflections on Marxism, history, and contemporary politics*. Basingstoke: Palgrave Macmillan.

Churchill, W. S. (1986). *The Second World War, Volume IV: The hinge of fate*. Boston: Houghton Mifflin.

Clarke, P. F. (2009). *The last thousand days of the British empire: Churchill, Roosevelt, and the birth of the Pax Americana*. New York: Bloomsbury Press.

Clingingsmith, D., and Williamson, J. G. (2004). *India's de-industrialization under British rule: New ideas, new evidence*. National Bureau of Economic Research Working Paper 42.

Clingingsmith, D., and Williamson, J. G. (2008). Deindustrialization in 18th and 19th century India: Mughal decline, climate shocks and British industrial ascent. *Explorations in Economic History, 45*(3), 209–34.

Coase, R. H., and Wang, N. (2012). *How China became capitalist*. Basingstoke: Palgrave Macmillan.

Cohen, B. J. (1998). *The geography of money*. Ithaca, NY: Cornell University Press.
Cohen, S. P. (2004). *The idea of Pakistan*. Oxford: Oxford University Press.
Cohen, P. A. (1974). *Between tradition and modernity: Wang T'ao and reform in late Ch'ing China*. Cambridge, MA: Harvard University Press.
Cohen, P. A. (1978). Christian missions and their impact to 1900. In D. Twitchett and J. Fairbank (Eds.), *The Cambridge history of China, Vol. 10: Late Ch'ing, 1800–1911, Part I* (pp. 543–90). Cambridge: Cambridge University Press.
Coleman, D. (2012). Nehru Appeals for JFK's Help in Fighting China. *History in Pieces*. Retrieved from https://historyinpieces.com/research/nehru-jfk-sino-indian-war.
Coll, S. (2005). *Ghost wars: The secret history of the CIA, Afghanistan, and bin Laden, from the Soviet invasion to September 10, 2001*. New York: Penguin.
Corbridge, S., and Harriss, J. (2008). *Reinventing India: Liberalization, Hindu nationalism and popular democracy*. Cambridge: Polity Press.
Cordesman, A. H., and Lin, A. (2014). *Chinese strategy and military power in 2014: Chinese, Japanese, Korean, Taiwanese and US perspectives*. Washington, DC: Center for Strategic and International Studies.
Cumings, B. (1996). The world shakes China. *The National Interest* (43), 28–41.
da Silva, F. R. (2011). Dutch and Portuguese in western Africa: Empires, merchants and the Atlantic system, 1580–1674. Leiden: Brill.
Dai, Y. (2011). *A concise history of the Qing Dynasty, Vol. III*. Singapore: Silkwood Press.
Daly, J. W. (2020). *How Europe made the modern world: creating the great divergence*. London: Bloomsbury Academic.
Dar, F. A. (2014). *Jinnah's Pakistan: Formation and challenges of a state*. New York: Oxford University Press.
Darby, P. (1987). *Three faces of imperialism: British and American approaches to Asia and Africa, 1870–1970*. New Haven, CT: Yale University Press.
Darwin, J. (2005). *Britain and decolonisation: The retreat from empire in the post-war world*. Basingstoke: Palgrave Macmillan.
Das, T., Mathur, C., and Richter, F.-J. (2005). *India rising: Emergence of a new world power*. Singapore: Marshall Cavendish International (Asia).
Davies, M., and Ryner, M. (2006). *Poverty and the production of world politics: Unprotected workers in the global political economy*. Basingstoke: Palgrave Macmillan.
Day, A. F. (2013). *The peasant in postsocialist China: History, politics, and capitalism*. Cambridge: Cambridge University Press.
de la Garza, A. (2014). The Mughal battlefield: Personnel, technology, and tactics in the early empire, 1500–1605. *Journal of Military History, 78*(3), 927–60.
de la Garza, A. (2016). *The Mughal empire at war: Babur, Akbar and the Indian military revolution, 1500–1605*. London: Routledge.
Deming, L. (2010). *Development of China in the modern world system*. Singapore: Cengage Learning Asia.
Deming, S. (2011). *The economic importance of Indian opium and trade with China on Britain's economy, 1843–1890*. Whitman College Economics Working Paper 25.

Denemark, R. A., and Thomas, K. P. (1988). The Brenner-Wallerstein debate. *International Studies Quarterly, 32*(1), 47–65.

Denoon, D. B. (1998). Cycles in Indian economic liberalization, 1966–1996. *Comparative politics, 31*(1), 43–60.

Derbyshire, I. (1995). The building of India's railways: The application of Western technology in the colonial periphery, 1850–1920. In R. MacLeod and D. Kumar (Eds.), *Technology and the Raj: Western technology and technical transfers to India, 1700–1947* (pp. 177–215). New Delhi: SAGE Publications.

Des Forges, R. V. (1973). *Hsi-liang and the Chinese national revolution*. New Haven, CT: Yale University Press.

Desai, V. R. M. (1972). Industrialisation: Plans and policy programmes in the context of Indian development. In A. V. Bhuleshkar (Ed.), *Towards socialist transformation of Indian economy* (pp. 169–98). Bombay, India: Popular Prakashan.

Dhanagare, D. N. (2016). Declining credibility of the neoliberal state and agrarian crisis in India: Some observations. In B. B. Mohanty (Ed.), *Critical perspectives on agrarian transition: India in the global debate* (pp. 138–63). London: Routledge.

Digby, W. (1901). *"Prosperous" British India: A revelation from official records*. London: Unwin.

Dikotter, F. (2010). *Mao's great famine: The history of China's most devastating catastrophe, 1958–1962*. New York: Walker.

Dirlik, A. (1989). *The origins of Chinese Communism*. New York: Oxford University Press.

Dimaculangan, P. (2014). The Needham question and the great divergence: Why China fell behind the West and lost the race in ushering the world into the industrial revolution and modernity. *Comparative Civilizations Review* (71), 106–14.

Dong, B., Gong, J., Peng, K., and Zhao, Z. (2015). Little divergence: Evidence from cotton textiles in Japan and China 1868–1930. *Review of Development Economics, 19*(4), 776–96.

Dower, J. W. (2017). *The violent American century: War and terror since World War II*. Chicago: Haymarket Books.

Dreyer, E. L. (2012). Continuity and change. In D. A. Graff and R. D. S. Higham (Eds.), *A military history of China* (pp. 19–38). Lexington: University Press of Kentucky.

Dreyer, J. T. (2007). China's power and will: The PRC's military strength and grand strategy. *Orbis, 51*(4), 651–64.

Dutt, R. C. (1906). *The economic history of India in the Victorian age: From the accession of Queen Victoria in 1837 to the commencement of the twentieth century*. London: Routledge & Kegan Paul.

Duffy, M. (1980). *The military revolution and the state, 1500–1800*. Exeter: University of Exeter.

Dutt, R. C. (1950). *The economic history of India under early British rule*. London: Routledge and Kegan Paul.

Dutt, V. P. (1968). The first week of revolution: The Wuchang uprising. In M. K. Wright (Ed.), *China in revolution: The first phase, 1900–1913* (pp. 383–415). New Haven, CT: Yale University Press.

Duzgun, E. (2018). Property, Geopolitics, and Eurocentrism: The "Great Divergence" and the Ottoman Empire. *Review of Radical Political Economics, 50*(1), 24–43.

Eacott, J. (2016). *Selling empire: India in the making of Britain and America, 1600–1830*. Chapel Hill: University of North Carolina Press.

Ebrey, P. B., Walthall, A., and Palais, J. B. (2009). *East Asia: A cultural, social, and political history*. Boston: Houghton Mifflin.

Economic survey of Pakistan 1961–1962. Rawalpindi: Ministry of Finance, Government of Pakistan.

Economic survey of Pakistan 1971–1972. Islamabad: Ministry of Finance, Government of Pakistan.

Economic survey of Pakistan 1972–1973. Islamabad: Ministry of Finance, Government of Pakistan.

Economic survey of Pakistan 2013–2014. Islamabad: Ministry of Finance, Government of Pakistan.

El Tiby, A. M. (2011). *Islamic banking: How to manage risk and improve profitability*. Hoboken, NJ: Wiley.

Elvin, M. (1973). *The pattern of the Chinese past: A social and economic interpretation*. Stanford: Stanford University Press.

Elvin, M. (1996). *Another history: Essays on China from a European perspective*. Broadway, Australia; Honolulu, Hawaii: Wild Peony; Distr. by University of Hawaii Press.

Er, L. P., and Wei, L. T. (2009). *The rise of China and India: A new Asian drama*. Singapore: World Scientific.

Eraly, A. (2007). *The Mughal world: Life in India's last golden age*. Harmondsworth, UK: Penguin Books.

Esherick, J. (1976). *Reform and revolution in China: The 1911 revolution in Hunan and Hubei*. Berkeley: University of California Press.

Esherick, J. (1987). *The origins of the Boxer Uprising*. Berkeley: University of California Press.

Esteban, J. C. (2001). The British balance of payments, 1772–1820: India transfers and war finance. *The Economic History Review, 54*(1), 58–86.

Fair, C. C. (2014). *Fighting to the end: The Pakistan army's way of war*. New York: Oxford University Press.

Fair, C. C., Crane, K., Chivvis, C. S., Puri, S., and Spirtas, M. (2010). *Pakistan: Can the United States secure an insecure state?* Santa Monica: RAND Corporation.

Fairbank, J. (1978). The creation of the treaty system. In D. Twitchett & J. Fairbank (Eds.), *The Cambridge history of China Vol. 10: Late Ch'ing, 1800-1911, Part I* (pp. 213–63). Cambridge: Cambridge University Press.

Farooqi, M. (1972). *Pakistan: Policies that led to break-up*. New Delhi: People's Publishing House.

Farooqui, A. (2005). *Smuggling as subversion: Colonialism, Indian merchants, and the politics of opium, 1790–1843*. Lanham, MD: Lexington Books.

Fenby, J. (2014). *Will China dominate the 21st century?* Cambridge: Polity Press.

Fincher, J. H. (1981). *Chinese democracy: The self-government movement in local, provincial, and national politics, 1905–1914*. New York: St. Martin's Press.

Fisher, M. H. (1991). *Indirect rule in India: Residents and the residency system, 1764–1858*. New York: Oxford University Press.

Fisher, M. H. (Ed.) (1994). *The politics of the British annexation of India, 1757–1857*. New York: Oxford University Press.

Fleurant, A., Perlo-Freeman, S., Wezeman, S. T., and Wezeman, P. D. (2016). *Trends in international arms transfers, 2015*. Retrieved from Solna, Sweden: http://books.sipri.org/files/FS/SIPRIFS1503.pdf

Flynn, D. O., and Giraldez, A. (1995). Born with a "silver spoon": The origin of world trade in 1571. *Journal of World History, 6*(2), 201–21.

Flynn, D. O., and Giraldez, A. (Eds.). (1997). *Metals and monies in an emerging global economy*. Aldershot: Variorum.

Flynn, D. O., and Giraldez, A. (2010). *China and the birth of globalization in the 16th century*. Burlington, VT: Ashgate.

Foster, J. B. (2013). Why ecological revolution? *Monthly Review, 61*(January 2010), 1–18.

Foster, J. B., Clark, B., and York, R. (2010). *The ecological rift: Capitalism's war on the earth*. New York: Monthly Review Press.

Frank, A. G. (1996). India in the world economy, 1400–1750. *Economic and Political Weekly, 31*(30), PE50–PE64.

Frank, A. G. (1998). *ReOrient: Global economy in the Asian age*. Berkeley: University of California Press.

Frank, A. G. (2000). Around the world in eighty years. *Journal for the Comparative Study of Civilizations, 5*, 45–98.

Frank, A. G. (2007). *World accumulation 1492–1789*. New York: Algora.

Frank, A. G. (2014). *ReOrienting the 19th century: Global economy in the continuing Asian age*. Edited by R. A. Denemark. Boulder: Paradigm.

Frank, A. G., and Gills, B. K. (1993). *The world system: Five hundred years or five thousand?* London: Routledge.

Frank, A. G., and Gills, B. K. (2000). The five thousand years: World system in theory and praxis. In R. A. Denemark, J. Friedman, B. Gills, and G. Modelski (Eds.), *World system history: The social science of long-term change* (pp. 3–24). London: Routledge.

Frankel, F. R. (2005). *India's political economy, 1947–1977: The gradual revolution*. 2nd edition. New York: Oxford University Press.

Friedman, J., and Chase-Dunn, C. K. (2005). *Hegemonic decline: Present and past*. Boulder: Paradigm.

Friedman, M., and Friedman, R. D. (2002). *Capitalism and freedom*. Chicago: University of Chicago Press.

Frobel, F., Burgess, P., Heinrichs, J., and Kreye, O. (1981). *The new international division of labour: Structural unemployment in industrialised countries and industrialisation in developing countries*. Cambridge: Cambridge University Press

Fumagalli, A., and Mezzadra, S. (2010). *Crisis in the global economy: Financial markets, social struggles, and new political scenarios*. Los Angeles: Semiotext(e). Distributed by the MIT Press.

Galtung, J. (1971). A structural theory of imperialism. *Journal of Peace Research, 8*(2), 81–117.

Gandhi, R. (2013). *Punjab: A history from Aurangzeb to Mountbatten.* New Delhi: Aleph.

Gao, Y. (2012). *China as the workshop of the world: An analysis at the national and industry level of China in the international division of labor*. London: Routledge.

Garavini, G. (2012). *After empires: European integration, decolonization, and the challenge from the global south, 1957–1986.* Translated by R. R. Nybakken. New York: Oxford University Press.

Gardezi, H. N., and Rashid, J. (Eds.). (1983). *Pakistan, the roots of dictatorship: The political economy of a praetorian state*. London: Zed Press.

Garthoff, R. L. (1966). *Sino-Soviet military relations*. New York: Praeger.

Gilpin, R. (2012). *War and change in world politics*. Cambridge: Cambridge University Press.

Gitter, D. (2016). Is China's period of strategic opportunity over? *The Diplomat*, May 28. Retrieved from http://thediplomat.com/2016/05/is-chinas-period-of-strategic-opportunity-over/.

Goitein, S. D. (1974). *Letters of medieval Jewish traders*. Princeton, NJ: Princeton University Press.

Goldman, M. (1994). *Sowing the seeds of democracy in China: Political reform in the Deng Xiaoping era*. Cambridge, MA: Harvard University Press.

Goldman, M., and MacFarquhar, R. (Eds.). (1999). *The paradox of China's post-Mao reforms*. Cambridge, MA: Harvard University Press.

Goldstone, J. A. (2009). *Why Europe? The rise of the West in world history, 1500–1850*. Boston: McGraw-Hill Higher Education.

Gommans, J. J. L. (2002). *Mughal warfare: Indian frontiers and high roads to empire, 1500–1700*. London: Routledge.

Gommans, J. J. L., and Kolff, D. H. A. (2001). *Warfare and weaponry in South Asia, 1000–1800*. New York: Oxford University Press.

Gordon, S. (1993). *The Marathas, 1600–1818*. Cambridge: Cambridge University Press.

Gray, J. (1998). *False dawn: The delusions of global capitalism*. New York: The New Press.

Greenberg, M. (1969). *British trade and the opening of China, 1800–42*. Cambridge: Cambridge University Press.

Gujral, M. L. (1979). *Economic failures of Nehru and Indira Gandhi: A study of 3 decades of deprivation and disillusionment*. Ghaziabad, India: Vikas.

Gungwu, W. (1998). Ming foreign relations: Southeast Asia. In D. Twitchett and F. W. Mote (Eds.), *The Cambridge history of China, Vol. 8: The Ming dynasty, 1368–1644, Part II*. Cambridge: Cambridge University Press.

Gupta, N. (2005). Partial privatization and firm performance. *The Journal of Finance, 60*(2), 987–1015.

Gurley, J. G. (1976). *China's economy and the Maoist strategy*. New York: Monthly Review Press.

Habib, I. (2006). *Indian economy, 1858–1914*. New Delhi: Tulika Books.

Habib, I. (2013). *Indian economy under early British rule, 1757–1857*. New Delhi: Tulika Books.

Habib, I. (2014). *The agrarian system of Mughal India, 1556–1707*. 3rd edition. New York: Oxford University Press.

Hall, K. R. (2011). *A history of early Southeast Asia: Maritime trade and societal development, 100–1500*. Lanham, MD: Rowman and Littlefield.

Hamilton, C. J. (1919). *The trade relations between England and India, 1600–1896*. Calcutta: Thacker, Spink & Co.

Hancock, G. (1994). *Lords of poverty: The power, prestige, and corruption of the international aid business*. New York: Atlantic Monthly Press.

Hanneman, T., and Gao, C. (2016). Record deal making in 2016 pushes cumulative Chinese FDI in the US above $100 billion. *Rodium Group*, December 30. Retrieved from http://rhg.com/notes/record-deal-making-in-2016-pushes-cumulative-chinese-fdi-in-the-us-above-100-billion.

Harvey, D. (1990). *The condition of postmodernity: An enquiry into the origins of cultural change*. Oxford: Blackwell.

Harvey, D. (2005). *A brief history of neoliberalism*. New York: Oxford University Press.

Hassan, M. (2013). Pakistan "received $25.91b" from US since 9/11. *The Nation*, June 27.

Hatano, Y. (1968). The new armies. In M. C. Wright (Ed.), *China in revolution: The first phase, 1900–1913*. New Haven, CT: Yale University Press.

Heydarian, R. J. (2014). *How capitalism failed the Arab world: The economic roots and precarious future of Middle East uprisings*. London: Zed Books.

Hinnebusch, R. (2011). The Middle East in the world hierarchy: Imperialism and resistance. *Journal of International Relations and Development, 14*(2), 213–46.

Hobbes, T. (1985 [1651]). *Leviathan*. Edited by C. B. Macpherson. Harmondsworth, UK: Penguin Books.

Hobson, J. M. (2004). *The Eastern origins of Western civilization*. Cambridge: Cambridge University Press.

Hobson, J. M. (2015). The Eastern origins of the rise of the West and the "return" of Asia. *East Asia, 32*(3), 239–55.

Hodgson, M. G. S. (1974). *The venture of Islam: Conscience and history in a world civilization, Vol III: The gunpowder empires and modern times*. Chicago: University of Chicago Press.

Hoffman, P. T. (2015). *Why did Europe conquer the world?* Princeton, NJ: Princeton University Press.

Hopkins, T. K., and Wallerstein, I. (1996). *The age of transition: Trajectory of the world-system, 1945–2025*. London: Zed Books.

Hossain, H. (1988). *The company weavers of Bengal: The East India Company and the organization of textile production in Bengal, 1750–1813*. New York: Oxford University Press.

Hout, W., and Meijerink, F. (1996). Structures in the international political economy: World-system theory and unequal development. *European Journal of International Relations, 2*(1), 47–76.

Hsiao, L.-l. (1974). *China's foreign trade statistics, 1864–1949*. Cambridge: East Asian Research Center, Harvard University.

Hung, H.-f. (2009). Introduction: The three transformations of global capitalism. In H.-f. Hung (Ed.), *China and the transformation of global capitalism*. Baltimore: Johns Hopkins University Press.

Huntington, S. P. (1996). *The clash of civilizations and the remaking of world order*. New York: Simon and Schuster.

Husain, I. (1999). *Pakistan: The economy of an elitist state*. New York: Oxford University Press.

Husain, N. A. (1987). Pakistan-U.S. security relations: Arms sales, bases, and nuclear issues. In L. E. Rose and N. A. Husain (Eds.), *United States-Pakistan forum: Relations with the major powers* (pp. 1–14). Lahore: Vanguard.

Hussain, E. (2013). *Military agency, politics, and the state in Pakistan*. New Delhi: Saṁskṛiti.

Hutchins, F. G. (1967). *The illusion of permanence: British imperialism in India*. Princeton, NJ: Princeton University Press.

Ichiko, C. (1980). Political and institutional reform, 1901–1911. In J. Fairbank & K.-C. Liu (Eds.), *The Cambridge history of China, Vol. 11: Late Ch'ing, 1800 to 1911, Part II* (pp. 375–415). Cambridge: Cambridge University Press.

Ikram, S. M. (1989). *History of Muslim civilization in India and Pakistan: A political and cultural history*. 4th edition. Lahore: Institute of Islamic Culture.

Irfani, S. (2004). Pakistan's sectarian violence: Between the "Arabist Shift" and Indo-Persian culture. In S. P. Limaye, R. G. Wirsing, and M. Malik (Eds.), *Religious Radicalism and Security in South Asia* (pp. 147–70). Honolulu: Asia-Pacific Center for Security Studies.

Irogbe, K. (2013). Global political economy and the power of multinational corporations. *Journal of Third World Studies, 30*(2), 223–47.

Irvine, W. (1994). *The army of the Indian Moghuls: Its organization and administration*. Delhi: Low Price Publications.

Ishfaq, M., and Chaudhary, M. A. (1999). Fiscal deficits and debt dimensions of Pakistan. *The Pakistan Development Review, 38*(4), 1067–80.

Jabeen, M., and Mazhar, M. S. (2011). Security game: SEATO and CENTO as instrument of economic and military assistance to encircle Pakistan. *Pakistan Economic and Social Review, 49*(1), 109–32.

Jacobson, H. K., and Oksenberg, M. (1990). *China's participation in the IMF, the World Bank, and GATT: Toward a global economic order*. Ann Arbor: University of Michigan Press.

Jain, P. C. (2012). *Economic determinants of India's foreign policy: The Nehru years (1947–64)*. New Delhi: Vitasta Pub.

BolithoJalal, A. (1994). *The sole spokesman: Jinnah, the Muslim League and the demand for Pakistan*. Cambridge South Asian Studies, Vol. 31. Cambridge: Cambridge University Press.

Jalal, A. (1990). *The state of martial rule: The origins of Pakistan's political economy of defence*. Cambridge [England]; New York: Cambridge University Press.

Jalal, A. (1994). *The sole spokesman: Jinnah, the Muslim League and the demand for Pakistan*. Cambridge South Asian Studies, Vol. 31. Cambridge: Cambridge University Press.

Jalal, A. (1995a). Conjuring Pakistan: History as official imagining. *International Journal of Middle East Studies, 27*(1), 73–89.

Jalal, A. (1995b). *Democracy and authoritarianism in South Asia: A comparative and historical perspective*. Cambridge: Cambridge University Press.

Janin, H. (1999). *The India-China opium trade in the nineteenth century*. Jefferson, NC: McFarland.

Jo, Y. H. (2011). The capitalist world-system and US cold war policies in the core and the periphery: A comparative analysis of post-World War II American nation-building in Germany and Korea. *Journal of World-Systems Research, 17*(2), 428–55.

Jones, E. L. (2003). *The European miracle: Environments, economies, and geopolitics in the history of Europe and Asia*. Cambridge: Cambridge University Press.

Judge, J. (1997). *Print and politics: "Shibao" and the culture of reform in late Qing China*. Stanford: Stanford University Press.

Kang, D. C. (2012). *East Asia before the West: Five centuries of trade and tribute*. New York: Columbia University Press.

Kaura, U. (1977). *Muslims and Indian nationalism: The emergence of the demand for India's partition, 1928–40*. New Delhi: South Asia Books.

Kaushik, D. R. (2005). Military synthesis in South Asia: Armies, warfare and Indian society, c. 1740–1849. *The Journal of Military History, 69*(3), 651–90.

Kemp, T. (2013). *The climax of capitalism: The US economy in the twentieth century*. London: Routledge.

Keylor, W. R. (1996). *The twentieth-century world: An international history*. New York: Oxford University Press.

Khan, A. (1999). Ethnicity, Islam and national identity in Pakistan. *South Asia: Journal of South Asian Studies, 22*(s1), 167–82.

Khan, A. H. (2015). *From Sufism to Ahmadiyya: A Muslim minority movement in South Asia*. Bloomington: Indiana University Press.

Khan, F. H. (2012). *Eating grass: The making of the Pakistani bomb*. Stanford: Stanford University Press.

Khan, H. (2005). *Constitutional and political history of Pakistan*. New York: Oxford University Press.

Khan, I. A. (2004). *Gunpowder and firearms: Warfare in medieval India*. New York: Oxford University Press.

Khan, M. (1999). The political economy of industrial policy in Pakistan, 1947–1971. University of London School of Oriental and African Studies Working Paper 98.

Khan, M. A. (1969). *Friends not masters: A political autobiography*. New York: Oxford University Press.

Khan, M. H. (1981). *Underdevelopment and agrarian structure in Pakistan*. Boulder: Westview Press.

Kick, E. L., and Davis, B. L. (2001). World-system structure and change: An analysis of global networks and economic growth across two time periods. *American Behavioral Scientist, 44*(10), 1561–78.

Kissinger, H. (2012). *On China*. New York: Penguin.

Klein, T. (2012). Rethinking the origins of "Western" imperialism in China: Global constellations and imperial policies, 1790–1860. *History Compass, 10*(11), 789–801.

Kohli, A. (1989). *The state and poverty in India*. Cambridge: Cambridge University Press.

Kohli, A. (2004). *State-directed development: Political power and industrialization in the global periphery*. Cambridge: Cambridge University Press.

Kohli, A. (2011). *Democracy and development in India: From socialism to pro-business*. New York: Oxford University Press.

Kohli, A. (2012). *Poverty amid plenty in the new India*. Cambridge: Cambridge University Press.

Kux, D. (2001). *The United States and Pakistan, 1947–2000: Disenchanted allies*. Baltimore: Johns Hopkins University Press.

Lalvani, K. (2016). *The making of India: The untold story of British enterprise*. London: Bloomsbury Continuum.

Landes, D. S. (2015). *Wealth and poverty of nations: Why some are so rich and some so poor*. United Kingdom: Little, Brown Book Group, 2015.

Lardy, N. R. (1987a). The Chinese economy under stress, 1958–1965. In R. MacFarquhar and J. Fairbank (Eds.), *The Cambridge history of China, Vol. 14: The People's Republic, Part 1: The Emergence of Revolutionary China, 1949–1965* (pp. 360–97). Cambridge: Cambridge University Press.

Lardy, N. R. (1987b). Economic recovery and the 1st five-year plan. In R. MacFarquhar and J. Fairbank (Eds.), *The Cambridge history of China, Vol. 14: The People's Republic, Part 1: The Emergence of Revolutionary China, 1949–1965* (pp. 144–84). Cambridge: Cambridge University Press.

Lebowitz, M. A. (2004). What keeps capitalism going? *Monthly Review, 56*(2), 19–26.

Lee, R. E. (2013). *The longue durée and world-systems analysis*. Albany: State University of New York Press.

Levi, S. C. (2016). *Caravans: Punjabi Khatri merchants on the Silk Road*. Harmondsworth, UK: Penguin Books.

Li, J., and Wang, L. (Eds.) (2014). *China's economic dynamics: A Beijing consensus in the making?* London: Routledge.

Li, M. (2008). *The rise of China and the demise of the capitalist world-economy*. London: Pluto Press.

Lieberthal, K. (1987). The Great Leap Forward and the split in the Yenan leadership. In R. MacFarquhar and J. Fairbank (Eds.), *The Cambridge history of China, Vol. 14: The People's Republic, Part 1: The Emergence of Revolutionary China, 1949–1965* (pp. 293–359). Cambridge: Cambridge University Press.

Lipietz, A. (1987). *Mirages and miracles: The crises of global Fordism*. London: Verso.

Liu, G.-G., Wu, J.-L., and Zhao, R.-W. (1979). Relationship between planning and market as seen by China in her socialist economy. *Atlantic Economic Journal, 7*(4), 11–21.

Liu, Y. (2007). *The Dutch East India Company's tea trade with China, 1757–1781*. Leiden: Brill.

Lorge, P. A. (2005). *War, politics and society in early modern China, 900–1795*. London: Routledge.

Lorge, P. A. (2012). Water forces and naval operations. In D. A. Graff and R. Highman (Eds.), *A military history of China*. Lexington: University Press of Kentucky.

Lucarelli, B. (2004). *Monopoly capitalism in crisis*. Basingstoke: Palgrave Macmillan.

Luthi, L. M. (2008). *The Sino-Soviet split: Cold War in the communist world.* Princeton, NJ: Princeton University Press.

Macaulay, T. (1995 [1835]). Minute on education. In B. Ashcroft, G. Griffiths, & H. Tiffin (Eds.), *The post-colonial studies reader* (pp. 428–430). Routledge Publishers.

Macaulay, T. B. 1835. *Minute on Education.* in Sharp, H. E. (Ed.), and Board of Education. (1965 [1920]). *Selections from Educational Records, Part I (1781–1839).* Calcutta: Superintendent, Government Printing; Reprint. Delhi: National Archives of India. (p. 107–17).

MacLeod, R., and Kumar, D. (Eds.). (1995). *Technology and the Raj: Western technology and technical transfers to India, 1700–1947*. New Delhi: SAGE Publications.

Maddison, A. (1971). *Class structure and economic growth: India and Pakistan since the Moghuls*. London: Allen and Unwin.

Maddison, A. (2001). *The world economy: A millennial perspective*. Paris: Organisation for Economic Co-operation and Development.

Maddison, A. (2003). *The world economy: Historical statistics*. Paris: Organisation for Economic Co-operation and Development.

Maddison, A. (2005). *Growth and interaction in the world economy: The roots of modernity*. Washington, DC: AEI Press.

Maddison, A. (2007). *Chinese economic performance in the long run*. Paris: Organisation for Economic Co-operation and Development.

Mahmood, M. (1977). The pattern of adoption of green revolution technology and its effect on land holdings in the Punjab. *Pakistan Economic and Social Review, 15*(1/2), 34–68.

Mahtaney, P. (2007). *India, China and globalization: The emerging superpowers and the future of economic development*. Basingstoke: Palgrave Macmillan.

Malcolm, J. (1826). *The political history of India from 1784 to 1823*. London: J. Murray.

Malekandathil, P. (2010). *Maritime India: Trade, religion and polity in the Indian Ocean*. New Delhi: Primus Books.

Malekandathil, P. (2013). *The Mughals, the Portuguese, and the Indian Ocean: Changing imageries of maritime India*. New Delhi: Primus Books.

Malik, I. H. (1991). *US-South Asian relations, 1940–47: American attitudes towards the Pakistan movement*. New York: St. Martin's Press.

Mandel, E. (1975). *Late capitalism*. Translated by J. D. Bres. London: Humanities Press.

Mansingh, S. (2006). *Historical dictionary of India*. Lanham, MD: Scarecrow Press.

Mao, S. (1965). *Selected works of Mao Tse-Tung, Vol. 2*. Peking: Foreign Languages Press.

Mao, Z. (1975). *Selected works of Mao Tse-Tung, Vol. 4*. Peking: Foreign Languages Press.

Mao, Z. (1977). *Selected works of Mao Tse-Tung, Vol. 5*. Peking: Foreign Languages Press.

Marino, R. (2014). *The future BRICS: A synergistic economic alliance or business as usual?* Basingstoke: Palgrave Macmillan.

Mark, C.-K. (2013). *China and the world since 1945: An international history*. London: Routledge.

Marshall, P. J. (1968). *Problems of empire: Britain and India, 1757–1813*. London: Allen and Unwin.

Marshall, P. J. (Ed.) (2005). *The eighteenth century in Indian history: Evolution or revolution?* New York: Oxford University Press.

McCartney, M. (2011). *Pakistan: The political economy of growth, stagnation and the state, 1951–2009*. London: Routledge.

McIntyre, W. D. (1998). *British decolonization, 1946–1997: When, why, and how did the British empire fall?* New York: St. Martin's Press.

McKercher, B. J. C. (2006). *Transition of power: Britain's loss of global pre-eminence to the United States, 1930–1945*. Cambridge: Cambridge University Press.

McMichael, P. (2000). World-systems analysis, globalization, and incorporated comparison. *Journal of World-Systems Research, 6*(3), 68–99.

McNally, D. (2009). From financial crisis to world-slump: Accumulation, financialisation, and the global slowdown. *Historical Materialism, 17*(2), 35–83.

Meemamsi, G. B. (1993). *The C-DOT story: Quest, inquest, conquest*. Noida, India: Kedar Publications.

Menzies, G. (2008). *1421: The year China discovered America*. New York: William Morrow.

Merchant, M. (2015). Why Shashi Tharoor is right on Britain's colonial debt to India. *DailyO*, July 23. Retrieved from http://www.dailyo.in/politics/minhaz-merchant-shashi-tharoor-oxford-union-address-congress-britain-colonialism-monsoon-session-parliament/story/1/5168.html.

Michael, F., and Chang, C-L. (1966). *The Taiping rebellion: History and documents, Vol. 1, History*. Seattle: University of Washington Press.

Mielants, E. H. (2005). The rise of European hegemony: The political economy of South Asia and Europe compared, A.D. 1200 to A.D. 1500. In C. Chase-Dunn and E. N. Anderson (Eds.), *The historical evolution of world-systems*. Basingstoke: Palgrave Macmillan.

Mielants, E. H. (2008). *The origins of capitalism and the "rise of the West."* Philadelphia: Temple University Press.

Mills C. W. (1958). *The causes of world war three*. New York: Simon and Schuster.

Miskimin, H. A. (1977). *The economy of later Renaissance Europe, 1460–1600*. Cambridge: Cambridge University Press.

Mitcham, C. J. (2005). *China's economic relations with the West and Japan, 1949–79: Grain, trade and diplomacy*. London: Routledge.

Mitchell, B. R. (2013). *International historical statistics: 1750–2010.* Palgrave McMillan, Basingstoke, Hampshire.

Modelski, G., and Thompson, W. R. (1988). *Seapower in global politics, 1494–1993*. Basingstoke: Palgrave Macmillan.

Mohanty, B. B., and Lenka, P. K. (2016). Neoliberal reforms, agrarian capitalism and the peasantry. In B. B. Mohanty (Ed.), *Critical perspectives on agrarian transition: India in the global debate* (pp. 164–95). London: Routledge.

Mokyr, J. (2002). *The gifts of Athena: Historical origins of the knowledge economy*. Princeton, NJ: Princeton University Press.

Mokyr, J. (2009). *The enlightened economy: An economic history of Britain, 1700–1850*. New Haven, CT: Yale University Press.

Moore, B. (1966). *Social origins of dictatorship and democracy: Lord and peasant in the making of the modern world*. Boston: Beacon Press.

Moore, R. J. (1999). Imperial India, 1858–1914. In W. R. Louis and A. Low (Eds.), *The Oxford history of the British empire, Vol III: The nineteenth century* (pp. 422–46). New York: Oxford University Press.

Moosvi, S. (2008). *People, taxation, and trade in Mughal India*. New York: Oxford University Press.

Moosvi, S. (2010). *People, taxation, and trade in Mughal India*. Oxford; New York: Oxford University Press.

Moosvi, S. (2015). *The economy of the Mughal empire c. 1595: A statistical study*. New York: Oxford University Press.

Morse, H. B. (1926). *The chronicles of the East India Company trading to China, 1635–1834*. Oxford: Clarendon Press.

Mortimer, R. (1974). *Indonesian communism under Sukarno: Ideology and politics, 1959–1965*. Ithaca, NY: Cornell University Press.

Mosley, L. (1962). *The last days of the British Raj*. New York: Harcourt, Brace and World.

Mukherjee, A. (2010). Empire: How colonial India made modern Britain. *Economic and Political Weekly, 45*(50), 11.

Mukherji, R. (2008). The political economy of India's economic reforms. *Asian Economic Policy Review, 3*(2), 315–31.

Munir, M. (2005). The judicial system of the East India Company: Precursor to the present Pakistani legal system. *Annual Journal of International Islamic University Islamabad, 14*(1), 53–68.

Murphy, E. (2013). *The making of terrorism in Pakistan: Historical and social roots of extremism*. London: Routledge.

Musharraf, P. (2006). *In the line of fire: A memoir*. New York: Simon and Schuster.

Myers, R. H. (1965). Cotton textile handicraft and the development of the cotton textile industry in modern China. *The Economic History Review, 18*(3), 614–32.

Myers, R. H. (1991). *Two societies in opposition: The Republic of China and the People's Republic of China after forty years*. Stanford: Hoover Institution Press.

Nambiar, R., Mungekar, B., and Tadas, G. (1999). Is import liberalisation hurting domestic industry and employment? *Economic and Political Weekly, 34*(7), 417–24.

Naughton, B. (1993). Deng Xiaoping: The economist. *The China Quarterly, 135*, 491–514.

Naughton, B. (2007). *The Chinese economy: Transitions and growth*. Cambridge, MA: MIT Press.

Nayak, S. (2015). *Global financial crisis: Genesis, policy response and road ahead.* New York: Springer.

Nayar, B. R. (2001). *Globalization and nationalism: The changing balance of India's economic policy, 1950–2000*. New Delhi: SAGE Publications.

Nayar, B. R. (2007). Globalization and India's national autonomy. In B. R. Nayar (Ed.), *Globalization and politics in India* (pp. 346–83). New York: Oxford University Press.

Nef, J. U. (1941). Silver production in Central Europe, 1450–1618. *Journal of Political Economy, 49*, 575–91.

Nehru, J. (1959). *The discovery of India*. Garden City, NY: Anchor Books.

Newell, P. (2012). *Globalization and the environment: Capitalism, ecology and power*. Cambridge: Polity Press.

Nicholas, D. (1999). *The transformation of Europe, 1300–1600*. New York: Arnold.

Noman, O. (1988). *The political economy of Pakistan 1947–85*. London: KPI.

North, D. C., and Thomas, R. P. (1973). *The rise of the Western world: A new economic history*. Cambridge: Cambridge University Press.

Oak, M., and Swamy, A. V. (2012). Myopia or strategic behavior? Indian regimes and the East India Company in late eighteenth century India. *Explorations in Economic History, 49*(3), 352–66.

Office of the Secretary of Defense (2015). *Annual Report to Congress: Military and Security Developments Involving the People's Republic of China 2015*. (D-117FA69). Washington, DC: Department of Defense.

O'Leary, G. (1998). *Adjusting to capitalism: Chinese workers and the state*. Armonk, NY: M.E. Sharpe.

Organski, A. F. K. (1968). *World politics*. New York: Alfred A. Knopf.

Ortmann, S. (2014). The "Beijing Consensus" and the "Singapore Model": Unmasking the myth of an alternative authoritarian state-capitalist model. In J. Li and L. Wang (Eds.), *China's economic dynamics: A Beijing consensus in the making?* London: Routledge.

Osmani, S. (2005). *The impact of globalization on poverty in Bangladesh*. International Labour Organization Policy Integration Department Working Paper 65.

Overbeek, H., and van Apeldoorn, B. (2012). *Neoliberalism in crisis*. Basingstoke: Palgrave Macmillan.

Paine, S. C. M. (2003). *The Sino-Japanese War of 1894–1895: Perceptions, power, and primacy*. Cambridge: Cambridge University Press.

Palat, R., Barr, K., Matson, J., Bahl, V., and Ahmad, N. (1986). The incorporation and peripheralization of South Asia, 1600–1950. *Review (Fernand Braudel Center)*, 171–208.

Palat, R. A. (2010). World turned upside down? Rise of the global South and the contemporary global financial turbulence. *Third World Quarterly, 31*(3), 365–84.

Pan, R. (2015). China's WTO membership and the non-market economy status: Discrimination and impediment to China's foreign trade. *Journal of Contemporary China, 24*(94), 742–57.

Panagariya, A. (2005). India in the 1980s and the 1990s: A triumph of reforms. In W. Tseng and D. Cowen (Eds.), *India's and China's recent experience with reform and growth* (pp. 170–200). Basingstoke: Palgrave Macmillan.

Panagariya, A. (2014). India and China: Trade and foreign investment. In N. C. Hope, A. Kochar, R. Noll, and T. N. Srinivasan (Eds.), *Economic reform in India: Challenges, prospects, and lessons* (pp. 96–138). Cambridge: Cambridge University Press.

Pant, H. V. (2008). *Contemporary debates in Indian foreign and security policy: India negotiates its rise in the international system*. Basingstoke: Palgrave Macmillan.

Papanek, G. F. (1967). *Pakistan's development: Social goals and private incentives*. New York: Oxford University Press.

Parker, G. (1976). The "Military Revolution," 1560–1660—a myth? *Journal of Modern History, 48*(2), 196–214.

Parker, G. (1996). *The military revolution: Military innovation and the rise of the West, 1500–1800*. 2nd edition. Cambridge: Cambridge University Press.

Parthasarathi, P. (2011). *Why Europe grew rich and Asia did not: Global economic divergence, 1600–1850*. Cambridge: Cambridge University Press.

Parthasarathi, P., and Wendt, I. (2009). Decline in three keys: Indian cotton manufacturing from the late eigthteenth century. In G. Riello and P. Parthasarathi (Eds.), *The spinning world: A global history of cotton textiles, 1200–1850*. New York: Oxford University Press.

Pati, B. (Ed.) (2007). *The 1857 rebellion*. New York: Oxford University Press.

Pati, B. (Ed.) (2012). *The great rebellion of 1857 in India: Exploring transgressions, contests and diversities*. London: Routledge.

Patnaik, P. (2015). The Nehru–Mahalanobis strategy. *Social Scientist, 43*(3/4), 3–10.

Patnaik, P., and Chandrasekhar, C. P. (2007). India: Dirigisme, structural adjustment, and the radical alternative. In B. R. Nayar (Ed.), *Globalization and politics in India* (pp. 218–40). New York: Oxford University Press.

Patnaik, U., and Patnaik, P. (2015). Imperialism in the era of globalization. *Monthly Review, 67*(3), 68–81.

Paulino, S., Uliafnova, A., and Wan, G. H. (2010). *The rise of China and India: Impacts, prospects and implications*. Basingstoke: Palgrave Macmillan.

Pei, M. (2016). *China's crony capitalism: The dynamics of regime decay*. Cambridge, MA: Harvard University Press.

Perelman, M. (2011). *The invisible handcuffs of capitalism: How market tyranny stifles the economy by stunting workers*. New York: Monthly Review Press.

Peterson, V. S. (2003). *A critical rewriting of global political economy: Integrating reproductive, productive, and virtual economies*. London: Routledge.

Petras, J. F., and Veltmeyer, H. (2013). *Imperialism and capitalism in the twenty-first century: A system in crisis*. Farnham: Ashgate.

Polanyi, K. (2001). *The great transformation: The political and economic origins of our time*. Boston: Beacon Press.

Pomeranz, K. (2000). *The great divergence: China, Europe, and the making of the modern world economy*. Princeton, NJ: Princeton University Press.

Postone, M. (2007). Theorizing the contemporary world: Robert Brenner, Giovanni Arrighi, David Harvey. In R. Albritton, R. Jessop, and R. Westra (Eds.), *Political economy and global capitalism: The 21st century, present and future* (pp. 7–24). Anthem Press.

Prabhakaran, M. P. (1990). *The historical origin of India's underdevelopment: A world-system perspective*. Lanham, MD: University Press of America.

Prakash, O. (1998). *European commercial enterprise in pre-colonial India*. Cambridge: Cambridge University Press.

Prakash, O. (2004). *Bullion for goods: European and Indian merchants in the Indian Ocean trade, 1500–1800*. New Delhi: Manohar.

Preston, D. (2000). *The boxer rebellion:The dramatic story of China's war on foreigners that shook the world in the summer of 1900*. New York: Walker.

Princen, T., Manno, J. P., and Martin, P. L. (Eds.) (2015). *Ending the fossil fuel era*. Cambridge, MA: MIT Press.

Przeworski, A. (1991). *Capitalism and social democracy*. Cambridge: Cambridge University Press.

Purcell, V. (1963). *The Boxer Uprising: A background study*. London: Cambridge University Press.

Pursell, G. (1992). Trade policies in India. In D. Salvatore (Ed.), *National trade policies* (pp. 423–58). New York: Greenwood Press.

Qadir, A. (2014). Parliamentary hereticization of the Ahmadiyya in Pakistan: The modern world implicated in Islamic crises. In G. Ganiel, H. Winkel, and C. Monnot (Eds.), *Religion in times of crisis*. Leiden: Brill.

Quanxi, G. (2014). Revolution, reform and constitutionalism: The evolution of China's 1982 Constitution: An Interpretation Based on Political Constitutionalism. *Peking University Law Journal, 2*(1), 27–57.

Quibria, M. (2010). *Aid effectiveness in Bangladesh: Is the glass half full or half empty?* Paper presented at the seminar organized by Department of Economics, University of Illinois.

Qureshi, I. H. (1965). *The struggle for Pakistan*. Karachi: University of Karachi Press.

RAND Corporation (1989). *Long-term economic and military trends, 1950–2010*. Santa Monica: RAND Corporation.

Rashid, A. (2002). *Taliban: Islam, oil and the new great game in central Asia*. London: I.B. Tauris.

Rawlinson, J. L. (1967). *China's struggle for naval development, 1839–1895*. Cambridge, MA: Harvard University Press.

Ray, I. (2014). *Bengal industries and the British industrial revolution (1757–1857)*. London: Routledge.

Raychaudhuri, T. (1999). *Perceptions, emotions, sensibilities: Essays on India's colonial and post-colonial experiences*. New York: Oxford University Press.

Raza, R. (1997). *Zulfikar Ali Bhutto and Pakistan: 1967–1977*. New York: Oxford University Press.

Rees, J. (2006). *Imperialism and resistance*. London: Routledge.

Reid, A. (1988). *Southeast Asia in the age of commerce, 1450–1680, Vol I: The lands below the winds*. New Haven, CT: Yale University Press.

Reinert, E. S. (2010). *How rich countries got rich and why poor countries stay poor*. London: Constable.

Richards, J. F. (1993). *The Mughal empire*. Cambridge: Cambridge University Press.

Rizvi, H. A. (1993). *Pakistan and the geostrategic environment: A study of foreign policy*. New York: St. Martin's Press.

Rizvi, H. A. (2003). *Military, state and society in Pakistan*. Lahore: Sang-e-Meel Publications.

Roberts, M. (1995). The Military Revolution, 1560–1660. In C. J. Rogers (Ed.), *The military revolution debate: Readings on the military transformation of early modern Europe* (pp. 13–36). Boulder: Westview Press.

Roberts, P. E. (1916). *A historical geography of the British dependencies, Vol. VII, Part I: History to the end of the East India Company*. New York: Oxford University Press.

Robinson, W. I. (2011). Globalization and the sociology of Immanuel Wallerstein: A critical appraisal. *International Sociology, 26*(6), 723–45.

Rose, S. (2010). *For all the tea in China: How England stole the world's favorite drink and changed history*. New York: Penguin.

Rosenberg, N., and Birdzell, L. E. (1986). *How the West grew rich: The economic transformation of the industrial world*. New York: Basic Books.

Rosenthal, J-L., and Wong, R. B. (2011). *Before and beyond divergence: The politics of economic change in China and Europe*. Cambridge, MA: Harvard University Press.

Rowe, W. T. (2012). *China's last empire: The great Qing*. Cambridge, MA: Belknap Press of Harvard University Press.

Roy, D. (1998). *China's foreign relations*. Lanham, MD: Rowman and Littlefield.

Roy, K. (2011). *War, culture, and society in early modern South Asia, 1740–1849*. London: Routledge.

Roy, K. (2014). *Military transition in early modern Asia, 1400–1750: Cavalry, guns, government and ships*. London: Bloomsbury.

Roy, K. (2015). *Warfare in pre-British India, 1500 BCE to 1740 CE*. London: Routledge.

Roy, K. D. (2005). Military Synthesis in South Asia: Armies, Warfare and Indian Society, c. 1740–1849. *The Journal of Military History, 69*(3), 651–90.

Roy, T. (2002). Economic history and modern India: Redefining the link. *Journal of Economic Perspectives, 16*(3), 109–30.

Roy, T. (2006). *Traditional industry in the economy of colonial India*. Cambridge: Cambridge University Press.

Roy, T. (2009). Did globalisation aid industrial development in colonial India? A study of knowledge transfer in the iron industry. *Indian Economic and Social History Review, 46*(4), 579–613.

Roy, T. (2012a). India and the world economy: 1757–1947. In C. Ghate (Ed.), *The Oxford handbook of the Indian economy* (pp. 33–55). New York: Oxford University Press.

Roy, T. (2012b). *India in the world economy: From antiquity to the present.* Cambridge: Cambridge University Press.

Rudra, A. (1964). Relative rates of growth: Agriculture and industry. *The Economic Weekly*, November 7.

Rueschemeyer, D., Huber, E., and Stephens, J. D. (1992). *Capitalist development and democracy*. Chicago: University of Chicago Press.

Ruvalcaba, D. E. M. (2013). Inside the BRIC: Analysis of the rise of the semiperipheral character of Brazil, Russia, India, and China. *Austral: Brazilian Journal of Strategy and International Relations, 2*(4), 141–73.

Saikia, Y. (2014). Ayub Khan and modern Islam: Transforming citizens and the nation in Pakistan. *South Asia: Journal of South Asian Studies, 37*(2), 292–305.

Sanchez-Triana, E., Biller, D., and Nabi, I. (2014). *Revitalizing industrial growth in Pakistan: Trade, infrastructure, and environmental performance*. Washington, DC: World Bank Group.

Sanderson, S. K. (2005). World-systems analysis after thirty years: Should it rest in peace? *International Journal of Comparative Sociology, 46*(3), 179–213.

Sarkar, P. (1992). De-industrialisation through colonial trade. *Journal of Contemporary Asia, 22*(3), 297–302.

Sarkar, S. (2013). Bhadralok aspirations and the quest for technical knowledge, 1830–1900. In D. Kumar, J. Bara, N. Khadria, and C. R. Gayathri (Eds.), *Education in colonial India: Historical insights* (pp. 99–124). New Delhi: Manohar.

Sattar, A. (2017). *Pakistan's foreign policy, 1947–2016: A concise history*. 4th edition. New York: Oxford University Press.

Sauvant, K. P. (2009). *The rise of transnational corporations from emerging markets: Threat or opportunity?* Cheltenham: Edward Elgar.

Schwartz, B. I. (1951). *Chinese communism and the rise of Mao*. Cambridge: Harvard University Press.

Scott, D. (2008). *The Chinese century? The challenge to global order.* Basingstoke: Palgrave Macmillan.

Scott, D. (2009). *China and the international system, 1840–1949: Power, presence, and perceptions in a century of humiliation*. Albany: State University of New York Press.

Screpanti, E. (2014). *Global imperialism and the great crisis: The uncertain future of capitalism*. New York: Monthly Review Press.

Seats, E. (1987). The commodity structure of East-West trade and its implications. *Michigan Journal of Economics, 8*(1), 20–35.

Sen, K. (2008). *Trade, FDI and industrial transformation in India*. Paper presented at the "Emerging Trends and Patterns of Trade and Investment in Asia" research workshop at the 9th Global Network Conference, Brisbane, Australia.

Sen, S. (1998). *Empire of free trade: The East India Company and making of the colonial marketplace*. Philadelphia: University of Pennsylvania Press.

Sengupta, M. (2009). Making the state change its mind: The IMF, the World Bank and the Politics of India's Market Reforms. *New Political Economy, 14*(2), 181–210.
Seth, V. K. (2014). Debate on de-industrialization revisited: The process of decline of traditional flexible manufacturing. *Global Business Review, 15*(3), 597–610.
Shah, A. (2014). *The army and democracy: Military politics in Pakistan*. Cambridge, MA: Harvard University Press.
Shao, W. (1991). *China, Britain, and businessmen: Political and commercial relations, 1949–57*. Basingstoke: Macmillan.
Sherman, S. (2009). China in three geographical contexts. In G. K. Trichur (Ed.), *The rise of Asia and the transformation of the world-system* (pp. 59–68). Boulder: Paradigm.
Shih, M.-W. (2001). *The rise of China in world-system perspective.* Doctoral Dissertation, State University of New York at Binghamton.
Siddiqa, A. (2017). *Military Inc.: Inside Pakistan's military economy*. London: Pluto Press.
Siddiqa-Agha, A. (2003). *Pakistan's arms procurement and military buildup, 1979–99: In search of a policy*. Lahore: Sang-e-Meel Publications.
Silverman, J. (1972). The ultimate objective of Nehru's socialism. In A. V. Bhuleshkar (Ed.), *Towards the socialist transformation of the Indian economy*. Bombay: Popular Prakashan.
Singh, J. (2010). *Jinnah: India, partition, independence*. New York: Oxford University Press.
Singh, K. (1979). Pakistan, India and the bomb. *New York Times*, July 1, p. E21.
Singh, N. K., and Srinivasan, T. N. (2013). Federalism and economic development in India: An assessment. In N. C. Hope, A. Kochar, R. Noll, & T. N. Srinivasan (Eds.), *Economic reform in India: Challenges, prospects, and lessons*. New York: Cambridge University Press.
Singh, N. K., and Srinivasan, T. N. (2014). Federalism and economic development in India: An assessment. In N. C. Hope, A. Kochar, R. Noll, and T. N. Srinivasan (Eds.), *Economic reform in India: Challenges, prospects, and lessons*. Cambridge: Cambridge University Press.
SIPRI yearbook 1971: armaments, disarmament and international security. (1971). Oxford: Oxford University Press.
SIPRI yearbook 1972: armaments, disarmament and international security. (1972). New York: Humanities Press.
SIPRI yearbook 1978: armaments, disarmament and international security. (1978). London: Taylor & Francis Ltd.
SIPRI yearbook 1986: armaments, disarmament and international security. (1986). Oxford: Oxford University Press.
SIPRI yearbook 1994: armaments, disarmament and international security. (1994). Oxford: Oxford University Press.
Sklair, L. (1991). *Sociology of the global system*. Baltimore: Johns Hopkins University Press.
Sklair, L. (1997). Social movements for global capitalism: The transnational capitalist class in action. *Review of International Political Economy, 4*(3), 514–38.

Sklair, L. (2001). *The transnational capitalist class*. Oxford: Blackwell.
Skocpol, T. (1977). Wallerstein's world capitalist system: A theoretical and historical critique. *American Journal of Sociology, 82*(5), 1075–90.
Skocpol, T. (1994). *Social revolutions in the modern world.* Cambridge: Cambridge University Press.
Smith, J. C. (2016). *Imperialism in the twenty-first century: Globalization, super-exploitation, and capitalism's final crisis*. New York: Monthly Review Press.
Smith, N., and Harvey, D. (2008). *Uneven development: Nature, capital, and the production of space*. Athens: University of Georgia Press.
Snyder, D., and Kick, E. L. (1979). Structural position in the world system and economic growth, 1955–1970: A multiple-network analysis of transnational interactions. *American Journal of Sociology, 84*(5), 1096–26.
Sobhan, R. (1965). Strategy for industrialization in Pakistan. In A. I. Qureshi (Ed.), *Third five-year plan and other papers: Papers read at the 12th Pakistan Economic Conference held at Peshawar from March 1 to 3, 1965*. Rawalpindi: Pakistan Economic Association.
Solar, P. M. (2013). Opening to the East: Shipping between Europe and Asia, 1770–1830. *The Journal of Economic History, 73*(3), 625–61.
Srinivasan, T. N., & Tendulkar, S. D. (2003). *Reintegrating India with the world economy*. Washington D.C.: The Institute of International Economics.
Stander, S. (2009). The absorptive class. In P. Zarembka (Ed.), *Why capitalism survives crises: The shock absorbers* (pp. 11–45). Bingley, UK: JAI.
Stander, S. (2014). *Why war: Capitalism and the nation-state*. New York: Bloomsbury Academic.
Stephen, M. D. (2014). Rising powers, global capitalism and liberal global governance: A historical materialist account of the BRICs challenge. *European Journal of International Relations, 20*(4), 912–38.
Stiglitz, J. E. (2015). *The great divide: Unequal societies and what we can do about them*. New York: W. W. Norton.
Stone, I. (1984). *Canal irrigation in India: Perspectives on technological change in a peasant economy*. Cambridge: Cambridge University Press.
Streusand, D. E. (2011). *Islamic gunpowder empires: Ottomans, Safavids, and Mughals*. Boulder: Westview Press.
Strikwerda, C. (2000). From world-systems to globalization: Theories of transnational change and the place of the United States. *American Studies, 41*(2/3), 333–48.
Stuart-Fox, M. (2003). *A short history of China and Southeast Asia: Tribute, trade and influence*. London: Allen and Unwin.
Studer, R. (2015). *The great divergence reconsidered: Europe, India, and the rise to global economic power*. Cambridge: Cambridge University Press.
Subrahmanyam, S. (2012). *The Portuguese empire in Asia, 1500–1700: A political and economic history*. Malden, MA: Wiley-Blackwell.
Subramanian, A. (2008). *India's turn: Understanding the economic transformation*. New York: Oxford University Press.
Sweeney, S. (2011). *Financing India's imperial railways, 1875–1914*. London: Pickering and Chatto.

Tang, Y., Xu, J., and Zhang, X. (2017). China's investment and rate of return on capital revisited. *Journal of Asian Economics, 49*, 12–25.

Teiwes, F. C. (1987). Establishment and consolidation of the new regime. In D. C. Twitchett (Ed.), *The Cambridge history of China, Vol. 14: The People's Republic, Part 1: The emergence of revolutionary China, 1949–1965*. Cambridge: Cambridge University Press.

Terlouw, C. (1992). *The regional geography of the world system: External arena, periphery, semiperiphery, core*. Netherlands Geographical Studies. Utrecht: Koninklijk Nederlands Aardrijkskundig Genootschap.

Terlouw, C. P. (1993). The elusive semiperiphery: A critical examination of the concept of semiperiphery. *International Journal of Comparative Sociology, 34*(1), 87.

Terlouw, K. (2002). The semiperipheral space in the world-system. *Review (Fernand Braudel Center)*, 1–22.

Tewari, M. M. (1982). *External resources and economic development in India*. Delhi: B.R. Publishing.

Tharoor, S. (2016). *An era of darkness: The British empire in India*. New Delhi: Aleph.

Third Five-Year Plan. (1961). New Delhi: Government of India Planning Commission.

Thomas, R. G. C. (1978). *The defence of India: A budgetary perspective of strategy and politics*. Delhi: South Asia Books.

Thomas, S. C. (1984). *Foreign intervention and China's industrial development, 1870–1911*. Boulder: Westview Press.

Thompson, W. R., and Reuveny, R. (2010). *Limits to globalization: North-South divergence*. London: Routledge.

Thorner, D., Thorner, A., and Bhattacharya, S. (2005). *Land and labour in India*. New Delhi: Chronicle Books.

Tomlinson, B. R. (1979). *The political economy of the Raj, 1914–1947: The economics of decolonization in India*. London: Macmillan.

Touraine, A. (2014). *After the crisis*. Translated by H. Morrison. Cambridge: Polity Press.

Tracy, J. D. (Ed.) (1990). *The rise of merchant empires: Long-distance trade in the early modern world, 1350–1750*. Cambridge: Cambridge University Press.

Trichur, G. K. (2009). *The rise of Asia and the transformation of the world-system*. Boulder: Paradigm.

Trocki, C. A. (1999). *Opium, empire, and the global political economy: A study of the Asian opium trade, 1750–1950*. London: Routledge.

Twitchett, D. C., and Mote, F. W. (1998). *The Cambridge history of China, Vol. 8: The Ming dynasty, 1368–1644, Part II*. Cambridge: Cambridge University Press.

Van Hamme, G., and Pion, G. (2012). The relevance of the world-system approach in the era of globalization of economic facts and networks. *Geografiska Annaler: Series B, Human Geography, 94*(1), 65–82.

Varoufakis, Y. (2011). *The global minotaur: America, the true origins of the financial crisis and the future of the world economy*. London: Zed Books.

Venkataramani, M. S. (1982). *The American role in Pakistan, 1947–1958*. New Delhi: Radiant.

Vitali, S., Glattfelder, J. B., and Battiston, S. (2011). The network of global corporate control. *PloS one, 6*(10), e25995.

Vohra, R. (1974). *The Chinese revolution, 1900–1950*. Boston: Houghton Mifflin.

Volscho, T. (2015). The revenge of the capitalist class: Crisis, the legitimacy of capitalism and the restoration of finance from the 1970s to present. *Critical Sociology*, 1–18.

Vries, P. (2015). *State, economy and the great divergence: Great Britain and China, 1680s–1850s*. London: Bloomsbury Academic.

Wakeman, F. (1978). The Canton trade and the opium war. In D. Twitchett and J. Fairbank (Eds.), *The Cambridge history of China, Vol. 10: Late Ch'ing, 1800–1911, Part I* (pp. 163–212). Cambridge: Cambridge University Press.

Waley-Cohen, J. (2014). *The culture of war in China: Empire and the military under the Qing Dynasty*. London: Bloomsbury Academic.

Wallerstein, I. (1974). The rise and future demise of the world capitalist system: Concepts for comparative analysis. *Comparative studies in society and history, 16*(04), 387–415.

Wallerstein, I. (1979). *The capitalist world-economy*. Cambridge: Cambridge University Press.

Wallerstein, I. (1984). *The politics of the world-economy: The states, the movements, and the civilizations*. Cambridge: Cambridge University Press.

Wallerstein, I. (1990). Antisystemic movements: History and dilemmas. In S. Amin, G. Arrighi, A. G. Frank, and I. Wallerstein (Eds.), *Transforming the revolution: Social movements and the world-system*. New York: Monthly Review Press.

Wallerstein, I. (1991). *Geopolitics and geoculture: Essays on the changing world-system*. Cambridge: Cambridge University Press.

Wallerstein, I. (1992). The West, capitalism, and the modern world-system. *Review (Fernand Braudel Center), XV*(4), 561–619.

Wallerstein, I. M. (2000). *The essential Wallerstein*. New York: New Press : Distributed by W.W. Norton.

Wallerstein, I. (2002). The itinerary of world-systems analysis; or, how to resist becoming a theory. In J. Z. Berger and M. Zelditch Jr. (Eds.), *New directions in contemporary sociological theory* (pp. 358–76). Lanham, MD: Rowman and Littlefield.

Wallerstein, I. (2003). The end of the beginning. Retrieved from http://www.hartford-hwp.com/archives/10/075.html.

Wallerstein, I. (2004). *World-systems analysis: An introduction*. Durham, NC: Duke University Press.

Wallerstein, I. (2006). Islam in the modern world-system. *Sociologisk Forskning, 43*(4), 66–74.

Wallerstein, I. (2009). Crisis of the capitalist system: Where do we go from here? *Memorial Lecture to the Harold Wolpe Trust*.

Wallerstein, I. (2011a). *The modern world-system I: Capitalist agriculture and the origins of the European world-economy in the sixteenth century*. Berkeley: University of California Press.

Wallerstein, I. (2011b). *The modern world-system II: Mercantilism and the consolidation of the European world-economy, 1600–1750*. Berkeley: University of California Press.
Wallerstein, I. (2011c). *The modern world-system III: The second era of great expansion of the capitalist world-economy, 1730s–1840s*. Berkeley: University of California Press.
Wallerstein, I. (2013). *Does capitalism have a future?* New York: Oxford University Press.
Wakeman, F. (1978). The Canton trade and the Opium War. In D. Twitchett & J. Fairbank (Eds.), *The Cambridge history of China Vol. 10: Late Ch'ing, 1800–1911, Part I* (pp. 163–212). Cambridge: Cambridge University Press.
Wang, D. (2013). US-China trade: 1971–2012: Insights into the US-China relationship. *The Asia-Pacific Journal, 11*(24), 1–15.
Wang, Q. E. (1999). History, space, and ethnicity: The Chinese worldview. *Journal of World History, 10*(2), 285–305.
Waseem, M. (2007). *Politics and the state in Pakistan*. 3rd edition. Islamabad, Pakistan: National Institute of Historical and Cultural Research, Centre of Excellence, Quaid-i-Azam University.
Waters, M. (2009). *Globalization*. London: Routledge.
Weeks, J. (2014). *A global approach to the global financial crisis*. Paper presented at the Izmir University of Economics Workshop on "The Great Meltdown of 2008: Systemic, Conjunctural or Policy-Created?"
Weiss, A. M. (1991). *Culture, class, and development in Pakistan: The emergence of an industrial bourgeoisie in Punjab*. Boulder: Westview Press.
Westad, O. A. (2012). *Restless empire: China and the world since 1750*. New York: Basic Books.
Whitcombe, E. (1972). *Agrarian conditions in northern India*. Berkeley: University of California Press.
White, L. J. (1976). *Industrial concentration and economic power in pakistan*. Princeton, NJ: Princeton University Press.
Whiting, A. S. (1954). *Soviet policies in China, 1917–1924*. New York: Columbia University Press.
Wilkins, M. (1998). Multinational corporations: An historical account. In R. Kozul-Wright and R. Rowthorn (Eds.), *Transnational corporations and the global economy* (pp. 95–133). Basingstoke: Palgrave Macmillan.
Wilkinson, S. (2015). *Army and nation: The military and Indian democracy since independence*. Cambridge, MA: Harvard University Press.
Wills, J. E. (1974). *Pepper, guns, and parleys: The Dutch East India Company and China, 1622–1681*. Cambridge, MA: Harvard University Press.
Wills, J. E. (1998). Relations with maritime Europeans, 1514–1662. In D. Twitchett and F. W. Mote (Eds.), *The Cambridge history of China, Vol. 8: The Ming dynasty, 1368–1644, Part II*. Cambridge: Cambridge University Press.
Wilson, J. E. (2016). *The chaos of empire: The British Raj and the conquest of India*. New York: PublicAffairs.

Wolff, R. D., and Resnick, S. A. (2012). *Contending economic theories: Neoclassical, Keynesian, and Marxian*. Cambridge, MA: MIT Press.

Wolpert, S. A. (2009). *Shameful flight: The last years of the British empire in India*. New York: Oxford University Press.

Wolpert, S. A. (2011). *India and Pakistan: Continued conflict or cooperation?* Berkeley: University of California Press.

Woodruff, P. (1954). *The men who ruled India*. New York: St Martin's Press.

World Bank. (1996). *India: Five years of stabilization and reform and the challenges ahead*. Washington, DC: The World Bank.

World Trade Organization (WTO). (2001). WTO successfully concludes negotiations on China's entry. *WTO News* press release, September 17. Retrieved from https://www.wto.org/english/news_e/pres01_e/pr243_e.htm.

Wright, M. K. (Ed.). *China in revolution: The first phase, 1900–1913*. New Haven, CT: Yale University Press.

Xiaoping, D. (1984). Building a socialism with a specifically Chinese character. *The People's Daily*, June 30.

Xie, Y., and Zhou, X. (2014). Income inequality in today's China. *Proceedings of the National Academy of Sciences, 111*(19), 6928–33.

Xu, Y.-C. (2012). *The political economy of state-owned enterprises in China and India*. Basingstoke: Palgrave Macmillan.

Yagi, K., Yokokawa, N., Hagiwara, S., and Dymski, G. A. (2013). *Crises of global economies and the future of capitalism: Reviving Marxian crisis theory*. London: Routledge.

Yokokawa, N. (2013). Cyclical crisis, structural crisis, systemic crisis, and future of capitalism. In N. Yokokawa, S. Hagiwara, and G. Dymski (Eds.), *Crises of global economies and the future of capitalism: Reviving Marxian crisis theory* (pp. 127–50). Routledge.

Zaheer, H. (1994). *The separation of East Pakistan: The rise and realization of Bengali Muslim nationalism*. New York: Oxford University Press.

Zaidi, S. A. (2005). *Issues in Pakistan's economy*. New York: Oxford University Press.

Zestos, G. K. (2016). *The global financial crisis: From US subprime mortgages to European sovereign debt*. London: Routledge.

Zhao, S. (2004). *A nation-state by construction: Dynamics of modern Chinese nationalism*. Stanford: Stanford University Press.

Zurndorfer, H. T. (2011). Cotton textile manufacture and marketing in late imperial China and the "Great Divergence." *Journal of the Economic and Social History of the Orient, 54*(5), 701–38.

Zwart, P. d. (2016). *Globalization and the colonial origins of the great divergence: Intercontinental trade and living standards in the Dutch East India Company's commercial empire, c. 1600–1800*. Leiden: Brill.

Index

Page references to figures and tables are italicized.

About the Author

Samee Lashari studied political science at Northern Arizona University as a Fulbright Scholar, graduating in 2017 with a PhD, and then joined South Texas College as a lecturer. He has also taught at the University of Texas Rio Grande Valley and Texas A&M University. Currently, he is a professor of government at Houston Community College. His work on issues related to Pakistan and South Asia has been published in various edited collections and journals.